THE
SECRET HISTORY
OF
ST⊕NEHENGE

Ancestral Mysteries and Lost Civilisations

MARIA WHEATLEY

Published by Celestial Songs Press, 2023

Marlborough,
Wiltshire, SN8 4AF

TheAveburyExperience.co.uk
EsotericCollege.com

Email: mariawheatley@aol.com
Telephone +44 (0)1672 511427

A CIP record for this book is available from the British Library.

ISBN 978-0-9560733-8-9

Cover design: Ewan Warmbath
Editing and formatting: Roma Harding

Unless otherwise credited all illustrations
and photographs are my own with the exception of
Fig. 87 Ewan Warmbath
Figs. 111, 112, 115, 117, 121-125, 132, 134, 137 & 272 Richard Cardew
Figs. 64, 71, 104, 238 & 277 Copyright free stock (Pixabay)

Printed by
DolmanScott
www.dolmanscott.com

For the Ancestors of Stonehenge

Thank you to Chris Kelly for his initial editing and to Caroline Morgan, Fiona Hughes and Maureen Walton for their illustrations. Michelle Hood, Martin Morrison, Trevor Hallett, John Harris, Paul Goddard and Busty Taylor for their photographs. Also to Jonathan Womack for the cover design concept. Appreciation to Busty for his support during the research, and to Roma Harding for the finalising and formatting of this book.

Rodney Hale calculated the astronomical position of Alphecca at Stonehenge. Mathematical harmonic musical intervals and the caustic beam were calculated by Richard Cardew who sadly died in December 2022. I enjoyed being taught sacred geometry and harmonics by Richard. His YouTube channel is https://youtube.com/@richardcardew3980.

Foreword

I am very proud to support and promote Maria Wheatley's latest book *The Secret History of Stonehenge*. I have known Maria for several years and have been very impressed by her astonishing and insightful knowledge about ancient locations in Britain, such as Stonehenge, the Avebury complex and Silbury Hill to name but a few of the many locations thoroughly investigated in this new and enlightening book.

A second generation dowser and geomancer, as well as studying the Neolithic and Bronze Ages at Oxford university, Maria and her colleagues have successfully questioned the conventionally assumed age of such sites as Stonehenge.

Equally as impressive, she sheds light on the ancient elongated headed people of ancient Britain, a subject largely ignored by conventional academia. It appears that these people of nobility existed prior to the arrival from Europe of the Beaker people, who largely invaded the elongated headed peoples' territories around 2500 BC. The ensuing conflicts and interaction between these two distinct peoples resulted in the extermination of the elongated headed ones and the takeover of their cherished sacred places. This led to a transformation of Stonehenge.

The Secret History of Stonehenge is a must read for anyone interested in the history of Great Britain and the lives of our ancient ancestors.

Brien Foerster

Author of
Elongated Skulls of Peru and Bolivia: The Path of Viracocha

CONTENTS

"One of the best-kept secrets of Stonehenge's geomantic activation is the geodetic magic square. When it manifests in the Earth it becomes a 'gateway' and it can be opened, closed or its frequency raised by the power of 5, 10, or 15. The magic square became associated with the Lo Shu square of Feng Shui, but silently it gives access to other earth-realms far beyond its customary use in the art of placement."

Dennis Wheatley

Chapter 1

Sacred Britain

Ancient cultures worldwide developed a complex network of megalithic sites: pyramids, obelisks, dolmens, standing stones, stone circles and vast megalithic temples were constructed throughout the prehistoric world. Serving various purposes from astronomical predictors to seed germination, they were magnificent and multifunctional. (Selected sites were located over complex earth energy patterns, complementing their musical harmonics and celestial alignments in a manner that was mathematically complex, yet artistically inspired.) Major power sites such as Stonehenge were ingeniously encoded to aid manifestation, to hear faint oracles and to heal the sick—the vestiges of which are still active and can be experienced today as a divine gift to us from a long-lost civilisation. Prehistoric civilisations, whose ruins are preserved in earth and stone, developed sophisticated technological cultures. Many of the megalithic temples were constructed where the natural forces of the earth are intense and highly concentrated, and we shall see how prehistoric geomancers utilised these invisible currents that move beneath and above the Earth's surface. This esoteric knowledge, still employed in China as *Feng Shui*, was incorporated into European megalithic temple complexes to unite Heaven with Earth and to harness celestial and terrestrial power. To marvel at the rising Sun at Summer Solstice at Stonehenge and other sites is awe-inspiring, and, as you will see, the hidden geomantic purpose behind the alignment is ingenious. Once fully encoded, these monuments became active and the resulting phenomena were spectacular. Traces of this system have been researched by academics, archaeologists, mathematicians and non-academics alike, such as dowsers, healers and sensitives. Our combined research provides a holistic insight into the hidden dynamics of ancient sites.

In contrast to the discord brought about by religious division in the past few centuries, it is possible that a megalithic culture once united humankind in spiritual accord. The unifying principle was a magical, spiritual understanding that knew no racial or religious boundaries as its esoteric teachings spoke directly to the human soul. Stonehenge was a vital component in a worldwide global system; looking at its original physical identity, which was quite different from what we see today, brings a fresh insight to its spiritual meaning and purpose. Set aside the old-fashioned interpretation of Stonehenge created by dry academic archaeologists and allow a new view to unfold as you witness first-hand the achievements of our ancestors; there is far more to Stonehenge than we are told. For example, stones which did not fit neatly into the accepted model were buried and, rightfully, should be raised. We will also explore numerous sacred sites as we journey across the ancient world and encounter many wonders and energies that bring us intimately closer to their sacred purpose and, more importantly, how we can benefit from them today. We will also meet a long-lost Neolithic civilisation, builders of numerous prehistoric sites—their otherworldly appearance is an ill-fitting truth suppressed over the years by incredulous scholars. Legendary locations and mythical beings from the distant past draw us closer to acknowledging and understanding these facts. The secret history that emerges is even stranger than fiction.

Sacred Isle, Mystical Britain

To ancient people, Britain was a sacred land, a place of enchantment and the dwelling place of the gods. By 6000 BC Britain had become separated from mainland Europe and was considered to be uniquely sacred. Within the confines of the island, an ancient occult tradition developed of equal potency and authenticity to Egypt, India and Tibet capable of revealing to us today a history as majestic as has ever been seen or told. Accounts of strange marvels circulated among its European neighbours that hint at the regard for Britain as a land of mystical fascination. Procopius, the Byzantine historian, who flourished in the sixth century (AD 500-565) refers in his *De Bello Gothic* to a late form of belief in Britain's mysterious reputation. Accordingly, fishermen from the Breton coast were compelled to ferry over the invisible shades of the dead. At midnight they would be awakened by a tap at the door and hear a low voice call their name. A strange force attracted them to the shore where they found their empty boats, yet the waters rose to the bulwarks as if they were overloaded. More than a day and a half's sailing could be achieved in just one hour. When they reached the British shore, the souls departed as a loud voice called out the names of those who had disembarked, and their boats once more rose in the sea.

The sacred Hindu texts the Puranas, composed in Sanskrit, refer to direct communication between India and Western Europe, which they called *Varaha Dwipa*. England was known to them as *Sweta Saila* or 'Islands of the White Cliffs'. The Greeks of Alexandria had great respect for the ancient British priesthood, with its reputation for cosmological knowledge and profound wisdom; Clement of Alexandria wrote that the Pythagoreans took their philosophy from the Druids, as proven by the sophisticated geometry found in ancient British stone monuments. Julius Caesar spoke of the Druids with admiration, stating that they "lectured on the stars and their motion, the magnitude of the earth and its divisions and on natural history."

Undoubtedly, the Druids inherited their esoteric tradition from an earlier Bronze Age priesthood, who likewise inherited it from their predecessors. Mystical Britain has a lineage that stretches back to the

THE SECRET HISTORY OF STONEHENGE

prehistoric. Stonehenge stands unique among Britain's monuments and is unlike other megalithic temples. So great was the mystery of its origins that there still remains much to be discovered—its secret history will change how we view ancient Britain. Our Upper Palaeolithic or Late Stone Age ancestors (50,000-10,000 years ago) lived in a very different-looking Europe. The land we know as the British Isles had yet to be formed as it was still connected to Europe by the Doggerland landmass. According to geophysicist Dr Robert Schoch, ten to twelve thousand years ago the British Isles were born when a cataclysmic solar plasma outburst caused the ice sheets to melt and sea levels to rise dramatically, flooding Doggerland.

Archaeology allows us insight into the distant past. For example, Burrington Coombe, located in the limestone rock of the Mendip Hills in Somerset, southern England, is one of the earliest scientifically dated cemeteries in Britain. Inscribed crosses found on the cave walls of Aveline's Hole are believed to have been carved by the Mesolithic people just after the last Ice Age. Nearby, the cathedral-like caverns of Gough's Cave, some 2 miles (3.2 km) long, contained the skeleton of 'Cheddar Man', who lived nearly nine thousand years ago. Archaeologists describe Mesolithic (between Palaeolithic and Neolithic) people as nomadic, roaming the land following cattle herds and hunting game for survival. We can disregard this as a sole image of the distant past, as my geomantic research tells a different story. The Mesolithic people carefully selected specific locations for their future megalithic sites. We shall learn that it appears the landscape was mapped out and ground plans were prepared by a complex geophysical survey of the British Isles. This may sound unbelievable, yet the evidence is indisputable. Archaeologists have noted that certain Neolithic monuments, such as long barrows and causewayed enclosures, were sited upon Early Mesolithic locations and places of activity. From these studies has emerged the identification of invisible soil boundaries and intersection points at which two aquifer layers reach the surface; where chalk meets green sand is an example in southern England. During long barrow excavations these highly significant geological boundaries were identified by geologists but largely ignored by archaeologists.

Mesolithic Monoliths

The people of the Mesolithic era were the first to raise standing stones that marked the location points of underground aquifers and geological soil boundaries. Yet this achievement is repeatedly credited to the later Neolithic culture. In the early-19th century, eighteen out of the sixty-nine or so long barrows on the Salisbury Plain were excavated, and it was noted that at the base of many of these barrows fragments of sarsen stone formed a pavement or floor. Furthermore, 'pits' that had been cut neatly into the solid chalk bedrock were very similar to stone socket holes and rarely contained burial deposits. In the Stonehenge environs, stone floors were found at Bole's Barrow, King Barrow, Heytesbury North Field Barrow, Knook Barrow and a number of other barrows. According to archaeologist David McOmish, "pits that are constantly found beneath the mounds appear to begin the entire mound process." Other barrows, such as at Wor Barrow in Dorset, and in Lincolnshire, conceal similar pits. Seemingly unexciting, these tell a story, long forgotten. Situated on the outer regions of Salisbury Plain, Arn Hill Long Barrow, near Warminster, is an unusual long barrow; inside, a sarsen standing stone was found at the end of a stone pavement. Its position was very similar to where the pits occurred in other mounds, making it likely these were in fact stone sockets that once supported Mesolithic monoliths. A new sequence of prehistoric activity now emerges since carbon dating of the Salisbury Plain pits suggests a time span, McOmish argues, of "several centuries [that] could separate the use of the pits for possible standing stones from any covering long barrow event." Later, during the Early Neolithic, some of these standing stones were broken up by the long mound builders and recycled for use as flooring. Archaeologist Timothy Champion was the first to note that all European Neolithic causewayed enclosures are located where two aquifer layers emerge and meet, producing high levels of electromagnetic energy.

Together, these findings lead me to suppose that monoliths preceded the earliest barrows and were deliberately placed as markers of sites of power. Identifying underground geological features embodied deep meaning; the standing stones raised by the Mesolithic people stood unmolested for centuries. This culture was highly intelligent and had an extraordinary awareness of the Earth. Recent evidence shows they created a thriving community close to where Stonehenge would be raised centuries later. In the 1960s, three Mesolithic post holes found in Stonehenge's old visitors' car park

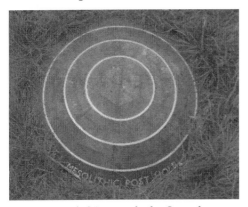

were grossly misinterpreted by archaeologists. The width of the holes suggested timber posts 14 ft (4.3 m) high, weighing several tons. These post holes were excavated by amateur archaeologists, Lord and Lady Vatcher, who interpreted the standing timbers as totem poles. Rather than randomly placed posts, the timbers were aligned to-

Fig. 1 Mesolithic post hole, Stonehenge.

wards the Spring and Autumn Equinoxes—their positions show astronomical awareness and an understanding of the annual movement of the Sun. This flawed excavation raised many questions and concerns. In 1988, some thirteen years after the initial discovery, a fourth posthole was found, suggesting that important features had been missed. Most archaeologists agree that the Vatchers were not qualified excavators, but their amateur interpretation of *totem pole* has stuck ever since, thus robbing the ancient builders of an important achievement. Were the posts simply totem poles or, as my dowsing suggests, the remains of a small section of a much larger timber structure, such as a wooden temple complex with an eye to the heavens?

Situated about a mile (1.6 km) to the east of Stonehenge is Vespasian's Camp, an Iron Age hillfort, shown in *Fig. 2*, which was once a Druidic ceremonial centre, dating to 500 BC. In 2005, archaeologists excavated a low-lying hollow northeast of the camp, known as Blick Mead, and unearthed a Mesolithic building—the oldest known construction in the Stonehenge landscape. This find is unprecedented, as it was believed that no such structure should exist. It was

6

initially interpreted as a 'home base' or campsite, which people returned to seasonally. Over 10,000 Mesolithic implements were excavated in remarkably pristine condition; the flint blades are still razor-sharp as proven when some of the archaeologists even cut their fingers on them. We know that a nearby spring was revered as sacred, likened to Lourdes in France, and numerous Mesolithic deposits were placed in the warm, steaming spring water. Its sacred status continued to be revered throughout the millennia, demonstrated by the fact that deposits from the Neolithic, Bronze and Iron Ages were found alongside ritual deposits of the later Romano-British period. This had always been hallowed ground. Mesolithic people lived here for over 1,500 years spanning 6250-4700 BC. This was no seasonal camp, for over sixty generations lived, thrived, worked and worshipped here, at a magical, sacred healing spring in the vicinity of what would come to be known as Stonehenge.

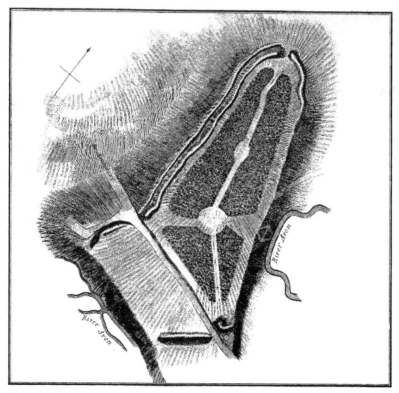

Fig. 2 Vespasian's Camp, close to the Mesolithic settlement.

The Mesolithic People

So, who were the Mesolithic people and what did they look like? According to archaeologist Sue Anderson, Early Mesolithic people had long skulls, high brow ridges, large jaws and they had muscular bodies. In Europe, she says, "two physical types were identified: long-headed with protruding noses, and round-headed with flat faces." According to archaeologist Marija Gimbutas, the early Europeans were hybrids of Neanderthal man with their long skulls, large jaws and prominent brow ridges, and Cro-Magnon man that had rounder skulls. This produced a natural hybrid race of human beings with long skulls and large jaws. We will soon meet these ancient long headed people, see what they really looked like and explore the monuments they raised as we delve deeper into Britain's forbidden history.

Chapter 2

The Long Headed Civilisation ~ Ethereal Looking Human Beings

During the Neolithic era (5500-2500 BC), Mesolithic sites and monoliths were redeveloped and monumentalised. Although Mesolithic people placed standing stones on leys, deep underground aquifers and soil boundaries, the Neolithic long headed culture were the first to really utilise ley lines and earth energies. One thousand years later, during the Chalcolithic (Copper) and Bronze Ages (c2500-700 BC) the megalithic builders would also align their constructions, including stone circles, standing stones, round barrows and earthworks, upon the original Neolithic ley and earth energy network.

Mainstream archaeologists have largely dismissed the long headed culture. Even though Victorian archaeologists and anthropologists meticulously took measurements of their skulls and skeletons, never once did they reconstruct or reassemble what they had found. Had they done so, our modern ancestors would have seen a human being that looked radically different from ourselves, with a somewhat otherworldly, ethereal appearance. This long headed civilisation of the British Isles, and some parts of Europe, may have been the genesis of folkloric beings such as elves, pixies and the fey; indeed, their appearance offers the possibility that they were a completely different species. Associated with the European long headed civilisation are dolmens, long barrows, cairns, causewayed enclosures, rondels, timber halls, coves and cursus monuments.

In southern England, long barrows were constructed of two main types: the *chambered long barrow* that was used in two phases, firstly as a temple and then for burial deposits; and an *unchambered long barrow* or *cenotaph* that was without internal chambers. Visually striking, these enigmatic cenotaph long mounds were integral to a seed enhancement agricultural programme, which I will describe in more detail in later chapters.

Origins of the Long Barrow

Long barrows have a lineage stretching back to the Mesolithic era. Many scholars suggest that the common trapezoid shape originated from the Danubian and the Linearbandkeramik (LBK) cultures. Built of massive timber posts with wattle and daub mortar, these rectangular longhouses ranged from 30-147 ft (7-45 m) long and between 16.5-30 ft (5-7 m) wide. Clive Bonsall, of the University of Edinburgh, noted that the shape of Early Mesolithic longhouses of Lepenski Vir was inspired by the 2,227 ft (679 m) high Treskavac mountain, as the trapezoidal shape of its summit looks similar to the longhouse or barrow. Omnipresent and eternal, this bare porphyritic cliff dominates the landscape. Located in Serbia, in the central Balkan Peninsula, Lepenski Vir is one of the oldest Mesolithic civilisations in Europe. Certainly, the Danubian longhouse influenced the LBK culture that continued to construct longhouses for both the living and the dead during the Late Mesolithic period. Its standardised shape became the framework for British Neolithic long barrows.

Nearly eight hundred years before stone circles were raised, the long headed culture of Wessex constructed timber longhouses at sites such as Avebury Henge—one stood at the centre of the southern inner circle. According to archaeologist Lisa Brown of Bath University, a similar structure was found beneath West Kennet Long Barrow; timber structures were also found at the heart of Stonehenge, where, as we shall see, stood an enigmatic wooden temple. Other structures, such as large timber halls that preceded the feasting halls of the Dark Ages, have recently been unearthed. In 2013, four longhouses were excavated at Kingsmead Quarry, in Kent, as well as sites at Hazelton North and Ascott-under-Wychwood in the Cotswolds, which are associated with longhouses and long barrows. Later, in Chapter 5, I will discuss the timber longhouse that was found at Avebury.

Fig. 3 A reconstruction of a Neolithic long house.

Stonehenge's Long Barrows

Inspired by the LBK longhouse design, the Neolithic long headed people raised over sixty-nine long barrows close to Stonehenge, each taking, archaeologists estimate, over 5,000-man hours to complete. Of these, sixteen surviving barrows are sited within 4 miles (6.43 km) of Stonehenge. The long headed people constructed several different types of chambered long barrow; one style which is known as the *Cotswold Severn barrow* is found all over southern England. Internally, this consists of a main passage with side chambers likened to the cruciform design of a church or cathedral. The chambered mound's outermost layer was chalk white, which would have stood out spectacularly against the lush green landscape. Two well-known reconstructed long barrows in southern England are at West Kennet, near Avebury in Wiltshire, and Wayland's Smithy on the Ridgeway near Uffington, Oxfordshire, both boasting megalith chambers.

Fig. 4 Wayland's Smithy Long Barrow.

However, the majority of long barrows on the Salisbury Plain in the Stonehenge area contained timber chambers that appeared far more rectangular in shape and structure. The outer section of the long mound would also have been constructed of chalk. I can imagine the timbers painted in bright golden and red ochre colours, which can be found in abundance in the Avebury and Stonehenge landscapes.

Royal Burials

Across the British Isles, most chambered long barrows contained numerous communal deposits, sometimes of as many as 40-80 individuals. The Stonehenge environs was, however, different. Here, many long barrows contained only one primary burial. I suggest that this was the final resting place of the spiritual and royal elite of Stonehenge.

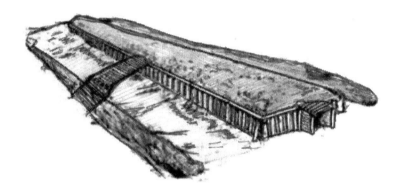

Fig. 5 A Stonehenge long mound. Based on the findings of Fusssell's Lodge Long Barrow, near Stonehenge.

You are about to encounter the forgotten Neolithic people of Stonehenge, disregarded by mainstream academics. A veil of darkness has engulfed their memory but now, for the first time, their story is told. In my booklet *The Elongated Skulls of Stonehenge* (2016), I describe my initial findings of the long headed people, who appeared to have been murdered and placed into long barrows that surround Stonehenge. However, I now believe this to have been eclipsed by further research, which reveals an even stranger, more complex history.

Located on the southeastern edge of Salisbury Plain, an unassuming track now used by the military takes us to the final resting place of a Neolithic queen or high priestess. My book drew attention to the long barrow, following which people came to pay their respects and placed ribbons and strips of cloth on a nearby tree—such regard for our ancestors warms my heart, mindful to use natural materials. When I first investigated the mound, it was easily accessible. Then,

in 2021, the military placed 'No Entry' and 'Out of Bounds' signs (*Fig. 6*) and erected a new fence denying access. Military establishments surround Stonehenge and occupy a large area that I can only liken to Area 51 in America. I climbed over the fence and to my horror discovered the whole barrow was covered in a wire mesh, like a Faraday cage. The official explanation was this was due to badger intrusion.

Fig. 6 The barrow now has 'No Entry' and 'Out of Bounds' signs.

The Neolithic High Queen

As I have previously stated, the High Queen's long mound on Salisbury Plain is Britain's largest long barrow. Known as Tilshead 2 or the 'Old Ditch Barrow', its unexciting name hides a majestic legacy. Swelling out of the eastern slopes of Breach Hill, near Tilshead, the barrow is 390 ft (118.6 m) long, 119 ft (36.2 m) wide, and 11 ft (3.3 m) high. It contains seventy times the volume of any other barrow on Salisbury Plain, its 430,000 cubic ft of chalk and earth fifteen times the size of lesser long mounds. Its sheer size and presence in the landscape is quite extraordinary.

The primary burial was discovered by excavations in the early 1800s by Sir Richard Colt Hoare (1758-1838) and William Cunnington (1754-1810). Orientated towards the Summer Solstice Sunrise, this largest and most spectacular barrow in Britain was the final resting

Fig. 7 The largest long mound in England, Salisbury Plain.
Photograph: Busty Taylor.

place of a high profile, long headed woman, shown above in *Fig. 7*. Compared to contemporaneous funerary practices, this burial was lavish. There were only flat graves for the commoners, a far cry from the well-designed long barrows that housed the corporeal remains of the elite. Evidence presents a violent end for this Neolithic woman. Close to her 'flexed' body (the skeleton placed in the foetal position) was a pile of burnt flints and, as archaeologist Aubrey Burl (1926-2020) observed, "nearby was an incomplete cremation deposited there while the bones were still hot." Both inhumations were found at the northeast end of the mound, the body covered by a cairn of flints and the cremation sat on a platform of flints—a platform cremation. Within the long barrow was an unusual round mound containing animal bones. Secondary burials had also been placed within the mound; near the southwest, three human skeletons were deposited 1½ ft (0.45 m) above the floor near a cavity in the chalk. Further excavation of the old surface level by Colt Hoare revealed that at the base level of the mound was a deep pit. Even after 5,000 years of being buried beneath tons of chalk and earth, this woman appeared perfectly preserved, "as if it had been done with a chisel," commented the original excavator. I speculate, based on evidence given earlier, that this pit was actually a socket hole cut into the chalk bedrock that originally housed a Mesolithic standing stone. Hoare and Cunnington respectfully returned her skull and skeletal remains to the mound, and left her to rest in peace. Indifference followed.

Sixty years later, she was abruptly disturbed and unceremoniously dug up by Dr John Thurnam, the medical superintendent of the Wiltshire County Asylum, who had a long history of involvement with archaeology and craniology—the study of skulls. He retained her skull for his studies and from that point on she was destined never to return to her grave. Thurnam amassed around one hundred skulls from the graves of our Neolithic ancestors, and after his death the collection was sold. Today, the skull of the Stonehenge High Queen, shown in *Fig. 8*, lies in a cardboard box in a storage facility, miles away from her noble tomb. I went to see her to apologise for this. I said a prayer and felt her longing for the land she knew. On top of her skull was branded the label 'Tilshead Old Ditch', for she is nameless, and the story of her people has never before been told. Until I became interested, no-one realised that the greatest mound ever constructed in prehistoric Britain was raised in her honour. Today, her mound lies in a military firing zone. It was only recently that military tanks stopped driving over it, practising their exercise manoeuvres. Thankfully, the site is now protected by large wooden posts denying the military their intrusive climbs. My heart wishes that one day this noble Neolithic queen will be returned to her glorious long mound, to rest in peace once more upon the Plain she knew so well.

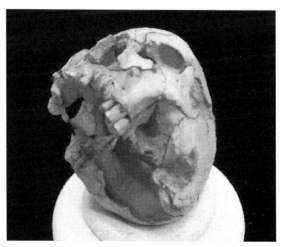

Fig. 8 The High Queen showing the sheer length of her skull. Estimated 5 ft tall (1.52 m).

A Neolithic High King

Memories of the long headed men, women and children linger in the monuments they left behind, and I soon realised that the High Queen's single burial was not so rare after all. Several other Neolithic long mounds in the Stonehenge area also housed important single burials; some of these mounds are spectacular and can still be visited today. At other sacred places, such as in the area around Avebury, the Yorkshire Wolds and Wales, for example, single long barrow burials are unusual. Could it be that this radical difference in burial deposits and funereal rites provides evidence that Stonehenge was the royal capital of the long headed ruling elite? I think so. Close to Stonehenge stands the exceptionally well-preserved Winterbourne Stoke Long Barrow; measuring 240 ft (73 m) long, 72 ft (23 m) wide and 10 ft (3 m) high, it is still an imposing presence in the landscape. Winterbourne Stoke is a prehistoric cemetery containing some of the finest examples of Neolithic and Bronze Age barrows in Wessex. In 1863, when Winterbourne Stoke Long Barrow was excavated, a single male burial was found in the flexed position, mirroring the Neolithic queen's burial posture. Certainly, his skull (see *Fig. 9*) was very hyper-dolichocephalic (long and elongated), but unlike the Neolithic queen, it showed no signs of violence and this man had lived his full term. The excavator noted that he must have had

> "...a high-status lifestyle as his teeth were all present, beautifully white and with scarcely a trace of erosion on their crowns, due to the individual's rich diet of unrefined foodstuffs."

Caesar informs us that Britain's Iron Age elite consumed "milk and flesh"; this type of diet may have been an inherited tradition from the Neolithic long headed ruling elite, accounting for hardly any tooth erosion. The High King was buried at ground level, accompanied with a flint implement 8 in (20.3 cm) long, which has been interpreted as a phallic-like object. Six secondary burials, one man, one woman and four children, with a plain urn-shaped food vessel, were also found 2 ft (0.60 m) from the top of the mound.

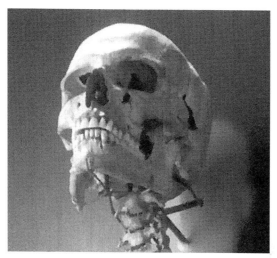

Fig. 9 The skull of the High King, described as hyper-dolichocephalic.

Oriented northeast-southwest, many researchers and authors have suggested that the long mound faced the Summer Solstice Sunrise. However, this is also the orientation of the moon's most northerly rise and, interestingly, the majority of chambered mounds located around Stonehenge face eastwards, looking towards the arc along which the moon rises. Astronomical alignments often predetermined a long mound's location; for example, Fussell's Lodge long barrow on the outskirts of Salisbury Plain, shown in *Fig. 5*, was placed upon the site of an earlier barrow that incorporated complex lunar sightings. Burl calculated that nine out of ten barrows in the Stonehenge area were associated with the rising or setting of the moon. The ancients must have known this orientation marked the placement of both the Sun and the Moon in the heavens, perhaps symbolising masculine and feminine balance and equality.

Stonehenge Shamans: the Tilshead Long Barrows

The long barrows at Tilshead are amongst the largest mounds constructed in prehistoric Britain. Those close to the Neolithic queen contained rare grave goods, such as pointed and carved red deer antlers or ox skulls, which I suggest are regalia belonging to the Neolithic shaman and denote their spiritual status. As we shall see later, Professor Stuart Piggott (1910-1996) noted that certain Middle

Bronze Age grave goods pointed to the interment of a shaman, which is not dissimilar to my own observations of Neolithic burials. For instance, Tilshead 1 long mound, the 'Kill Barrow', lies within the military firing zone, therefore access is denied. It measures 170 ft (51 m) long and faces the Winter Solstice Sunrise. Opened in 1865, the barrow yielded a unique platform cremation; interestingly, the burnt bones, some only partially charred, were found covered in a substance resembling mortar and others were stained a vivid green-blue colour, although chemical tests showed no traces of copper.

At Alfred's Castle, an Iron Age hilltop enclosure in Wiltshire, archaeologists believe a timber structure they uncovered to be a 'witch doctor's healing house', and that the skull they found interred, coated in green malachite, was to show shaman status. Tilshead 4, known as the 'White Barrow', is a well-preserved long mound 255 ft long (77 m) by 156 ft (47.5 m) wide and 8 ft (2.4 m) high. Although it has never been fully excavated, finely pointed deer tines (antler tips) were found next to a skull and indicate, I suggest, shaman status.

Fig. 10 Stag tine used by a Stonehenge shaman.

A short distance away, another long barrow contained a shaman. Tilshead 5, known as 'Lodge Barrow', housed two skeletons, next to which were placed the skull of a short-horned ox (the first domesticated cattle) and several deer tines. Another ox skull was carefully positioned at the base of the barrow's western end. Tilshead is the unique resting ground of at least eight or nine shamans. To the southwest of Stonehenge lies Sherrington Long Barrow, where four skeletons were placed close to a purposefully built cist in the chalk that also held an ox skull with a small, pointed wand-like piece of deer tine. These burial deposits reveal the forgotten spiritual legacy of a long-lost culture. (Generally speaking, archaeologists are not experienced or interested in considering ritual activity, leaving that to the anthropologists—revealing a rift between the two once closely related disciplines that were kin.)

Alton Down Long Barrow: Figheldean 31

Another forgotten member of the Stonehenge long headed elite was lovingly placed beneath a long mound, Figheldean 31, known today as 'Alton Down Long Barrow'. Located southeast of the Neolithic causewayed enclosure called 'Robin Hood's Ball', it measures 148 ft (47 m) long, 2.28 ft (0.7 m) high, and tapers from 40 ft (15 m) to 29 ft (12 m) in width. This area of the Salisbury Plain was once a peaceful place, but today Army artillery drowns out the birdsong and spoils any tranquillity. Most long barrows on the Plain contain timber chambers; unusually, Figheldean 31 probably had a megalithic chamber, as three large sarsens lie disregarded in the ditch. Left alone and undisturbed by the early antiquarians, this long mound escaped invasion until, fatefully, it was opened on 8th September 1864, by Thurnam. Aggressive digging allowed him to reach the base of the barrow where he found a very strange looking skull and,

despite its unusual characteristics, he failed to document its gender. He did record, however, that there was a single interment of a flexed skeleton "doubled up in the black earth and whose bones had been separated before the interment." His trained eye noted that the skull and bones were "remarkable for their peculiarly eroded character". Can we infer from this that they were ancient long before being placed in the mound? If that were the case, then it suggests that a Mesolithic long headed ancestor was placed inside a Neolithic long

Fig. 11 The location of Alton Down Long Barrow.

mound. We see the bones and not the flesh of the departed and need to remember that an influential long headed person was laid to rest within this regal mound. For thousands of years, the rising Sun at Winter Solstice bathed the mound in a pale golden light. Regrettably, in the early 1900s on military instruction, the mound was made ruinous to be transformed into an army shelter. The entire central part was removed, leaving just the fringe of the long mound; a sorrowful disfigurement which cruelly robbed it of its millennia-old beauty.

Many other long mounds housed single burials, such as the megalithic chambered long barrow at Tidcombe, near Chute, in Wiltshire, as well as Winterbourne Stoke 53. At nearby Everley, Fittleton Long Barrow may have been the resting place of a female shaman or high priestess; lying by her side were the remains of a *Bos longifrons* (short-horned ox) and a huge set of deer antlers. In life, this long headed woman may have been a spiritual leader and the burial deposits her shamanic tool kit—such finds are exceptionally rare in Neolithic long barrows. Today, like so many other long mounds, Fittleton, on the northeast edge of Salisbury Plain, is overgrown with weeds, thistles and large shrubs that strangle and hide the mound, making it hard to find. Deep tank tracks run close to the mound just missing the chamber's end, and danger signs warn civilians of the perils of the Plain.

Bole's Barrow: A Noble Young Prince

Standing within the live ammunition military zone on Salisbury Plain, this barrow can never be visited. Bole's Barrow once housed a prestigious long headed male burial. Often called Bowlsbury, the origin of the name is unknown as the only historical reference is from Andrews' and Dury's large 1773 map of Wiltshire. Impeccably preserved, despite millennia of adverse weather and potential erosion, the barrow stands over 10 ft (5.8 m) tall and is 150 ft (48.4 m) long and 94 ft (28.6 m) wide. It has survived for so long due to its unusual internal structure which consisted of 5.9 ft (1.8 m) high sarsens and bluestones, both of the type that would be used at Stonehenge one thousand years later. Clearly, these people were

Fig. 12 Antiquarian illustration of a Long Barrow.

moving stone across vast distances long before Stonehenge Phase 1. This stone layer was capped by 4.5 ft (1.4 m) thick of pure white chalk, its outline resembling the roof of a house.

Cunnington's keen eye noted the two ends of the mound created a fine beauty and symmetry that united the manmade structure with the contours of the landscape. Deep within Bole's Barrow, about 39 ft (11.9 m) from the eastern end, an oblong cist was placed exactly perpendicular to the axis of the barrow, its brilliant white chalk grave-pit containing the primary burial. The bones were of a distinctly different colour to the secondary burials and a ghostly grey soil, clearly different to any other soil used in the barrow's construction, filled the 2 ft (0.60 m) deep chalk cist. A large sarsen was placed on top of the skeleton, crushing it; careful restoration revealed a "well-formed young adult male" with an exceptionally long skull. Cunnington remarked, "the barrow was raised in his honour." There can be little doubt that this young man was a noble, perhaps equivalent to a prince or priest? Time and again, across the Plain, evidence of long barrows containing single burials repeats itself, and few have ever questioned why—until now.

Meet the Murdered
Apart from the Neolithic High Queen of Tilshead 2 long mound, who showed signs of being murdered, none of the other single interments—and they are numerous—presented any sign of unnatural death. Yet, as we shall see, this did not apply to others. Excluding the single royal burials described so far, numerous long barrows in the region of Stonehenge gave up evidence that one or more murder victims were placed next to a primary single interment that had

apparently died of natural causes. Stonehenge appears to be a focal point for this peculiar type of burial practice, compared to other parts of England. So, what was going on? When I wrote my first booklet regarding the initial discovery of the elongated skulled people of Stonehenge, my research into the discovery of remains showing signs of a violent death suggested there had been some kind of war or conflict, perhaps between the tall and, as some authors have suggested, the giant-like round-headed Beaker immigrants. However, I have revised this view; a scrupulous re-evaluation of the skulls alongside fresh evidence shows that the history of the long headed culture was more than just conflict and murder; signs of ritual activity suggest something much stranger, which seems to have included ritual execution.

We read that a high prince was laid to rest with dignity in Bole's Barrow, which was constructed of impenetrable chalk, rock and heavy stones that made digging problematic. It took Hoare and Cunnington and four labourers three days to dig out a small section measuring 6 ft x 10 ft (1.82 x 3 m). Finally, fourteen skulls were recovered, of which three were smashed, possibly after death, whilst others showed signs of damage at the time of death. Digging made the heavy stones unstable, and some weighing up to 200 lbs (90.7 kg) had fallen on the workmen, hindering the excavation. Despite this, before the dig was abandoned, they managed to find a deep hole in the ground, possibly where a Mesolithic standing stone had once marked the soil boundary. Cunnington was no grave robber and he always respectfully returned the skeletons to their resting place. But then, in 1864, along came John Thurnam (1810-1873), who took much less care in adding to his growing—some would say obses-sive—collection of skulls. At Bole's Barrow he pushed his sharp spade ruthlessly into the mound and dug up several 'cleft' skulls including one of a young girl, also "four perfect skulls", telling us that not everyone had been murdered. More recent archaeological analysis shows that four of Thurnam's ten or eleven cleft skulls had been damaged after burial, making a probable two that indicated potential signs of violence. Selfishly, he collected every bone he unearthed, leaving the barrow he thought completely empty, and stole his way home with his hoard before nightfall. Even doctors can be superstitious, and on moonless nights the Plain descends into blackness when the wind can often sound like an otherworldly groan. By day and by night, this long mound housed more secrets; unknown to Thurnam and other excavators, numerous skeletons remained deep within—old Britons still at peace, for the time being.

Years passed before a new generation of archaeologists came along: the grandsons of William Cunnington, William Junior and Henry, were now digging into barrows on the Plain with youthful vigour. Following in their grandfather's footsteps, they returned to Bole's Barrow and this time no stone was left unturned. Scarring the mound forever, it took four workmen five days to dig a massively oversized trench, a total length of 82 ft (24.9 m), so deep that it penetrated the natural chalk bedrock in complete violation of a sacred site. Primarily seeking skulls, they did not expect to find a mound within a mound, and this is what their trench exposed: an undisturbed section and an unusual conical shaped mound of flint, earth and sarsen, among which they found a later deposit of three skulls. The Cunningtons' report is more detailed and reliable than Thurnam's and further digging revealed sixteen more individuals. The younger William remarked, "the majority of these, there can be no doubt, were killed by severe cleavage of the skull." One of these skulls was elongated. The greater part of its left temporal bone had gone, possibly due to injury, and another long skull showed damage to the left temple. On another skull, the upper part of the cap had been cut clean off and three more victims showed that a blow had been inflicted above the left eye. One of these displayed signs of bandaging in infancy, creating a cephalic index of 72.0 and producing a dolichocephalic shaped skull, whilst others were naturally elongated. Such wounds suggest close-up combat and certainly these victims would have seen their attackers. Six others were also despatched with a sharp instrument that had cut through the nasal bone. One had suffered a painful wound to the left cheek, another was beheaded. Their killers had shown no mercy, as three small children were cruelly killed; one can only hope these poor souls were saved the terror of seeing others killed before them. It is notable that these murder victims were given an honourable burial, just like the high prince. Murder or war victims are often left in situ after the event, so it is interesting to consider why these people were buried with dignity and honour. This will be explored further.

Not far from Bole's Barrow stands Norton Bavant 13 Long Barrow, also located within the military no-go danger zone of the Plain and has a similar history. Strikingly prominent on the hilltop, this barrow that faces the Equinox Sunrise is 180 ft (55 m) long, 90 ft wide (27.4 m) and 9 ft high (2.7 m). An excavation in 1866 revealed a primary burial of an extremely long headed (hyper-dolichocephalic) person that displayed no signs of violence, and their body was honoured by being placed on the floor of the mound. However, elsewhere a confused mass of jumbled skeletons was found spread over a larger area. This consisted of the remains of eighteen people: eight men, five women and five children, whose skulls all showed signs of having been murdered by a blow to the head.

Tilshead Lodge Barrow: Tilshead 5
Close to Tilshead 2, the resting place of the Neolithic High Queen, are numerous long mounds that also contained both murdered and non-murdered burials. Tilshead 5 is a long barrow situated west of Tilshead Lodge, measuring 173 ft (52.7 m) long by 60 ft (18.2 m) wide, at a height of 5 ft (1.5 m) with visible side ditches. Orientated towards the Equinox Sunrise, it was excavated first by Hoare and Cunnington who found a secondary Saxon burial of a skeleton lying west to east, just under the turf near the eastern end. When Thurnam reopened the mound on 1st September 1865, he discovered two flexed skeletons. One skull, probably from the primary burial, displayed no violent wounds. Close to this body were red deer antlers and cattle skull deposits, which, as previously mentioned, may be the signature deposits of a spiritual leader or healer—a shaman. Nearby, the other skeleton was pulled taut, occupying 1.5 cubic ft (0.04 m), and showed visible signs of violence.

Close by is another well-built, robust long barrow, which until recently was in the middle of a tank drive and has survived heavy

Fig. 13 One of the Tilshead Long Barrows.

vehicles riding over it during manoeuvres. After decades of constant torment, it is remarkable that the mound is still 4 ft (1.25 m) high! Despite this, not one bone was crushed, so credit is due to the engineering skills of the long headed mound builders. Their solid design which consisted of a "core of black earth" and layers of chalk and earth, capped by chalk, kept the mound intact. Of the two flexed inhumations it contained, one skull revealed a violent attack—yet another murder victim—and the other showed no sign of violence. Both bodies were laid to rest with dignity in the same flexed position. A shallow area close to the centre of the mound indicated the presence of an underlying structure, possibly a longhouse.

More Stonehenge Murders: Together We Sleep Forever
Facing the Midwinter Sunrise and located on the appropriately named 'Slay Down', is Tilshead 7. This housed the remains of nine long headed persons. Now covered with thick undergrowth and needle-sharp brambles, despite its position inside the military danger zone the long mound is still whole, measuring 210 ft (64 m) long by 78 ft (23 m) wide. At a depth of 5 ft (1.5 m) near the east end were found the remains of eight closely packed skeletons, described by excavators as

> "...strangely cemented together, so closely as to show that if not interred after the decay or removal of the flesh, the bodies must have been packed together as closely as possible in the sitting or crouching position."

The heart feels what the mind cannot, and I sense these three men and three women were couples, some of whom had children. Their lives came to an end in an act of utter violence—all were murdered —sadly, their attacker(s) did not spare a baby in its first year or a two-year-old toddler. Beneath the carnage, another high queen, or member of the long headed elite, presented no signs of violence; her flexed body was placed in the foetal position as if awaiting rebirth in the otherworld. In the name of science, and ever greedy for yet more skulls to stockpile, Thurnam not only took the long headed queen in whose honour the mound had been raised, he also pulled the couples and their children from their resting place. No longer would they lie intimately close to one another with their beloved children. Science can be cold—ice cold. On a chilly winter's day, beneath a dark, brooding slate-grey sky, I got as close to the barrow as the military would allow and I apologised to the lingering memory of the families that once slept alongside the High Queen or priestess. Rarely does an archaeologist ever apologise for the ransacking of mounds, and most would rather speculate and project their theories onto the ancestral landscape than take five minutes to listen in silence, to sense times past and pay their respects to the dead— people whose remains are about to become artefacts in a museum or a boxed collection somewhere. Hoping that my thoughts and feelings would be carried on the wind and reach them, I felt their energy and swore to them that I would give them their voice.

The Giant's Grave

There are too many mounds to name, but I wish to relate one more example that contained both murder victims and a non-murdered primary burial. It lies on Milton Hill, on the edge of the northern limits of Salisbury Plain, near Pewsey. As so often found, the Giant's Grave Long Barrow is placed dramatically on the skyline, boasting outstanding and unspoilt views across the landscape, and is pleasantly located within an accessible part of the Plain. Go there and see, it is well worth a visit! The mound, oriented towards the Summer Solstice Sunrise, is 315 ft (96 m) long, 66 ft (20 m) wide and stands 7 ft (2.13 m) high. On my first visit, I experienced a strong and uplifting sense of 'Spirit of Place', which reawakened my deep sense of a long-lost ancestral landscape. The individual memorialised was brutally attacked, yet another victim of a violent death. However, three other skeletons showed no such signs. The location is not far from Nether Avon 6 Long Barrow. Until 2012, Nether Avon was a military establishment and today its public face is that of the 'Joint Services Parachute Centre', which masks the fact it contains an underground base. This long mound is oriented S/SE-N/NW. Lying within, faces up towards the heavens, were two primary burials; once again, only one had been violently murdered.

Cranial Deformation

Within this pattern, an astonishing fact emerged that gave a vital clue to solving this cold case murder mystery. Overlooked and seemingly *unnoticed* by archaeologists, the evidence found represented an ancient secret, hidden in plain sight. Co-existing in the Neolithic era were two distinct types of long headed people, one with an exceptionally long skull whose type exhibited no signs of violence, and lesser-long headed with skulls that displayed a much rounder occiput. It was these people who were the victims of violence. Shockingly, even very young children, as well as older children and teenagers, were murdered along with their parents. The evidence for murder and/or sacrifice is compelling, and throws up the interesting question of why some people were violently killed, while others who lay in close proximity were left intact, apparently at peace when they died, often of natural causes?

Examination of British Neolithic skulls notes that while the long skulls are natural, the longer elongated skulls show a marking that crossed the skull immediately behind the coronal suture or a coronal depression; this was probably the result of cranial deformation in infancy due to binding that would have covered the head and been carried under the jaw. By this means the coronal region and sides of the skull were constricted and compressed, producing a longer skull. The depression was the width of two fingers, and my research indicates that this practice is unique to the long (and round headed) British elite. However, in ancient Briton the ruling elite commonly used cranial deformation to display royal status, making them instantly recognisable. There are numerous examples of coronal depressions from chambered barrows, including in north Wiltshire at West Kennet Long Barrow and at Tilshead, and in Gloucestershire at Uley, Nympsfield and Lugbury long barrows. Scottish examples come from Aberdeenshire and Orkney (Birsay), where, interestingly, it is a striking feature in the skulls of women. Further examples are found at Cladh nan Druidhneac, Iona. In Wales, examples come from Mewslade, and skulls found at East Ham, London, show distinct traces of a coronal depression. *Fig. 14* below shows the cranial deformation of the High Queen of Stonehenge compared to a lesser-long headed skull from Nutbane Long Barrow, in Hampshire (*Fig. 15*), which is of natural skull length.

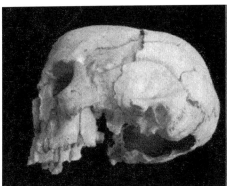 

Fig. 14 The longer skull of the High Queen showing cranial deformation. Tilshead 2 Long Barrow.

Fig. 15 Non-cranial deformation (lesser long headed). Nutbane Long Barrow, Hampshire.

Skull Sizes

The relative proportion of the breadth and length of a skull is known as the cephalic index. Those that range from 65-70 on the index are exceptionally long and narrow; the name given to these types of skulls is hyper-dolichocephalic. At 70-75 they are labelled dolichocephalic. Skulls with an index ranging from 75-80, considered to be the most common type, are mesaticephalic. The next group contain skulls with indices from 80-85, and these are called brachycephalic (round skulled); the roundest skull type, from 85-90, are hyper-brachycephalic. The distinguishing features of this latter group are excessive elongation, flattening of the parietal bones and a squared skull base. When viewed from behind these skulls give a laterally compressed appearance, which are the features of cranial deformation enhanced by a sagittal suture—sometimes elevated into a notched ridge—although hair would have probably camouflaged this unusual feature. It is noteworthy that almost identical coronal depressions are found in dark skinned people. Certainly, Mesolithic 'Cheddar Man' had dark skin and blue eyes, making it likely that the coronal markings were natural. In the 19th century, Professor Karl Ernst von Baer observed that the long skulls he considered undistorted also had a shallow depression behind the coronal suture. Nonetheless, two types of long headed people were living side by side and, in certain areas, especially around Stonehenge, the lesser-elongated were enslaved.

Hyper- and Lesser-elongated Skulls: West Kennet Long Barrow

Atmospheric and inviting, the Neolithic reconstructed West Kennet Long Barrow, sited close to Avebury, was, in 1665, still surrounded by small edging sarsen stones. Today, only a few survive at the eastern end. The mound is orientated east-west targeting sunrise at the Equinoxes, when at dawn a wide shaft of sunlight would have illuminated the stone passageway and the far western chamber. Likewise, when the full moon rose directly in the east, its silvery light would have shone down the passageway. Within the long mound are five spectacular megalithic chambers that feel alive and full of energy. Among the first to enter the mound in modern times was the indomitable Thurnam, who cleared the chalk rubble infill from the large western chamber, about 8 ft (2.4 m) long by 9 ft (2.7 m) wide, and nearly 8 ft (2.4 m) high. Inside, he found six skeletons in a crouched or sitting posture, five of which were probably males from 17 to 50 years of age, the sixth an infant. With one exception, they were of small stature, and four hyper-elongated skulls showed no signs of violence. One of these was around 35 years old, 5 ft 7 in (1.73 m) tall, and his skull was exceptionally narrow with a distinguishing prominent ridge in line with the sagittal suture, as described. This had a flat and narrow back, only 5¼ in (15.2 cm) wide, illustrated in *Fig. 26*. Another male skull was strikingly similar, suggesting they were related—in all probability, brothers.

Fig. 16 West Kennet Long Barrow housed a hyper-long skull of a 35-year old man.

Two lesser-elongated skulls had frontal sutures that gave a much broader and less elongated form. Unlike the hyper-elongated skulls, they displayed a full and rounded occiput, making them noticeably different. In *Fig. 17*, artist Caroline Morgan followed the dimensions in size, length and diameter to reproduce the skull's outline appearance. For simplicity, the ridge has been omitted to emphasise the pyramidical point at the centre of the skull, which is another unusual feature of the exceptionally long headed people.

In ancient Britain, as mentioned, the hyper-long headed culture was probably a ruling elite, the Neolithic royalty, aristocracy or priestly class, while the lesser-elongated skulled people may have been the serving class sacrificed at the obsequies of their rulers, in a similar fashion to those found in some Egyptian tombs. This seems more likely than to consider they were being killed in conflict. During the Iron Age in Gaul, around the time of Julius Caesar, slaves or dependents were killed over the grave of their chiefs; it was a willing sacrifice, such was their deep belief in the afterlife. A similar rite may have been practiced in Neolithic Britain. Excavating Bole's Barrow, the younger Cunningtons noted: "It would appear as if the males of a small tribe had been sacrificed, young and old together." In 2015, I suggested that the long headed murders had been committed by tall and robust Beaker immigrants, although most murderers do not bury their victims with honour. Honouring the dead in this way suggests shared spiritual or religious beliefs, or a mutual set of social and moral obligations.

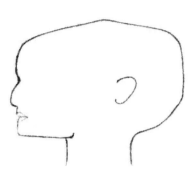

Fig. 17 Side view of a hyper-long headed male from West Kennet Long Barrow. *Illustration:* Caroline Morgan.

Fig. 18 Lesser-long headed from West Kennet Long Barrow.

New Evidence

Three hundred and fifty Neolithic skulls, mostly from southern England, were recently analysed in the context of understanding violence in prehistory. According to the archaeological research of R J Schulting and Michael Wysocki, a high proportion of healed depression fractures could suggest a non-lethal domestic ritualised context for such violence. It was noted that 2% of fatal head injuries were caused by interpersonal or inter-group violence, and that 4-5% had healed. *Fig. 19* shows the extent of confirmed cranial trauma discovered across Neolithic Britain in England, Wales and Northern Ireland. Although the researchers state that some of the killings were caused by inter-group violence, or different regional communities attacking one another, they failed to notice the most important facts: the hyper-elongated skulls exhibited no sign of inter-group violence, whilst a large percentage of the lesser-elongated skull types dis-played extreme violence. They were also all buried together.

Fig. 19 Cranial trauma in the British Isles.

Non-Noble Burials

Long barrow burial deposits do not account for the entire Neolithic population at any given locality. Archaeologists suggest there was probably a secondary form of flat grave burial, which is still prac-

ticed today. Alternatively, as is highly likely, cremation deposits were placed in rivers which have always had their own mythology surrounding death and the afterlife. The remains of a small boy, thought to be around seven years old was found buried in a ditch encircling Windmill Hill causewayed enclosure, near Avebury. He displays a hyper-elongated skull type, which can clearly be seen in *Fig. 20*.

Fig. 20 Hyper-elongated skull of a seven-year-old child.

The Long Mounds of Gloucestershire and Staffordshire

One curious and distinctive characteristic of several examples of long barrow that grace the Gloucestershire landscape is a forecourt crafted by two large projections of the mound, hence their identity as *horned barrows*. Belas Knap Long Barrow, shown below in *Fig 21*, is one of the finest examples, having a 'false' entrance.

Fig. 21 Belas Knap Long Barrow.

An indication of what this false entrance might have meant can be found in ancient Egypt, where tombs often had entrances to the *Duat* or Underworld; it was believed the recently departed could travel back and forth through the burial chamber. A deep shaft led to an underground chamber called a *mastaba*, where an adjacent room was stocked with food and items for use in the afterlife, while the walls were decorated with scenes depicting various daily activities in life. Mastabas were also built with a chapel, including a sacrificial altar. A false door was created through which the souls of the deceased could travel in and out of the burial chamber. Similar beliefs could have governed burial practices in Gloucestershire, which may explain the use of a false entrance. Interestingly, at Belas Knap a long headed male and a round headed male were deposited together behind the false entrance. A clear distinction between their skulls can be seen in *Fig. 22*. Here, as found elsewhere in southern England, the same strange burial rites were being practiced and reveal the lesser-elongated skull people suffered violent deaths.

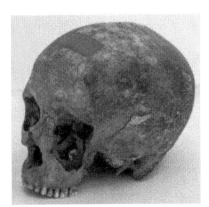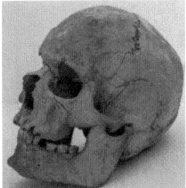

Fig. 22 Left: typical long headed male. Right: round headed male from the false entrance.

Mirroring the examples near Stonehenge, deep in the chambered long barrow of Rodmarton, situated about 6 miles (9.6 km) to the southwest of Cirencester, Gloucestershire, an exceptionally long headed man was found alongside several lesser-elongated headed people. Commonly known as Windmill Tump, Rodmarton Long Barrow is nearly 187 ft (57 m) long and 9 ft (2.7 m) high in places, surrounded by a modern dry-stone wall. Today, this peaceful place is surrounded by fields of cereal crops and shielded by trees. The barrow contained three stone-lined chambers; those to the north and south had unusual and magnificent portholes—a circular hole cut into the stone giving restricted access into the chamber. The workmanship was so extraordinary, one wonders what tools were used to cut through the solid stone to create this hole. When the Rev Samuel Lysons (1806-1877) of Rodmarton began excavations in 1863, to his surprise he found the north chamber intact and undisturbed. Looking around he saw seven upright stones holding up a single capstone, estimated to weigh around eight tons. Sadly, the porthole stones have long since disappeared and only his account reminds us of the long headed peoples' unusual megalithic design. Later, I will discuss the meaning of these porthole stones. At one time, the dark,

narrow gallery leading to the entrance was formed of horizontal dry- stone walling; inside were thirteen or fourteen long headed people, all of whom were deposited in a crouching posture. The skulls, many of which were encrusted with stalagmites, were of six or seven men, three or four women, and three long headed children of around two, three and twelve years old. The adult males, who, calculated by the length of the thigh bones which measured 17-17.5 in (43-44.5 cm), and the tibiae 14-14.5 in (35.5 cm),

Fig. 23 Long headed children were found at Rodmarton. *Illustration:* Fiona Hughes.

were middle aged and approximately 5 ft 4 in (1.64 m) in height, although "endowed with powerful and vigorous frames." The thigh bones of the women were 15-16 in (38-40 cm), giving them a height of 5 ft (1.52 m). Some of the men had three cervical vertebrae showing signs of arthritis, a condition which was also found in the long barrows of Uley, Nympsfield, in Gloucestershire, and at Winterbourne Stoke, near Stonehenge.

Three male skulls and one female skull were exceptionally long, narrow and well preserved. One skull of a man of around 50 years old at the time of his death, was one of the most hyper-elongated discovered, having a cephalic index of 72. This is slightly less than the skull from nearby Uley Long Barrow and another from Long Low Long Barrow, near Wetton in Staffordshire, both of which measured 71. Viewed from above, the long and ovoid form was more pronounced than other elongated skulls and is very striking. Furthermore, the smallness of the back and base, the head's occipital region, at only a little over 5 in (13 cm) in breadth, is astonishingly small. As we shall see, other facial and bodily features gave these people a distinctly mythic, ethereal appearance.

Wanton Murder

Four lesser-elongated skulls, males aged from 30-50 years, had horrendous wounds and heavy gashes that were inflicted during their lifetimes. One man endured such a violent attack that his skull suffered a straight cut that sliced through the top part of his skull; the whole of the frontal and anterior halves of the two parietals indicated the edges of the wound were sharp. Although short in stature, this man had a large and robust physique with muscular and heavy features. Despite such a gruesome killing, this man was buried with honour; his sliced-off skull was carefully placed in its correct anatomical position, and he was placed in a sitting crouched position, as if staring at the chamber's entrance—perhaps guarding the barrow for his master. Another, with a lesser-elongated skull, also suffered brutal violence; the frontal and right parietal sections of his skull gashed in various directions. Yet another took the brunt of an aggressive attack; the fragments of his skull so numerous that we might suppose the wounds were inflicted in sheer wantonness. Yet, these people were all buried with grave goods that must have held meaning and value in life. They included shards of thin black pottery, a small fragment of a green stone that was smooth and polished, a large flint with flakes broken off, and two finely worked leaf-shaped flint arrowheads that were probably ceremonial. These Neolithic burial deposits offer us an insight into the lives and beliefs of the long headed elite.

Fig. 24 Uley Long Barrow. *Photograph:* Paul Goddard.

Uley and Lugbury Long Barrows

Uley Long Barrow is situated on the brow edge of the Cotswolds in Gloucestershire, overlooking the Severn Vale, and is well worth a visit. In 1821 and 1854, Thurnam was joined by a Mr E A Freeman and together they broke open the mound. A contemporary illustration shows that an excessively large section of the southern side was opened up. Thurnam estimated the mound to be about 120 ft (39.6 m) in length, 85 ft (26 m) in greatest breadth and 10 ft (3 m) in height. The entrance is formed by a large flat stone, which in certain light resembles an elongated head and neck resting on upright stones at each side. A small opening led to a central gallery around 22 ft (6.7 m) in length, 4.5 ft (1.37 m) wide and 5 ft (1.5 m) in height, and on each side of the central gallery are two chambers. Thurnam reported that the chambers on the north side "no longer exist, being in a ruinous condition when it was first discovered." The sides of the gallery and the chambers are carefully constructed of large slabs of oolitic limestone placed on their edges, and the space between filled with a dry wall of small stones. The same technique of dry-stone walling is still employed today, as seen throughout the Cotswolds. In the interior were the remains of thirteen long headed people, six of whom were in the central gallery. They had been disturbed, possibly millennia ago, but one skeleton was found squatting three feet inside the entrance, retaining its original posture. Another person, near the far end of the gallery, had been deposited on their back. Inside Chamber 1 were four skeletons, including one of a woman; in Chamber 2 were pieces of pottery, charcoal, and parts of one human skeleton; and in the ruinous Chamber 3 were two more skeletons. Over this chamber, about six inches from the surface and near the highest part of the cairn, was a secondary skeleton from the Late Roman period. Only two skulls from Uley Long Barrow were preserved, one of a man and the other a nameless child; the rest are missing or possibly, one imagines, kept somewhere in a box in a private or museum collection.

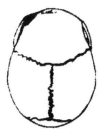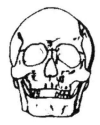

Fig. 25 Uley, skull of a long headed male.

The illustration above in *Fig. 25* is of the skull of a mature man who lived to be around 65 years of age. Described as being of "great thickness and large capacity," it is remarkable for its length in proportion to its breadth and showed signs of cranial deformation. The pyramidal aspect in the front view of the skull shows a central ridge present along the median line. The other skull found, missing its lower jaw, was of a small child of perhaps nine or ten years of age. The child's skull had the same lengthened form as the elderly man's; perhaps it is comforting to think they were laid to rest together. All of the lesser-elongated adults appear to have been killed by a blow to the head—a theme repeated at Lugbury Long Barrow.

Lugbury Long Barrow stands about two hundred yards from the Fosse Way, a Roman road which follows one of four main prehistoric thoroughfares in England. One can imagine legionnaires contemplating this ancient monument as they marched to fight the native Celts. Although the site is now a ghostly outline of its former glory, it is still worth visiting. On his travels in the 17th century, John Aubrey came across this long mound. Inside was a stone paved cist for a young man who was carefully laid on his right side, with his head facing west and his knees drawn up. Within other chambers the bodies appeared to have been packed closely together in crouched or sitting postures. Chamber 1 held seven female long headed skeletons; Chamber 2 appeared never to have been used or had been robbed of its contents, as not a fragment of bone was found; Chamber 3 contained nine skeletons, all men, and fragments of a ninth skull; and Chamber 4 held what could have been two families —four adults, two possibly of each sex—and four children placed closely together. There are many examples of both types of long headed people across Great Britain.

Fig. 26 The remains of Lugbury Long Barrow.

My final example comes from Long Low Long Barrow near Wetton, in Staffordshire, as it tells a different story to the others. In this area of England, the lesser-elongated headed people were not murdered and appear to have lived in harmony with their hyper-long headed counterparts. Excavated in 1849, this long barrow was striking in that it had rounded terminals, or round barrows, at each end. The chamber was 7 ft (2 m) long by 5 ft (1.52 m) wide, with a beautifully paved floor, as shown in *Fig. 28*. Inside and lying undisturbed were the remains of thirteen people, from infancy to the infirm, with

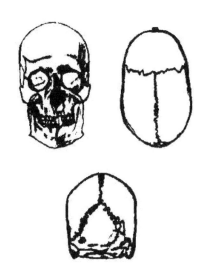

several women placed close to the centre. At the centre was the body of a man with an exceptionally elongated skull, shown in *Fig. 27*. Moreover, as with the long headed skulls of southern England, it displayed flattening of the parietal bones, a result of cranial deformation. Close by was a woman and a little girl of about seven years old, both long headed and with exactly the same features; probably related, they too experienced cranial deformation. Skulls found in the neighbouring county of Derbyshire, in the barrows of

Fig. 27 Male long headed skull from Long Low Long Barrow.

Bole Hill on Bakewell Moor, Stoney Lowe, Brassington Moor, Ringham Low, Five Wells Hill and Taddington are all of the exceptionally long headed kind.

Fig. 28 Paved chamber at Long Low Long Barrow.

A Mythical Appearance

To see a Neolithic hyper-long headed person today, we might think they had walked out of a Sci-Fi movie. Striking facial features and unusual bodily stature made the long headed people stand apart from the round headed European Beaker people, whose skulls were shaped more like we would expect to see today. A modern human head is on average one-eighth proportion of the body. Neolithic skulls were longer but of smaller proportion to body length, one-tenth in size and remarkably narrow, making their heads look small on a long body. The Neolithic long headed ratio of skull length to vertical height is 1:36-1:20 as opposed to 0:85-0:90 in modern humans, making the long headed skull longer than its height compared to a modern skull that is slightly higher than its length. Another peculiar feature is that the back of the skull was much rounder compared to a modern skull. In general, long headed people had small straight noses, a very strong jawline and rounder foreheads. As previously mentioned, along the sagittal suture was a raised ridge bringing the skull up to a point, whereas the top of a modern skull is gently rounded. The sides of the long headed skull, the parietal bones, appeared flat with a distinctive squareness at the base, hence the term given by artist and antiquary Daniel Wilson as 'coffin-shaped'.

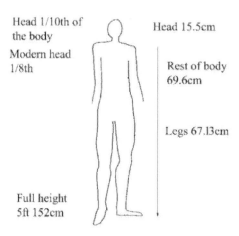

Fig. 29 The body proportions of a long headed person.
Illustration: Caroline Morgan.

Even stranger, the position of their ears added to an otherworldly look. Due to the strong jawline and length of the skull, the ears were set further back giving an elfin-like appearance. This was emphasised by large, deep-set eyes. In a few examples, such as at West Kennet Long Barrow, skulls were also found with unusual dental characteristics, where no canine teeth were present; they were all more or less of equal size like a child's milk teeth.

Several reports included the curious observation of "small or non-existent ossicle ridges." I spoke to a colleague who is a doctor about this, who informed me: "I'm not sure what ossicle ridges are. Today, ossicles refer to the three tiny bones of the middle ear. In older days, ossicles were 'small bones' but this doesn't sound correct from an anatomical point of view." But what if it *was* anatomically correct? If so, with small inner ear bones (if indeed that's what is being referred to), and with ears set back, could they hear different audio ranges and frequencies? Without further in-depth medical study, much remains speculative and uncertain. Anthropologists also noted that numerous femur bones had what appeared to be an extra muscle attachment: "The two upper lips of the linea aspera [produced a] prolonged spiral round into the anterior intertrochanteric line." This occurred in both sexes, which indicates that some sort of prolonged physical activity developed this extra muscle attachment, resulting from, for example, carrying heavy loads in a zig-zag or sideways fashion, perhaps due to moving heavy stones. It is a fact that at sites such as Avebury and Stonehenge, the largest stone settings were invariably Neolithic and were thus moved by the short yet strong, long headed people.

Fig. 30 Ryedale woman, tiny long skull. *Illustration:* Caroline Morgan.

A typical example of a hyper-long headed skull—a woman's—comes from a long barrow in Ryedale, North Yorkshire. She had a small frame and was only 4 ft 8 in (1.46 m) tall with characteristically small features. As previously mentioned, although their heads were elongated they were remarkably small in proportion to their bodies. This woman was only 35 years old. Her skull, shown in *Fig. 30*, was 7 in (17.7 cm) long and her face only 4½ in (11.4 cm). She would have looked exceptionally petite with strange ear placements, curiously familiar to us from mythic fiction (*Fig 31*). Perhaps stories of elves and pixies originated from a distant memory of the long headed Neolithic people?

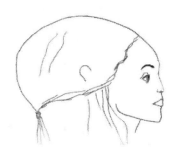

Fig. 31 Curiously familiar from mythic fiction.
Illustration: Caroline Morgan.

In Irish mythology, the Tuatha Dé Danann are seen as a supernatural race that can interact with humans in the mortal world, although not always for good. However, after losing a battle, legend says they moved underground into the barrows and mounds, and so became the fairies of Ireland, consigned to the Underworld (people of the mound, fairy mounds), where they became known as the 'sidhe'. Interestingly, as legend attests, the Tuatha Dé Danann are associated with Neolithic passage tombs, such as at Newgrange and Four Knocks, which were seen as portals to the otherworld. That the ethereal looking long headed were found in long mounds may be the origin of this age-old legend; the long headed *were* the Tuatha Dé Danann.

Fig. 32 A long headed woman.
Illustration: Fiona Hughes.

An exceptionally long skull was unearthed from a long mound that still survives today in the Ryedale district. This woman was ceremonially placed into a long mound and though only a fragment of her skull survived, measurements taken have allowed her memory to live on. Her long, yet small skull was 8.3 in (20.3 cm) long, and with a height of 6 in (15.2 cm).

Her age at death is estimated to be 60 years. Among the bone fragments was a portion of lower jaw; numerous excavated Neolithic jaws show a great thickness in the molar region and a noticeably small chin. If her jaw was similar to that of the High Queen of Stonehenge, shown in *Fig 33*—as it probably was—this may explain her low and retreating forehead, referred to as a very low 'basis cranii' (base of the skull). Similar looking skulls and jaw bones found at Stoney Littleton Long Barrow in Somerset, were referred to as 'fronte valde depressa'.

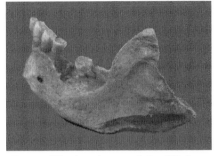

Fig. 33 The jaw bone of the High Queen of Stonehenge.

The Rudstone Long Barrow

Parts of the county of Yorkshire, as with the land around Stonehenge, appears to have been a centre for the long headed megalithic people. One of the most unusual long mounds in the British Isles can be found on the chalk downland of East Riding; its combination of a long mound, replete with burial deposits and an adjoining cenotaph unchambered mound, is unprecedented. The monument consists of two long mounds joined together to form a V-shaped earthen structure: the north mound 210 ft (64 m) long, 75 ft (22.8 m) 45 ft (13.7 m) wide, and 4 ft (1.2 m) high at the eastern end. Officially described as a *linear earthwork*, it contained a cremation area with disarticulated human bones and a possible secondary cremation with Anglo-Saxon pottery. No burials were found in the unchambered mound to the south. Undoubtedly, the north mound housed the elite of the community. Sited just half a mile (2.2 km) away, stands the tallest menhir in the British Isles, the Rudstone Monolith. Towering just over 25 ft (8 m) tall with a circumference of 16.4 ft (5 m), and weighing an estimated 26 tons, this stone was probably transported from Cayton Bay, about 9 miles (16 km) to the north. Today, it stands Pagan and proud in Rudstone's Christian churchyard. In 1773, the standing stone was capped with lead to protect its tip against erosion, which was of course unnecessary. Excavations in the 18th century concluded that the stone extended as deep below as it was above ground. Perhaps, some of the long headed occupants of the nearby long barrow were responsible for transporting and raising this giant monolith. One man buried within the Rudstone barrow was described by excavators as "small in stature but muscular and well-built." Like the Wor Barrow man in Dorset, his skull, shown below in *Fig. 34*, was exceptionally narrow.

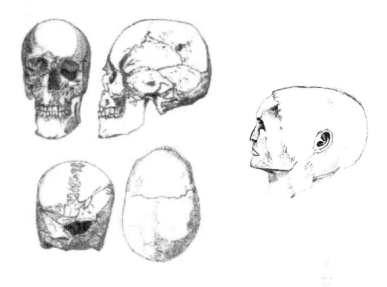

Fig. 34 Left: Very elongated and narrow skull from the Rudstone Long Barrow. Right: Using the same measurements a side profile of the Rudstone male with setback ears. *Illustration* Caroline Morgan.

Recently Lost Knowledge and Suppressed Disclosure

Studying the measurements of the long headed people documented in archaeological reports, one thing became apparent to me: many of the illustrations were not drawn to the correct scale, even though the measurements were clearly listed. An illustration by Caroline Morgan of an elongated skull that she drew to the *precise* scale, using the exact measurements originally recorded, is shown in *Fig. 36*. Note that her skull is longer than the archaeological illustration, shown in *Fig. 35*. It should also be noted that this happened more than once, to the point where I suspect that information regarding the Early Neolithic peoples' true appearance was being deliberately

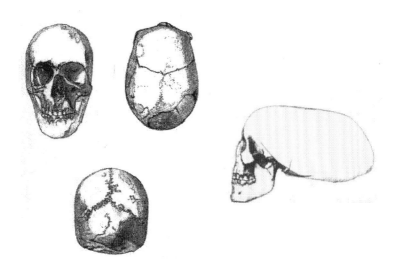

Fig. 35 Left: Victorian drawing of the skull. Right: Using the same measurements reveals a longer skull (repressed information). *Illustration:* Caroline Morgan.

suppressed. One reason for this could be that it challenges the orthodox view, and thus our understanding of the prehistoric past. Such is the academic pride in dividing categories that whenever something new comes along that doesn't quite 'fit' there is a tendency, as novelist Jeanette Winterson puts it, to avoid tricky encounters by familiarising or trivialising it, either by attempting to categorise the un-identified with existing species or rejecting it altogether. So, whether this evidence has been deliberately dis-regarded, or simply ignored since the 19th century, and because in a funding-driven world no-one knows how to treat such 'exotic' data, it remains an open question. *Fig. 36* gives a com-parison of the longest skull from West Kennet Long Barrow with a modern-day head size.

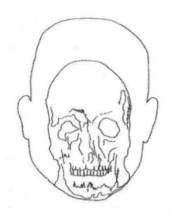

Fig. 36 A small, narrow long skull compared to a modern-day head. *Illustration:* Caroline Morgan.

Britain's Earliest Long Headed Mummy

Thousands of years before the Egyptians mummified their elite, the long headed Wessex culture practiced mummification. Wor Barrow, a long mound that lies within Cranborne Chase in Dorset, an area renowned for its prehistoric archaeology, shows how some of the dead were treated in unusual ways. This barrow was constructed for long headed males, six of whom were under the age of 45 when they died, while the sex of the seventh person could not be determined. Heights ranged from 4 ft 10 in to 5 ft 9 in (1.20-1.55 m) tall. The tallest, Burial 4, was a later deposit, its long skull shown in *Fig. 37* and its narrowness in *Fig. 38*. I pointed out to the curator how small the skull was and he agreed, "its small proportions are striking". Without a doubt, the tallest individual conforms to the long headed body type: the skull is longer but in smaller proportion to body length.

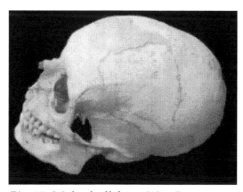 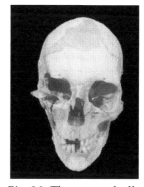

Fig. 37 Male skull from Wor Barrow, showing its length. Child-like in size.

Fig. 38 The same skull showing its narrowness.

However, the most unusual burial is Burial 8, which was placed in the barrow's ditch; a body that had been tightly wrapped and preserved for between 30 and 130 years before it was deposited in the barrow, making it the earliest known 'mummy' in Britain. Possibly this person was sacrificed, or met with a violent end, caused perhaps by an arrowhead; nonetheless, for more than a century this unburied mummy was revered in some manner. Another of the males gave evidence of a congenital or developmental syndrome, which would have shown itself as a facial disfigurement and possibly a physical disability requiring the use of some form of a crutch.

Chapter 3

Medical and Spiritual Trepanation

Surgeons in the Neolithic era performed a variety of operations on the body, including the brain. One of these was trepanation, a surgical intervention where a hole is drilled into the skull, then incised or scraped using surgical tools presumably made of flint or, later, of bronze. To date, more than 1,500 trepanned skulls have been found throughout the world, from Europe to North America, Russia, China and South America, particularly in Peru. The surgeon drilled into the skull to remove a piece of bone, exposing the dura mater without damage to the underlying blood vessels, meninges and the brain. That people survived demonstrates a level of expertise on the part of the practitioner, but to fully understand the operation let us meet the Neolithic patients and uncover their surgical past.

Many hypotheses have been put forward to explain the reasoning behind such an operation, from the removal of entities that cause epilepsy, to a simpler medical need to provide some form of relief. One theory, published in 2015 by Miguel A Farias in the medical journal *Surgical Neurology International*, argues that unconsciousness was regarded by Neolithic people as a 'dead' state and that trepanning a skull would bring the person back to life, 'undead' as it were. Reading through the various theses and from compelling evidence I have gathered from existing literature so far, I conjecture that in the Neolithic the primary reason for the operation was due to characteristics unique to long headed people and their desire to achieve a higher state of consciousness. Starting from a clue that has received no prior attention, I have uncovered a rare and extraordinary surgical procedure that the European long headed people performed— this is a strange cranial 'marking' which changed the physical appearance of the individual, making them instantly recognisable.

This should be considered less in terms of a medical practice but as part of a long-forgotten sacred rite.

L'Homme Mort: the European Trepanation Capital

Our journey begins at one of the major trepanation capitals of Europe, in the Lozère region of France, where the discovery was made in one place of a hundred and fifteen trepanned skulls—Neolithic cranial surgery on a grand scale. Excavated in the late-19th century, human use of the sepulchral hypogeum-like caves of L'Homme Mort has been dated to the Early Neolithic. Silent, very still and intensely dark, these caverns housed numerous burial deposits thought to predate megalithic dolmens and burial chambers. The skulls found were hyper-dolichocephalic—very long and elongated. This did not surprise the excavators who were familiar with seeing and handling such skulls. A surprise did await them, however. Upon handling one particular skull in the dimly lit chamber, an excavator's thumb slipped into a perfectly formed hole. A colleague called out in the darkness, as he too had found a 'holed' skull. They immediately carried the skulls outside into the light when, for the first time in nearly six thousand years, evidence of prehistoric surgery was revealed to modern man. Leading the excavation, Dr Barthélémy Prunières soon realised the significance of the 'hole' and began to study the trepanned skulls, most of which were long headed. Certainly, the antiquity of the cave indicates that the first Neolithic surgeons were of the long headed civilisation. However, the operation was also performed on a small proportion of mesocephalic (middle sized—not elongated—but not quite fully round) skulls, as well as round skulled people, although these may have been secondary deposits.

Hauntingly atmospheric, the vast sepulchral caverns of Baume-Chaudes in Lozère, rise up to a mesmerising cathedral-like interior. The southernmost caverns terminate in a deep well-like chamber, measuring 82 ft (25 m) long by 13 ft (4 m) wide, and housing copious burials. In the late-19th century, excavators collected the remains of over three hundred people of various ages, both male and female, and sixty skulls, just under one third of which were trepanned.

Ceremonially placed amongst the remains was a circular, perforated shamanic relic made from the skull of a deer—probably an amulet or spiritual tool. All of the human skulls were hyper-long headed, similar in shape and length to their Palaeolithic ancestors. Out of the sixty trepanned skulls, not one was brachycephalic or mesocephalic. Noted characteristics were the broad frontal region of the skulls with a large cranial capacity, and their height, calculated by using the mean length of fifteen femur bones, gave an estimate of 5 ft 3 in (1.6 m), almost the same height as the long headed people of Stonehenge. These ancient cranial remains show unequivocally that the first surgeons were long headed.

Les Grotte du Petit Morin: Cavern of the Goddess

Yet more trepanned skulls were found close to the dolmens of Lozère, in the Joches area of Coizard, north-eastern France. Within the eternally dark labyrinth of Petit Morin's caverns lies a vast necropolis that unites more than thirty hypogeal chambers. Hollow-ed out of the solid chalk to provide a sacred space for both ritual and burial, the only link to the outside world from these womb-like chambers is by an 'entry-passage' of walkways. Such passageways have a deep feminine significance, linking the descendants to their ancestors—from this world to the otherworld—time present to time past. Imagine walking silently along a dimly lit passageway lead-ing into chalk white quadrangular chambers, some as large as 21.52 sq ft (2 sq m). Carefully etched onto one of the chamber walls is the famous image of a goddess, or matriarchal mother, as shown in *Fig. 39*. The thick base of the figure becomes thinner and rounder to-wards the top, the head stylised following the artistic style of their Palaeolithic ancestors, symbolising her everlasting nurturing protec-tion within the darkness.

Fig. 39 Carved image of a goddess, or matriarchal mother.

50

According to Lithuanian anthropologist Marija Gimbutas (1921-1994), who specialised in goddess mythology, hypogea symbolise the uterus emphasising rebirth and the divine feminine. The site at Petit Morin and other hypogea at Mornouards, Mesnil-Sur-Orge (Essonne), Font Vielle and Bouches-du-Rhone, were all situated close to dolmen complexes which probably inspired their location. During the late-19th century, neuro-anthropologist Paul Broca selected fifty-two skulls to examine from the caves of Petit Morin. Out of twenty-eight male and twenty-four female skulls, only four were rounded with an index of not less than 83. Ten were dolichocephalic, lesser-elongated, with an index not exceeding 75; the remainder were graded between these two extremes. Remarkably, in the late 1880s, French archaeologist Joseph Baron de Baye (1853-1931) excavated more than a thousand burials in the valley of Petit Morin, removing numerous skulls and other relics to his château for his own personal collection. Thereafter, an expert team of European doctors and anthropologists studied the French skull collections to try and understand the reasoning behind Neolithic trepanation.

Holes in the Archaeological Theory

For centuries, trepanation was interpreted as a shamanic practice for the purpose of creating an exit route for demonic seizure-inducing possession. Yet, close examination of the skulls tells a different story. I contend that the practice of trepanation crosses two main areas: the first is the *physical* treatment of wounds and medical conditions; the second is *metaphysical,* to achieve a transcendent state of consciousness by improving cerebral blood circulation, which decreases with age. The more elongated skull type was especially susceptible to circulation problems.

Before we explore esoteric reasons for the operation, let us look at the medical conditions that were treated. In studying the skulls at Petit Morin, it was noted that of several trepanned skulls, it was clearly performed as emergency surgery. If the patient suffered a skull fracture, trepanation enabled the removal of shattered pieces of bone, and could reduce liquid substances (blood, water or pus) beneath the skull. In his paper, *On Trepanning the Human Skull in*

Prehistoric Times (1882), recorded in the proceedings of the Scottish Society of Social Anthropology, Robert Munro tells of a Professor Parrot who described a case of trepanation from a Neolithic cemetery at Bray-sur-Seine:

> "The tissues surrounding the perforation in the skull exhibited some special pathological phenomena and he observed that the inference of the operation had been performed solely for a surgical purpose, probably to give an exit for accumulated pus. … Around the seat of the operation, there was evidence of an extensive osteitis, the cause of which he assigned to a traumatic wound."

The paper goes on to say the subsequent researches of Dr Parrot and other experts confirmed earlier observations by Dr Pruniéres, that occasionally the operation was performed for purely surgical purposes.

Fig. 40 A trepanned skull from Sardinia.

Treatment of Diseased Bone and Osteitis

From the seemingly primitive rock-shelter of Entre-Eoches, near Angouleme, in France, emerged a sophisticated surgical treatment. A small number of trepanned skulls provided unmistakeable evidence that the operation had been performed to remove a section of diseased bone. Other skulls suggested that it was used to treat certain diseases of the bone, such as osteitis (inflammation). One trepanned skull found in Marne showed extensive disease of the frontal and parietal bones. On the left parietal, a small section of healthy bone stood out at the centre of the depressed portion of the diseased area, offering a strong contrast. The diseased bone was thin and had broken in two or three places in the process of extraction; no trace was left of the coronal suture which the disease had entirely obliterated. The opening of the frontal and left parietal bones was of the usual oval shape and had been performed partly on healthy and diseased bone. The edges of the aperture were perfectly healed, showing the patient survived the operation long enough for this to happen. The disease, which was probably an exfoliative osteitis, likely came about as the result of trauma as there was a depression on the frontal bone which could have been caused by a weapon.

When Dr Parrot carefully examined a piece of trepanned skull from one of the dolmens of Port-Blanc, Saint-Pierre de Quiberon, Morbihan in Brittany, the opening indicated to him that the bone was removed on one side by a scraping process, while the other side revealed an abrupt edge as if a cutting instrument had been used: "The operation had been as neatly executed as if it had been performed by one of our most distinguished surgeons."

The Stonehenge Brain Surgeon

To the east of Stonehenge, an excavation from a round barrow, known as Amesbury 71, revealed a well-built man who had survived trepanation. When another trepanned skull and fragment were re-examined, bone samples from the round barrow known as Amesbury 51 suggested a Bronze Age surgeon was treating a terminal and almost incurable disease that still haunts humanity today. This barrow was excavated in 1881, just a stone's throw from Stonehenge, by Colt Hoare and Cunnington. The duo noted that the body was "big-boned and with perfect white teeth" and the skull, displaying a trepanned section, was very well-preserved. Roger Watson, the Documentation Officer at Devizes Museum in Wiltshire, reassessed the evidence and concluded that a surgical procedure had probably taken place sometime between 2000-1600 BC. He notes:

"...a young man underwent a major surgical operation, perhaps for a brain tumour, that involved the cutting away of a disk of bone measuring 1.25 in (32 mm) in diameter from his cranium."

Whilst excavating (or rather ransacking) the Stonehenge barrows, Thurnam sometimes mistook trepanned skulls as 'cleft' skulls. As noted earlier, Bole's Barrow on Salisbury Plain housed a primary inhumation of an extremely long headed male confirming that his skull had been trepanned—alongside was found a 5 in (12.7 cm) skull roundel, the removed section of the trepanned hole. More examples were unearthed at Fussell's Lodge Long Barrow. This verifies that the first British surgeons, as in France, were the Neolithic long headed people.

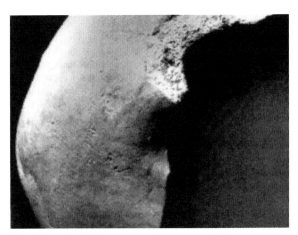

Fig. 41 A healed trepanation wound from a skull found at Fussell's Lodge Long Barrow.

Skilful Surgeons: Avoiding Brain Damage

In Bougon, western France, are the Bougon tumuli. Standing among a group of five Neolithic barrows is the incredible and unforgettable Tumulus 'A' that feels active and alive. Dated to 4800 BC with a diameter of around 137 ft (42 m), its centre is 16½ ft (5 m) high. Inside the barrow, south of the mound's centre is a large rectangular chamber measuring 25½ ft (7.8 m) across, with a height of over 8 ft (2.2 m). The magnificent stonework requires close inspection as the chamber walls contain artificially shaped (dressed) orthostats, with gaps filled by dry-stone walling, a common feature of numerous long barrows, passage graves and court tombs across Europe. Before reaching out to touch the stonework, please close your eyes and ask the ancestors for permission to interact with the site, in order to align with the ever-present whispers and ancestral energy. A gargantuan capstone weighing 90 tons covers the chamber, supported by two stalwart stone pillars that also serve to subdivide the chamber.

The long headed of the Neolithic era were small people, only around 5 ft (1.52 m) tall, yet they moved the heaviest of stones. In 1840, an excavation by archaeologists who discovered the Bougon tumuli found around two hundred skeletons in three distinct layers, separated by stone slabs. Unfortunately, the vague reports prevent a detailed chronology. Accompanying finds included flat and round-bottomed pottery, beads, pierced teeth, chains of seashells and stone tools, including a diorite mace. At the base level, which normally represents the oldest burial layer, was the skull of a man who had undergone three trepanations during his lifetime. During the first, a circular disk was removed from the left occiput at a precise angle to skilfully avoid brain damage, showing that the Neolithic surgeons were anatomically aware, also of potential brain injury caused by intrusion. Two operations followed near the top of the skull and the edges were perfectly cicatrised (healed). In imparting a timeless and spiritual ambience, this stone temple personified sacred space for centuries. Such was its charm and reverence that a thousand years or so after its construction, it was used for further burials by people of a completely different culture.

Elongated Trepanned Skulls: Lisbon, Portugal

From deep within a sacred cave situated on the bank of the Tagus, near Lisbon, Portugal, in a place known as Casa da Moura, a large quantity of human bone was found. At least one hundred and fifty individuals were placed within the safety of these caves. Although most of the bones were decayed, three or four complete skulls confirm they were elongated. On the upper part of one mesocephalic skull, one of the parietal bones had a deep groove in the form of a pointed ellipse, 2 in (5 cm) long by ¾ inch (1.9 cm) wide. The upper plate had been sawn through by a sharp implement. The intention of the surgeon was to gain access to the brain, but for some reason the operation was abandoned—the patient must have died as there was no sign of healing.

Fig. 42 Almemdres Dolmen of Portugal. Phase 1: constructed by the long headed civilisation.

Phase 1 of the Almemdres Dolmen (stone circles), a Portuguese site worth visiting, was constructed by the long headed civilisation and later extended in the Bronze Age. In 2020, my guide informed me that, like at Stonehenge, the stone complex was soon to be cordoned off, prohibiting public access. I was blessed to be able to interact and touch these wise old stones that have witnessed so much.

A Standard Operation

Close inspection of hundreds of reports reveals that trepanation was a standardised procedure. Strikingly so, as the apertures made are uniform in size and rarely do the dimensions differ. They are nearly always elliptical, between 1-2 in (25.4 mm) by approximately one third of an inch (6-10 mm), with oblique edges. The operation appears to have been performed on both sexes and on all parts of the head except the forehead, usually the parietal bones. Great care was taken by the surgeons not to disfigure the skull; the trepanned sections were always covered by the hairy scalp to avoid any noticeable disfigurement. The procedure shows that the surgeon always knew the correct location and size of the incision, implying trained practitioners. We have seen that the operation was used for various medical purposes, from the removal of bone to relieving pressure on the brain. However, I suggest that due to the elongated skull shape, many people suffered from a persistent condition which trepanning could relieve. One woman's experience may explain why…

Trepanation and Higher Consciousness

In 1970, Amanda Feilding, Countess of Wemyss and March, drilled a hole in the top of her head, believing this would bring about a higher state of consciousness. She says it did. Amanda was inspired by Dr Bart Hughes, who, in 1962, advocated trepanation as a means of achieving a transcendent state. She claims "something is lost" when parts of the skull encasing the brain fuse together as we grow older. According to most medical specialists, beyond the anecdotal there is no evidence that this is true. Amanda's thought-provoking hypothesis is that trepanation improves cerebral circulation by allowing the *full heartbeat* to express itself inside the cranial cavity— this is otherwise hindered once the cranial bones close in childhood. She adds that to compensate for the relative loss of circulation, humans developed an internal system of control of blood flow to the brain, which identifies with the development of 'ego' and the origins of language. Trepanation frees the flow, allowing people to achieve and sustain a higher state of consciousness—a similar state as that experienced by children before their cranial bones fuse.

In 2004, Amanda began a collaboration with Russian scientist Yuri Moskalenko, whose research on patients with cranial lesions shows evidence of blood flow changes. This is part of an investigation on changing intracranial dynamics with age, looking at ways to increase cranial compliance which, they theorise, might help to limit the detrimental changes associated with ageing. Amanda reported feeling better immediately after the operation, and claims it uplifted her, gave her more energy and made her more buoyant. However, over time, this faded, so she had another larger hole drilled on the right-hand side of her head by a doctor in Mexico City. To ensure that the wound would not grow over, a piece of wax was inserted to inhibit bone growth. The uplifting and spiritual feelings she experienced before were similar after the second surgery. Her husband, a former Oxford University professor, who once taught the future US President, Bill Clinton, also had a hole made in his skull. Amanda was 27 years old when she performed her first trepanation. Bravely, she used an electric foot-operated dentist's drill, applied a local aesthetic to her scalp and taped glasses to her face to prevent blood from dripping into her eyes. Using a mirror for guidance, she then bore a hole about half an inch (1.27 cm) wide in the top of her head just above the hairline, while a friend filmed the procedure. One surgeon who observed the video footage said she could have killed herself in the process. It is *definitely not* advisable to try this at home.

While it has been demonstrated that trepanation was performed as a medical intervention, the majority of trepanned long skulls displayed no signs of trauma to justify the operation for that reason. I noted numerous elongated skulls from all over England and France showed a distinctive sign of premature obliteration (early fusing) of the sutures (see *Fig. 43*). The Rudstone man of East Riding, Yorkshire, is a good example. His sagittal suture closed along the inner table of the

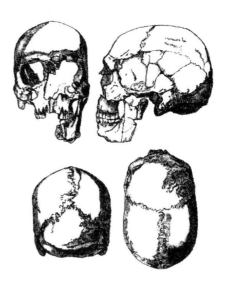

Fig. 43 Male skull with premature closure of the sutures.

skull and is completely denticulated or finely toothed, a condition also observed in two other skulls from long barrows nearby. Premature obliteration of the sutures appears to be consistent with the long skull phenomenon, and numerous examples can be cited. The Rodmarton male skull, for example, shows the sutures are quite distinct externally but appear to be obliterated internally. At Five Wells Long Barrow, in Derbyshire, one skull of an individual about 35 years old showed premature obliteration of the sagittal suture, which is entirely effaced. Likewise, in the case of one of the most elongated skulls I have ever seen, a woman from Ryedale, North Yorkshire, had her sutures prematurely closed, and younger members of the long headed culture show similar premature closure. It was initially surmised that this premature closing caused synostosis, an elongation of the brain as the sutures close, meaning the brain does not grow at right angles to them. Another opinion claimed this was prevented by ossification of the sutures. Regardless, the premature closure of the sagittal sutures is clear, and would have inhibited the heartbeat in the head. Moreover, this must have been more pronounced in an elongated skull than Amanda would have experienced with her shorter and rounder skull. It certainly would have been a dynamic sensation, offering the potential to produce feelings of intense spiritual insight and higher consciousness.

Hyper-Long Headed Examples of Trepanation

My inspection of trepanned skulls deposited in long barrows confirms that the most elongated were trepanned. As noted earlier, the primary interment at Bole's Barrow was the longest skull having undergone trepanation, while other lesser-elongated skull types had not. This is repeated at Rodmarton and at Fussell's Lodge, along with numerous other long barrow examples in Yorkshire. In contrast, Bronze Age brachycephalic skulls, and those from other periods, frequently display an open coronal suture when compared to the long headed skull type of the same age group.

I conclude that trepanation (trephination) was a surgical procedure mainly applied to long headed individuals to counteract the effect of premature obliteration of the sutures. It was probably reserved for a select group of people, such as the ruling elite and priestly class. Its benefit was to experience spiritual elevation, higher consciousness, and the *heartbeat in the head* that the closure of the sutures prohibit. Thousands of years ago, trepanation allowed, as Amanda Feilding experienced, uplifting and enhanced spiritual feelings.

Perhaps it was a way to directly commune with Gaia and other deities. Occasionally, children were selected for trepanation. Broca's keen eye noted that one skull was unsymmetrical because the sagittal suture was out of the meridian line and bent towards the trepanned area. This deviation was evidently due to the operation having been performed while the bones were sufficiently plastic enough to heal. As noted, the sutures of the skull tend to become firmly united with age, whereas in a young child the remains of the sutural membrane still exist, making separation relatively easy. *Fig. 44* shows the left parietal bone of a long headed child that has been operated upon, diminishing the arch on that side. As this child grew older, the right parietal bone en-croached considerably over the median line, indicating the young age of the child at the time of the operation. I will show compelling evidence that this child, who grew into a young adult, was revered after death.

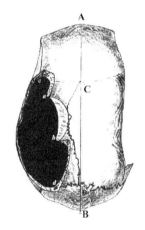

Fig. 44 Childhood trephination.

Pain Relief

Amanda Feilding sensibly applied local anaesthetic to her scalp to ease the pain of the procedure. But did the Neolithic surgeons pro-vide their patients with local anaesthetic, an application of antiseptic or painkillers? Dated to around 4200 BC, the Cueva de los Murciéla-gos, a cave system at Albuñol, Granada, in southern Spain, was used as a sacred burial ground. Found alongside the burials were woven grass bags that contained a large quantity of opium poppy capsules. The opium poppy, the source of morphine and heroin, was domes-ticated by prehistoric Europeans in the Western Mediterranean. During the Neolithic period it appears that its cultivation spread westwards, as indicated by numerous finds of opium poppy seeds in Switzerland and Germany. The seeds may have been used to relieve pain as well as to create altered states of consciousness.

Fruity alcohol, in conjunction with psychoactive substances, was also consumed by our ancestors; one or both substances may have been taken not only for medicinal purposes, but also to enhance religious experience. Dioscorides, writing in the first century AD, mentions wine mixed with extracts of the mandrake plant as the standard surgical anaesthetic of his day. Ancient Egyptian mythology tells of an incident in which the god Ra overcomes the goddess Hathor by stupefying her with mandrake beer. Beer and wine were brewed by the pre-dynastic Egyptians, early Sumerians and ancient Britons. Human beings have always sought and revered ochre for its medicinal properties as well as for its uses in dying and art. Its efficacy, largely as an antiseptic and antihemorrhagic agent, was well known throughout the Western and Eastern worlds. Whatever pain relief was used, the trepanation procedure was often carried out more than once—sometimes as many as four times—and those who underwent the operation were almost certainly revered; their skulls became the object of veneration and amulet crafting.

Chapter 4

Posthumous Trepanation
~ the Mark of a Priestess

Whether in life or death, those who experienced trepanation were honoured. After being laid to rest in a prestigious mound, an additional trepanation procedure was usually performed. Meticulous examination of numerous skulls has revealed unmistakable signs of posthumous trepanation. Sadly, with little recent documentation on this matter, and academic discourse a rarity, it seems so often that archaeological excavation and taxonomy skills eclipse their imagination. Certainly, the evidence that 5,000 years ago trepanation was common practice, even after death, deserves attention. Post-mortem trepanation is distinguishable from that performed on a living person by several characteristics: the aperture is generally larger and its outline more irregular; the surrounding edge is perpendicular or at a slight angle to the skull's surface and presents a series of separate cuts or saw marks, depending on the type of instrument used. Further, the extraction was rougher, often leaving crude gashes and scratches on the surrounding bone, as if done by an untrained person rather than a skilled surgeon. Though it is understandable that more care would be taken when trepanning a live subject. To an expert, the cuts also have a fresh appearance and never show any cicatricial (healing) deposits.

Sacred Bone, Holy Amulets

Intriguingly, post-mortem trepanations invariably took any prior operation into account. The same post-mortem procedure was repeatedly performed; the healed edge of the trepanned skull was selected and a section close to its edge removed, possibly for use as a healing bone amulet—according to the laws of sympathetic magic, an object that shares properties with another has influence over it.

Deep within the burial caves of L'Homme, Lozère, an unusual burial arrangement was unearthed. A trepanned skull was ceremoniously placed in a central position, encircled by other skulls. Several trepanation procedures had occurred after death; the original trepanation had been performed in childhood, and this person had lived to a mature age. Sometime after death, large portions of the skull were cut out as close to the old operation as possible. Later, two further trepanations were performed, making a very large hole and gap, as shown in *Fig. 45*.

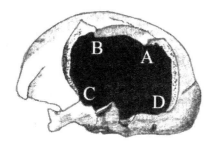

Fig. 45 Skull with multiple post-mortem trepanations.

Fig. 46 Trepanned skull. A-B is a healed area.

Post-mortem trepanation may have been a religious rite. It appears that fragments of the skull, especially those portions near to the old operation, became treasured relics and were used as polished bone pendants. Perhaps the trepanned individual was revered as saintly, or a Neolithic version thereof. Earlier, the childhood trepanation of the Cibournios skull was examined and, as *Fig. 44* shows, A-B is the healed edge of the surgical trepanation. Large post-trepanation sections were taken from A-C as well as from B-D. Likewise, *Fig. 46* shows healed areas with removed sections.

People would return to the burial deposit and extract sections of the deceased's skull. The idea that a section of the skull showing signs of healing in itself had healing power is consistent with two basic forms of magical action: *Contagious* is the magic of contact, where influence passes from one object to another; and *sympathetic* works (often at a distance) on the principle of shared properties. A more modern variation explains how, to Catholics (and non-Catholics), the bones of saints carry miraculous powers as holy relics. Alternatively, the post-mortem portion of skull may have been adopted as a relic worn by the priesthood, or by a Neolithic doctor, used as a ritual healing object or simply revered as a talisman. To the later Celtic Iron Age peoples of France, the head was seen as a vassal of the soul; if this was an inherited tradition from their Neolithic and Bronze Age ancestors, a bone amulet may have represented part of the soul of that person, serving as a direct link to their otherworldly ancestor.

Roundels and an Autopsy

The trepanned section from the original operation is known as a 'roundel', from the Old French word *ro(u)nd*. Numerous examples of roundels are found buried with individuals. Several of these from southern France, especially the Parisian basin, show the object had been perforated, suggesting it was worn as an amulet or pendant, either in life by the person who had undergone the successful operation, or after death by relatives, descendants, or admirers.

In the 1960s, a rescue excavation on behalf of the Ministry of Works was carried out at Amesbury 51 Bronze Age round barrow by Paul Ashbee. This barrow, one of the Cursus Group near Stonehenge, had been previously ploughed, severely reducing its size to approximately 60 ft (18.2 m) in diameter and 4 ft (1.2 m) in height. Cunnington was the first to notice a large piece of skull about 3 in (7.6 cm) wide in the loose soil, which he described as having been "sawed off". This was the case, and Ashbee's excavation saved the roundel.

Fig. 47 Selection of roundels.

Could there be another explanation for post-mortem trepanation, one that blends the world of ritual with a more scientific approach? Post-mortem sections of a trepanned skull from the Bougon tumulus indicated no concern for protecting the cranial contents. This person may have undergone an autopsy after death, as a large portion of the frontal and parietal bones were cut away, as *Fig. 48* shows.

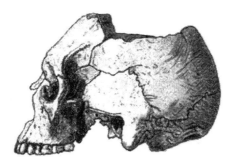

Fig. 48 Bougon skull, showing signs of a possible autopsy.

Early excavations of the Allée couverte de Dampont, a covered passage grave in Val-d'Oise, unearthed two polished stone hatchets along with scrapers, borers, flint flakes, bone pointers, portions of deer tine, a conical shell (patella) pierced at the apex with three small holes, and pottery fragments. Amongst a quantity of human remains were three fragments of trepanned human skulls. The first revealed a partially cicatrised perforation on the right temple, measuring 1 in x 1 in (2.5 cm x 2.5 cm). The second posthumous trepanation was on the left side of a skull, unusually of an elongated 3 in (7.6 cm) portion of bone from the temporal region. The third may have been a cranial amulet of an irregularly shaped portion with a partially cut margin.

Mysterious Operation
One of the more bizarre, trepanned skull examples comes from a tumulus at Deux-Sèvres, western France. It belonged to an elderly man and showed the operation was only partially performed during his lifetime and then suspended, to be completed at or immediately after death. Careful examination of the skull revealed that the instrument used to perform the operation was made of metal and that the

method of manipulation was a gentle sawing action. Why the operation was completed after death is difficult to fathom; it may have been performed according to a spiritual belief, since a medical purpose seems pointless. Of course, these concerns are conflated when we consider the believed necessity for safe passage to the afterlife. What follows is a brief summary of other notable examples.

In the late 1880s, excavations were undertaken of two tombs in Strupčice, Czech Republic. Inside, the remains of cremated bodies and skull fragments showed traces of trepanation. The edges had healed, suggesting patients lived on for some time after the operation. In Poland, a roundel was found that was evidently worn as an amulet. In Northern Europe, from a burial site in Borreby, Denmark, a skull was found missing large pieces, presumably taken for ritual purposes. Another skull from beneath a dolmen at Noes, on the Danish island of Falster, had undergone a large trepanation, and archaeologists noted evidence of a posthumous section. At a site in Roknia, in Algeria, sometime between 1843 and 1852 the French General, Louis Faidherbe, discovered two trepanned skulls dating from "a remote antiquity". One had healed, the other had not.

Other examples from the Americas and Russia demonstrate that the trepanning operation was a worldwide phenomenon. The practice declined, however, from the Middle Bronze Age. Its zenith was reached during the long headed Neolithic era, at a time when there was no distinction made between natural science and metaphysics. Surgical operations may have been accompanied by ritual ceremonies, safeguarding the patient on subtle levels. Such practices are no longer thought relevant by most doctors today, yet are still performed by shamans, perhaps the whispered vestiges of a forgotten Neolithic rite.

The Mark of a Priestess

Our knowledge of prehistoric surgery is limited to operations that involved bony tissue, for that is usually all that remains of the physical body. Is it possible, then, that other forms of healthcare and practice have gone unnoticed by archaeologists? One particularly intriguing operation, a rare cranial surgical procedure probably reserved for the Neolithic elite or priesthood, that has not been documented until now, brings us closer to understanding the strange ritual customs of this era.

In order to better comprehend this procedure, we need to explore the Seine-Oise-Marne, or SOM culture, which is the name given by archaeologists to those at the heart of the transitional phase from the Neolithic to the Chalcolithic (Copper) Age, within the border-lands of France and Belgium. From the fourth millennium BC, and lasting for some thousand years, this megalithic civilisation con-structed the unique *gallery grave*. This featured a distinctive *porthole slab* which was incorporated into the long mound, separating the entrance from the burial chamber. Porthole megalithic structures occur across Central Europe, giving a unique cultural and spiritual identity to the ceremonial landscape. Whether coincidental or not, I noted that trepanned 'holed' skulls are often found in porthole burial chambers of the Seine-et-Oise region in France and else-where; this symbolism binds the two. Several Swedish megalithic

stone cists also have a port-hole feature, in Germany are known as a *Selenloc* or 'soul hole'. One interpre-tation of their purpose is that the holes were created with the intention of releasing the soul of the deceased person. Mean-while, in the British Isles, holed stones such as Cornwall's Men-an-Tol (meaning 'stone of the hole') and the 8 ft tall Long Stone at Minchinhampton, in Gloucestershire, were believed to have healing properties.

Fig. 49 The Long Stone, Minchinhampton.

In England, porthole long barrows are rare, but in the Cotswold county of Gloucestershire are two fine examples at Avening and Rodmarton. As we saw earlier, antiquarians recorded that Rodmarton Long Barrow was associated with long headed burials and a vicious murder. For centuries, the mound was cruelly mutilated to the point of savage destruction; regrettably, the northern and southern port

Fig. 50 Porthole entrance, Rodmarton Long Barrow.

hole slabs were destroyed. A perfectly trepanned skull was found in one of the chambers, deliberately positioned to stare through the porthole, guarding the ancestors—everything had meaning, nothing was by chance. Another trepanned skull was found at nearby Bisley Long Barrow. Yet another porthole was recorded at Bridestones Long Barrow on Cloud Hill, near Congleton, Staffordshire, which is certainly worth visiting—the red and white standing stones create a stunning contrast.

An Unexplained Operation: Dolmen de la Justice d'Epône

Returning to Seine-et-Oise, held within the quiet porthole dolmens were more than just trepanned skulls. Over the next few pages, I will describe another procedure: radical surgery that altered a person's appearance and may have been an attempt to distinguish them from other members of the community. This operation was performed in a specific area lying northwest of Paris, between the rivers Seine and Oise. Examples can be dated to the Neolithic, but others may have been missed because they were either misidentified or overlooked, for reasons discussed above. Excavated in 1881, the Dolmen de la Justice d'Epône, near Mantes, had its burial deposits intact. Pottery, stone implements and ornaments were unearthed, in addition to about sixty skeletons, including twelve skulls. Of these, three female skulls were set aside as being truly remarkable. Each displayed an identical marking that was due to a surgical procedure performed in the region of the vertex—the head's upper surface. In each case, the scar had healed to form a distinctive suture-aligned T-shape or cross, in which the vertical portion of the 'T' is associated with the central sagittal suture; the crossbar, or the top of the 'T', is associated with the lambdoid suture above the occipital bone at the back of the skull. It was noted that the antero-posterior branch begins precisely above the anterior curve of the frontal bone, which follows the sagittal suture and terminates near the obelion (the point of the sagittal suture, level with the parietal foramen, where the transverse branch is encountered), as if these were used as markers. This is made clearer in *Fig. 51*.

To our distant ancestors, the skull's sutures may have held a profound metaphysical meaning. Perhaps they were perceived as 'mystical lines' along which spiritual energy flowed? What is certain is that the scar evident upon the skull was the result of a lesion made during the person's lifetime. It was deep enough to directly affect the periosteum, that is, a membrane covering the surface of the bones. Searching through the documentation of excavated skull collections, three other female skulls also show this strange, distinctive T-marking.

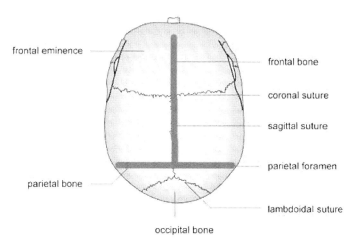

Fig. 51 The top of a skull showing how the 'T' marking is aligned upon the sutures.

Fig. 52 Conflans-Sainte-Honorine with an unusual stone feature.

Trepanned and T-marked Skulls: Conflans-Sainte-Honorine

Three other marked skulls were respectfully placed within the megalithic dolmens of Epône, Conflans-Sainte-Honorine and at Feigneux. In the nearby sanctuary of Vauréal, excavators found a trepanned skull with a large depression in the frontal bone and this had healed remarkably well, although a section had been removed by post-mortem trepanation. Also at Vauréal was a female skull with a distinctive T-marking. An account of the burial finds here can be found in a late-19th century book by the Marquis de Nadaillac, *Manners and Monuments of the Prehistoric Peoples* (1892), which describes five skulls placed neatly in a row. One skull of a woman lay close to a beautiful necklace made of round pieces of bone and slate, on which hung a small jadeite axe amulet. Across the Channel in the Manton mound (round barrow) near Marlborough, Wiltshire, a miniature dagger, just a few inches long, was found next to the skeleton of a mature woman. Later, we will discover that this was part of a shaman's medical kit.

Another extraordinary female T-marked skull was unearthed at the megalithic site of Conflans-Sainte-Honorine (see *Fig. 53* below). Originally this passage grave was raised at the confluence of the rivers Seine and Oise. However, more recently it has been moved to Saint Germain in Paris and reconstructed exactly as found. A unique feature of this porthole monument is that the oval opening had a stone specifically designed for closure, illustrated in *Fig. 52*. Was this a common design for porthole slabs? Astonishingly, the woman's skull had healed but not completely, due to the unusual width of the lines forming the T-shape. On other skulls bearing the T-mark, the lines were much thinner. Studies suggest that the operation was probably performed in one session, and in a continuous line across the head.

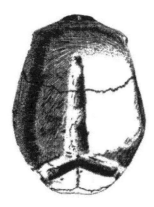

Fig. 53 Female T-marked skull
from Conflans-Sainte-Honorine.

Fig. 54 The skull of a high
priestess of Champignolles.

Nearby, from the Neolithic sepulchral cave of Feigneux, a hyper-elongated double-trepanned skull was excavated that showed traces of an operation both before and after death. Another long headed woman revealed a T-mark, and the diploe was uncovered by either a wound or possibly an infection that had eventually healed. None of these skulls indicated any pathological problem that could account for the operation. All these women were healthy individuals who were selected for an extraordinary operation, which was probably performed in childhood.

Details of the Operation

Tracking down T-marked skulls has not been easy. However, George Grant MacCurdy's 1905 paper 'Prehistoric Surgery—a Neolithic Survival', published in *American Anthropologist*, reported that one woman's skull underwent two operations: a T-marking and a trepanation. As the former had no obvious medical purpose, we can assume it must have been a metaphysical one. As the character of the lesions indicate they were made in childhood, this suggests that as a young girl she had been selected for the T-marking operation and one imagines that she led an extraordinary life. She was laid to rest in a peaceful dolmen passage grave at Seine-et-Oise. A cast of her skull clearly shows the T-marking and trepanned holes. The reason for the latter operation is usually given as treatment for epilepsy or depression, rarely in the pursuit of higher consciousness or advancement of the soul. Seen in a new light, as a little girl showing psychic or spiritual tendencies, the T-section operation was performed in the service of her gifts. The trepanning may have been done in later life to compensate for the premature closing of her skull's sutures. Perhaps she underwent trepanation in order to maintain her psychic powers and on a physical level to improve cerebral circulation, which is lost in adulthood after the closure of the cranial bones.

Other Markings

Not all of the skull markings found near Paris were T-shaped. Late-19th century excavators found eighteen skulls in a single dolmen, one of which stood out as it bore a bold marking following the hairline from front to back. To those examining the skull, this was clear evidence that the marking was a variant of the same general type of T-shape; it also showed (albeit uncertain) signs of trepanation. Another skull—not trepanned—had an unusual oval scar in the region of the bregma, the point on the skull where the coronal suture is intersected by the sagittal suture. Lying close by were three trepanned skulls, a considerable ratio of cranial interventions for a tomb that contained no more than forty skeletons. The original meaning of the T-mark is long forgotten, but it seems that it could have been interpreted as a sigil—an inscribed symbol considered to have magico-religious power—the mark of a high priestess. Selected at a young age for her healing or prophetic ability, this again may have been performed to activate the individual's intuitive and psychic ability. It is possible that to prehistoric people the skull represented the part of the body that 'carried' intelligence and spirituality. Equally, the T-mark could have signified any number of things from royalty, warfare, penal justice, or simply the horrific branding of a slave. We can be assured that the T-mark would have changed that person's appearance. However, because the remains were placed within a prestigious monument, this suggests a high-ranking individual.

Making the Mark More Distinctive

One telling observation I noted is that the T-mark on the scalp made by the operation often followed the natural partings of the hair. One example followed the median line on the forehead to the whorl at the crown, rather like a centre parting of combed hair, whilst two others descended laterally from the crown on either side. Interestingly, the T-mark is not dissimilar to the 19th-century Parisian fashion of combing the hair into a T-shape, illustrated in *Fig. 55*, which offers a visual impression of how a Neolithic high priestess might have looked. The T-mark would have exaggerated the hair parting, making it wider and more noticeable; a dramatic look created by braiding the hair or arranging it in a suitable style to show off the 'T'.

Fig. 55 Victorian hair parting.

Nature offers a colourful palette that was utilised by ancient peoples. Ochre was widely used to paint the temple interiors at the Ness of Brodgar, Orkney, giving a warmth of colour to the cold, grey stone walls. Perhaps, for full moon ceremonies, the priestess enhanced her T-marking by applying white chalk paste along the parted lines, making them glisten in the moonlight. The yellow and red hues of ochre may have been used for sunrise, sunset or at lunar eclipse ceremonies. A dramatic blue can be extracted from woad, which has been used as a permanent dye in early and modern times, perhaps to decorate the hairline at important events.

A Surgical Instrument

How did the ancients perform operations such as trepanation and T-marking? Flint can be razor sharp and made into effective surgical instruments. Eight miles (13 km) northeast of Stonehenge on Snail Down stands a vast Bronze Age round barrow cemetery, containing thirty-three mounds. One of the largest, at 97 ft (29.5 m) across and 11 ft (3.3 m) high, produced a Beaker cremation with another more unusual item, shown in *Fig. 56*. Interpreted by archaeologists as a cloak pin, this was secured with cloth in a wood-lined sheath and carefully placed alongside a spearhead. That it was encased and presumably carried around, suggests it was more instrumental than ornamental, perhaps even surgical? Adding plausibility to this, it was left as part of a cremation burial, and had a roundel alongside it.

Fig. 56 A surgical instrument?

Fractures and Amputations

Most archaeologists argue that prehistoric operations on the skull were carried out to treat individuals who had suffered head trauma, most likely in combat. Certainly, evidence suggests that surgeons probably performed trepanation to remove splinters of skull bone and relieve pressure from clots forming from broken blood vessels. However, trepanation and the T-mark operation may also have been performed to counteract the closing of the sutures and to experience states of higher consciousness. Several skulls showed fractures that were effectively set and perfectly healed. Other medical conditions were also being successfully treated by Neolithic doctors. This goes against a general idea that Neolithic communities were 'primitive', and thus lacking any medical or other sophisticated knowledge. Writing in 1875 in a medical journal, a respected doctor and professor of his era noted:

"The fractures [were] set with a neatness which gives us a very high opinion of the skill of the Neolithic bone setters. The setting of one fracture at the lower end of the tibia and of another at the neck of the femur, are not inferior to what we should expect from the most skilful surgeons."

Not far from the T-marked priestesses, at Buthiers-Boulancourt, about 40 miles (65 km) south of Paris, archaeologists reported evidence of surgery in an Early Neolithic tomb dated to c4900-4700 BC. Advanced awareness of anatomy and medical knowledge had been applied to remove the left forearm of an elderly man. The amputation was clean and the wound successfully healed, indicating that antiseptic treatment and aftercare were applied. Neolithic amputations have also been found in Sondershausen, Germany, and Moravia in the Czech Republic. The skeleton of a 6 ft (1.82 m) tall, mature Mesolithic man who lived during the Linearbandkeramik period, was found in a prestigious grave containing various goods including a schist axe, a flint pick and the remains of a young animal. The absence of a forearm and hand bones suggested it had been amputated, and further analysis showed the arm had been cut above the elbow. It did not reveal any associated infection, suggesting the operation had been conducted in a sterile environment. Certainly, tests revealed that the patient survived the operation and, although he suffered from osteoarthritis, he lived a long time afterwards. Despite the amputation, his grave indicated that this man remained an honoured part of the community.

Advanced Surgery and Dentistry

Rene Noorbergen, in his book *Secrets of the Lost Races* (1977), revealed that in 1969 the Soviet Academy of Sciences noted that a number of central Asian skeletons showed signs of sophisticated surgery. This led to an extraordinary discovery. To the astonishment of scientists, there were clear signs that heart surgery had been performed. The ribs had been expertly cut, an opening made, and the uncut ribs spread apart by retraction. Today, this is known as the 'cardiac window' allowing surgeons to perform accurate and life-saving heart surgery. The bony deposits on the cut ribs indicated that the patient survived three to five years following this extremely complicated operation. Surgery such as this shows an intimate knowledge of blood flow, anatomy, hygiene and the importance of aftercare.

These examples given show that major surgical procedures were more common than is generally presumed. Another facet of Neolithic healthcare is dentistry. A Neolithic tooth from a tomb in

Hulbjerg, Denmark, shows that it had been drilled. The probable reason for this was the infection of a cavity, which resulted in a painful abscess. Closer analysis with a scanning electron microscope, comparing the Neolithic hole with that of a modern drilled tooth, confirmed that it had been drilled in life, not after death. Furthermore, it revealed a similarity between ancient and modern drilling methods. So, the operation would have been successful, and the patient relieved of pain.

Fig. 57 Neolithic dentistry.

From all this we can infer that Neolithic physicians and their spiritual leaders could have worked together to create what today we might refer to as a holistic healthcare system. Points of the earth that emit healing energy and negative ion emissions would supply power to places where healthcare was administered. Earth energies that release healing frequencies are timed by the moon's phases. Accordingly, planetary placements would have been incorporated into the prehistoric surgeon's medical agenda. Archaeologists should re-examine not just the skulls and bones of our ancestors but their lives and beliefs, as magic, medicine, mathematics, geomancy and astronomy were seen as one science or bank of knowledge, entwining and enriching their lives and souls. Let us give Neolithic people the credit they deserve for being one of the first civilisations that paved the way for future societies.

Chapter 5

Stonehenge and the Moon

We have discussed the Neolithic people and now I want to explore the secret history of the most iconic stone circle in the world—Stonehenge—the spiritual capital of the long headed civilisation. It has a long history. Around five hundred years *before* the stone circles were raised, the long headed culture constructed timber monuments at sites we now know as Stonehenge, Stanton Drew and Avebury. In 2017, a ground-penetrating radar and soil-resistance survey discovered one of Avebury's best kept secrets. Detected at the centre of Avebury's southern inner circle were several large, buried sarsen stones. Also, as previously mentioned, a Neolithic timber longhouse 23 x 23 ft (7 x 7 m) and a nearby timber circle were identified. Dated to c3800 BC, the longhouse was labelled a 'domestic unit' as Peterborough pottery was found at the old surface level. However, I suggest that the structure was a timber temple.

From the moment the Late Mesolithic culture raised a tall timber post in the southeast sector, Avebury was considered hallowed ground, a land inhabited by gods and spirits—it is unlikely that this structure was used for profane purposes. Centuries later, to commemorate the location of the timber temple, the huge Obelisk standing stone and a square stone setting, consisting of large silver sarsen stones set next to small orange-red sarsen stones, was raised. Likewise, as early as 3500 BC, a vast timber temple complex stood on the site of Stonehenge. Ancient astronomers noted that the landscape of Stonehenge has a unique celestial latitude of 51°11′ N (51°18′), where the Midsummer Sun rose in the northeast at right-angles to where the extreme northern moon sets in the northwest. Another place which shares this alignment is the Neolithic Goseck Henge in Germany.

The first feature raised at Stonehenge were the timber buildings that stood within the circular earthwork, shown in *Fig. 58*. Remarkably, these were accessed by a roofed timber passageway—the long headed architects went to extraordinary lengths to conceal the goings-on inside Stonehenge from the non-initiated.

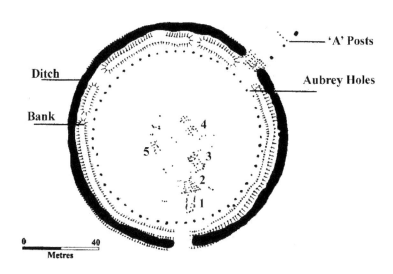

Fig. 58 Stonehenge's timber temple complex.

From 1919-26 Lt Col William Hawley (1851-1941) and R S Newall (1884-1978) excavated most of the south-eastern half of Stonehenge and unearthed what they thought to be five timber circles. More recently, archaeologists Mike Pitts and Rosamund Cleal reassessed these findings and concluded that the settings consisted of rectangular timber structures and various post settings. These structures, which I suggest were *temple shrine rooms*, were accessed from the southern causeway entrance, where one would walk through a small gap in a wooden screen and then down a dark timber corridor to approach the rectangular timber temples. Burl noted that:

> "Five exceptionally large timber posts stood diagonally across the entrance zone in the south, which was set at an angle, making it impossible for anyone outside to see down the long corridor. Restricting access even further, the far end was crossed by a long façade of nine large posts, three stood to the west, three at its end like giant gateposts and three stood to the east."

The timber screen ensured total privacy for whatever took place inside the temples. Timber structure 1 is a roofed passageway some 13 ft (4 m) wide and 10-12 ft long (3-3.66 m) that turns first to the left and then to the right, then along a second corridor around 12 ft long (3.66 m) which leads to timber temple 3, possibly through other passageways and screened areas to temples 4 and 5. These were likely roofed structures alongside timber posts. Mike Pitts reports:

> "There are indeed a lot of post holes, and some are very large, but there is no sign of a circular building. The nearest we get to any coherent 'structures' are rectangular arrangements. It may be that there were some buildings, but also we can imagine memorial posts, posts hanging with bones or offerings, fences controlling what people or spirits could see or where they could go. At this stage in its long history, 4900-4440 years ago, Stonehenge was dedicated to funeral ceremony, the earth replete with the dead, the space above alive with spirits."

Nearly a century has passed since the ceremonial corridors and timber structures were unearthed, and the mystery that Hawley began to unravel remains unsolved. Burl comments:

> "The people who raised the posts and laid out the zig-zag of torturous passages to shield the centre clearly wished to have their ceremonies concealed from the outside world."

So, what was going on inside of Stonehenge? Screened from the outside world, the timber buildings were in constant use. Hawley noted that the entrance corridor was frequently used:

> "…the ground was very flinty and hard from traffic over it, as though the area had been subjected to constant trampling."

The late Marija Gimbutas hypothesised that the Mesolithic and Early Neolithic civilisations of Europe were a goddess culture that constructed 'house-temples' and shrines. Remains of Neolithic shrines are found at sites across Eastern Europe: for example, one large prehistoric shrine, 753 sq ft (70 sq m) in size, was discovered at the site of Sabatinivka II in Moldavia, western Ukraine, assigned to the Cucuteni culture c4800-4600 BC. The inner features of a stone floor entrance, a bread oven, an altar measuring 9 x 19.6 ft (2.75 x 6 m), and a life-sized throne, were probably used by a priestess who oversaw the proceedings. Many figurines were found, one holding a baby snake while others were armless, resembling a snake goddess.

Malta's Neolithic temples of Tarxien and the Hypogeum both housed large and small goddess statues. Centuries earlier, Apollo, god of healing and light, became associated with the temple at Delphi in Greece, its chief deity the Earth goddess, Gaia. Staying within these European spiritual parameters, the timber temples of Stonehenge may have been goddess shrine rooms reserved for a feminine priesthood. It could be that the temples were painted in ochre shades of red, gold, and brown, each temple designated for a specific purpose, alive with people and spiritual energy.

Constructing the Henge Earthwork

Archaeologists are unsure if the ditch and bank earthwork surrounding Stonehenge today was contemporary with the timber
structures, although in all probability the earthwork preceded them.
It was an engineering accomplishment that created a huge barrier,
as the height of the chalk bank blocked the view from anyone outside—yet again, the emphasis was on secrecy within a sacred place.
Constructing the henge, one of the most unusual henges ever
constructed in the ancient world, was a Herculean task. Unlike other
henges, Stonehenge consisted of a circular internal bank, an outer
ditch, and an additional lower outer bank—which was broken in the
northeast and south by two causeway entrances. In 1877, Sir W M
Flinders Petrie (1853-1942) measured the circle on the inside of the
ditch to be 340 ft (104 m) in diameter, the bank 20 ft (6 m) wide and
6-8 ft (1.82-2.44 m) high. A survey undertaken for William Camden's
Britannia in 1610, stated that the henge bank was 10 ft (3 m) wider,
so we can presume it was also higher over two hundred and fifty
years earlier. Typically, a Wessex henge bank was constructed from
quarried chalk blocks and pieced together to form a solid bank wall
or formed from chalk rubble. Not at Stonehenge. The henge was
carved out of the solid chalk bedrock to form a smooth white 'basin'
with no rough edges; imagine a massive bowl with a lower outer
bank, a ditch and a higher internal bank. Raising the area within the
henge would have created an elevated platform, an ideal stage for
ceremonial performances. In Ireland, some henges were scooped out
around the edge of the bank leaving a convex arena like an upturned
saucer. Mayburgh, near Penrith in the Lake District, was similar.

Archaeologists say that Stonehenge's henge bank was constructed
of chalk rubble edged with chalk blocks for support, although an
eyewitness to an archaeological dig disagrees. The late Tom Gorrey,
who was a well-known and widely respected Stonehenge guide and
custodian of the site for more than twenty years, was present at the
famous 1954 excavation of the earthwork, conducted by Professors
Richard J C Atkinson (1920-1994) and Stuart Piggott (1910-1996). The
excavation revealed that:

"...instead of being composed of loose chalk as would be expected in such a bank, it was made up of solid chalk integral with the surrounding ground, which appeared to have been cut away to a lower level in order that the mound should be formed."

If this eye-witness account is correct, it begs the question of whether deer antlers were used to extract the vast circle-like henge, with a circumference of nearly 900 ft (274 m), from the solid chalk bedrock or was another form of advanced instrumentation employed? Although the tall henge bank concealed an inner area, additional screening was added. The discovery of postholes in sections along the bank indicate there was once an outer fence. Reaching a total height of 15 ft (4.5 m), the height of the bank and fence prevented outsiders from using the bank to stand on and kept the uninvited away. Whilst we are spoon-fed an archaeological mantra that a Wessex henge bank should appear as 'a gleaming chalk white bank set against a lush green landscape', my vision is different. I imagine that a henge brings a colourful and creative element—Stonehenge's chalk bank may have been an artistic blank canvas.

A prototype henge was discovered in 1987 underneath Max Gate in Dorchester, Dorset, the house built and lived in by Wessex author Thomas Hardy in 1885. Named 'Flagstones', part of this henge was unearthed and destroyed when a bypass was built in the 1980s. Hardy had previously unearthed a 'Druid' stone while digging a well, and some of the henge remains under the garden of the house and surrounding area. Flagstone's ditch diameter of 328 ft (100 m) was almost identical to that at Stonehenge and contained sarsen and local sandstone slabs covering prehistoric burials. These holes may have formerly sited standing stones. Built c3300-3000 BC, Flagstones was artistically decorated with symbols carved onto vertical chalk walls, including concentric circles, spirals, chevrons, criss-cross and parallel lines. Concentric circles and spirals are patterns emitted by underground water and would be recognised today by professional water diviners; the exact same motifs appear on chalk plaques and Neolithic Grooved Ware pottery.

Later we will see that Stonehenge was sited above a large aquifer that emits a spiral pattern and six concentric circles of dowseable energy. If the henge had such carvings, they may have been a visual acknowledgment of the earth energies present within the monument. For important ceremonial events, the symbols might have

Fig. 59 Red chevrons may have been painted on the chalk bank.

been painted with ochre, which was in demand from the Early Upper Palaeolithic period onwards. Ochre is the name commonly given to iron ore, haematite, goethite and limonite, used as a source of red, yellow and brown pigments, respectively.

The use for millennia of red ochre colourant for body art and to colour the bones of the departed, has been widely documented. For example, at the 250,000-year-old Acheulian rock shelter in Beçov, Czechoslovakia, archaeologist J Fridich found a flat stone used to prepare ochre powder. Preliminary dating of an ochre mine in South Africa's Wonderwerk Cave may date back as far as 350,000 or even 400,000 years. In the Mousterian levels of the Pech de l'Azé cave site in France, François Bordes discovered abundant signs of red and yellow ochre as well as manganese, which produces the black pigment used by the Neanderthals. The excavation of an ochre mine in Lovas, Hungary, dated c40,000 to 30,000 years ago, was interpreted by its excavators as a concerted effort to extract material for paint. When ammonia is added to ochre paste it stains chalk, stone and wood like paint, although it is not permanent. My own experiments with ochre demonstrate that wood and chalk painted with golden ammonia-free ochre paste, and exposed to harsh winter weather conditions, can remain vibrant for at least two months. On the Ness of Brodgar, Orkney, Neolithic artisans left behind small ochre paint pots used to stain colour on the inner temple walls.

From Wood to Stone

For around five hundred years, ceremonial activity was conducted within Stonehenge's hidden timber temples, until dramatic changes occurred around 3300-3100 BC. The timber structures, screens and corridors were dismantled, and Stonehenge was transformed into a large stone circle. Newcomers with fresh ideas and trade links forging new alliances, were probably influencing the area. They initiated concerted efforts that would change Stonehenge from a transient timber structure to more permanent stone.

Welsh bluestones were selected to construct a large stone circle that archaeologists call 'Stonehenge Phase 1'. According to author John Burke, these bluestones are three times more magnetic than other stones found in the British Isles, thus boosting the stone circle's energy field. In one of the oldest stories of its origins, Geoffrey of Monmouth, in his *History of the Kings of Britain* (AD c1136), describes how Stonehenge was reconstructed using the stones from the Giants' Dance in Ireland, a stone circle located on the legendary Mount Killaraus. Here, Merlin dismantled the circle and shipped the stones to Amesbury on Salisbury Plain, using the force of 15,000 men, having first defeated the Irish and captured the stones. According to legend, Merlin wanted the stones of the Giants' Dance for their magical and healing properties, so Stonehenge was built to commemorate the death of the Britons treacherously killed by Saxons during peace talks at Amesbury. Although this 900-year-old legend is mainly fantasy—Saxons did not arrive in prehistory and none of Stonehenge's stones came from Ireland—the fact that its 'bluestones' come from Wales has led to speculation that there may be some grain of truth in Geoffrey's mythical history.

Excavations have shown that some of the bluestones originated in West Wales from a stone circle called Waun Mawn, which was partially dismantled and re-erected at Stonehenge. A similar conclusion was reached in the late-18th century by William Cunnington, the first to propose that Stonehenge's bluestones were dismantled from an older monument and moved over 180 miles to the east. He writes:

> "There can be little doubt that the small monoliths are older than the outer circle and trilithons, and why may they not have composed a very ancient circular temple before they were brought to Stonehenge?"

Later, in 1923, geologist Herbert Thomas established that the spotted dolerite bluestones at Stonehenge originated in the Preseli Hills of West Wales, where he suspected they formed a "venerated stone circle". Subsequently, in 2010 a team of archaeologists led by Mike Parker Pearson, explored this idea. Parker Pearson points out in his book *Stonehenge* (2013), that the Early Neolithic ancestors of the Nevern Valley in Wales probably brought the tradition of megalithic construction to this part of Britain, as well as transporting the bluestones. Using standing stones dismantled from Waun Mawn and possibly other stone circles, the ancient builders raised the bluestone circle at Stonehenge. The diameters of Stonehenge Phase 1 and Waun Mawn are nearly identical: the identification of two bluestone quarries at Craig Rhosyfelin and Carn Goedog in the Preseli Hills indicates the stones had been quarried c3400-3000 BC, centuries before Stonehenge was erected. It was found that stone socket Hole 91 at Waun Mawn matches Stonehenge's bluestone 62 base shape. The six stone holes and four surviving standing stones at Waun Mawn may have once formed part of a large circle of 30-50 stones. From the centre of this circle, the Midsummer Sun rose within the entrance formed by stone Holes 9 and 21. Having originated in West Wales and later reincarnated at Stonehenge, the bluestones were raised to create Britain's most sophisticated lunar stone circle.

Fifty-six dark bluestones were set in a large stone circle with a diameter of 284.8 ft (86.8 m), against a predominantly brilliant white henge bank. We might imagine an aesthetic choice in this contrast of colouring, reflecting the yin-yang of Eastern tradition. I must point out a curious fact, which is that the first stone to be set at Stonehenge was not raised, it was buried. In 1920, Hawley found deep within Aubrey Hole Number 1, "a gritty and non-glittering sandstone". This rarely mentioned buried stone is known as 'Stone OU 9' and bluestone Number 1 was placed upon it. Visually stunning and smooth to the touch, the bluestones were midnight blue intermingled with small white flecks of crystal, called feldspar. Stonehenge Phase 1 was beautiful, each stone polished to appear like the star-spangled sky. Today, lichen and weathering camouflage the former splendour of the bluestones that now appear dull, aged and grey.

Some were dotted with pink flecks and others exhibited a distinctive olive-green tone, adding an extra dimension of colour. Additionally, the stone circle consisted of two post settings, marked 'A' in *Fig. 60* below, and aligned to the Northern Major Moonrise, which I will discuss shortly. Sharing the same axis, beyond the entrance and running southwest-northeast, stood the Heel Stone and a line of former standing stones that survive as stone Holes 'B' and 'C', which provided a second sightline towards the Northern Moonrise.

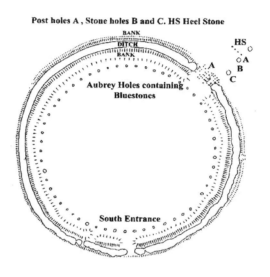

Post holes A , Stone holes B and C. HS Heel Stone

Fig. 60 Stonehenge Phase 1: contemporary with Bluestonehenge.

Fig. 61 Bluestonehenge near West Amesbury.

Another smaller contemporary bluestone circle, later discovered, was raised 1.5 miles (1.60 km) towards West Amesbury, close to the River Avon. Bluestonehenge (see *Fig. 61*) contained a circle of 25-30 standing stones, 33 ft (10 m) across, surrounded by a henge set on a ramped mount. In total over 80 bluestones were moved from Wales.

Midsummer Madness

Revering the goddess aspect of creation, the long headed matriarchal society worshipped the Earth and the Moon as a representation of the goddess. Around five thousand years ago, from the centre of the bluestone circle, a rare moonrise could be seen. The Heel Stone, commonly associated with the Midsummer Sunrise, was however an accurate lunar marker, originally erected to mark the midpoint position of the 18.61-year lunar Metonic cycle. Astronomers recognised this because the Heel Stone was erected at 51°18', which is over a degree and nearly 6.5 ft (2 m) further from the correct position had it been intended as a solar Midsummer marker, whereas the lunar alignment was *exact*. Later, during Stonehenge Phase II (orthodox dating c2500 BC), the northeast entrance was widened, placing the Heel Stone *close* to where the Sun rose at Midsummer; "although" remarks Burl, "this redesign was never precise being over a degree out." Richard Atkinson in his book *Stonehenge* (2013) states:

"The Heel Stone is the subject of one of the most popular and persistent misconceptions concerning Stonehenge, namely that it marks the point of sunrise on Midsummer Day for an observer stationed at the centre of Stonehenge, or the Altar Stone. Actually, it does nothing of the sort. It is true, admittedly, that at the present day the Midsummer Sun in its eastward-slanting climb, does pass over the Heel Stone, with a little less than half its disc showing above the horizon. But it does this only some appreciable time after true sunrise, that is, the moment at which the first gleam of light appears on the horizon as the upper margin of the Sun creeps above it. True sunrise, in the sense, will not take place over the point of the Heel Stone until about the year AD 3260."

Night of the High Moon

Repeatedly, every nine years when the moon reached its midpoint position, it would rise over the tapering crest of the Heel Stone when the original narrow north-eastern entrance framed the entire event. Surrounding the Heel Stone, approximately 12 ft (3.6 m) from its base, was a circular ditch contemporary with the raising of the Heel Stone. This ditch—half of which now lies forgotten beneath grass—seems to have been a symbolic rather than a physical barrier, as it was refilled and rammed with chalk rubble very shortly after it was dug. Everything at Stonehenge had meaning; the Heel Stone and its chalk white moon-like circle created an enclosed arena, perhaps reserved for the priestesses who stood by the Heel Stone to celebrate this rare lunar event. An even rarer lunar event that must have been high on the ceremonial agenda was the 'Night of the High Moon', the longest night of the moon's Metonic cycle. According to astronomer Gerald Hawkins (1928-2003), the High Moon occurred at three intervals of 19, 18 and 19 years, which added together makes 56, the number of bluestones at Stonehenge. The night of the High Moon is the time when the same phase of the moon is repeated on the same date of the year within an hour or so of its cycle—it would have been associated with night-time ceremonies and celebrations.

An ingenious design that brought the light of the High Moon to the stone circle explains one of Stonehenge's most unusual features. Many stone circles are surrounded by a henge: a ditch and bank, with the ditch on the inside and the bank on the outside, creating a circular or oval enclosure. Numerous theories have been proposed to explain why henges were constructed, and one of the most popular is that the earthwork provided an inner arena for ritual activity, separating the sacred from the profane on the outside. Stonehenge stands unique among henges as the bank is on the *inside* and the ditch on the *outside*, with an additional smaller external bank. There is no archaeological explanation as to why it was constructed in this way. Mathematician Richard Cardew suggests the answer lies in *reflection*. Rarely constructed in a perfect circular or oval shape, a henge often consists of several 'arc' sections; one reason for this states that these were the result of the bank being built in various sections. We propose, however, that the *purposefully* constructed arcs served a specific design function. When activated by the light of the Full Moon, the arcs can produce a visual phenomenon. Exploring this unusual lunar alignment and its effects allows us to re-live pre-historic lunar rites and the lost theatrical wonders of Stonehenge Phase 1.

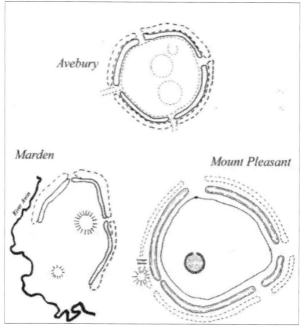

Fig. 62 Examples of henge 'arcs' or corner sections.

Chalk white henge monuments with arcs or corner sections can potentially act as a gigantic lens that can produce an optical visual phenomenon called a 'caustic'. This is a curve, or surface, upon which each of the parallel light rays is at a tangent and typically produces a curve of concentrated light. These shapes often have 'cusp singularities', a singular point of the curve, which acts like a spotlight, as shown in *Fig. 63*. The word *caustic* comes from the Latin via Greek and implies burning (combustion). The intensity of light increases near the caustic, yet it is not intense enough to actually cause burning. A familiar sight produced by this effect is a rainbow. The bright colours occur at the caustic surface and the light rays are concentrated near the cusp, where the intensity can be expected to be higher. A caustic light cusp is the focal point of a reflecting surface, halfway between the vertex and the centre of the curvature. We hypothesise that certain henge arc sections at Stonehenge produced a caustic light pattern. For this to occur, certain criteria are required: a bank on the outside, which is one of its unusual design features, a reflective surface and a light source. Chalk is highly reflective especially when polished to produce a sheen. When the Full Moon shone onto the brilliant white chalk arc section, it would have

Fig. 63 Light rays produce a curve of concentrated light.

created a spotlight effect that acted like a mirror, the arc reflecting a thin caustic contour line of moonlight onto the ground. The only requirement for this to happen is a chalk floor, and we have already established that the floor of the bluestone circle was sculpted from solid chalk bedrock to create a white inner arena. Stonehenge Phase 1 produced a light show or backdrop for theatrical rituals, and mathematical calculations reveal the length of the caustic line and the timing of past events.

Midwinter Light Show

At Stonehenge, on the longest night of the High Moon as the Sun set, the Full Moon rose over nearby Lark Hill. While it is impossible to see into the past, we can envisage a group of long headed people standing within the enclosure that surrounded the Heel Stone. Having timed their astronomical calculations to perfection, others stood in awe at the centre of the large bluestone circle. Today, computer software has replaced the gifted Neolithic mind, whose unlimited mathematical capacity needed no such assistance. To describe the rare event of the most Northerly Moonrise, the timings are computer calculated based on a previous alignment at Stonehenge on 5th-6th December 2006. The table below gives the date, time, azimuth, altitude and average change in degrees altitude per hour, throughout the long night of winter's High Moon.

Event	Date	Time	Azimuth	Alt Deg/hr
Rise	5/12/06	15:47	41	-0.8
East-ish	5/12/06	18:00	65	15.2 11
Due East	5/12/06	20:27	90	36.7 10
Due South	6/12/06	00:55	180	66.8 20
Due West	6/12/06	05:23	270	36.8 20
Set	6/12/06	10:05	319	0.8 10

Calculations by *Heavens-Above http://www.heavensabove.com*

The movement in azimuth (direction round from due north) is not constant with time during the night. It is faster when the moon is in the south and less so when it is in the east or west, due to the angle the lines of declination make with the horizon. Using these calculations, the moon does not reach due south until nearly an hour after midnight. This is because the time of the Full Moon was 00:25 on 5th December, a full day earlier, and so for this particular lunar event the moon is not due south at midnight as one would expect. During the Neolithic, on a dark December afternoon, the most northerly Full Moon rose at around 4 pm, and it would reach the eastern sector of the henge bank at 8.27 pm when the visual effects would have begun. The moon's light once shone on the opposing western section of the chalk bank either between bluestones 34 and 35, or upon stone 34, creating a soft caustic spotlight; the mirror effect would reflect a delicate and slender line of moonlight onto the chalk floor. Mathematically, the length of the light beam is half the radius of the henge, creating a soft flow of light that reached towards where the Y Holes would be dug some 1,300 years later. Perhaps the memory of the caustic light beam defined their location? Suddenly, after just 8-10 minutes, the caustic light would disappear… but not for long. Two hours later it would have lit up the henge bank and reflected a small path of moonlight, possibly targeting Station Stone 93 and gently brightening part of its outer face.

This is the year of the High Moon when the moon reaches its maximum and most extreme northerly zenith at 00.55 (invariably midnight) and aligns perfectly to the southern causeway entrance (see *Fig. 65*). Due to the wide gap in the henge bank, created by the northeast entrance, the final caustic beam would appear when the moon reached due west. At around 05.23 am, bluestone 6 or 7 may have been illuminated by moonlight casting a final caustic spotlight and a linear line of light towards the Y Holes. Over five thousand years ago, when the chalk floor and henge were in pristine condition, it would have looked as if the Full Moon, a white land circle, had brought the light and power of the moon to Stonehenge. Young or old, high status or otherwise, whoever attended this event must have felt themselves part of the most eventful night in prehistoric Britain. Slowly moving around the henge, each soft caustic light effect would have enhanced the drama of ritual and, for us, this offers a new insight into the wonders of Stonehenge. Our calculations show that the caustic light phenomenon could theoretically occur at every Full Moon. However, the best viewing time would be during the long dark winter months when the Full Moon is high and bright, especially around Midwinter. In 3000 BC the moon rose at 41°43' True North (TN), and in 2500 BC at 41°53' (TN) in its 18.61-year cycle. Archaeological evidence supports the assertion that the moon's cycle, from its Major, Midpoint to Minor rising, was recorded by Stonehenge's astronomers.

Fig. 64 Moonlight reflects on water, snow and chalk.

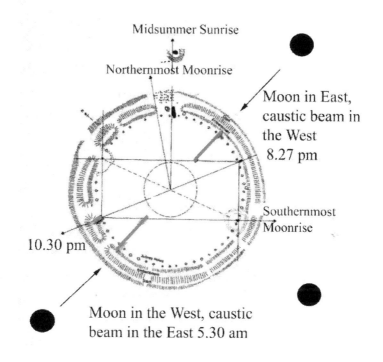

Fig. 65 Caustic beam and timing of the Night of the High Moon.

Long before the bluestone circle was raised, timber posts known as the 'A' posts were erected to mark the moon's changing position over 18.61 years, which would eventually define the width of the northeast 'lunar' entrance, shown in *Fig. 66*. The henge bank and its reflective properties accentuated the moon's light, and this would explain why the Stonehenge architects constructed the bank on the *inside*, unlike any other henge monument. However, unless the chalk was regularly cleaned, polished or replaced, this ritual would be short-lived. Experimental archaeology has shown that chalk earthworks soon become extensively grassed over, covered with thick scrub and weed growth. Although our calculations have shown that light phenomena, as described, is possible, and our working model brings this aspect of the past alive, some may see Stonehenge's caustic light show as too imaginative. How dull the study of the past would be if we are deprived of such possibilities.

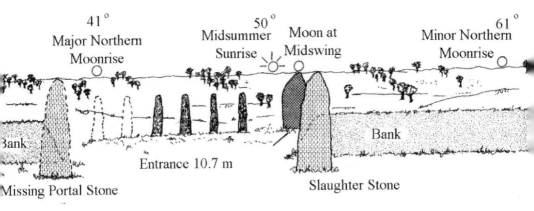

Fig. 66 Accurate lunar alignment over the Heel Stone.

Both entrances were dedicated to the Moon goddess. At midnight on the Spring and Autumn Equinoxes, when the Full Moon reached its zenith, the Moon aligned perfectly with the southern causeway entrance.

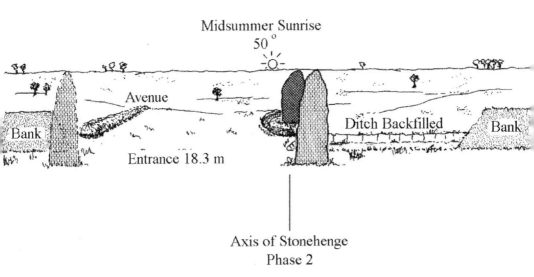

Fig. 67 Inaccurate Summer Solstice Sunrise. The position of 50° is now some 6.5 ft (2 m) away from the correct 'solar' position.

Eclipse Predictor

To the ancients the bluestone ring may have represented the ecliptic, the imaginary circle around the heavens along which the Sun and the planets appear to follow. In 1964 Gerald Hawkins made a model to show how Stonehenge was a lunar and solar eclipse predicting computer. However, the most accurate model was produced in 1966 by British cosmologist Sir Fred Hoyle, who calculated that eclipses could be foretold at Stonehenge if the system began at a Full Moon. The first point of Aries is bluestone number 14, shown in *Fig. 68*. The point S represents the position of the Sun, the solar longitude; M is

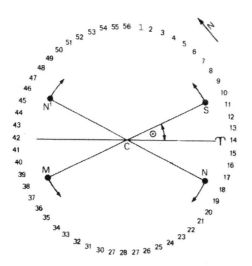

Fig. 68 Eclipse predicting model.

the Moon projected on to the ecliptic; N^1 is the descending node of the Moon; N is the ascending node; and C is the centre, the position of the observer. The Moon's Nodes are invisible (mathematical) points where the orbit of the Moon crosses the ecliptic, and take into account the relationship between the Sun, Moon and Earth. When these markers move in partic-

ular directions in real time, the bluestone circle transforms into an eclipse predicting stone circle. The Sun makes one circuit per year and the Moon one circuit per lunar month. When the Moon is at N (ascending node), a Solar Eclipse occurs when the Sun is within 15 degrees of N; and a Lunar Eclipse occurs when the Sun is within 10 degrees of N^1. When the Moon is at N^1, a Solar Eclipse will occur if the Sun is within 15 degrees of the Moon, and a Lunar Eclipse if it is within 10 degrees of the opposite end of the line of lunar nodes. Although this may not have been the intention of the monument builders, it appears that the bluestones could foretell eclipses even when only half of them would actually be visible from Stonehenge.

To accurately determine eclipses, Hoyle said the markers would have to be moved in this fashion, with the Sun moving anticlockwise two bluestones every 13 days, the Moon anticlockwise two bluestones every day, and N and N^1 moving three holes every day. However, the most spectacular eclipse occurs when a Full Moon coincides with Midwinter, and a blood-red Full Moon rises above the crest of the Heel Stone.

Eclipses exert a powerful influence upon earth energies, and this may have been the main reason why the ancients wanted to predict them. My dowsing research on eclipses dates back to 1999, when I was part of a research team determining the influences of a total Solar Eclipse on earth energies and underground water (such as a geospiral energy pattern). We noted that at the moment of totality, the *geodetic* system of earth energies, including some grid and ley lines as well as earth currents, appear to momentarily lose their dowseable energy field. Sometime after the event, the energy pattern returns and there is an increased energy surge, rather like a 'reboot', which might have been utilised by the ancients.

Callanish and the Moon Priestess

Sharing a feminine prehistoric heritage, numerous megalithic sites incorporated lunar alignments. One of the most breathtaking, Callanish stone circle that stands on the Isle of Lewis, in Scotland's Outer Hebrides, was discovered by the late Margaret Curtis. The layout of the monument is similar to a Celtic cross, making it a highly unusual design. Margaret noticed that the surrounding landscape and the stone circle were aligned to the Moon and would have produced one of the most awe-inspiring alignments in the Neolithic world. I went to Callanish in 2006 to see this alignment for myself. On the Isle of Lewis there is a remarkable hill range in the form of a woman lying on her back, creating a mountainous image of a voluptuous goddess. Local people call her 'Sleeping Beauty' or in Gaelic *Cailleach na Mointeach*, which translates as 'The Old Woman of the Moors'. Multiple prehistoric stone circles in the area of the Callanish circle, dating back some 5,000 years, were positioned to align to Sleeping Beauty and the Moon.

Fig. 69 Callanish stone circle. *Photograph:* Busty Taylor.

Every 18.61 years, when the Full Moon is at its most extreme south-erly position, a series of spectacular lunar alignments occur. The honey-coloured Moon, low on the horizon, rises over the breast of the Sleeping Beauty and slowly moves along her body. The contours of the hill make the bright full orb disappear and then reappear, intensifying the unfolding event. At moonset, approximately 2-5 hours later, the Full Moon passes through the central Callanish stones, and, if a person is stood on the rocky hillock at the higher southern end of the site, he or she will appear silhouetted *within* the Moon. Imagine seeing the silhouette of a priestess, the top of her head touching the highest point of the Moon's orb, with outstretched arms touching the sides of the Moon and her body and legs within the golden orb.

Margaret calculated that a small human figure fits perfectly within the orb, but then suddenly and dramatically,

> "...gradually grows bigger and bigger, altering your sense of perception and enhancing your sense of wonderment, until the person is twice the size of the Moon."

Then, when the imagery vanishes, the person stands alone upon the elevated hillock. This is megalithic theatre at its finest. She says:

"We saw this rare and spectacular event in June 1987 with friends from across the world. None of us will ever forget the beauty of that calm, clear summer night. Even after years of scientific study, we had never anticipated the wonder and drama of the event itself. The most awe-inspiring moment of all was when the Moon reappeared inside the circle."

In 2006, sadly I didn't get to see the grand finale due to cloud cover, but I did meet Margaret and I saw the Moon rise across the body of the Sleeping Goddess, as if touching the hill range to reawaken 'The Old Woman of the Moors'. I will never forget the magic and awe of Callanish.

Moon Stones of Brittany

Further afield, across the English Channel, stand the giant menhirs of Brittany, which attracted the attention of Alexander Thom (1894-1985). Thom determined that it was British lunar rather than solar sites which almost always targeted the largest upright standing stones. The most impressive of the single menhirs in Europe is Le Grande Menhir Brisé, Er Grah or *Men-er-Hroeg* (the Fairy Stone), near the French town of Locmariaquer. It had fallen before 1727 and today is recumbent, broken into five large pieces, with one piece missing. Estimated to weigh in excess of 344 tons (350 metric tons), it would have stood over 66 ft high (20 m). Several other large menhirs still stand in Brittany, ranging from 30-40 ft (9-12 m) in height. At Carnac, which means 'Cemetery of the Bones', several hundred upright stones are aligned in an easterly direction for more than 3 miles (5 km), making this the greatest concentration of megalithic remains in Europe. They begin in the west at the village of Ménec, the 'Place of the Stones' and flow like a megalithic river eastward through Kermario, the 'Place of the Dead', to Kerlescan, and at one time extended as far as the river Crache. The entire stone settings fall into these main groups.

Having noted that in Britain tall stones provided a backsight or foresight to lunar alignments, Thom proposed that the geometric design of Le Ménec, Kermario and the Kerlescan stone rows, with their associated outlying menhirs, created a huge lunar observatory that centred on the giant stone of Er Grah. The Major and Minor lunar standstills targeted certain standing stones several miles away, creating an astronomical ceremonial landscape centred on the Moon. One of the tallest stones in Europe, if not the world, is Kerloaz menhir, which is 40 ft (9.5 m) tall after losing 6.5 ft (2 m) to a lightning strike, two hundred years ago. Standing on the top of a hill, on a clear day it is visible from more than 18.5 miles (30 km) away.

Stonehenge and the Goddess of Reincarnation

Clearly, in both Britain and France, the moon and a dark night were essential ingredients for a Neolithic ritual performance. Celestial goddess energy was ever-present at Stonehenge, radiating its stellar influence from one constellation that took centre stage. To the Iron Age culture, it was not an almighty father God who received the souls of the departed into his heavenly abode, it was originally a goddess. Corona Borealis, the Greek Northern Crown or 'Crown of the North Wind', a semi-circular constellation that the British Celts associated with the goddess Arianrhod, was the 'silver circle',

daughter of the great mother goddess Don and her consort Beli. Arianrhod is a lunar goddess of the seasons, of time and tides, who weaves the destinies of humankind. Her domain is the rotating island of Caer Sidi in Corona Borealis, a silver castle at the back of the North Wind, where the souls of dead kings, poets, heroes, warriors and magi-

Fig. 70 Arianrhod, associated with Stonehenge.

cians await the goddess and her female attendants to decide their fate before being reincarnated. Corona Borealis was the Pagan heaven and Arianrhod a primal figure of feminine power, a goddess of reincarnation. Legend says that poets and astrologers learnt their wisdom from the stars of Caer Sidi, the stars of knowledge that rule over the mysteries of life and death. Arianrhod is the guide of the souls of the great heroes and heroines from this world to the next and back again, on their journey through the uncharted dark realms to conquer death and darkness and be reborn.

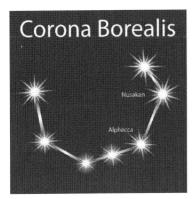

Fig. 71 The constellation of Corona Borealis.

In 3035 BC, at midnight when the Equinox Sun rose and set due east and west, Caer Sidi, the goddess Arianrhod, was directly above Stonehenge when the brightest star of the constellation, Alphecca (Gemma), was at the exact zenith and centre of the bluestone circle. Seeing the Corona Borealis, the Celtic Pagan heaven, above the stone circle must have held meaning and mystical fortitude. To ascend to heaven needed the assistance of the celestial star bird, Cygnus the Swan, which to the Celts was the grey lag goose that carried the soul beyond the North Wind. Perhaps ceremonies that involved rebirth and destiny were performed to coincide with Alphecca, the brightest star in Corona Borealis at the zenith on Spring Equinox, a time when nature is likewise reborn and the onset of lighter nights assured.

Stonehenge is a multifaceted diamond with many usages, guises and portals to be activated at different times of the year. To the Celts, rebirth and reincarnation were not merely concepts but a profound visual event; shooting stars were seen as souls returning to Earth to be reborn. According to Catherine Tennant, author of *The Lost Zodiac* (1995), the meteors known as the Coronides fell from the starry semi-circle of the goddess from mid-April to the end of June, a time of mystical rebirth. Medieval Cabalists predicted the fate of nations and cities by observing the stars vertically overhead, which they formed into sacred words in accordance with a variant of Hebrew called the *Celestial Alphabet*; the words formed indicated the 'Fate of Place'. To ancient astronomers, the position upon the terrestrial globe of a city, sacred site or temple, had a direct relationship to its heavenly longitude, especially at the zenith. At certain times of the year, stars or planets directly overhead would influence the location below. At midnight on the Spring Equinox, like the all-seeing eye of the goddess, Alphecca was exactly overhead connecting the blue-stone circle to Arianrhod, the goddess of reincarnation (see *Fig. 72*).

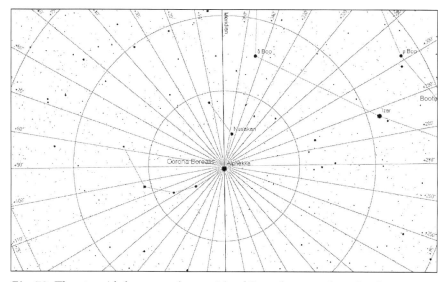

Fig. 72 The star Alphecca at the zenith of Stonehenge when the Sun rose due East and set due West. *Calculations:* Rodney Hale.

There is supporting archaeological evidence that Stonehenge Phase I was built by a matriarchal society. During re-excavation of Aubrey Hole number 7, a chalk socket of one of the 56 bluestones, the burials of considerably more women were found than men, suggesting that women were especially important to the monument. Christie Willis, of the Institute of Archaeology, University College London, worked on the project and confirmed that the remains found were of at least fourteen women and nine men, all young adults or older. Radiocarbon dating revealed that they were deposited in several ceremonies from about 3100 BC to at least 2140 BC. These were the people who truly understood Stonehenge, and they left behind clues to a great puzzle that we are still piecing together; one of the strangest mysteries being the little-known fact that the magnificent bluestone lunar temple was suddenly abandoned.

Chapter 6

Stonehenge As Never Before Seen

For over three hundred years, Stonehenge's bluestone circle was impeccably preserved, its ditches cleared of debris and the stones well-maintained. Abruptly, fate intervened and around 2900-2800 BC the site was abandoned. Archaeologist J Evans concluded, "on a local scale, it seems clear that this episode reflects human abandonment of the site." Left to ruin, the vast henge was no longer immaculate and over a long period of time vegetation and weeds grew all over the site and choked the once clean chalk bank. In 1921 it was suspected that something very unusual suddenly happened here, when an excavation revealed that parts of the henge bank had toppled into the ditch, smothering its life. This left Phase 1 in a state of decay, which spread across the entire site. Hawley found that trees had grown on the eroded bank and agricultural areas on the Salisbury Plain became a wilderness; the most complex lunar henge in Britain was deserted and left to rot. Men, women and children left the area, and without people stone circles are deprived of their life blood. Why the long headed people abandoned Stonehenge remains a mystery, but around one hundred and fifty years later people returned to the Plain, but not to Stonehenge. Instead, a new monument was constructed that overlooked Stonehenge's 56-bluestone circle. Climate change occurred around 2900 BC and parts of the British Isles experienced a long drought, other places a wetter climate. Despite the Herculean task of moving the bluestones from Wales, perhaps Stonehenge was 'blamed' for changing weather patterns and crop failure. Maybe its rituals no longer appeased the gods, and it was deemed a 'no-go' area.

Burl noted that a new henge was constructed just over half a mile away (1.4 km). From here, the long headed people would have stared towards a decaying Stonehenge with its hauntingly familiar, forlorn-looking stones. Today, what became known as Coneybury Henge survives as a ghostly cropmark, yet around five thousand years ago it was constructed on land sloping gently to the south, the enclosure's interior cut back into the hillside to create a level platform. Echoing the design of Stonehenge's earlier timber structures, it had an entrance to the northeast. Excavations from its ditch suggest a construction date of 2800-2600 BC. Over 700 post and stake holes were discovered, perhaps from timber buildings and a wooden circle. Additionally, an arc of large timber posts was placed concentrically to the inner edge of the ditch, possibly forming a circle or a horseshoe arc. Large amounts of cattle bone and lithic material, along with Grooved Ware and Beaker pottery, indicative of carcase preparation and cooking, was excavated.

Several Grooved Ware pots excavated in Scotland, from Balfarg Henge, in Fife, were found to have held black henbane, a powerful hallucinogenic, and other similar

Fig. 73 Figsbury Ring, near Stonehenge.

pots contained alcohol. Grooved Ware was also found at Stonehenge Phase 1 bluestone circle, Durrington Walls and at nearby Figsbury Ring (*Fig. 73*), all of which adds to the picture of human interaction with these sacred sites. Perhaps, coinciding with climate change there was some kind of energy 'overload' at Stonehenge and so it was left. Much remains unknown.

Archaeologists have calculated that around one hundred and thirty years after the construction of Coneybury Henge, people returned to Stonehenge. Whatever the circumstances that forced the long headed people to abandon the area may have instilled a 'taboo' regarding the bluestone circle, and so Stonehenge was to be transformed. The long headed people began restoring the site by clearing the scrub and weeds and dismantling the large bluestone circle. The white chalk henge bank that stood around 6-9 ft (1.8-2.7 m) high was repaired, and once again a secretive inner realm from uninvited intrusion was created. Guarding the entrance, three tall megaliths, known as the Slaughter Stone and its two partners, now blocked the internal view from the northeast passage. Sacred traditions resumed and the same centre that housed the early timber temple structures and the bluestone circle was reused some five hundred years later. The memory of centuries earlier recalled the position of the former lunar 'A' posts, which dictated the width of the old henge entrance; the newly repaired henge bank stopped just three strides short of it. New materials were selected to create the most unusual stone circle in the world. Sarsen stone, a form of sandstone, was chosen for the towering trilithons and the lintelled stone circle. The stone came from West Woods, near Marlborough, and in a superhuman effort was moved over 15 miles (30 km) to the site of what would become the iconic structure we have come to know today. Only two stones, Stone 26 and Lintel 160 that rested upon Trilithon 59-60, were from elsewhere. Adding to the mystery of Stonehenge, the visible stones that scattered West Woods were bypassed; only sarsen stone that had never seen the light of day was chosen. Professor Mike Parker Pearson points out that the stonemasons probably selected the buried sarsen stones which are silvery-pink in colour, as they were crust-free and therefore softer and easier to shape. Rediscovering the ancient past of our mythical ancestors allows us to understand the 'power of place' in many different ways; to relive past memories and reconnect to the monument in a more holistic way.

Ancient surveyors applied sophisticated geometry and mathematics in its construction, and this has been widely documented, but there is a hidden side to Stonehenge that has been over-shadowed by the work of mathematicians, astronomers and engineers. The land upon which Stonehenge stands is remarkable and it was geomantically decoded in immeasurable detail. Beneath Stonehenge is an exceptionally deep and highly active aquifer that releases energy, from which emerges numerous underground rivers and streams creating an invisible flowing waterscape of torrent power. Furthermore, this led geomancers to locate earth energies that would dictate the megalithic settings, certain stones placed above earth voltages making the temple highly charged. We will explore this aspect in more detail.

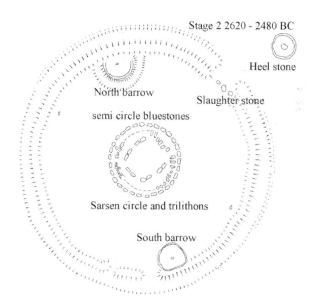

Fig. 74 Stonehenge Phase 2: standard depiction.

We all think we know the world-famous Stonehenge, its iconic stone circle instantly recognisable. However, I suggest that the original Stonehenge looked very different to what we see today. The first version of Stonehenge was highly symmetrical, although several of its large stone settings were removed in antiquity. *Fig. 74*, based on Parker Pearson's expertise, shows Stonehenge during the period 2620-2480 BC. I question this and invite you to join me on a quest to discover the lost identity of Stonehenge. Let us break free from the orthodox model and explore the past anew.

We are told the inner horseshoe setting contained five massive trilithons, yet Stonehenge may have contained an extra trilithon setting. Although now buried, its location is revealed here. We also know that Stonehenge is usually depicted as having one Altar Stone. However, I have found physical evidence to show there were once two striking Altar stones, as well as two D-shaped timber temples that housed two of the Station Stones. These are just some of Stonehenge's forgotten secrets. Enclosing the inner horseshoe and bluestone settings was a giant lintelled ring of thirty standing stones, surrounded by a white henge. This, as mentioned earlier, could have displayed inscribed symbols richly painted in ochre and woad. In memory of the ancestors, our journey to explore Stonehenge's lost secrets begins with the giant trilithons and their unusual properties —it's Stonehenge—but not quite as you know it.

Secrets of the Healing Trilithons

For engineering reasons, the trilithons were probably the first megalithic features to be raised; it would have been difficult to install them within an enclosed circle of smaller stones. Today, five massive trilithons create a horseshoe enclosure which opens to the northeast; yet originally, there may have been six. The first and second trilithons counting clockwise remain in situ and rise in height towards the giant Greater Trilithon, which stands to the southwest. Advanced engineering skills were required to raise the 90-ton trilithons, but this alone cannot account for Stonehenge's placement as the surveyors could have chosen anywhere on the Plain. I believe the main reason why the location was selected, on challenging sloping ground, was due to fast-flowing earth energies that can still be experienced today. Laser analysis of the stones reveals the subtlety of the stone dressing and shows the trilithons had been carefully matched for size, working and colour. For example, Trilithons 51-52 and 59-60 were once a silvery-pink colour, whereas Trilithons 53-54, 55-56 and 57-58 were paired orange and pink. These stones share the same architectural refinement as those of the outer circle and taper towards the top with a slight convexity, giving the illusion they are taller. The lintels are curved on both faces, the outer curve being more pronounced. Further analysis of stone tooling techniques hint at the possibility that the trilithons were prepared by a different group of people to those who constructed the lintelled stone circle. Archaeologist Francis Pryor, in his inspiring book *Stonehenge: The Story of a Sacred Landscape* (2018), suggests the trilithons may have been worked and shaped by a high-status group. I suggest they were the long headed nobility, the ruling elite of the day.

Trilithon 51-52: Magical Water

Appearing superhuman and god-like, the trilithons look down on us from on high. At the heart of Stonehenge, they formed a healing temple. I associate the trilithons with healing energies and magical properties that have been ignored by archaeologists and academics. One of the earliest examples documenting Stonehenge's healing powers comes from *The History of the Kings of Britain* by Geoffrey of Monmouth. Writing in the 12th century, he describes:

> "...in these stones is a mystery, and a healing virtue against many aliments... for they washed the stones and poured the water into baths, whereby those who were sick were cured. Moreover, they mixed confections of herbs with the water, whereby those who were wounded were healed, for not a stone is there that is wanting in virtue or leech-craft."

Centuries later c1690, antiquarian and father of archaeology, John Aubrey (1626-1697), whose name is familiar to us for his discovery of the 'Aubrey Holes', vestiges of some of the 56 stone holes of the Phase 1 bluestone circle, stated that pieces or powder of the stones, when placed in a well, kept toads away and the water pure. In 1701, Rev J Brome reported that if the stones were rubbed or scraped and water thrown upon the scrapings, they would heal any green and infectious wound or old sore. One trilithon at Stonehenge has mystifying properties that echo the accounts of both Monmouth and Aubrey: that when water is mixed with sarsen it has distinctive healing properties. Prior to the 1950s, Trilithon Stone 51 was known to have the strange ability to produce water. On its outer face there was once a deep hole 4 in (10 cm) wide that extended down into the stone for just over 2 ft (60 cm). Tom Gorrey, the custodian of Stonehenge for more than twenty years, was baffled that this stone's deep hole always contained *clear* water even during a hot drought. From

The water bearing hole now filled with concrete

Fig. 75 The water well.

the smooth water marking on the stone, presumably, for thousands of years, water frequently flowed from the hole, which can be seen in *Fig. 75*. On numerous occasions, Gorrey siphoned water from this hole and noticed that in a very short time it was full again. A local water diviner pondered upon the issue and pointed out that it could not be coming from below the ground and thought the water was produced by rain. However, for the hole to fill with rainwater it would need a considerable downpour with

the wind driving the rain in the 'right' direction, and, as Gorrey noted, this could be ruled out as when the hole was siphoned it simply filled up again. Another explanation proposed condensation as the cause. Accordingly, water would seep down from the top of the stone or lintel, possibly via a vertical crack. This lintel differs from the others, having a much more weathered appearance, in some places to a depth of several inches. One solution saw the water being created in the gaps under the lintel stones which are unusually wide and deep: "…should they not have been caused by weathering, they could have been made for the purpose of admitting air and assisting condensation." Certain stones condense water more readily than others, which is a property of sarsen stone and why it is considered unsuitable for housebuilding. However, I think condensation is highly unlikely and can be ruled out.

Similar to Stone 51, Nigel Pennick wrote of a stone basin called 'The Devil's Well' near Llanfihangel-y-Pennant in Wales, of which he observes, "with no obvious supply of water, [it] nevertheless is always full." We can have little doubt that Stone 51 and The Devil's Well both produced water that could have been viewed as sacred and/or healing. Belief that all life comes from water has been a staple of all religions since earliest recorded times, and water is still used in rituals today. However, there is no natural water supply within a mile of Stonehenge, making Stone 51's power to produce a small but permanent supply of water seem miraculous. Sadly, in modern times the sanctity of this stone's well was desecrated. In the early 1950s the water hole was being misused by visitors as a convenient place for the disposal of litter, so the Ministry of Works decided to fill the hole with cement and plastic to stop the water and rubbish overflowing. This criminally short-sighted action blocked the stone's sacred water source, preventing further investigation into this intriguing feature. Consequently, few people have heard of the water-producing standing stone, although the ancient tradition of mixing the 'powder' of the stones with water to heal wounds, ailments and to purify water, is widely known. I suggest that its origins lie in this stone's ability to produce water—magically. Imagine if the hole was unplugged to see if the miracle waters would once again return to Stonehenge!

Trilithon 59-60: Healing Power

Standing opposite Trilithon 51-52 is Trilithon 59-60, and together they create an extraordinary stone setting. Interestingly, its lintel (L160) is the only one in the entire stone circle not to have been sourced from West Woods. While its origin remains unknown, it was probably sourced from the Valley of the Stones, near Marlborough. Stone 60 is one of the most unusual stones in the entire complex—if not the world—as it once had a rough back and a notable 'pregnant swell' over what used to be a space big enough for three people to squeeze into, or two people to sit. There are many examples of megaliths that can be sat on, such as the Devil's Chair at Avebury, or the chair-like ledge at Gors Fawr stone circle in Wales. But at Stonehenge you could actually sit *inside* a standing stone, which is remarkable. Undoubtedly this so-called 'cave' was once used for ritual and healing purposes.

Atkinson did some fine restoration and resetting of the fallen stones, but he also made some terrible mistakes. According to Master Dowser Guy Underwood's personal notes, which I have inherited, Stone 60's unique feature was destroyed by the Ministry of Works in 1959. I suggest this was to stop people interacting with such a curious internal feature. This stone was designed to be entered, a unique feature now lost. Underwood recalled that in 1959, when Stone 60 was straightened—it was leaning slightly—it began to crack and as a result was filled with a crude block of dark concrete, scarring its sandstone beauty (*Fig. 76*). An eyewitness told him that when the stone was forced perpendicular by crane and chain, as it cracked it emitted a 'strange' sound. Some blamed the wind on Salisbury Plain, but I feel it was the stone 'groaning'. Archaeologists argue that Stone 60 had several holes that weakened it so that when it was moved, it broke with the strain. The unusual look of this stone was said to be caused by weathering, yet no other standing stone at Stonehenge has such bizarre weathering. Atkinson informs us:

> "...when sandstone was still and all manner of creatures burrowed in it, [leaving] disturbed areas that are softer than the surrounding rock, and thus [it] weathers more easily."

Fig. 76 Stone 60 before and after the cement disfigurement.

Stone 59: the Spine Stone

Stone 59 lies broken in three pieces, numbered 59a, b and c. It must have fallen inwards before AD 1574, when antiquarian drawings show it recumbent. This stone is nonetheless unique as no other trilithon at Stonehenge displays such an unusual feature: along the middle of the stone are two raised areas that look like purposefully carved 'spines', which is why I call stones with one or two spine ridges a *spine stone*. At Avebury Henge, one human-sized stone has a prominent

Fig. 77 The Spine Stone: Stone 59.

central spine ridge running from the top of the stone to its base. Archaeologists, such as Atkinson, call this feature 'broad tooling' and suggest that it was made in this manner in preparation for finer smoothing which was never carried out, but this seems no more likely than any other explanation.

Stonehenge is regarded as one of Britain's finest stone temples and as one of the most important sacred sites of the ancient world. Planning, design and construction must have taken very many years, so it is unlikely that the stones were left in a poor and unfinished state. Stonehenge was the ancestor's pride and glory, therefore it follows that any such marks must have had significance and meaning. Over thirty years ago, we noted that Stone 59 emits dowseable energy that flows along the stone's spine feature. When standing upright it may have assisted in balancing the chakra system, achieved simply by placing one's spine directly against the spine of the stone, aided by the spine ridge being at human height. Even today, if you place your hand, palm down, a few inches above the ridge, you can feel heat radiate from the ridge of the stone. Another carved spine stone can be found at Beltany stone circle in County Donegal, Ireland.

Fig. 78 A trilithon setting close to the Greater Trilithon.

The Fall of Trilithon 57-58

On 3rd January 1797, farmworkers ploughing the land half a mile from Stonehenge thought there had been a terrible earthquake. The silence was broken only when they felt a mighty concussion in the ground. Later that day, the workmen realised that 90 tons of Trilithon 57-58 had crashed to the ground. Adept at raising stones to balance and stand effortlessly, the ancients did not dig deep sockets, and, despite the shallow socket depth, the trilithon had stood perfectly well for over 4,500 years, so why did it fall? Apparently, in the autumn of 1796, travellers waiting for a local fair wanted to get out of the bitter southwest wind and rain that lashes across the Plain, so they dug a shelter at the side of Trilithon 57-58. The hole was never filled in, weakening the trilithon's stability and eventually caused it to fall. Stone 58 fell flat, but Stone 57 was left tilted at an angle, and was subsequently misused by boys sliding down its inner face and damaging the fine stone with their heavy Victorian hobnailed boots. One hundred and sixty-one years later, the stones were re-erected, but they were displaced by 7.8-11 in (20-30 cm) too far to the southwest, no longer showing a symmetrical relationship with its opposite twin.

Ancient Writing or Symbols?

Over five hundred years ago, in Elizabethan times, it was recorded that a strange artefact was found at, or close to, Stonehenge. This baffled London's most learned scholars who failed to agree on its interpretation. William Camden, author of *Britannia*, the first detailed historical account of Great Britain, published in Latin in 1586 (translated into English in 1610), wrote:

> "I have heard that in the time of King Henrie the Eighth, there was found neere this place [Stonehenge] a table of metal, as it had been tin and lead commixt, inscribed with many letters, but in strange a Caracter, that neither Sir Thomas Eloit, nor master Lilye Schoole-master of Pauls, could read it, and therefore neglected it. Had it been preserved, somewhat happily might have been discovered concerning Stonehenge, which is now obscured."

Archaeologists have suggested that the artefact was a lead cursing tablet, inscribed with Roman characters. Yet, Roman lettering would have been familiar to English scholars. In the 1660s, the antiquarian John Aubrey mused:

> "The inscription in Lead found at Stonehenge which Mr Lilly the Schoolmaster, and Sir Tho. Eliot could not read, might be made by the Druides."

Angered by the loss of the tablet, Stukeley wrote in 1724:

> "But eternally to be lamented is the loss of that tablet of tin, which was found at this place… inscrib'd with many letters… No doubt it was a memorial of the founders, wrote by the Druids, and it had been preserv'd till now, would have been an invaluable curiosity."

If there was a lead or tin tablet associated with Stonehenge, where was it originally located? The brief description by Camden, from an earlier source, states that it was found near Stonehenge. Perhaps it had been moved from another location? Many years ago, I spoke about one place that may have housed the tablet, and which could also explain an unusual carving on Stone 57. Today, smothered in lichen, the carving is hard to see. Archaeologists describe a "figurine and the haft of an axe", yet it is rectangular in shape, as shown in *Fig. 79*. Originally, the stone carving could be seen at head height and there is a similar but smaller carving on the fallen Lintel 121, just behind Stone 57. Possibly, during the Bronze Age, the tablet, which may have contained some information about Stonehenge, was placed upon Stone 57. This rectangular-shaped carving appears similar to stone carvings found in Brittany; another interpretation is that they represent the goddess. Sometime later, the tablet may have been placed in a round barrow dating from the Late Bronze Age. Certainly, around a thousand years after this stone had been raised, carvings of axes and daggers were etched into the inner face of the stone, as shown in *Fig. 80*.

Fig. 79 Rectangular carving of Stone 57.

Fig. 80 Carvings on the inner face of Trilithon Stone 53.

The Greater Trilithon 55-56

Dominating Stonehenge, the Greater Trilithon Stones 55 and 56 stood 24 ft (7.3 m) high, 8 ft (2.4 m) above the lintels of the surrounding circle. Weighing a total of around 95-100 tons, the Greater Trilithon had presence. The grading in height of the five trilithons was designed to direct the observer's eye towards this taller trilithon and

Fig. 81 The Greater Trilithon: Stone 56 stands in the centre.

the southwest. Standing on the former astronomical axis line and aligned to the Winter Solstice Sunset, one's attention is drawn away from the warmth of the Summer Solstice Sunrise. Due to the high henge bank, the only view that could be seen from outside the stone circle was the very top of the Greater Trilithon's lintel, teasing the uninvited to ponder upon what was happening behind the secluded henge wall. Fully dressed, polished and pristine, the trilithons were a colourful pair, one appearing an orange colour and its partner a silver-pink, glistening crystal-like in their seductive charm when touched by the light of the Sun or Moon. Today, the tall Trilithon 56 is still silver-coloured and smooth to the touch. However, most of the sarsen stones are a ghastly greenish colour as lichen smothers and hides their former splendour. The Greater Trilithon was, alas, restored in the wrong place, approximately 23.5 ins (60 cm) south-west of its original position. Anthony Johnson, author of *Solving Stonehenge: The New Key to an Ancient Enigma* (2008), states that it "is rotated approximately nine degrees anticlockwise from the perpendicular of the axis." What a shame the holy inner sanctum has three misplaced stones, and that two were damaged in attempting to restore the trilithon's settings.

Long ago, one of the Greater Trilithon stones fell, striking the ground with a massive thud. A sketch dating to AD 1575 showed Stone 55 recumbent, broken in two halfway along its length. At almost 33 ft (9 m) long, with over 8 ft (2.5 m) of its length embedded in its chalk socket, this stone was a mismatch with its partner. Stone 55 had been

Fig. 82 The club foot of Stone 55.

paired with Stone 56 that was 10 tons lighter and only 24 ft (7.3 m) long, placed just 4 ft (1.2 m) into a chalk socket. To counteract the difference in height, the bottom of this stone was shaped into a 'club foot' (*Fig. 82*). When Stone 55 fell, its partner 56 was pulled out too and leaned for hundreds of years. Possibly, Stone 55 may have been selected for the reason it had powerful dowseable 'positive and negative' energy polarities, but it did contain a design 'flaw' and eventually fell asunder. In 1812, Colt Hoare illustrated the leaning Stone 56 (see *Fig. 83*). In 1660 it was leaning 75°, in 1720 by 70°, in 1870 by 66° and in 1901 it was 60.5°, by which time it was resting dangerously on Bluestone 68 and might have caused further damage to the tall bluestone. So, in 1901, English mining engineer William Gowland straightened it.

Fig. 83 The badly leaning Greater Trilithon.

Mysterious Lunar Holes

Certain lintel carvings are not easily explained and so have tended to be ignored. Situated high above ground level and therefore out of sight, the circular indentation on top of Lintel 29-30 is intriguing. Clearly carved and worked, it has been interpreted as a hollow 'cup mark', shown in *Fig. 84*. Interestingly, this indentation is perfectly aligned to the 'Night of the Longest Moonlight' at the most Northerly Moonrise; it is unlikely this is coincidental. It may be that the marking was intended for the moonlight to course through, or to be 'captured' and 'absorbed' *into* the lintel and the stones below. This is a lunar stone.

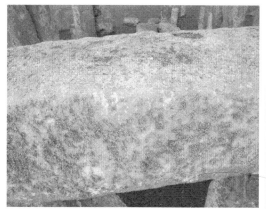 

Fig. 84 Indentation of Lintel 29-30 marks the night of the longest moonlight. *Fig. 85* Deep mortise holes.

Said to be one of the biggest blunders in the making of Stonehenge, are the circular holes on the Greater Trilithon's 16.5 ton lintel. Deep mortise holes are visible on the eastern face (see *Fig. 85*) that match the large tenons on top of Stone 56. On the western face are shallower depressions, apparently the start of mortise holes which have been interpreted as 'errors'. The masons simply got the holes wrong, flipped the giant stone over and started again! Another implausible suggestion is that the shallow holes may have held another stone lintel, but that too is not feasible as it would have been far too heavy for Stone 55—the shorter and weaker partner of the Greater Trilithon—to support. Interpreting the shallow depressions of Lintel 156 as a 'mistake' on their grandest and tallest trilithon is to insult

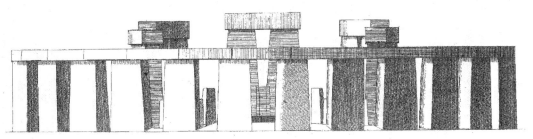

Fig. 86 The upper window created by the outer circle and the Greater Trilithon.

the intelligence and ability of our ancestors. Everything at Stonehenge had meaning. Imagine if the indentations were not intended for the human eye but were to be seen by the two eyes of heaven, the Sun and the Moon, connecting Stonehenge to the celestial light that imbued the lintels with power. Professor John North noted that the Greater Trilithon is designed to capture two celestial events: in its lower window the setting Winter Solstice Sun and the Minor Southern Moonset in its upper window; both appear between the Greater Trilithon and the lintelled stone circle, as shown in *Fig. 86*. North calculated that as the moon set, its last glint within the slit would gradually shift, day by day, from the right-hand end to the left, and then reverse (see *Fig. 87*). Thus, the Greater Trilithon united the Sun and the Moon as one.

Fig. 87 The Moon in the window box.

Stonehenge has a long-forgotten protracted lunar ritual that occurred at Winter Solstice, and which coincided with the Minor Southern Moonset. During the Winter Solstice period of any Southern Lunar Standstill, the Dark Moon always coincides with the week of Winter Solstice sunsets, creating a visual drama second to none. Dark Moon is an astronomical term for the last waning crescent moon that rises in the east just before dawn, after which the Sun rises. We have seen how the Greater Trilithon captures the Sun at Midwinter and the moon at its standstill in its upper and lower windows. This is also

Fig. 88 Dark Moon (no Moon/New Moon) and waxing Crescent Moon.

the time of the Dark Moon and, in this case, the start of the longest night. Dark Moon rises honey-coloured in the east and each night it gets thinner and thinner until it disappears before one or two moonless nights occur. After which, the thin crescent of the waxing moon can be seen in the west. You can see Dark Moon—no moon—followed by the waxing crescent moon, each month (*Fig. 88*). In modern Pagan terms, Dark Moon represents the Crone aspect of the goddess, and I suggest this protracted lunar ritual represented to the ancestors death, rebirth, fertility and renewal, once celebrated at Stonehenge by the lintelled standing stone in the east.

The Jewel of Stonehenge

In 1620, Inigo Jones stood at the centre of Stonehenge. He saw a recumbent green sandstone lying flat, which he named the 'Altar Stone', believing it to be a Druid altar. Now known as Stone 80, originally it stood upright, but then, centuries ago, Trilithon Stone 55 collapsed and broke into two pieces, now identified as 55a and 55b. What happened was 55a and its 10-ton lintel pressed the Altar Stone firmly into the ground, partially burying it, as shown in *Fig. 89*. Burl states that the Altar Stone is 16 ft (4.87 m) long by 3.5 ft (1.06 m) wide, and 2 ft (0.60 m) in depth. It was raised 10 ft (3.04 m) from the geometrical centre of Stonehenge, where it marked a powerful earth energy zone (discussed later). Rich in colour and bejewelling Stonehenge, the Altar Stone is a pale green sandstone, flecked with shimmering mica and small pieces of garnet. Originally, it was highly polished, smooth to the touch, and would have glistened like a precious gemstone. Today, while all plans and surveys of Stonehenge show a single Altar Stone, I am challenging this orthodoxy. The Altar Stone may not have stood alone and could, I believe, have had a partner. There is documented evidence to support this view. Imagine, for a moment, at the heart of Stonehenge two central stones standing close together as a pair, mirroring the other pairs of trilithons and creating a twin-like symmetry. Over three and a half centuries ago, a historical account states that one of the Altar Stones was uprooted and carted away. Tracking down physical evidence for a second long-lost Altar Stone was not an easy task, but I have managed to gather tangible proof of its existence.

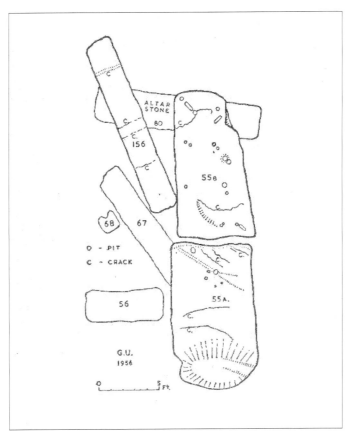

Fig. 89 Survey of the Altar Stone by Guy Underwood.

Evidence of a Second Altar Stone

The Altar Stone is uniquely composed of a fine-grained pale green sandstone and no other stone at Stonehenge is like it. Significantly, chips of a *different* grey-green micaceous sandstone have been found in the soil on the site and fragments unearthed. Hawley and Atkinson thought the stone was sourced from an outcrop of the Cosheston Beds on the shores of Mill Bay, Milford Haven, South Wales. However, modern analysis by geologist Rob Ixer located an outcrop in West Wales, at the Senni formation of Lower Palaeozoic sandstone. Nonetheless, the sandstone chips were clearly darker and greyer in colour than the surviving pale green Altar Stone. This could be physical evidence of an unknown, missing sandstone, sourced from West Wales, that once stood at the heart of Stonehenge.

One of the first people to dig at Stonehenge in the vicinity of the Altar Stone(s) was George Villiers, 1st Duke of Buckingham. In 1620 he visited Stonehenge when James I of England was staying at Wilton House, near Salisbury, the seat of the Earls of Pembroke. Whilst digging at the centre of Stonehenge, Buckingham found a large 6 ft (1.8 m) deep hole that may have been the stone hole for the second Altar Stone. Atkinson argued that this stone hole WA3359 may have been the socket for a pair of tongue and grooved bluestones, which when slotted to-gether formed one large stone the size of the Altar Stone. Tongued bluestone Stone 66 remains buried, though the grooved bluestone Stone 68, shown in *Fig. 90*, still stands. Instead of fitting together two blue-stones to create a makeshift Altar Stone twin, it would seem more likely that the Stonehenge masons simply quarried another exquisite sandstone as a partner to the original. Imagine two very tall green sand-stones, one darker than the other, standing side by side at the heart of

Fig. 90 The grooved bluestone.

Stonehenge. This presents an architectural possibility that is ignored by mainstream archaeologists. During the same dig, Buckingham also found horns, "batter-dashes", rusty armour, arrowheads, stag and oxen bones, and other rotten bones.

Additional and compelling evidence for a second Altar Stone comes from the Royal Architect, Inigo Jones (1573-1652). In 1620 he completed the first survey of Stonehenge for King James I, in which he stated that at the centre of Stonehenge was a stone that appeared very similar in width and height to the surviving Altar Stone. It seems likely that Jones was referring to a second Altar Stone at the centre of Stonehenge, which he refers to as 'the Cell'. Colt Hoare, in his *Ancient History of Wiltshire, Vol. 1* (1812), informs us:

> "In the inmost part of the Cell, Mr Jones observed a stone (which is now gone) appearing not much above the surface of the earth, and lying towards the east, four feet broad, and sixteen feet long."

It is highly unlikely that these identical measurements of the Altar Stone are coincidental. Some years later, during the mid-1600s, another antiquarian report regarding the second Altar Stone surfaced. This was in one of John Aubrey's volumes of *Monumenta Britannica*. Aubrey had been told of its fate by Randal Chaldicot, Rector of Bishopstone, a village close to his home at Broad Chalke, Wiltshire. Presumably, this man of the cloth was telling the truth when he told Aubrey:

> "Phillip, Earl of Pembroke, Lord Chamberlayne to King Charles I, successor of James I, did say 'that an Altar Stone was found in the middle of the Area here and that it was carried away to St James'.'"

It is worth mentioning, as an aside, that antiquarian Sir Richard Colt Hoare, born at Stourhead, purchased Glastonbury Tor in 1786. In 1804 he funded the restoration of the St Michael church tower, all that remained of the 14th-century stone church.

Stolen by Royal Command?

Commissioned by Henry VIII, St James's Palace, the main London residence of the monarchy from 1530-1698, was second only to the Palace of Whitehall. King James I (1566-1625), famous for sponsoring the translation of the King James Bible into English, the best-selling book in history, was a complex character and bisexual; his lover allegedly George Villiers, the Duke of Buckingham. In 1590, three hundred Scottish witches had been tried for plotting the murder of the king as James VI of Scotland. He is known to have been highly superstitious, and suffered from a perpetual and morbid fear of a violent death. Desiring to understand witchcraft and possibly to use their tricks against those he feared, James began to study witchcraft and magic. His research into the ancient art was published in 1597 in three books titled *Daemonologie*, detailing his opinions on the subject in the form of a Socratic dialogue between the sceptic Philomathes and the knowledgeable occultist Epistemon, who reveals many aspects of witchcraft and sorcery. The book ends in a strange and sickening account of the North Berwick witch trials, an action based on the evidence of Dr John Fian, the alleged head of a coven whose confession was painfully drawn with the use of thumbscrews, the Boot (a horrendous design of blades thrust into the lower legs), and by ripping out his fingernails.

Curiously, the first people to dig and survey Stonehenge knew one another and were involved either in witchcraft or the trials. The witch hunt fever that was to flourish under the self-appointed Witchfinder General, Matthew Hopkins, heightened the king's anxiety. Inigo Jones travelled across Europe with a wealthy member of the aristocracy, Francis Manners (1578-1632), and witnessed witch trials and horrendous mass burnings. His brother, Roger Manners (1576-1612), the 5th Earl of Rutland, was Jones' wealthy patron. In 1620 Buckingham married Katherine, daughter of Francis Manners, now the 6th Earl of Rutland, against her father's objections. One of their daughters, Mary Villiers, was to become much loved by the king. At the age of 12, she married 15-year-old Charles, eldest son of the 4th Earl of Pembroke. Due to the king's affections, the duke gained power and influence. Members of Parliament noted that

England was "not now governed by a monarchy, but by a triumviri, whereof Buckingham was the first and chiefest, the prince the second, and the king the last." Buckingham could do what he liked, and during the height of the witch hunt Manner's servants were accused of killing his sons at Belvoir Castle (the seat of the Dukes of Rutland) and were sentenced to death. Yet, Buckingham was employing 'cunning folk' (witches), who believed in the power of ritual, herbs, stones and stars, and I think Buckingham did too. He was known to have enlisted the services of Richard Napier, the astrologer physician who treated the Earl's younger son. Another cunning man, Pierce Butler, who possessed 'strange faculties', was also in his service. According to a 19th-century account, when James was dying, an extraordinary ritual was performed to rid the king of his illness. As he lay on his deathbed, in excruciating pain, a ritual to lessen his suffering was to transfer his pain to the body of an animal. A young pig had been selected for the rite and was dressed in the clothes of a human baby. The Duchess of Buckingham played the part of midwife to the baby pig, which had been baptised before being chased out of the room. It is deeply ironic that a monarch who had devoted so much of his life to stamping out all traces of witchcraft should have taken part in a blasphemous ritual in attempting to prolong his own days on earth.

I strongly suspect that Buckingham took the second Altar Stone for his beloved king. The evidence for a missing stone is unambiguous; Aubrey states that it was 'carried away' to St James's in London. The only person to have dug at length at Stonehenge's centre before Aubrey was Buckingham, who frequently stayed with the king in London. Buckingham also became connected with the philosopher Francis Bacon, known for developing a scientific and spiritual approach to the discovery of Nature's secrets. Years after Bacon's death, the Royal Society was based on his epistemological legacy.

The Stone of Scone, also known as the 'Stone of Destiny', and often referred to as the Coronation Stone, is an oblong piece of red sandstone that has been used for centuries in the coronation of the monarchs of Scotland and later the monarchs of England, although whether the present stone is the original is questionable. Could the green-grey sandstone have been used in a similar manner by King James I? Or did the architect Inigo Jones, Surveyor of the King's Works, incorporate the missing Altar Stone into the foundation of one of his buildings, such as the Banqueting Hall at Whitehall, renowned for its Pagan masked balls that a growing Puritanism disapproved of? Another suspected location is the Queen's House at Greenwich, one of Jones' first designs. Or perhaps the stone stayed in Wiltshire, integrated into the grounds of Wilton House, seat of the Earls of Pembroke, where King James enjoyed visiting? The memory of the missing Altar Stone never faded.

Fig. 91 Limestone stones at Berwick St James, near Stonehenge.

Centuries later, in September 1865, members of Wiltshire Archaeological Society referred to the second Altar Stone that had been 'carted away' and they wanted to find it. The following year, William Cunnington, grandson of William Cunnington senior, believed he had found a report of the missing Altar Stone, and immediately wrote to the Clerk of Works at St James's Palace, who replied, "No such stone now exists here." The trail had gone cold. Then, in 1933, G M Engleheart had an idea that St James's Palace may have been mistaken for Berwick St James, a village about four miles from Stonehenge. He postulated that the second Altar Stone had been turned into a stone bridge, a common practice during that era. This is consistent with what John Aubrey had been told by Mrs Mary Trotman, that someone living in Bishopstone had taken a large stone from Stonehenge to make a bridge. Engleheart thought the stone had been re-erected at the corner of a street in the village of Berwick St James. But he was mistaken, as the stones are limestone and not sandstone, as shown in *Fig. 91*. Published in the *Salisbury Journal* on 3rd March 2007, this story was retold by Dennis Price, who claimed to be a Wessex archaeologist and said he had discovered the exact whereabouts of the missing Altar Stone at Berwick St James. However, it turned out that Price was a kitchen employee at Wessex Archaeology rather than a qualified archaeologist. It was fake news. More than three hundred years after the first observation of the second Altar Stone, the search continues.

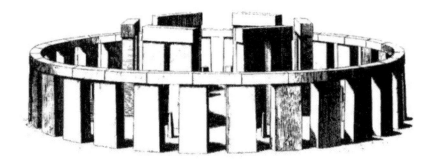

Fig. 92 Greater Hexagon plan of Stonehenge by Inigo Jones (1620).

The Missing Trilithon

I shall shortly describe how the *dual* Altar Stones symbolically repre-sented a male and female deity that were said to 'occupy' Stone-henge and whose powers culminated at Winter Solstice. Meanwhile, Inigo Jones speculated that there was an additional trilithon, and from his 'Greater Hexagon' plan, illustrated above in *Fig. 92*, he suggested that Stonehenge in design consisted of four intersecting equilateral triangles inscribed within the circumference of the circle, resulting in the need for a sixth trilithon to complete the symmetry of the hexagon. Aubrey, a widely respected antiquarian, visited Stonehenge some fifty years after Jones, and he too was unsure of the correct number of trilithons. One of his surveys speculates there were two 'missing' trilithons, their position shown in the bottom sector of *Fig. 93*, making seven in total. Certainly, early antiquarians who documented and surveyed Stonehenge repeatedly reported a missing Altar Stone, and possibly one or more missing trilithons. Unlike modern-day archaeologists, Jones and Aubrey questioned what the innermost sanctum of Stonehenge actually looked like, and so do I.

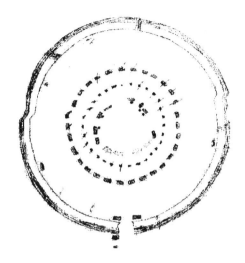

Fig. 93 John Aubrey's plan of Stonehenge (1666).

Between 1719-25 William Stukeley (1687-1765) paid many visits to Stonehenge and drew the monument in several detailed sketches. He also compiled a reconstruction based on what he saw amidst the ruins. For nearly 300 years, Stukeley's model prevailed as the correct representation of Stonehenge. His drawing of the leaning Greater Trilithon and Trilithons 57-58 before they fell, the smashed lintel of Trilithons 59-60 as well as Trilithons 53-54, are shown in *Fig. 94*. Stukeley also drew an inner horseshoe of bluestones, but recent excavations now show this to have been an oval. One of his contemporaries, architect John Wood the Elder (1704-1754), disagreed with some of his findings and questioned his measurements. Stukeley was confident that his version of Stonehenge was correct as it was based on what he could see. Prior to his drawings, as we have seen, earlier antiquarians questioned the number of trilithons at the heart of Stonehenge. If there *was* another trilithon, why didn't Stukeley or Wood record it? Was it lying ruinous outside the monument, or had it been partially buried?

Fig. 94 William Stukeley's drawing of the Stonehenge trilithons (1724).

Whilst surveying ancient sites, we do know that Stukeley often failed to record or observe stone settings. In the Avebury environs, he overlooked a satellite stone circle called the 'Falkner Ring' which once consisted of twelve red-hued sarsen stones and was discovered by Mr Falkner of Devizes in 1840. Stukeley also muddied the waters over the Beckhampton Avenue by drawing standing stones that simply did not exist, combining what he could see with what he imagined was once there, for which he produced no evidence.

The Buried Trilithon

Photographer and author Pete Glastonbury informed me some years ago that "a trilithon was buried in 1928". Under Hawley's directive, between 1919-26 the southeast area of Stonehenge was savagely stripped to the chalk bedrock, the Aubrey Holes and the Y and Z Holes (discussed in a later chapter) were located, and Stones 1, 2, 6, 7, 29 and 30 were straightened. Could Hawley's team have been responsible for the burial of the trilithon simply because it did not fit the known and believed model as presented by Stukeley? More importantly, if Glastonbury is correct, then why was it buried and not restored like Trilithon 57-58? A photograph provided by Glastonbury shows an arrow pointing to the buried trilithon's known secret location (see *Fig. 95*). Questioning the accepted model and imagining the Stonehenge of our ancestors has led to identifying long-lost stones that lie on the periphery of existence in a twilight zone. Nonetheless, if there is a large trilithon setting that lies hidden, a simple excavation would surely disclose the truth. In all probability, Stonehenge may have looked radically different to what archaeologists now suggest. There is the distinct possibility of a second green sandstone Altar Stone, conceivably a sixth trilithon, and we will soon encounter timber temples that once housed a sarsen stone. Alternatively, do we stay in the comfort zone of conformity and settle for William Stukeley's and Professor Richard Atkinson's model?

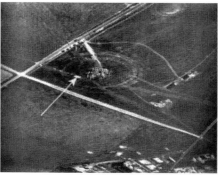

Fig. 95 The buried trilithon's secret location, hidden from view.

Paired Symmetry

Megalithic symmetry made possible Stonehenge as a stone temple of balance and harmony. The trilithons formed facing pairs and an additional trilithon would have created an opposing partner to the Greater Trilithon. The long headed masons are known to have re-arranged the 56 bluestones that were dismantled from Phase 1. One interpretation is that the bluestones were reset as a double arc. Entirely invisible on the surface today, these were one of the most important archaeological discoveries at Stonehenge. Between 1954 and 1956, Professors Atkinson, Piggott and Stone excavated a segment of the bluestone circle between Stones 32 and 33 that stands inside the present-day bluestone circle, and identified what they called the 'R' Holes. Further excavations located the 'Q' Holes on the outside of the present-day bluestone circle. Looking into the socket holes, where numerous bluestone chippings were found, they gazed into the past and realised they had unearthed a section of Stonehenge that had not been seen since 2500 BC. Hawley had noticed some of these anomalous holes before but had not realised their significance. Forming a concentric arc that extended from Stone 46 clockwise to Stone 34, the position of twelve pairs of Q and R Holes were excavated, and it was estimated that there were in total twenty-two pairs that formed a bluestone arc, as shown below in *Fig. 96*.

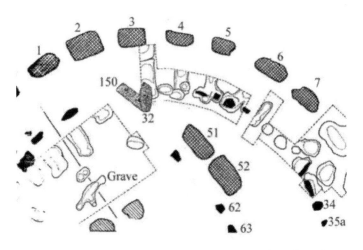

Fig. 96 The bluestone concentric arc excavation showing the former stone holes.

Atkinson noted that the total number of bluestones outnumbered those that could have stood in the concentric Q and R stone setting. He surmised that if the spacing was continued, it would equate to 38 pairs of bluestones forming a concentric circle with additional entrance stones. Sockets for two to three bluestones were found behind the Greater Trilithon and further sockets were found close to Trilithons 57-58 and 59-60, supporting the idea of a concentric circle. In an email correspondence, Professor Mike Parker Pearson told me:

> "We don't know if they [the bluestone sockets behind the greater trilithon] were part of a larger Q and R bluestone circle (which is how I have interpreted them), or if they sat in isolation, (which is how English Heritage depicts them)."

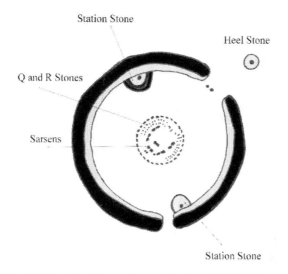

Fig. 97 Model of Stonehenge by English Heritage.
The bluestone arc and stone settings.

This model is shown above in *Fig. 97*. Atkinson calculated that the mean diameters of the concentric stone circles would be 74 ft (22.5 m) and 86 ft (26.2 m) respectively. A simple, yet important clue, making the bluestone concentric circle highly likely, is that the number of bluestones from the Aubrey Holes and Bluestonehenge total 83, and the number in the large concentric bluestone rings are 76 with six additional stones flanking the entrance, making a total of 82.

Entering Stonehenge in the Late Neolithic was a grand affair as there were once inliers that formed a bluestone avenue. Today, one walks through just two bluestones (see *Fig. 98*), but originally the spotted dolerite entrance stones, Stones 31 and 49, were once part of a 17 ft (5.18 m) long avenue containing four pairs of bluestones that led into the monument. Either side of the entrance were three standing stones that created another line 11 ft (3.35 m) long. Next to entrance Stone 49 is recumbent Stone 48 (R37 on *Fig. 99*), a rhyolite bluestone of a dark blue-grey colour displaying delicate flows of thin parallel white lines, creating a beautiful contrast to the more plentiful spotted dolerite stones. Pairs of bluestones standing 6 ft (1.8 m) high encircled the monument, forming a bluestone concentric circle of contrasting colour and texture.

Fig. 98 Stonehenge today: the bluestone entrance containing a male phallic shaped stone (left) and a female diamond shaped stone (right).

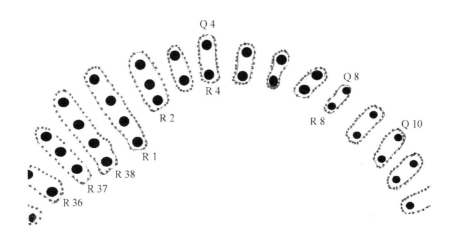

Fig. 99 Atkinson's excavation of the bluestone avenue entrance.

The Four Main Types of Bluestones

Four and a half thousand years ago, the bluestones displayed their multi-coloured splendour. Today, weathering and lichen have made the bluestones and the sarsen stones appear uniformly grey and dull. Bluestones are so-called because of their colour; in dry weather they are bluish-grey but when wet after rain acquire a noticeably bluer tinge. Bluestone is a generic term that describes the Welsh bluestones, but there are several varieties and colours that are, petrologically speaking, entirely different. Spotted dolerite is the most common type of bluestone found at Stonehenge, which is a coarse-grained crystalline rock of bluish-grey colour, speckled with irregular nodules of white or pink feldspar, usually about the size of a pea, or smaller. Geological identification, by Rob Ixer and Richard Bevins, reveals the spotted dolerite stones came from Carn Goedog and Carn Breseb, on the northern side of the Preseli Mountains.

Fig. 100 The bluestones are of human height.

Several bluestones displayed different colours that dramatically stood out from the spotted dolerite variety. Stones 44, 45 and 62 are dark blue, like the midnight sky, known as 'unspotted dolerite' and have no feldspar spots. Quarried from Craig Rhosyfelin, rhyolite bluestone is a form of volcanic lava of a dark blue-grey colour, and instead of being spotted has a delicate flow of thin white parallel lines. Five surviving examples are Stones 48 and 46, which still stand and form diametrically opposite pairs to Stones 40 and 38, plus 32e which is now buried. Never mentioned because they are no longer visible are five stumps of a softer volcanic ash variety: these are

Stones 32c, 33e, 33f and two unnumbered fragments between Stones 40 and 41. Exceptionally smooth to the touch and dark olive-green in colour, they were once visible within the stone circle. However, due to their softness and vulnerability to weathering, these became stumps and now lay buried and forgotten. Stones 33e and 33f stood close to each other, probably forming opposing pairs. One stone within the bluestone circle was especially powerful: Stone 40g is a below-ground stump and its energy has been capped. This unusual sandstone, loaded with mica, had a lead cover placed over it that lessens its high vibrational resonance. Mica in stone, rather like quartz, enhances its energy; to cap it violates the stone's sacred identity. The lost technology of how the bluestones were actually set into the chalk indicated a sophistication that astonished Atkinson. Each socket hole consisted of a central trench with a deep cavity at either end "as though a great dumbbell had been pressed into the chalk," noted Burl. The trench chalk was still clean, fresh looking and brilliant white, but the socket holes contained dirtier chalk caused by the falling earth when the stones had been removed.

Seen in its entirety, Stonehenge was once a magnificent temple containing highly polished and multicoloured stones. The Altar Stones, one pale and one dark green, flecked with garnet and glistening mica, stood alongside the dark blue-grey bluestones with white parallel stripes. Midnight black bluestones were set against dark olive-green stones, and bluestones peppered with white and pink spots contrasted with the tall silver-pink sarsens. This aesthetic quality is part of Stonehenge's lost identity.

Spooky Bluestones and Storms

Brian Davison, former Inspector of Ancient Monuments at Stonehenge, recounted how, on 15th October 1987, a team from the University of Bristol took drill samples from ten bluestones. Stone 65 still bears the scar of the diamond drill bit, and flake samples were taken from a further five of the inner bluestone oval. There was a lot of mock apprehensiveness because of the many stories of storms brewing up from nowhere and bad luck following the tampering with the stones.

"We joked and said, well, you know, even if people don't see us, the gods will see us and we'll be struck down. Well, we finished our work about 9 o'clock at night, and cleared away, and said, well there you are, it's all superstition. Nothing's happened. No thunderbolts. No claps of thunder. But that was October 1987. Six hours later, we had the hurricane known as The Great Storm of 1987 that was a violent extratropical cyclone with hurricane force winds, the like of which has never been seen since, and was not predicted by weather forecasters!"

More Lost Features: Decorated Timber Temples

Designing one of the wonders of the ancient world, the long headed people created a version of Stonehenge that is hardly ever talked about—this is a sad truth concerning its history. Within the henge once stood two D-shaped timber temples; their foundations now lie hidden beneath the north and south barrows. Nearly a century ago,

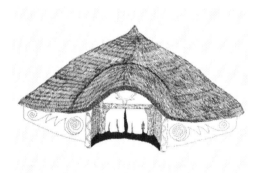

Hawley discovered that within the D-shaped buildings were smooth, yellow plaster floors, and each temple housed a sarsen Station Stone that may have been used for healing purposes and would have been revered; certainly, these stones must have been seen as special. To complement this, some of the structure's timbers

Fig. 101 Artist's impression of the timber temple that housed a Station Stone.
Illustration: Fiona Hughes.

were, perhaps, richly painted with ochre for secret or intimate ceremonies. The northeast-southwest axis line of the trilithons was also incorporated into the rectangular arrangement of the four Station Stones, the southeast-northwest section of which aligns to the Southern Major Moonrise as well as to the Northern Major Moonset, forming an astronomical alignment that brought, symbolically and physically, celestial energies to the stones.

Constructed of wattle and daub, a traditional way of building until medieval times, the rooms were well designed. Parker Pearson speculates that the southern D-shaped building was "presumably a roofed gathering place for people." English Heritage's survey team suggested that because of the bank and ditch 'kink' around the building, it is exceptionally old. This may therefore have been the first structure ever raised at Stonehenge—only further excavations will reveal its true age.

The Sarsen Circle

Finally, the sarsen circle was raised in all its circular perfection. As previously mentioned, the sarsens when first worked would have been a stunning a mixture of silver with a pink tinge that glistened in the Sun and in moonlight. The original number of uprights in the circle was thirty, but only sixteen remain in position (1-7, 10, 11, 16, 21, 23, 27-30), while nine others are either leaning or have fallen (15, 19 and 26). The remaining sarsen stones (13, 17, 18, 20 and 24) are missing. The main concentration of missing stones is in the south-western section—the direction of the setting Midwinter Sun. All of the sarsen stones were sculpted into a rectangular shape with an average width of 7 ft (2.13 m) and a thickness of 3-4 ft (0.9-1.2 m), the flatter side of the stone facing inwards. The stones taper towards the top, some in a convex curve, creating an optical illusion of straightness. Standing 13.5 ft (7.16 m) tall, excavation has revealed they are buried to a depth of 4-5 ft (1.21-1.52 m), making the overall length 18 ft (5.48 m). Stone 11 in the south is a smaller stone that was broken in antiquity and stood just 8 ft (2.4 m) high. Positioned with considerable accuracy to make a perfect circle, the centres of the stones are equally spaced at intervals of 10.5 ft (3.2 m), which allows for the variation in width of the standing stones. Creating a wider entrance into the ring, Stones 1 and 30 were spaced 1 ft (0.30 m) wider than the rest in adjacent pairs.

The ancient long headed masons overcame a significant engineering problem: Stonehenge is situated on sloping ground, which fell 6 in (15 cm) from south to north, and 1.3 ft (39 cm) from west to east, yet a perfect ring of 30 heavy sarsen stones with curving lintels formed a circle, the tops of which were never more than 4 in (10 cm) from the horizontal. The accuracy in achieving this on sloping ground was guaranteed by placing Stone 30 at the entrance almost 1 ft (30 cm) shallower in the ground than Stone 10 to the south, where the land was lower. The perfectly curved lintels once fitted together so tightly it would have appeared as a seamless complete circle, the stones as close together as other mortarless ancient stone blocks of which it is said a credit card cannot be fitted between the masonry. Today, only five lintels remain in position, each weighing between 3-5 tons, 10.5 ft (3.15 m) in length, and between 3.5 ft (1.04 m) and 2.5 ft (0.73 m) thick. Every lintel was skilfully carved on the inner and outer side so that it followed the curve of the circle. To see this, simply stand near the entrance against Stone 27 and look along the inner face of

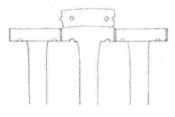

Fig. 102 Lintel workmanship.

the three lintels, where the curve is most pronounced. It is often assumed that the lintels simply balance on the tops of the uprights, but they are securely locked in position by mortice and tenon joints. Each upright has a pair of small projecting knobs or tenons on its upper surface, one for each of the two lintels it supports. These lintels have a corresponding pair of round pits, or mortices, on their respective undersides.

So familiar is the image of Stonehenge that we tend to overlook the skilled workmanship of the masons who made the top of the uprights exceptionally flat, smooth and level. As an extra safeguard against lateral movement, the edges on the inner and outer faces of the lintels were slightly raised, the lower edges being cut away to make a symmetrically sloping edge that rests in tight dish-like beds. Additionally, each lintel is jointed to its neighbour by a tongue and groove (or toggle) joint, which can be seen on fallen Lintel 122. Great care and attention must have been taken in order to get the upper surfaces of the lintels horizontal and level with each other. Imagine being at this unique stone circle when the last lintel was set in place as stone pressed against stone, hearing it slot into place.

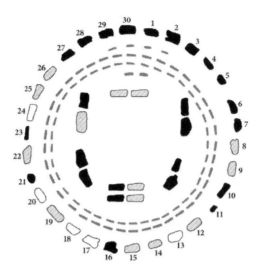

Fig. 103 Stonehenge with two Altar Stones, a possible sixth
trilithon, the bluestone concentric circle and entrance stones.

Stonehenge now stood forming a colourful, symmetrical stone monument containing a possible extra trilithon, the Altar Stones, the
Heel Stone and the concentric bluestone circle, as shown above in
Fig. 103. The temple was now complete, and the stage was set for
powerful rituals to be performed. Francis Pryor wrote that the
bluestones appeared "human [in] size" and felt their "presence".
Perhaps, the giant, taller than life trilithons may have been seen as
super-human, even god-like, with their ability to communicate to
the long headed priesthood in so many ways. Exploring the secret
language of the stones and their mystical properties can open a
portal, perhaps just a little, allowing a glimpse of age-old rituals.
Soon, I will explore millennia-old clues that hint at the ceremonies
that could have occurred within the enchantment of Stonehenge.

Chapter 7

An Oracle and Healing Temple

The fundamental question about Stonehenge that has never been fully answered is why was it built, for what purpose? Archaeologists inform us that the monument was primarily a focus for death rites and ancestral worship. Mike Parker Pearson is one of these, adding that it also "served to unite distant communities such as the Welsh and Wessex cultures." Stonehenge can be likened to a multi-faceted diamond and, as with a church or temple that serves its community in honouring births, marriages and deaths, likewise, in its heyday, Stonehenge had multiple roles. With its distinctive lintelled circle and inner stone trilithon setting, it was raised to create Britain's foremost healing and oracle centre, as emulated centuries later at Delphi in ancient Greece. As late as the mid-18th century, Stonehenge was thought to have aural power; it was a place where one could hear the voice of a deity. Captivating pilgrims from all over the ancient world, Stonehenge was the megalithic jewel in Albion's crown.

The Power of Stone

For millennia, various cultures have revered stones, gems and crystals, believing them to possess an innate power. In ancient Egypt and Babylon, statues became a 'residence' for the god or deity that was thought to inhabit that particular stone block or statue. The Old Testament tells of the Ten Commandments carved in stone, and Islam's Mecca is where devout pilgrims worship the Black Stone, the *Ka'ba*. Today, most gemstones are seen as benevolent or having healing properties. Exquisite, polished Neolithic jade axes were sculpted for ceremonial use and undoubtedly represented

Fig. 104 Stone contained the life-force of the deity.

status, strength and power. In the Bronze Age, men and women wore amber imported from Estonia and English jet from Whitby Bay, fashioned into beautiful, high-status necklaces. Some standing stones were believed to bring good luck; for example, it is said that Welsh drovers took chippings from a monolith called the King Stone at the Rollright Ring, in Oxfordshire, to bring them good fortune. Repeatedly, the early medieval cleric, Geoffrey of Monmouth, told of how the stones at Stonehenge had "a healing virtue against many

Fig. 105 The omphalos at Delphi.

ailments," and we have seen that holed stones were believed to possess healing properties. At Delphi, in ancient Greece, a temple was built to house the *omphalos*, the most sacred stone at the centre of their world (see *Fig. 105*). Across time and still influencing modern-day culture, stones are believed to hold power.

The power of stone cannot be underestimated and Don Robins' extensive research into its hidden properties demonstrates this. He claims that a stone's crystal lattice can be programmed to release sound or a 'ghostly' image. Robins investigated the Rollright Ring alongside Paul Devereux and other scientists, as part of the 'Dragon Project' in the late 1970s. Dr Robins, who holds a PhD in Solid State Chemistry, was a faculty member at London University's Institute of Archaeology, and developed the technique of electron spin resonance as a powerful tool for archaeological analysis of food remains. His articles in *Nature and Science, The Times* and *New Scientist* have helped to make the study of energy anomaly research at ancient sites respectable. Robins is also widely respected for his analysis of the preserved mummified remains of an Iron Age (or Romano-British) young male, known as the 'Lindow Man', who experienced a brutal ritual sacrifice. I have studied Robins' work, and although he did not relate any of his research to Stonehenge in particular, I propose that certain stones at Stonehenge were aurally programmed, creating a temple that literally generated its own spiritual sound and power. This is because a standing stone's crystal lattice structure is analogous to a semi-conductor, as both have the capacity to store and transmit energy. Inside a stone's lattice structure are 'defects' which can be likened to islands that, in piezoelectric terms, can produce an electric current. Conversely, an electric current can produce a periodic defect, as utilised in quartz watches. Within a crystal lattice, these defect impurities and its hidden electrons provide the basis for a form of memory that can enable a stone to be programmed to store information. Robins surmises that electrons within a stone's lattice can produce a magnetic effect that may be used to encode and store images or sound that can later be released.

Most lattices have defects as a result of the incomplete or disordered population of ions that can produce 'wells' which house intruder ions and trap electrons. Intruder ions are present in all stones apart from the purest crystalline quartz and are commonly used in semi-conductor and solid-state laser technology. These cavities can be magnetic and house iron atoms, thus allowing incoming energy to be easily trapped, stored and transmitted. Free electrons moving in the lattice constitute an electric current—imagine active electricity moving within the seemingly still and motionless stone. Free electrons are found in most defect lattices, generated internally by radioactivity or in almost perfect crystals, by external forces such as cosmic rays. Ionising radiation scatters electrons across the lattice, and some fall into the defect centres to become trapped. Over time, these defect centres can release the trapped electrons and may be likened to ions carrying charges and messages through a nervous system. In semi-conductors, excitation will cause an electric current which can release electrons from their energy wells. Thus, stones and semi-conductors share similar properties. I contend that the ancients knew how to program a standing stone's lattice to store sound and images, utilising the defect lattice and its ability to memorise data. As we shall soon see, when Stonehenge was in fully functioning order, undoubtedly people came from far and wide to seek oracular guidance, for healing and to witness strange, faint sounds or mirage-like images released from the stones. Was this the source of the myth referred to by Bournemouth University's Head of Archaeology, Professor Tim Darvill, who posited that Stonehenge was a healing temple "occupied" by "a healing god"?

Programming Stone

Programming the defect lattice is a relatively simple process. Early research into stone programming was first explored by archaeologist and Master Dowser, Tom Lethbridge (1901-1971), who demonstrated how pebbles and stones can be encoded and 'charged' with a human 'bionic' field. Lethbridge discovered this when he picked up a pebble and dowsed over it and his pendulum continuously swung clockwise. He asked his wife to pick another pebble and his pendulum gyrated anti-clockwise. Lethbridge concluded that the pebble's crystal lattice structure somehow 'memorised' the bionic field of the person holding it and the polarity of that field. However, this memory was transient and after twenty-four hours the pebbles reverted to a neutral condition. Some weeks later, he visited an Iron Age hillfort and noticed that it was surrounded by beach pebbles used as sling stones in defence of the hillfort. He again dowsed the pebbles and found the majority had a male field charge and had been 'thrown' in anger. Lethbridge was puzzled by the fact that the pebbles had retained their bionic charge for over 2,000 years. Why hadn't they reverted to the neutral state? He considered the fate of a slingstone and concluded that when thrown, whether it hit or missed, it would suffer 'dynamic shock'. Could it be that this would lock the bionic charge into the pebble's internal lattice structure, probably for all time? He and his wife threw more pebbles at the garage wall, then verified his thesis by dowsing. After months of testing, the pebbles retained their bionic charge; 'dynamic shock' was the answer.

Dr J Havelock Fidler repeated Lethbridge's experiments and confirmed his findings. Fidler, an agricultural scientist, had an impressive academic background and he had read Zoology and Botany at Cambridge University. His methodical dowsing experiments showed that if a pebble was subjected to heat, it would retain the bionic charge; therefore, thermal shock was another charge retaining mechanism. But could the charge be successfully measured? Fidler found that if he held a pebble then gave it a light hammer blow, the diameter of rotation of the pendulum bob was small. After a heavy hammer blow, the swing diameter was much wider. He inferred from this that the degree of charging was directly proportionate to the degree of hammering. Ingeniously, he then built what he called a 'gyrometer' to measure the charges; this consisted of a light source shining onto a horizontal scale in graduated units of measure. When a charged pebble was placed in front of the light source and dowsed with a pendulum, this created a shadow of the pendulum's cord on the scale, which was measured in units he called *petrons*. Fidler could now properly measure the degree of bionic charging. Taking his ideas further, he found that a pebble's petron charge related to its size and mass; the larger the pebble or stone the greater the petron charge—this greater charge he called *lithon* power.

Our own experiments agree with Fidler in that a female-charged large stone placed in the vicinity of a male-charged smaller stone will induce an automatic aerial energy interaction between the stones. The female stone, having greater lithon power, could in a short time reduce the male stone's charge to zero, and then build up the female charge. In an energy interchange, the stone with the greater lithon power normally dominates other charged stones from a distance. Fidler established the wavelength amplitude of the energy by measuring the distance between peaks. If the energy travelled at the speed of light, as in the electromagnetic spectrum, then its frequency could be established quite simply by dividing the speed of light by the wavelength. Having determined all of this, Fidler discovered that charged stones released an aerial form of linear energy, rather like a ley line, which suggested to him that some leys were formed in this manner. As an agronomist, Fidler gained valuable insight into ley energy and its detrimental effects on living organisms. In a later chapter, we will discover how this energy can inhibit plant growth.

Lithon Power

In the sculpting process, the Stonehenge masons must have struck a stone thousands of times with stone mauls, each blow creating a dynamic shock which would have locked their own bionic field into the stone's crystal lattice for all time. Due to the scale of the stone and its beating, the resulting petron charge would have been high. Worked from rough-hewn stone into carefully crafted lozenge-shaped cross-sections, Stonehenge's huge trilithons were struck thousands of times by entire teams of masons. Because of the mass of these stones, their lithon power, especially that of the Greater Trilithon, the tallest in the circle, would have been enormous and energetically dominate the stone circle. To determine the gender of the individual masons, I dowsed all of the stones for petron charging and was surprised at the results. The

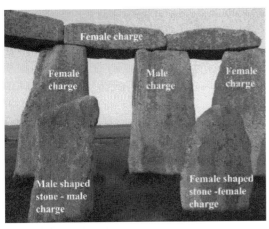

Fig. 106 The polarity of the entrance stones.

bluestones exhibited both male and female charges, but the greatest discovery was that the tall sarsen stones of the lintelled entrance to the stone circle alternate in equal male and female petron charges. So, when entering the monument, one is walking though male and female energy—an energy signature of balance (see *Fig. 106*). The Altar Stone, one of the most sacred stones at Stonehenge, has a female charge which demonstrates that skilled female masons worked this sacred stone. Most archaeological models portray men using large mauls to pound the stones; however, dowsing has revealed there was gender equality in their craftmanship.

Visual and Aural Programming

The encoding of the stones extends far beyond petron polarity charging. During their sculpting this may have been accompanied by visual and/or aural programming; a sound or an image projected onto the stone's lattice structure. Dr Robins states that a hammer and chisel can cause pressure on the defect lattice's magnetic properties to 'record' an image or a sound, and that a latent image may have been a peripheral phenomenon whereby the stone released something more akin to a ghost seen faintly from the corner of an eye. One reason why the stones at Stonehenge were sculpted may have been to provide a flattened surface on which to record an image or sound that could later be released. On occasions, along with others, I have glimpsed a faint image appearing close to the circle's centre, which may have been discharged from a standing stone's crystal lattice encodement.

Malta's Neolithic limestone temples are 'pitted', as shown in *Fig. 107*. This is usually interpreted as a decorative feature, but viewed in the context outlined they became the vital medium into which male and female charges were recorded, potentially alongside visual and audible phenomena.

Fig. 107 Pitted stonework, Malta.

The Hexham Heads

A strange encounter of an image associated with a sculpted piece of stone was witnessed by a well-respected archaeologist, Dr Anne Ross. In 1971, she was given two carved Celtic stone heads, coined the 'Hexham Heads' because they were found in the garden of a house in Hexham, Northumberland. At that time, Ross worked for the University of Southampton and was an acknowledged authority on Celtic artefacts, so her opinion was eagerly sought. On receipt of the heads, Ross placed them in her personal collection of artefacts, pending examination. Soon, strange happenings started to disrupt her life. Author Paul Screeton has investigated the Hexham Heads, and his book *The Quest for the Hexham Heads* (2012) is recommended for those who might wish to delve further into the mystery. In brief, the story goes that one night shortly after their arrival, Dr Ross woke up at 2 am feeling chilled and extremely frightened. Suddenly, she saw a shadowy outline of a tall, jet-black wolf-headed creature standing against the faint light of an open doorway in her bedroom. The creature moved into the corridor and, although scared, she felt compelled to follow it. She saw the tall figure clearly make its way down the stairs and head for the kitchen. Feeling overwhelmed by fear, she ran back upstairs to wake her husband and together they searched the house but found nothing. At this stage, the werewolf-like creature was not linked to the heads and was interpreted as a chance encounter. Later, Ross's daughter Berenice, on returning home from school to an empty house, also saw the creature and, although scared, like her mother she felt compelled to follow it. She watched as it vaulted over the stair banister and landed with a soft thud like an animal with padded feet, then simply vanished. More unnerving incidents occurred, and the 6 ft 6 in (2 m) tall, wolf-headed creature was reportedly seen by several members of the family. In researching the background history, Dr Ross discovered that when the two heads were unearthed from the garden, another strange creature had also been witnessed.

Vaguely skull-like in appearance, the first head was a greenish-grey colour that glistened with quartz crystals. Gaunt and bony, it had carved lines and an old, pitted surface with a masculine appearance.

It was crowned by a typically Celtic hairstyle, showing faint stripes. Both heads were about the size of a tangerine, the second one carved to give the more formidable and eerie appearance of an old woman with a strong beaked nose. The hair was severely combed back from its forehead into a bun. Unlike the male, this head revealed traces of red or yellow pigment. After both were found and taken into the Hexham house, the heads were linked to a series of poltergeist activity. They would move from one location to another, and at night neighbours witnessed a misty glow that marked their former resting place. An animal-headed creature, described as resembling a strange sheep-like man, similar to that witnessed by Dr Ross, was seen in the house next door. From then on, the black supernatural creature was firmly associated with the heads.

A twist in the tale caused a media sensation when lorry driver Desmond Craigie, former occupant of the house where the heads had been found, claimed to have made them for his daughter. One would imagine the sinister-looking toys were guaranteed to induce nightmares, rather than playtime pleasure. Further analysis found the dense quartz clustered stone was not, however, as described by Craigie. Eventually, the heads ended up in the possession of Dr Robins, who, in the presence of the old hag's head, felt a disturbing and overwhelming sense of menacing evil. Robins let astrologer and dowser Frank Hyde experiment with them. His dowsing pendulum apparently indicated the male head to be neutral and the hag's to be highly energised. When Robins left the heads with Hyde, the tale took another disturbing turn. After some time, he decided to contact Hyde to discuss his findings, but Hyde wasn't picking up the telephone or answering correspondence. Fate had intervened and shortly after receiving the heads, Hyde was said to have been involved in a car accident. Robins could trace neither him nor the heads; both had vanished. Unable to contact Don Robins to discuss megalithic memory-coding techniques, which I think my work has advanced, and the Hexham heads, I got in touch with Screeton. He told me that whilst writing his book, he too had tried to contact Robins and learnt that he had married a Russian woman and moved to Malibu, California—his exact whereabouts unknown.

The Hexham Heads is, nonetheless, a true story of how strange life-like images can be released from stone. Perhaps, as the Celtic heads were being carved, an image was projected onto the stone and, centuries later, a bizarre creature was sporadically released in the form of an entity, frightening all who encountered it.

Ultrasound and Standing Stones

Stone can also emit ultrasound. Prior to his disappearance, Robins, as part of the Dragon Project at the Rollright Ring, made several recordings of ultrasound at a frequency beyond most people's ability to sense. On one occasion at the King Stone, at dawn, the

Fig. 108 The King Stone, Rollright.

ultrasonic meter began pulsing, peaking for some seconds, before returning to inactivity, when it began pulsing in a steady rhythm which continued for some time. Why the King Stone generated this pattern was a mystery to Robins. He decided to monitor the stone for ultra-sonic pulsing for a year, and a pattern emerged. He found that pulsing was triggered by the dawn, under any weather conditions, and its intensity and duration varied over the year, peaking at the Equi-noxes. Throughout the monitoring of this ultrasonic pulse, the stone circle had remained ultrasonically silent, but the following year it awoke, and began to pulse rhythmically in a similar manner to the King Stone. What was going on? During one monitoring session, Robins recorded the ultrasonic pattern outside of the circle, but when he moved inside the circle the meter registered nothing. Had it malfunctioned? Robins thought this had ended the monitoring session, but as he made his way outside the circle, he noticed the rhythmic pulsing pattern had returned. So, he re-entered the circle and the meter registered the same ultrasonic silence. After several readings within and outside of the circle it seemed that inside was a zone of ultrasonic silence, and the noise returned outside. The stones were pulsing their ultrasonic sound waves outwards. Over a prolonged period of monitoring for anomalies, the Dragon Project researchers noted other curious recurring phenomena, such as sounds from the stones and the ground around them, subtle light effects, and other strange happenings such as the malfunctioning of quartz wrist-watches and alarm clocks used in the experiments. There was also the bizarre behaviour of animals at the site, including their sporadic refusal to go near certain megaliths.

Fig. 109 Maria dowsing the Rollright stones: sometimes they feel 'alive'. *Photograph:* Busty Taylor.

Like animals, some people are sensitive to the lower spectrum of ultrasound. Our hearing generally ranges between 20 to 20,000 Hz, although some people are sensitive to sound as high as 28,000 Hz. While for many people, witnessing a sunrise event is predominantly a visual experience, the same event in the past might have been quite a different experience. For example, could it be that the long skulled ancient Britons, with their ears set further back and a different brain size, could hear ultrasound issuing from the stones that you and I cannot? Hearing is the predominant sense in many indigenous cultures, whereas today in our modern visual world, seeing is the main sense that dominates our lives. We should not presume that at any ancient site our own experience of a sunrise event is identical to that of our ancestors—it may have been sensorially worlds apart.

Stone circles clearly held great importance in the Neolithic and Bronze Ages, so it is difficult to accept that their builders were unaware of any effect they created. At Stonehenge, they *only* selected stones that could be aurally programmed, and I suspect this was no coincidence. Within a stone's lattice are phonons that move through in streams, like a wave. It has been shown that drifting electrons in a piezoelectric material will lead to the formation of an acoustic-electric amplifier—many types of crystal and quartz crystal exhibit this natural phenomenon. This quality made sarsen stone a good choice for the giant trilithons and the outer lintelled stone circle; sarsen is a quartzite type of stone that has piezoelectric properties enabling sound waves to be effectively fed into its hungry lattice system, which could then conjure multiple effects with focused petron programming. At the centre of Stonehenge, to further increase sound or ultrasonic output, the masons selected an acoustic amplifying stone that served as an oracle. Magnetostrictive materials—that is, material capable of changing shape during the process of magnetisation—are found in lattice structures in semi-precious garnets, utilised as sound sources in a wide variety of applications from ultrasonic cleaners to microphones and loudspeakers. The latter is the commonest application that works on this principle; other applications developed with semi-precious garnet crystals are particularly effective at emitting ultrasound when subjected to a magnetic or electronic impulse. Flecked with mica and garnet, the pale green Altar Stone was undoubtedly selected for these qualities to ensure successful acoustic programming of its lattice.

Remarkably, as recently as three hundred years ago, it was believed that the Altar Stone could release faint audible sound, like megalithic murmurings. To Robins, one way of releasing an embedded sound or image within stone is to use the same mechanism that encoded it—sound. However, instead of hammering the stone as in the sculpting process, prayer or mantra could be used to release this data. The use of arcane language with syntactic and semantic parameters, coupled with prayer and ritual, or the repetition of words and chants as used in spells and incantations, is well known in magical practices. Focused intent alongside words may have been used to release programmed sound or a faint visual image that issued from the stones. I favour the former. Certainly, during their investigations, participants of the Dragon Project heard sounds coming from the stones as well as the ground around them.

Goddess Oracle

In 1747, John Wood the Elder's text, *Choir Gaure, Vulgarly Called Stonehenge, on Salisbury Plain, Described, Restored, and Explained,* recorded the monument as an oracular temple. An 18th-century architect, Wood designed the Royal Circus and Crescent in Bath, Somerset, connecting the layout in the form of a key to Queen Square. He also designed many other prestigious Georgian buildings including the city's Royal Mineral Water Hospital. Wood used his superior surveying skills to compile the most accurate survey of Stonehenge, which outshone William Stukeley's surveys of that era. Wood meticulously measured each stone's diameter, length and position within the monument, and made several important observations. He openly criticised Stukeley's mathematical errors and noted the principal and most accurate alignment at Stonehenge was lunar; therefore, the main deity in whose honour it was constructed was female, a goddess. Stukeley was annoyed by Wood's opinions as he saw the temple as solar, where white-clad male Druids (like himself) performed rituals at the Summer Solstice—a fanciful notion that has stuck ever since. Wood, however, later wrote extensively about Neo-Druidism. Burl agreed with Wood that certain standing stones within the henge are lunar/feminine, and he pointed out that the axe symbol found carved onto some of the sarsen stones is associated with the 'Protectresses of the Dead', adding that the Altar Stone is an image of "a woman protectress".

Since the Early Neolithic, when menhir statues of the protectress were raised in France, weapons have been associated with her. Aubrey Burl also notes other feminine stones such as the Stripple Stones of Cornwall and Ty-ar-Boudiquet in Brittany. Repeatedly, menhirs and standing stones were carved into female form, including at Kermene and Laniscar in Brittainy, where pillars were finely shaped with domed heads, tiny breasts and shrunken arms.

At Razet, 40 miles (64 km) from Reims, female images and axes were carved onto the chalk walls of subterranean chambers. At Stonehenge, the Altar Stone and its partner, now lost, were both green coloured, and since ancient times the colour green has been linked to growth, fertility, abundance, the heart chakra and is associated with the goddess Venus. Today, despite strong feminine symbolism, Stonehenge is wrongly perceived to be a masculine solar temple. However, in its holistic totality, it was a temple dedicated to the Moon *and* the Sun—to a lunar goddess as an oracle and to a masculine solar god of healing. Alignments to both the Sun and the Moon are incorporated into the layout of the monument which verify this. Encoded into stone, divination and healing were once key principles of Stonehenge. Wood seemed to underpin this idea 'In a letter to the Right Honourable Edward, Late Earl of Oxford, and Earl Mortimer', which forms the extended title of his book, when he says:

> "Some of those Images delivered Oracles, and thereby shewed Signs of Life; others in the Human and other Shapes moved with the slightest touch; and some cast their Eyes about as tho' they observed the Actions of all that approached them. Nor was the goddess singular in taking up her Habitation in a plain Block of Stone, since, among many other Instances, Pausanias tells us that Hercules as well as Cupid did the same; and that in one particular Place there were no less than thirty Square Stones which had the Names of so many Divinities."

Voice of the Goddess

Standing at the centre of Stonehenge, we have seen that the two Altar Stones represented an oracle stone and a healing stone. The oracular Altar Stone, with its garnet acoustic properties, may have been revered as the goddess immortalised in stone. Released by ritual, its 'voice'—sound either programmed or ultrasound—may have been invoked and interpreted by the long headed priestesses. Remnants of Stonehenge's oracular power survived for thousands of years and it was this that was eventually spoken of by Wood. Another oracle stone that is said to emit sound is Lia Fáil, the Stone

Fig. 110 The Stone of Destiny and the Mound of Hostages.

of Destiny, sited on the Inauguration Mound on the Hill of Tara, in Ireland. According to legend, all the kings of Ireland were crowned at this stone, and when the rightful High King put his feet upon it, the stone was said to 'roar' in joy.

Author Kathleen Herbert, in her fascinating book, *Peace-Weavers and Shield-Maidens: Women in Early English Society* (1997), writes that Roman historian, Cornelius Tacitus recorded in *Germania* (AD 98) that England was once a goddess worshipping country; this changed as Christianity became the dominant religion. The noteworthy fact about those he called the *Anglii* was that they were members of an alliance of goddess worshippers. Wood likened Stonehenge's oracle goddess to Diana, identified with the Greek Artemis of Ephesus in Turkey, whose vast temple was one of the 'Seven Wonders of the Ancient World'. The British equivalent could be the lunar goddess Cerridwen or Brigit, goddess of prophecy, divination, healing and occult knowledge, widely worshipped in times past. Brigit is associated with Artemis, the twin of Apollo, the god of prophecy, healing, music and light, and may be intimately woven into Stonehenge's long-lost history in more ways than one. Apollo's Temple at Delphi is famous for its Oracle and the priest-esses at Pythia, among the most powerful women in the Classical world. According to Diodorus, the mother of Artemis and Apollo was Leto, a beautiful British Titan goddess. Herbert says that Hyperborea relates to Britain and that Stonehenge was Apollo's temple; she also claims the twins were born in Hyperborea (not Kos):

"…for that reason, Apollo is honoured among them above all other gods; and the inhabitants [of Britain] are looked upon as priests of Apollo, after a manner, since daily they praise this god continuously in song and honour him exceedingly. And there is also on the island both a magnif-icent sacred precinct of Apollo and a notable temple which is adorned with many votive offerings and is spherical in shape. Furthermore, a city is there which is sacred to this god, and the majority of its inhabitants are players on the cithara; and these continually play on this instrument in the temple and sing hymns of praise to the god, glorifying his deeds."

Apollo's Celtic equivalent is the Sun god Lugh, who I suspect only later became identified with Apollo. Lugh was one of the most important Celtic gods, particularly in Ireland, and represented the solar light. Although originally seen as an all-wise, all-seeing deity, Lugh was later thought of as a great warrior and Irish cultural hero. According to legend, Apollo left Delphi in winter and chose to reside with the Hyperboreans at Stonehenge, where he *manifested* at two key times of the year. This, I suggest, was the result of stone pro-gramming which released a ghostly peripheral image, previously worshipped as Lugh. Apollo's manifestation at Stonehenge was recorded in the *Cog Almanacs* of England. Popular amongst rural communities, these almanacs provided an accurate perpetual calen-dar before the advent of printing and literacy. Surviving examples from the 17th and 18th centuries are of a square billet of wood with notches along four sides, corresponding to the (special) days of the year and displayed pictorial signs. For example, the Summer Solstice was represented by a big Sun symbol. Cog (or Clogg) Almanacs were still in use 1,300 years after the introduction of Christianity, yet depicted 71% Pagan feast days, the calendar being firmly rooted in pre-Christian times. It is recorded that on the Spring Equinox the god 'Apollo came to Stonehenge'. Perhaps, at dawn on that day when Apollo 'appeared', people would gather for healing. The other key healing day at Stonehenge was in the dead of winter.

Professor Tim Darvill and the late Geoffrey Wainwright (1937-2017) both suggest that "Stonehenge was a source and centre for healing, and not a place for the dead." Layamon, reporting in the *Brut* chronicle in the 12th century, said of Stonehenge:

> Magic powers they have
> Men that are sick
> Fare to that stone;
> and they wash that stone
> and bathe away their evil.

According to Darvill in the 21st century:

> "[the monument's] healing powers was at its most potent
> during the Winter Solstice, [they] believed that the henge
> was 'occupied' by Apollo, a prehistoric god of healing."

I associate Apollo/Lugh with the lost Altar Stone, an all-healing sacred stone and abode of the Sun god of healing. The Greek philosopher and historian Strabo, who lived in Roman times, pointed out that Iacchus, the daimon attendant and leader of the procession to the 'Mysteries of Eleusis', likewise appeared. Other gods were believed to manifest also. The Greeks believed in the real presence of a god who, if "external conditions were favourable, could manifest himself amongst them." This belief was also reflected in the hymn that Callimachus dedicated to Apollo, and to Dionysus in the play *Bacchantes* by Euripides. Once again, according to these accounts, Apollo could manifest in Greece and at Stonehenge.

Wood repeats the idea that a goddess could manifest by the Altar Stone:

> "...on all occasions to such as were to consult her in her
> Temple; and, from appearing as a Senseless Dead Stone
> above, seated herself so below as to convince her Votaries
> that she was really an Animal Body! Here then, My Lord,
> was the chief Miracle of the Work; and therefore to the Arch
> Priest, or perhaps to a Priestess of this Temple, Lucina,
> Diana, or Hecate."

Other historical accounts include Pliny, who assures us that the goddess Artemis appeared at Ephesus. In the fourteenth chapter of his thirty-sixth book, Pliny says that Ctesiphon (also the name of an ancient city), who was the architect of the Temple of Artemis:

> "…having been unable, by all his attempts, to place a heavy stone over the aperture that made the entrance of the temple drove him to despair, and he contemplated suicide. In response, the goddess set the stone in place herself, and that very night she appeared to Ctesiphon to tell him of it, and bid him live."

Lady Day

In pre-Christian times, close to the Spring Equinox, which was one of Lugh/Apollo's healing days, there was a special day called Lady Day. Throughout the British Isles, and until the 18th century, this day represented the start of the new year. In fact, to the City of London, and every financial institution in this country, it still does; the financial year runs not from 1st January, but from 5th April. Allowing for the eleven days lost in the calendar reforms of 1752 to align with Europe, this takes us to 25th March, Old Lady Day. Perhaps, on this day, the goddess was thought to audibly manifest at Stonehenge—her 'voice', transmitted through ultrasound or a shadowy image, was released from her stone. At the centre of Stone-henge, yin and yang energy personified by the two Altar Stones was once worshipped. Oracles were interpreted at this sacred site dedicated to the Sun god. Certainly, in medieval times, Stonehenge was still considered an important healing temple.

Living Stones

Two thousand years or so ago, standing stones were seen as being far more than just lumps of rock—stone was considered as having life-like and life-enhancing qualities. It is common in Western culture to view stones as being lifeless, inert lumps of rock, yet within there is perpetual activity. Their crystal lattice construction is geometrically arranged in a continuous, three-dimensional cubic form, in which every atom has what is called its 'official address'. A stone's lattice structure contains countless billions of atoms, but it is not static, there is movement and fluctuation within every stone. At a temperature of 21 degrees centigrade, for example, every single atom vibrates about its official address in the lattice at a rate of 10 to the power of 15 times per second, which is equivalent to a million billion times per second, at a speed beyond human comprehension. When the temperature is reduced, this vibration reduces in direct proportion. Only at an absolute low of 273°C do atoms become motionless. A stone's lattice consequently vibrates faster in summer than in winter, so it is attuned to seasonal variations. It could be argued, then, that on one level a megalith is experiencing the changing seasons and weather patterns. Through the continuous bombardment of cosmic rays, a stone's atoms are annihilated, and, in the process, high frequency gamma rays and free electrons are released, making a stone the equivalent of a vertical aerial, transmitting gamma rays into space. The freed electrons roam the corridors of the crystal lattice structure, where they may be captured by atoms deficient in electrons; some of these roaming electrons reach the stone's surface: these are known as exo-electrons. The cumulative effect of exo-electrons reaching the stone's surface produces a negative electrical charge. This is the reason why, when one touches a stone, you may, sometimes, experience a tingle in the hand, as the electric charge discharges through the body; but more importantly, the megalithic energy *enters* your own body.

Itzhak Bentov, in his fascinating book, *Stalking the Wild Pendulum: On the Mechanics of Consciousness* (1988), comments on several different levels of 'reality' that extend from minerals and plants to viruses and bacteria. These various realities can be expressed in graph form by plotting a 'quality' of consciousness against its 'quantity', or the number of responses a nervous system is capable of reacting to. A standing stone is said to have a 'mineral reality', which is the lowest level, beneath that of a virus and bacteria. This means that a stone may be vaguely aware of the presence of other stones, or of birds, animals and people in its immediate vicinity. In Bentov's thesis, a stone may be able to experience the emotions of such living things and to also record them, which implies that stones can be encoded by emotion. To give a simple example, a mouse being pursued by a bird of prey finds refuge in a stone with a recess in its base; the emotion of relief the mouse experiences could be encoded in the stone. Similarly, a stone may have a recess near its crest, which may attract birds to build a nest. The stone would then be exposed to the life-force and the emotions of the parent birds and their offspring; should such nesting occur many times, the emotion encoded would be intensified. So, it is theoretically possible for a megalith to experience changing temperatures, warmth and cold, as well as retaining some form of feeling or energy. Having interacted with particular standing stones at Avebury and Stonehenge ever since I was a young girl, I am aware that they know who I am.

According to folklore, some stones show human tendencies. For example, the Dancing Stones of Stackpole, Pembrokeshire, in Wales, three standing stones about a mile apart: one at Sampson Cross, the Devil's Quoit or Harold Stone, and another at Stackpole Warren, sometimes get together and go down to Saxon's Ford to dance until dawn. Other dancing stones include the Water Stone at Wrington, near Clevedon, which only dances at Full Moon on Midsummer's Day, and the Nine Stones of Belstone Common, in Devon, which dance daily at noon. On Midsummer's Eve, the stones of St Lythan's chambered cairn, South Glamorgan, whirl around three times and curtsey. Whilst other stones such as the Giant's Stone at Yetnasteen on Rousay, Orkney, walk each New Year's morning to the Loch of Scockness for a drink, and in County Wicklow, Ireland, the Motty Stone on Cronebane Hill, south of Rathdrum, is said to travel to wash at the Upper Meeting of the Waters once a year, on May Day morning.

The Roman historian Livy, born around 59-64 BC, records that a statue of Apollo once wept for three days and nights. To our ancient ancestors, stones and stone statues were alive and, as mentioned, contained the essence of the god or goddess they represented; their relationship was intimately profound. Many miracles have also been associated with the Virgin Mary. As teenagers, my brother and I once saw a painting of Mother Mary shed tears. Wherever the veil is thin, mysterious happenings can occur.

Moving Statues

The summer of 1985 saw a curious spate of 'moving statue' phenomena in Ireland. Across several different parts of the country, statues of the Virgin Mary reportedly moved spontaneously. For instance, in July, in Ballinspittle, County Cork, an observer claimed to have seen a roadside statue of the Virgin Mary suddenly move. Other occurrences soon followed at around thirty other locations. Not all of these apparitions were Marian, however, and some involved other divine figures appearing as stains on church walls. Thousands gathered at many of these sites, sometimes out of curiosity, or to gaze in wonder and pray. Up to 100,000 pilgrims were said to have visited the site at Ballinspittle in that first year alone, yet the Catholic Church remained highly sceptical and a bishop declared the phenomenon to be an illusion.

Bleeding images have also been reported, such as of the Holy Mother at a church in Mirebeau, France, which began bleeding from the traditional sites of stigmata, mimicking the wounds of Christ's Crucifixion. Blood tests conducted by London's Lister Institute indicated the blood to be of a rare human type—an elaborate hoax, one wonders? However, a more intriguing case occurred in 1975 when a 28 in (71.12 cm) plaster statue of Christ began to bleed. Now housed in the Episcopalian Church, Eddystone, Pennsylvania, according to the *National Enquirer* (January 20, 1976), the blood is human and of considerable age. Apparently, one investigator removed the solid plaster hands and found they continued to bleed profusely. Then, from the Jewish Kabbalah is the golem, a clay statue that comes to life when fed with paper bearing Kabbalistic formulae.

An interesting report of a strange encounter with a stone statue in the City of London, that momentarily came to life, was recalled in the book *Phenomena* (1977) by John Michell and Bob Rickard. Rickard describes numerous stories of moving statues and shares a news report that recounts a nervous breakdown suffered by a young guardsman on sentry duty at Windsor Castle, after seeing a nearby statue move. Following up on the story, Rickard contacted the army but was met with a stony response; he was refused permission to interview the guardsman as the incident had been dismissed and was considered officially closed.

To the medieval alchemists, phenomena from 'talking heads' to standing stones that move and statues that come to life, weep or bleed, are all examples that bring us tantalisingly close to the mysterious properties of some inanimate objects. Could it follow that prehistoric masons had the ability to programme and activate megaliths, knowing they held some kind of mysterious life force? I think they did and across time are guiding us to do so again, for the purpose of promoting peace and harmony within our public and private spaces and buildings.

Chapter 8

Musical Intervals

Mathematical Harmonics calculated by Richard Cardew
and interpreted by Maria Wheatley.

In traditional creation myths it is often said that the Creator first laid down a pattern of number as a fusion of music, mathematics, religion, geomancy, astronomy and poetry. Ernest McClain, whose mathematical harmonic system we follow, noted that in ancient Mesopotamia the gods were assigned numbers, encoding primary ratios of music—the gods' functions correspond to their numbers in his acoustic theory. Accordingly, the Sumerians created an extensive tonal and arithmetical model for the cosmos. The musical ratios that represented the gods were thus considered holy. As examples: Anil corresponded to the number 1/1 (60/60) written as (1); Enlil, 'god on the mountain', to 50 (5/6); and Ea/Enki to 40 (2/3).

Two thirds (2/3) represent the divine prime number 3 and musically is the perfect fifth. Importantly, 2/3 is the most powerful shaping force in music after the octave. Gilgamesh, the Sumerian hero, was '2/3rds god'. Simply put, musical harmonics are a mathematical expression of a fraction that equates to a musical interval. A musical interval is created when one note is played with another, by playing both together or one note after the other. An interval has a stronger effect on the listener, and its frequencies affect the body in different ways; it can engender profound healing. The perfect fifth 3/2 ratio was used by the medieval mystic Hildegard of Bingen in her musical compositions to express joy, openness and healing. In classical Chinese music the perfect fifth was considered to balance Heaven and Earth, yin and yang, and all classical Chinese music was based on this interval. Ancient natural science was also based on number and measure, as it is today. According to McClain, musical ratios are any ratio that uses only the numbers 1, 2, 3, 4 and 5, and must be combined only by multiplication. Musically, 1/1 is the still point, 2/1 the octave, 3/2 the perfect fifth, 4/3 the perfect fourth, 5/4 the major third, and 6/5 the minor sixth.

Pythagoras wrote of the *tetractys*, a sacred symbol drawn as a pyramid containing four dots at the base, then three, two and at the summit, just one dot. These four numbers form the divine proportions of 1/1, 2/1, 3/2 and 4/3, and their harmonics are found at ancient sites worldwide. Thousands of years before Pythagoras, a Greek mystic discovered the relevance of mathematical intervals and harmonics, which the long headed architects integrated into every earthen and stone setting at Stonehenge. The megalith builders used mathematical ratios in the construction of their stone circles and temples to create a relationship between sacred number, earth energies and heavenly bodies. We suggest that the megalithic architects used certain musical intervals to represent the Upper World of the Sun—time present, future, and heaven—and the Lower World of the Moon—the past, the Underworld, and the ancestors.

Music of the Spheres
Sacred for thousands of years, harmonic ratios are still found today in the overtone singing of the Tuva nomads, also in Gregorian chant. In 1619, Johannes Kepler explained in his *Harmonices Mundi*, written in Latin, that universal music or the 'Music of the Spheres' are musical intervals, and described the harmonies that relate to the motion of the six known planets of his time. Kepler believed that planetary intervals produce inaudible sound which can be heard only by the soul, and gave a "very agreeable feeling of bliss, afforded him by this music in the initiation of God." It is said that Pythagoras could hear these same planetary harmonies: the music of the spheres.

Modern mathematician Richard Cardew calculated the harmonic ratios of Stonehenge, the Sphinx Temple, Ireland's Newgrange, and at other sacred sites. In their mathematical silence, we suggest, like Kepler, the harmonics of a site can influence stone, consciousness and the human soul. We will demonstrate that an arithmetic-based tonal complexity underpinned Stonehenge's design, and that this encouraged a transcendental spiritual experience. Harmonics were integral to *all* of Stonehenge's concentric circular features, creating a spectacular sound-healing temple. It is possible, therefore, that a tonal system of instrumentation and/or vowel sound toning or overtone singing was performed using the same harmonic intervals that were associated with Stonehenge's various stone settings.

Music and Healing

Fabien Maman, a celebrated composer, healer and teacher, linked music with acupuncture. In 1977 he created the famous system of healing that used tuning forks rather than acupuncture needles. His seminal work demonstrates the healing effects of particular frequencies on the human body; in one experiment he found that playing musical intervals to cancer cells destroyed the cancerous cells. Each musical interval has its own unique balancing effect on the organs and at cellular level—each organ, bone and cell having its own frequency. If one organ is dissonant, this affects the whole body and balance can be restored using harmonic frequencies. As Itzhak Bentov points out, an illness is "out-of-tune behaviour of one or the other organs in the body." He explains that when a cell is stressed or diseased, its frequency changes and it begins vibrating discordantly. Thus, when a strong harmonising rhythm is applied, the malfunctioning cell might start beating in tune again. Just by playing the piano you can affect the energy of the universe—sound is energy. If you hit middle C key on a piano, its strings will vibrate at a pitch of around 256 Hz or cycles per second. Sound is vibration, and musical notes are vibration organised into a geometric grid of energy using twelve different qualities, or energy values. So, when you play middle C, every little bit of cosmic energy that vibrates to 256 cycles per second, or fractions of the soundwave generating that frequency, will vibrate in sympathy. For example, middle C will resonate to 256 x 2 = 512, 256 x 3 = 768, or lower divided by 2 = 128, and so on. All mathematical ratios resonate to the same frequency, making sympathetic connections across time and space. Thus, harmonics create a geometry of proportion and balance that can be sensed by the mind, body and soul.

Prehistoric knowledge and usage of musical ratios is evident; only the most harmonious intervals were incorporated into the diameters of major concentric stone circles and temples worldwide. These are: 2/1 the octave, 4/3 the perfect fourth, 3/2 the perfect fifth, 5/4 the major third, 5/3 the major sixth, and 8/5 the minor sixth. Dominant and single harmonics were also integrated into Egypt's pyramids. To give examples in the following ratios: the Bent pyramid 3/2, Red pyramid 3/2, Great pyramid 10/9, Khafre 4/3, Menkaure 9/8. Remarkably, all of these single pyramid ratios, as well as the Pythagorean ratios, are found in one place—at Stonehenge. More about these ratios will be discussed later.

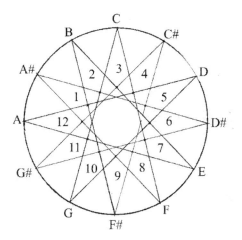

Fig. 111 The 12-pointed star with musical correspondences.

The 12-Pointed Star

From the first phase of what would become Stonehenge, harmonic ratios were integrated into the geometry of the site by creating a 12-pointed star, as shown in *Fig. 111*. This form of sacred geometry would go on to dictate the positions of the sarsen stone circle, the concentric bluestone circle (Q and R Holes) and the Z and Y Holes, shown in *Fig. 112*. In his seminal work, *A New View of Atlantis* (1969), John Michell demonstrates that the sacred geometry of Stonehenge, as well as Glastonbury's first wattle and daub church which he refers to as the 'New Jerusalem', contained a 12-pointed star and other related geometries. Michell was inspired by the sketches showing measurements of the layout of St Joseph's settlement in Glastonbury by Frederick Bligh Bond, who received them from the spirit of a medieval monk through automatic writing.

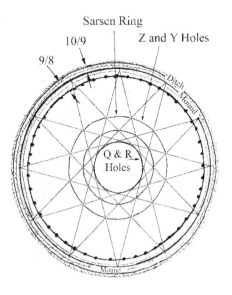

Fig. 112 The 12-pointed star and Stonehenge's harmonics.

The mathematical system and geometry used by Richard Cardew and myself in our analysis of Stonehenge, while based around a 12-pointed star otherwise differs greatly from Michell's. In our system, the star manifests by movement around a circle that contains twelve musical notes, which are universal qualities. The circle is empty until a starting point is found—say at 'F'—and we count seven notes clockwise, then draw a line from where we began at 'F' to end at 'C'. This process of clockwise counting in seven spaces is repeated until the 12-pointed star appears. Counting in sevens creates a mathematical ratio line of 3/2. This is because when any two notes are seven keys apart, such as F-F#-G-G#-A-A#, the harmonic ratio is 3/2, the perfect fifth, making an order of F, C, G, D, A, E, B. This represents the clockwise annual path of the Sun, the Upperworld, time present and time future.

However, there is a quicker way to make the 12-pointed star, which takes one on the darker, left-hand path of widdershins. This is the path of the Moon and entry into the Underworld of ancestral time past. So, in an empty circle containing the twelve notes, one finds a starting point at one of the notes and moves around the circle five paces anti-clockwise, then draw a line; repeat this process until the 12-pointed star is created. Each line drawn creates a mathematical ratio of the 4/3 harmonic, the perfect fourth. At Stonehenge, the Q and R Holes fit exactly into the centre of the 12-pointed star, which undoubtedly determined their position (see *Fig. 112*).

Harmonics of Stonehenge

Spanning 1,500 years, from the Late Neolithic to the Middle Bronze Age, harmonics were continually integrated into Stonehenge to create a sophisticated harmonic temple. Every circular setting made at least one harmonic with another, and each setting was designed to equate to a musical interval. During Phase 1, the ditch and chalk bank integrated the mathematical harmonic of 10/9, which is a minor tone. Additionally, the harmonic of 9/8, the major second, was created by the bank and bluestone circle (Aubrey Holes). Later, during Phase 2, the 9/8 harmonic was repeated with the placement of the Q and R Holes that held the bluestones. During Phase 4, the Q and R bluestone setting was redesigned into a bluestone circle and its diameter with the sarsen lintel stone circle created the 5/4 harmonic, the major third. In the Middle Bronze Age, the final phase of construction of Stonehenge, known as Phase 5, the digging of two rings of rectangular pits outside of the stone circle, the Z and Y Holes, were arranged in a double circle.

Parker Pearson points out that as well as antler picks, some of the holes contained other antlers that were antique, perhaps centuries old, when they were put into the holes. These holes were left open and gradually filled with fine silt blown in from outside. Atkinson suggested the Z and Y Holes may have been arranged as a spiral and were dug to hold some of the bluestones, but they were never used, and no-one has come up with a better idea to date. Unquestionably, the Z and Y Holes produce the most harmonics at Stonehenge: six in total, and this may have been the main reason why they were dug. For instance, the diameters of the Z and Y Holes produce the 4/3 harmonic, the perfect fourth; the Aubrey Holes to the Y Holes 8/5, a minor sixth; the Z Holes to the lintelled stone circle 5/4, the major third; the Q Holes to the R Holes 9/8, which can occur as a major second in two different frequencies; the Z Holes to Q Holes 3/2, the perfect fifth; and finally, the Y Holes to the Q Holes, which is the octave of 2/1. Stonehenge without doubt contains musical perfection and mathematical harmony.

Fig. 113 The major third created by the lintelled stone ring and the bluestone circle.

Experiencing Harmonics

Harmonics create the geometry of sacred proportion and were also incorporated into rituals and ceremonies. The mathematical ratios that were selected for Stonehenge's circular settings all correspond to a healing musical harmonic, which cannot be coincidental. We have already seen that Stonehenge was regarded as Lugh's/Apollo's healing temple and the harmonics would have intensified the power of the therapeutic dynamics, which were undoubtedly activated by a combination of sound toning and meditation. When Stonehenge is entered from either the southern entrance or the northeast cause-way, two harmonics are experienced. This is because the diameters of the ditch and the mound produce the harmonic 10/9, e.g., D/E, which is a minor tone. The next harmonic that would be encountered is the Pythagorean whole tone 9/8 or major second, e.g., C/D, created by the diameter of the white chalk bank and the large ring of 56 bluestones.

In the distant past, whilst standing in the interval gap created by the bank and the stone ring, men and women may have toned using the corresponding harmonic interval, synchronising perfectly with the encoded voice harmonic so that sound and temple became one. Alternatively, perhaps the ancestors were simply standing between the settings in meditative silence, sensing and attuning to the har-monic; as Kepler said, "inaudible sound that touches the soul." Sound energy researcher Kay Gardner says the interval of 9/8 "produces a feeling of lightness and has a mild dissonance." Inter-estingly, many sensitive people who I've taken into Stonehenge still sense 'dissonance energy' when they enter the monument. The major third 5/4 is also formed between the ditch and the bluestone ring, as 10/9 and 9/8 combine to make 5/4, which, as it occurs three times, is Stonehenge's primary harmonic. The most powerful of these is created by the diameters of the lintelled stone ring and the bluestone circle, as shown in *Fig. 114*. According to Fabien Maman:

> "…this interval touches the emotions and was used by Bach
> to touch the higher emotions, which can produce feelings
> of lightness, strength and joy."

In the same way, to raise the frequency of a church building as well as the congregation, the major third is used in religious music to evoke a higher emotional state of consciousness. At Stonehenge, its overall harmonic series suggests that one should leave behind any inharmonious energy *within* the 9/8 ratio, which encourages its release, clearing the way to fully experience the other harmonics, such as the spiritual energy and joy from the 5/4 harmonic of the lintelled stone ring and inner bluestone circle.

Experiments conducted by acoustic engineer Professor Trevor Cox of Salford University, appear to confirm that Stonehenge *was* a sound temple. Cox created a 3-D printed scale model, and he discovered that in pristine condition the stones could have amplified up to four decibels and created reverberation, which enhances the properties of music. Lower frequencies, says Cox, as spoken or sung at Stonehenge, would have sounded more base-like, "a bit like singing in the bathroom." Thus, lower tones would struggle 'to get through the gaps' in the large trilithons, whilst the higher ones would 'scatter'. Millennia ago, the long headed civilisation created the first major sound healing centre in prehistoric Britain, and it utilised an extensive harmonic tonal system synchronised with the site's circular settings, as described here. Today, the main harmonic that may be encountered for mediation, sound toning and healing purposes, is created by the sarsen stone circle to the bluestones, as well as the sarsen stone circle and the Z Hole positions.

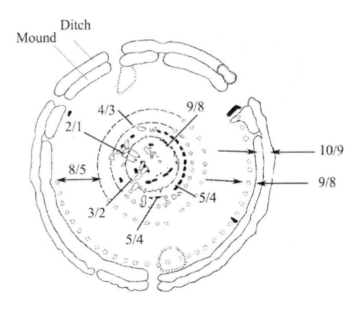

Fig. 114 The main harmonics of Stonehenge.

Ditch/mound: 10/9 is a minor tone.

Bank/bluestone circle: 9/8 major second (e.g., C/D). Fabien Maman says this interval brings tension between two polarities, creating movement that is used in modern classical music. To Kay Gardner this interval creates a feeling of lightness, openness and has a mild dissonance. The Q Holes/R Holes also resonate to 9/8.

Bluestone circle/sarsen circle, the ditch to the Aubrey Holes and the sarsen circle/Z Holes: 5/4 the major third (e.g., C/E). Richard Cardew considered that the traditional symbolism of the number 3 led to a harmony of divine perfection. Mary Elizabeth Wakefield and Michael Angelo state that this interval can possess sweetness, tranquillity, stillness and repose.

Bluestone circle/Y Holes: 8/5 minor sixth (e.g., C/A flat). Research by Gardner suggests this interval creates a feeling of poignancy.

Y Holes/Z Holes: 4/3 perfect fourth (e.g., C/F). The Sumerian gods and their functions were assigned a number corresponding to musical ratios; perhaps the Celts and ancient Britons had corresponding musical associations too. If so, the 4/3 harmonic resonates with the Moon, the goddess, the Underworld of the ancestors and time past. Kay Gardner says 4/3 also creates a feeling of serenity, lightness, and openness, and is used in Pagan songs such as *The Earth is Our Mother*. Fabien Maman feels the fourth interval gives a strong impression, rather like "awakening after a dream."

Z Holes/Q Holes: 3/2 perfect fifth (e.g., C/G). This is always seen as a desirable harmonic that expands energy in all directions and gives ease of flow. The perfect fifth relates to the Sun god, the Upperworld of time present, and time future.

Y Holes/Q Holes: 2/1 an octave (e.g., C/C an octave above), brings balance and the harmonious union of yin and yang. According to Wakefield and Angelo, "It is perhaps best exemplified by the sound of men's and women's voices singing together in unison."

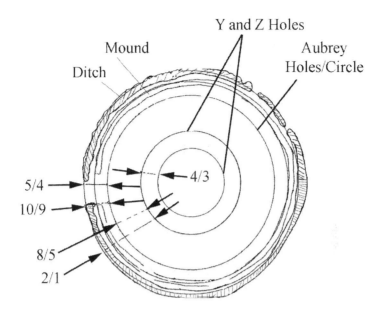

Fig. 115 Circular Harmonics at Stonehenge.

Throughout the ancient world, from India to Greece, music was regarded as having curative properties. The Greek philosophers Democritus (460-370 BC), remembered today for his atomic theory of the universe, and Theophrastus (371-287 BC), stated that some diseases of the body and mind can be cured or caused by music. A famous mass healing of the local community of the island of Lesbos occurred when Therpander and Arian played music, and Ismenia of Thebes was well known for curing sea divers of diseases with her uplifting music. Writing in 1651, the occultist Henry Cornelius Agrippa wrote:

> "...birds were allured with pipes and harts were caught the same. Fish in the lake of Alexandria are delighted with a noise and music has caused friendship between men and dolphins. The sound of the harp leads up and down the Hyperborean swans and melodious voices tame Indian elephants."

If sound toning using specific musical intervals was performed at Stonehenge, perhaps the entire temple was regarded as a sound healing sanctuary. Integrative oncologist Dr Mitchell Gaynor says:

> "If we accept that sound is vibration and we know that vibration touches every part of our physical being, then we understand that sound is heard not only through our ears but through every cell in our bodies."

Music teacher Jeff Rolka shows how easy it is to sing the solid E-vowel using the interval of the perfect fourth, so that it sounds both atmospheric and pleasing. The interval of the major third is the distance between two notes and, likewise, this interval can easily be sung using vowel sounds or overtone chanting, also produced using instrumentation. According to occult writer Murray Hope, the chakras are also associated with musical notes: the Base chakra C, Sacral D, Solar Plexus E, Heart F#, Throat G, Third Eye A, and Crown B. Harmonic ratios, as well as promoting healing, may have assisted the oracle aspect of Stonehenge, encouraging only the purest of prophecy to manifest. To the ancients, the sanctity that brought with it harmonics, healing, prophecy and wonder are the key characteristics of Stonehenge. Even in total silence, its divine mathematical proportions can influence the mind and soul. Sound healing is no longer dismissed to the status of an alternative healing practice, and it is now considered as a mainstream therapeutic treatment. Integrated into hospital treatment, music therapy is known to alleviate physical pain and enhance mental wellbeing. According to cognitive neuropsychologist and music therapist Thirumalachari Mythily, music therapy is today implemented in the areas of paediatrics to treat hyperactive children, and in geriatric care to help retrieve the memory of older people with neurological problems.

Origins of Britain's Perpetual Choirs
The Perpetual Choirs are first mentioned in the 1796 edition of a translation of *Fabliaux Tales,* which includes an English translation of the Welsh *Triads*. Three sites are given as the Perpetual Choirs of Britain: The Isle of Avalon (Glastonbury), Caer Caradoc (Salisbury),

and Bangor Iscoed (although disputed). In 1807, Iolo Morganwg (Edward Williams 1747-1826) compiled the *Triads of Britain,* translated from the Welsh by William Probert. Number 84 refers to the three choirs of Llan Illtyd Fawr (Llantwit Major, Glamorganshire), Ambrosius in Ambresbury (Amesbury, near Stonehenge), and Avalon (Glastonbury). Morganwg was an influential Welsh antiquarian and poet, a collector of medieval literature who compiled writings on Welsh history. He says:

> "...in each of these three choirs there were 2,400 saints; that is, there were a hundred for every hour of the day and the night in rotation, perpetuating the praise and service of God without rest or intermission."

However, after his death it emerged that Iolo Morganwg had forged several manuscripts, notably the parts of the *Triads* where the Perpetual Choirs are mentioned. John Michell (1933-2009), believing the manuscripts to be true, wrote his book *The Dimensions of Paradise* (1972), and identified an enormous ten-sided form of landscape geometry, nearly sixty-three miles across, in which numerous prehistoric and historical sites link up ten key points which centre around Whiteleaved Oak, on the borders of three counties: Herefordshire, Gloucestershire and Worcestershire. He refers to the same three locations, adding others that include Goring-on-Thames and Croft Hill, Leicestershire, a traditional site of ritual and popular assembly. Michell's 'Decagon of Perpetual Choirs' anchors on Stonehenge and its Summer Solstice Sunrise and Midwinter Sunset to "maintain the enchantment and peace of Britain." Diodorus, a much earlier source, states that Stonehenge was a city of choirs and that close to Stonehenge, or possibly at the monument itself, there is:

> "...a city that is there which is sacred to this god Apollo and the majority of its inhabitants are players on the cithara (an ancient Greek stringed instrument similar to the lyre), [which they] continually play in the temple and sing hymns of praise to the god, glorifying his deeds."

I suggest that the long headed people of Stonehenge were the first 'Circle of Perpetual Choirs' to sing praises to the god of the Sun 3/2 and the goddess of the Moon 4/3, aided by the musical harmonics skilfully incorporated into the monument.

Woodhenge: A Harmonic Dream Temple

Another site integral to the Stonehenge ceremonial complex is Woodhenge, which originally consisted of six concentric circles of timber posts. Varying in size and width, the towering posts may have been joined together by lintels, mirroring Stonehenge. We now know that it was not a roofed structure as there is no evidence of run-off water deposits. Sited not far from Stonehenge, next to the Durrington Walls super henge, Woodhenge was excavated and restored by Maud Cunnington (1869-1951) between 1926-29. Today, concrete markers show the former positions of timber posts, which may have been painted in white, red, gold and blue colours derived from chalk, ochre and woad, echoing those of the later Egyptian temples. We established the harmonic ratios of Woodhenge using Alexander Thom's data from his book *Megalithic Sites in Britain* (1967). Thom discovered the use of integral values of the Megalithic Yard (MY) which we can see often contain simple ratios. He determined the perimeter values of Woodhenge as 40, 60, 80, 100, 140 and 160. The ratios are 60/40 = 3/2, 80/40 = 2/1, 80/60 = 4/3, 100/80 = 5/4 ... and so on, shown in the table below.

Mathematical Harmonics of Woodhenge

Ring	Perimeter MY	Ratio	Ratio Value	Closest Ratio	Fraction
a	161.0	a/b	1.16	1.115	9/8 Major second
b	138.2	b/c	1.33	1.33	4/3 Perfect Fourth
c	104.2	c/d	1.31	1.33	4/3 Perfect Fourth
d	79.9	d/e	1.29		4/3 Perfect Fourth
e	61.3	e/f	1.55	1.6	8/5 Minor Sixth
f	39.4	d/f	2.03	2.00	2/1 Octave

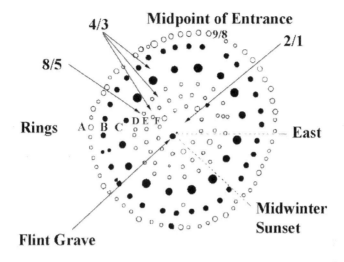

Fig. 116 Harmonics at Woodhenge.

Quite possibly, Woodhenge's ceremonies were led by women, as the dominant harmonic is the perfect fourth 4/3 (e.g., C/F), which corresponds to the Moon, the goddess and magic. Just as at Stonehenge, the entrance corresponds to the major second 9/8. This interval encourages one to let go of dissonant energy and to 'purify' before entering the sanctity of the inner circle, where the B, C and D rings are associated with the perfect fourth. Perhaps women stood within the 4/3 timber post recesses to interact with the encoded musical interval, either silently or with their own voices, to become one with the site's lunar energy. According to music teacher, Jeff Rolka:

> "...the perfect fourth as commonly used today in popular music is best suited to the [higher] female vocal range of alto."

Interestingly, Woodhenge repeats the 4/3 harmonic, whilst Stonehenge avoids it. We suggest the reason for this is because, as Trevor Cox pointed out, at Stonehenge the higher tones are diffused by the giant megaliths and "become more scattered". Perhaps, on a deeper level, this relates to Maman's remark about the perfect fourth's interval giving an impression like "awakening after a dream". In the past, it was thought that dreaming was based on the harmonic ratios of 2/1, 3/2 and 4/3. As previously mentioned, 4/3 occurs three times at Woodhenge and 2/1 is found at the centre, which begs the question: was Woodhenge utilised as a dream temple and, if so, does this explain why it is situated close to Durrington Walls ceremonial site and town, symbolically standing *outside* of corporeal time. Kay Gardner's statement is worth repeating at this point, that in sound healing the perfect fourth "brings serenity, lightness, and openness", and others have noted how it "touches the heart". Later, we will see that walking Woodhenge as a labyrinth creates a 2.5 coiled spiral which also resonates with the 4/3 harmonic.

Chapter 9

Pentatonic Temples and Stones

Mathematical ratios were integrated into sacred sites and temples to encourage spiritual growth and healing. During our investigations we have discovered that harmonics can generate numerical 'gateways' or 'portals', and Egypt has one of the most extraordinary harmonic portal temples in the ancient world. Music is magical as it can change into a higher energetic force. If you play a note on a piano, say F, and then look at which other piano strings seem to be vibrating in harmony, the strongest vibration will be the next F string up an octave: the vibration is double the original F. This doubling relationship is akin to cell reproduction, represented mathematically by the harmonic of 2/1 which is considered to be a 'female' energy. The next strongest vibration is the C above the second F. The transition from F to C is the 3/2 harmonic, and this is a 'male' harmonic because C is a 'new' note and relates to the path of the Sun. All of the twelve notes when they lie within one perfect doubling are termed an octave, and all harmonics above 2/1 change the note, but 3/2 changes the note with the *least* possible effort.

We demonstrated earlier that the 12-pointed star is developed by movement around a circle using the 3/2 harmonic, which represents all twelve musical notes. For example, when C is played it will create G, as it is male energy, a 3/2 overtone, then if G is played as the base note it will make D as its overtone, and so on: D makes A, A makes E, E makes B, B makes F#, F# makes C#, C# makes G#, G# makes A#, A# makes F. On a piano keyboard there are seven octaves, seven of each note, although F is at both the bottom and at the top, making eight F notes. These notes transport us from F through to C, G, D, A, E, B, F#, C#, G#, D#, A# before returning to F, and, like a dance—like life itself—it moves in rhythmic harmony. This is analogous to immortality as it does not quite return to the identical place (F) from where it began, so mathematically this dance will never end, eventually filling the entire circumference of the circle with perpetual harmony in motion.

Tritones: The Devil's Music

Pythagoras, the original source of our knowledge about harmonics, taught that the twelve notes are connected by a harmonic fraction, such as 2/1, 3/2 and 4/3, except, that is, when two notes are six notes apart. He called this harmonic discord *anathema*, a shut gateway, which today it is referred to as a *tritone*. Tritones are pairs of notes that are directly opposite each other and when repeated, return to the base note. In music theory, the tritone is defined as a musical interval composed of three adjacent whole tones (six semitones). F-B is the only tritone formed from the notes of the C major scale. It is a metaphor for a closed gateway where there is no resonance in the discord of time, often referred to as the 'Devil's Chord'—no dance or movement is possible. Mozart is a good example of how composers deliberately write tritone discords into their music; they are important because a single harmonic ratio such as 6/5, 5/4, 4/3, 9/8, 10/9 will join any given note, e.g., F, with every other note above and below it *except* for B, as it is a tritone. For example, F-F# is 16/15, F-G is 9/8, F-G# is 6/5, F-A is 5/4, F-A# is 4/3, but F-B is 7/5, which is not a harmonic. A musical scale is simply seven notes connected in a flowing sequence by the harmonic 3/2 until it reaches a tritone gateway of 7/5. To elaborate: the scale of C, in harmonic sequence, is F, C, G, D, A, E, and B. It stops abruptly at B, the first tritone B-F or F-B. The tritone F-B of 7/5 is a portal gateway because it stops the flow of the musical sequence and becomes, symbolically, a still point in time and space.

When a tritone occurs, it can influence the mind through dissonance and create slight anxiety, an otherworldly feeling and sensation, which is why musical tritones are used in horror films. The same disharmony is used, and indeed defines, great art. Tritones were associated with Egyptian royalty. For example, the Nemes Crown, a commonly depicted headdress worn by pharaohs, also known as the *khat* which means 'right', a single coloured or striped cloth with side pieces (lappets) that covers the whole crown and nape of the neck: notably, the blue and gold colour combination of Tutankhamen's iconic Nemes Crown, are a tritone apart. A gold or metal headband was often used to hold the material in place and secure ornaments such as the Uraeus or Ouraeus (meaning 'on its tail'), a stylised form of rearing cobra or vulture worn as a symbol of power and divine authority by the sovereign or royalty.

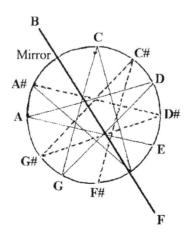

Fig. 117 The two pentatonic scales and the 'tritone mirror gateway' F-B.

The 12-pointed star containing all twelve notes has one portal gateway, which is produced by the tritones of F-B. Removing the tritone leaves the two ancient pentatonic scales of C, G, D, A, E and the remaining notes create F#, C#, G#, D#, A# (see *Fig.117)*. The gateway creates a mirror of each scale. A flute, believed to be 50,000 years old, was tuned to the pentatonic scale containing the five notes of C, G, D, A, E because when the tritone is absent the tension disappears, producing a pleasing sound. It has been suggested that these five notes may have been the first scale to be sung by proto-humans. Furthermore, early Gregorian chants contained pentatonic melodies, scales which are also found in traditional Native American, African and South Asian music. In ancient times, the notes F and B were often removed from the scale, leaving only five notes that can be played in any order and never produce an inharmonious tritone.

Pentatonic Scales

Pentatonic scales create peace and harmony and can ease emotional tension. Drawing the pentagram created by the geometry of the pentatonic scale can be inspiring; it is the magician's pentacle of power. To do this, draw a circle containing all twelve notes and starting at the gateway tritone note of F to enter the circle, count seven moves clockwise and draw a line to C; seven more moves connect the notes D, E, G, A, which is the pentatonic scale of C major; then exit the circle by the gateway of tritone B, the still portal in time and space. This creates a pentagram with the musical angles of 120 and 105 degrees, as shown in *Fig. 118*. Musically significant, 105 connects a tone to a major third; that is, a two-semitone interval to a three-semitone interval; 120 connects a two-semitone interval to another two-semitone interval. At first glance, the pentatonic long-legged pentagram looks out of proportion. Some academics automatically assumed it was just a badly drawn pentacle, but identical pentacles can be found illustrating 15th-century books on magick. To the magician, the pentatonic scale is an important magical tool possessing power for the evocation of a spirit or deity. Alternatively, imagine setting your intent and walking around a stone circle in this way. Each line walked flows with ease of the perfect fifth, making magical intent manifest effortlessly.

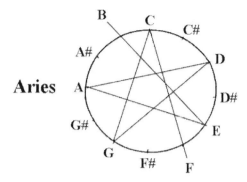

Fig. 118 The magician's pentatonic pentacle.

Pentatonic Standing Stones

At Avebury, the world's largest stone circle, several standing stones were selected for their pentatonic angle, some of which may have been enhanced by gentle sculpting. Even though the stones have been subject to weather erosion, the angles are nonetheless evident. The majority of standing stones (excluding those of West Kennet and Beckhampton Avenues) were studied for their overall shape and appearance. Our data shows that six stones were rather shapeless and rounded, nineteen had an angle of 105 degrees, eleven of 120 degrees (some had a combination), and where straight edges were still sharp the angles were within one or two degrees. At nearby West Kennet Long Barrow, two of the eight stones across the front are at 105 degrees—both at the left-hand end—and six display angles of 120 degrees, one having two 120-degree angles. Inside the chamber, six stones have obvious straight edges and obtuse angles, five are 105 degrees and one 120 is degrees. Finally, a single oblique stone at the entrance has an angle of 105 degrees. The actual notes that are close to these angles are 9/8 (which is a bit more), and 10/9 (a bit less). However, the interval that combines is 6/5, the minor third. As previously mentioned, 105 degrees connects a tone to a major third, that is a two-semitone interval to a three-semitone interval; and 120 connects a two-semitone interval to another two-semitone interval. Was this intentional? Pentatonic stones that display these ratios will resonate with that frequency, making sympathetic connections across the Avebury stone circle. In dowsing

Fig. 119 Pentatonic stone at the Ring of Brodgar, Orkney.

terms, it appears that people in the distant past have walked such lines leaving behind a *remanence* line. Many dowsers confuse these with energy lines. The majority of stones at the Ring of Brodgar on the Orkney mainland also show the pentatonic degree of 105 (see *Fig. 119*), as do some of the Callanish stones on the Isle of Lewis.

An interesting point about the use of the two pentatonic scales (F), C, G, D, A, E, (B) and (B), F#, C#, G#, D#, A#, (F) is that in terms of the zodiac of notes every single note of the pentatonic scale C, G, D, A and E is opposite its tritone note in F#, C#, G#, D#, A# i.e., C-F#, G-C#, D-G#, A-D#, E-A#. With no tritone, and therefore no discord, the gentle and soothing flow of energy can assist healing. When integrated into a circular or rectangular construct, the two scales of C and F# were probably used to enhance the evocation of the gods of the Upperworld or Underworld and to raise human consciousness. To the ancient Egyptians, as it was to many other cultures worldwide, F# was said to resonate with Mother Earth and was held sacred. The Native Americans of Oregon would play wooden flutes in F# to honour the Earth, and a similar flute found to be made from swan bone has been excavated in the Stonehenge environs, along with musical 'rattlers'.

The Pentatonic Sphinx Temple

To amplify High Magick, the ancient Egyptian architects integrated the pentatonic scales of C and F# into the Sphinx Temple, which is situated close to the front paws of the Sphinx on the Giza Plateau (*Fig. 120*). The pentatonic scale was so important in ancient Egypt that it is claimed by experts at Cairo Museum to be shown in hand gestures on the walls of the *mastabas*—an ancient Egyptian tomb consisting of an underground burial chamber with rooms above that are at ground level to store offerings.

In total, the two pentatonic scales create fourteen notes; this may relate to the fourteen reflections of the heavens in the Osiris myth, where Set cut Osiris' body into fourteen pieces and hurled them all over Egypt. One of the dynamics of a pentatonic scale is that it clearly shows the position of the F-B tritone which abruptly halts the flow of energy, creating a shut gateway. This can either be opened by the adept or used to meditate upon. It can also be sensed as it produces, through dissonance, slight anxiety, otherworldly feelings and sensations. Certainly, in some Western magical practices, the

pentatonic pentacle is used to invoke a mental or physical processional route within a temple or magic circle. The pentatonic scale of C is similar to a 'banishing pentacle' that can release unwanted energy. In addition, F# resonates with and heightens earth energies in the vicinity. In this instance, within the Sphinx Temple the upward pointing pentacle represents the realm of Ra, the Sun god, and the downward pointing pentacle the Underworld of Osiris— this has no association with black magic; it is, however, associated with the dead and the

Fig. 120 View of the Sphinx from the Sphinx Temple. *Photograph:* Michelle Hood.

ancestors of time past. A mirror axis flows down the centre of a pentatonic temple, which can be likened to a ley line: a powerful, energetic line of force. It seems highly plausible that Pentatonic Magick reached its height in Egypt over 5,000 years ago.

Invisible yet ever present, the pentatonic scales of F# and C combine to produce the 'Cat's Cradle', as shown in *Fig. 121*. Its meaning is unclear, but many sources note its popularity as a child's game for two players with a string tied in a circle that uses the fingers and hands to form different shapes and patterns. Other sources speculate

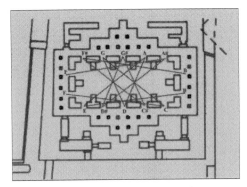

Fig. 121 The pentatonic scale of F#.

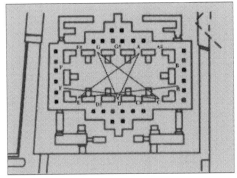

Fig. 122 The pentatonic scale of C mirrors the scale of F#.

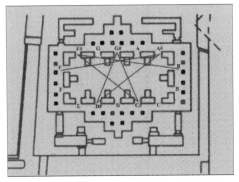

Fig. 123 The Sphinx Temple with both scales as 'the Cat's Cradle'.

that perhaps it is a reference to an old myth that cats steal the breath of babies in the cradle, which kills them. We suggest the cat's cradle is an ancient mystical symbol created by the two harmonic pentatonic scales and was integrated into the Sphinx Temple to be used for ritual evocation and manifestation. The Sphinx Temple shares harmonic acoustic similarities with Stonehenge, as the 5/4 harmonic occurs three times at both sites. Other harmonic ratios integrated into the Sphinx Temple include the perfect fifth (yang = Sun energy), and the perfect fourth (yin = Moon energy), determined by X/Y = 3/2, A/B = 18/17, B/C = 5/4, C/D = 5/4, D/E = 4/3 and D/F = 5/4, illustrated in *Fig. 124.*

Pentatonic Power

After decades of researching sacred sites, I sense, as I feel you do, there is more going on than the simplistic mantra: "It's all about death and the ancestors." Experiencing the energies of a site, connecting to the 'Spirit of Place', feeling a strong presence beyond one's rational understanding, touching the stones (as did those before us), all unite us to the past. As intangible as that may sound to an archaeologist, this is *our* realm now, where aspects of the past can be intuited as well as researched, and there were no limitations to the achievements and insights of our ancestors.

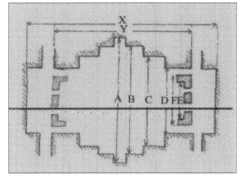

Fig. 124 Major harmonics of the Sphinx Temple.

I would like us to explore and expand upon previous interpretations of sites such as Stonehenge—together we can investigate the past anew, a prospect I find exciting. Mathematics proves to us that Stonehenge is an acoustic temple which may have been associated with a seasonal musical scale. Envisage the chalk henge circle as representing the ecliptic belt, which was first conceived of by English astronomer Sir Fred Hoyle (1915-2001). Imagine the circle contains the twelve zodiacal signs and twelve notes of a musical scale: F, C, G, D, A, E, B, F#, C#, G#, D#, A#. Millennia ago, at each of the four Quarter Days there could well have been a corresponding pentatonic scale in praise of the annual movement of the Sun. Each pentatonic scale corresponds to a musical sequence, and here we offer some examples which are illustrated in *Fig. 125*, showing the four Quarter Days are not arbitrarily placed but are the result of a mathematical ratio.

The Spring Equinox could correspond to C/G and A/E of the major C pentatonic scale C, D, E, G, A.

The Summer Solstice to A/E and C#/F# of the A pentatonic scale A, E, B, F#, C#.

The Autumn Equinox to A#/D# and C#/F# of the F# pentatonic scale F#, C#, G#, D#, A#.

The Winter Solstice would be A#/D# and C/G of the D pentatonic scale D#/A# and F/C/G.

Using the Aubrey Holes, the 5/3 ratio—which is a Fibonacci ratio—produces the four festival dates, and this ratio generates a square.

Furthermore, the mathematical link between the Aubrey Holes and the sarsen stone circle is also 5/3—this is a musical way of squaring the sarsen circle.

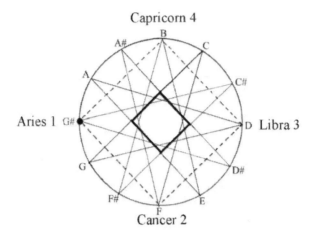

Fig. 125 The Solar festival dates generate 5/3 squaring the circle.

Pyramid Ratios

Musical intervals were also encoded into the pyramids of Egypt. Researchers and authors such as Rodney Hale, Andrew Collins and Christopher Dunn have studied the infrasound, ultrasound and Hertz frequencies within the Great Pyramid. Dunn recorded 439 Hz and 440 Hz, the latter being the most common, yet he says, "the coffer inside the pyramid is said to resonate with 438 Hz." Many theories rise out of the Giza Plateau to explain why the pyramids were built, and our research explores the measurements that generate the harmonics of sacred proportion within the pyramids and in the Kings Chamber. They incorporate the musical harmonics of 4/3 = perfect fourth/Moon, and 3/2 = perfect fifth/Sun. These are the two most important harmonics allowing the ease and flow of *any* energy, including earth, ley and grid, that is ever present. This is because harmonics above 2/1 change the musical note, though, as previously stated, the 3/2 harmonic changes them with the least possible effort. That any form of energy generated within a structure incorporating the 3/2 harmonic will flow and be distributed with ease and no resistance is a universal law. Ley lines and earth currents that flow through a 3/2 structure are not impeded and carrier lines unobstructed.

Measurement data used to calculate the harmonics, taken from the surveys of Mark Lehner via the website of Professor Ralph Greenberg, explains that to calculate a pyramid's ratio, its height is divided by the angle that a diagonal line makes with its base. The design differences possible for a square-based pyramid are limited; the edge slopes must all be equal, as must the face slopes, which are connected by the ratio $\sqrt{2}/1$. This is exactly six semitones. Richard Cardew and I demonstrate that the entire design of any square-based pyramid is encapsulated in a single harmonic ratio and musical scale.

Evidence for harmonic design equating to musical intervals is verified in the fact that the slopes of the five Egyptian pyramids: the Bent Pyramid, Red Pyramid, the Great Pyramid (Khufu), Khafre and Menkaure, all express a harmonic within a very small tolerance. The Great Pyramid produces a Pythagorean minor tone of 10/9 within one in ten thousand, meaning that the height was originally within a few centimetres of the exact ratio. The stepped-pyramid of Chichen Itza in Mexico, famous for the 7-coiled serpent shadow effect that appears at the Spring and Autumn Equinox, also has a Pythagorean 10/9 harmonic created by the outside steps and temple top. A common external harmonic at major sites is 10/9—when one walks into Stonehenge or mounts the steps of Chichen Itza, one is interacting with 10/9 harmonic energy. Khafre, the second largest pyramid on the Giza plateau, is believed to be the tomb of the fourth dynasty pharaoh Khafre, although many independent researchers disagree with the 'tomb' interpretation. Khafre's harmonic ratio gives a 4/3 harmonic interval of the perfect fourth. Earlier pyramids, such as the Bent Pyramid, has the harmonics of 1/1 and 3/2, the perfect fifth; the Red Pyramid 3/2; and Menkaure 9/8 the major second. These harmonics resonate with the soul and in their silence speak to those that sense their presence.

Fig. 126 The height of a pyramid divided by its base diagonal line determines its harmonic ratio.

The King's Chamber Harmonics

The King's Chamber in the Great Pyramid of Giza was constructed with mathematical precision. As at Stonehenge, its overall harmonic proportions are $4/2 = 2/1$ ($\sqrt{5}/\sqrt{5} = 2/1$), 5/4 the major third, 4/3 the perfect fourth, 3/2 the perfect fifth, the ratio of 5/3 which is nine semitones; further mathematical analysis shows that $5/2 \sqrt{5} = 10/9$. The ancient Egyptians knew the acoustic power of vowels. They believed that vowel sounds generate healing vibrations which could be achieved by toning. Toning manipulates the vowel sounds using the breath and the voice to make therapeutic sounds. Within a resonating structure, the healing influence of vowels could be amplified by toning or singing in unison with the musical interval associated with the monument. For example, men in the King's Chamber could have used the masculine interval of 3/2 between each vowel sound, and women the 4/3 harmonic interval associated with the feminine. Furthermore, studies of ancient Egyptian religious cult texts reveal that in many cases vowels or words were intended to be sung rather than spoken. The following quotation from Demetrius suggests that the sound of vowels continued to be important in the first century of the Christian era:

> "In Egypt, when priests sing hymns to the gods, they sing the seven vowels in due succession and the sound of these vowels has such euphony that men listen to it instead of the flute and the lyre."

According to Dr Lise Manniche, in her book *Music and Musicians in Ancient Egypt* (1991), the fact that singing took place in relation to the pyramids is confirmed in the following short title from Nikaure: 'Instructor of the singers of the Pyramid of King Userkaf'. This ascribed role may indicate that a group of singers were retained specifically to maintain song or chant-based rituals at the pyramid of Userkaf. It has already been established that certain Egyptian pyramids have two separate chambers producing two distinct sound frequencies; these frequencies, in turn, are believed to be amplified within the pyramid walls to create heightened fields of harmonic resonance which restore balance within the human body. Alongside toning, chanting or singing, applying the encoded musical interval would, undoubtedly, have assisted the healing process. As previously stated, a harmonic ratio such as 3/2 is dynamic as it allows energy to flow with uninterrupted ease—this interval relates to the Sun and time future. Vowel sound toning may have also been practiced at Stonehenge and at other monuments known for their reverberation qualities.

Chapter 10

The Music of the Earth

Various scientists and philosophers such as Pythagoras, Ptolemy and Kepler have throughout history assigned to the planets a tone. According to Kepler, each planet produced a musical tone that was proportional to its angular rate of movement around its orbit. In 1607, he came across Ptolemy's *Harmonics* and was pleased to discover he was following in the footsteps of the great Alexandrian astronomer. By 1618, Kepler had discovered the third law of planetary motion, and this extended the tonal range and emotional nuances of the singing planets the 'Music of the Spheres'. It is well known that numerical sequencing can be found in nature; biologists love sunflowers as they demonstrate the underlying mathematical rule shaping the pattern of life—the Fibonacci sequence—in which each number is the sum of the previous two (1, 1, 2, 3, 5, 8, 13, 21, 34, 55, 89, 144, 233, 377, 610…). The number of different clockwise and anticlockwise seed spirals on the face of a sunflower often form a pair of numbers from that sequence: 34 and 55, 55 and 89 or, in the case of very large sunflowers, 89 and 144. Although the mathematics seem perfect, plant biologists have not worked out a mechanistic model that fully explains how these seed patterns arise—not all sunflowers show perfect Fibonacci numbers, as real life is messy. Like a Mozart concerto, the gods have written imperfection into the mix. However, these numerical relationships can be found in a multitude of patterns in nature, from pineapples to pine cones.

If planets and plants reveal numerical sequences, I wondered if earth energies also contained mathematical ratios. I discovered something truly astounding about Gaia, bringing a new and dynamic interpretation of earth energies never before explored. This is that deep underground yin water can generate musical intervals. This occurs because aquifers, or deep powerful springs, emit a surface pattern of three or six concentric circles of earth energy called a *primary halo*, that can be likened to ripples on a pond. Undeniably, the diameters of a halo energy pattern can produce mathematical ratios, which I call the 'Music of Gaia'. Primary haloes produce the strongest tonal nuances as does the central *geospiral*, an energy pattern which is shown below in *Fig.127*.

Fig. 127 Concentric energy circles can produce harmonics.

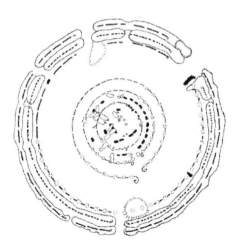

Fig. 128 Underwood's survey of Stonehenge's primary haloes.

Stonehenge Harmonics Revisited

Earlier, I described the harmonics of Stonehenge as decoded by the diameters of its circular features, but perhaps these values are *not* manmade mathematical measurements. In the late 1940s and early 1950s, Master Dowser Guy Underwood surveyed Stonehenge and discovered the primary halo pattern dictated its circular features, as shown in *Fig. 128*. I noted that the primary halo's concentric circles matched the mathematical harmonics that Richard Cardew has calculated. Thus, the spiral and circular earth energy patterns born of Gaia's waters *express* the mathematical values that were integrated into Stonehenge's architecture. Concentric stone circles are rare, there are only around thirty known examples in Britain. This scarcity, I suggest, reflects the infrequency of large geodetic primary haloes which are the invisible blueprints at major sites, most famously at Stonehenge. It must be noted, however, that not all primary halo patterns emit harmonics: I dowsed one about two miles (3.2 km) north of Stonehenge that was not expressing harmonic ratios. Likewise, not all concentric stone circles produce harmonics, such as the Druid's Circle in Cumbria. Here, the diameters of its concentric rings give the mathematical ratio of 3/1 which is not a harmonic.

Kepler wrote that the tonal expression of the planets could "touch the soul", which is how I feel about Gaia's tonal energy. Standing, sitting, or walking on musical earth energy imbues the body: body water, mind and soul with harmonic energy. I have enjoyed working with this expression of Gaia and benefited from its energy, and I want to share with you more of the wondrous world of Gaia's geodetic harmonics.

Woodhenge and Earth Harmonics

For decades Woodhenge has perplexed archaeologists because it was constructed just *outside* of the Durrington Walls henge complex, rather than inside to accompany the two other timber circles. Earth energies are the answer. Woodhenge is free to visit and easily accessible to the public all year round; it is a great place to experience harmonic primary halo energy. Its circular settings are set above six concentric primary haloes, as surveyed by Underwood (see *Fig. 129*). We discovered a magical way of walking Woodhenge that replicates its dominant harmonic of 4/3, and which encourages an extraordinary feeling of oneness with the site. Most people who visit simply walk in a straight line across the monument to its centre. However, only a small fraction of the site is encountered in this way, and I don't believe this was how the ancients interacted with the henge. I propose that Woodhenge was designed to be walked as a labyrinth, and in doing so *every* timber ring of the monument is experienced before reaching its centre.

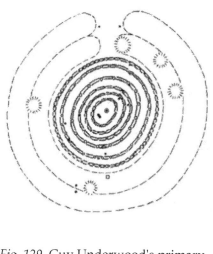

Fig. 129 Guy Underwood's primary halo survey of Woodhenge.

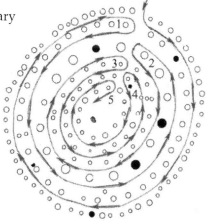

Fig. 130 The Woodhenge labyrinth.

Walking the Woodhenge Labyrinth

Labyrinth walking is an ancient practice used by many faiths for centering, contemplation and prayer. Combining the images of the circle and the spiral (mirroring the invisible primary halo and geospiral pattern), the labyrinth is a symbol for wholeness, representing a journey to our centre and back out again into the world. Encouraging a spiritual inner journey, labyrinths have a long history signifying growth and transformation; unlike a maze, its form has no dead ends and only one path. If you walk the Woodhenge Labyrinth in the manner I suggest, your steps will create a 2.5 coiled spiral, which is highly significant as this is the harmonic associated with the perfect fourth 4/3, Woodhenge's primary ratio. Creating this harmonic whilst walking the labyrinth puts you in resonance with its primary ratio, and thereby deeply connects you and your spiritual centre to Gaia's silent yet ever-present harmonic earth energy. For some, this can gently awaken the soul's divine purpose, whilst others emphasise a relaxing or healing experience.

This spiritual practice of walking the labyrinth can be experienced today by simply opening your senses and taking very slow and deliberate steps. Set your intent, be that in prayer or by asking a spiritual question to contemplate whilst walking to the centre. Enter Woodhenge by the two posts just outside of the site, and then take a left turn. After walking round the monument, return to where you started and take a right turn to Number 1, as indicated on *Fig. 130*. Having walked around these posts take a left turn at Number 2 followed by a right turn at Number 3, and finally a left turn at Number 4. You will arrive at the centre to find yourself close to the flint grave of a young Bronze Age child. Now listen for an answer to your question, or you may experience a deep revelation; after which slowly begin the return journey when you might pray or reflect further, and upon exiting give thanks to the ancestors and the guardian-child of the site. Sometimes, I might sit or lay down at the centre and ask for guidance or listen for an answer to my question, and graciously Woodhenge usually answers. Walking the labyrinth is a wonderful experience!

Fig. 131 Maria meditating by the Bronze Age flint grave after walking the Woodhenge labyrinth. *Photograph:* Busty Taylor.

Perfect Fifth Labyrinths

Some Cretan seven-path labyrinths may date as far back as the Early Bronze Age. Seven is the number of coils that contain all twelve notes of the 12-pointed star and creates a connection to the Sun, the 3/2 perfect fifth. When walked in a particular manner, the seven-path labyrinth becomes a 3.5 coiled processional pathway, a harmonic of the number seven.

Another example of a 3/2 labyrinth can be found in North America. The Hopi created the classical seven-path labyrinth as a symbol of the Earth Mother. This gives identity to the sacred in nature and honours the divine in all things. Walking a labyrinth, paired with intent which may include meditation, the human voice, instrumentation and/or performance, is to experience its geodetic harmonics. This can be alchemical, involving a magical process of creation, spiritual development and transformation.

Fig. 132 Based on the Cretan
labyrinth, a 3/2 harmonic.

Fig. 133 Hopi labyrinth, a 3/2
harmonic.

Harmonic Geospiral Energy

We saw earlier that by placing all twelve notes around a circle and
continually counting seven clockwise, this creates the spiral of fifths,
the 12-pointed star. The twelve notes become the zodiac and they
unfold to make seven octaves, seven coils. As previously demonstrated, taking five steps anti-clockwise around the twelve notes
creates a five-coiled spiral of 4/3, the perfect fourth.

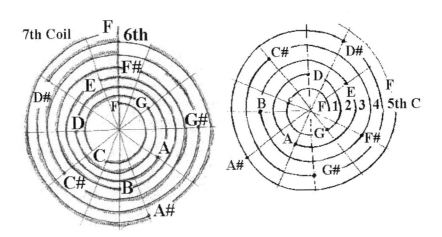

Fig. 134 Musical spirals: the perfect fifth and the perfect fourth.

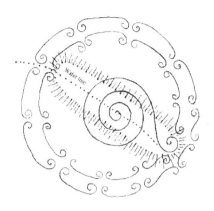

Fig. 135 The Bush Barrow's 3.5 coiled geospiral.

Geospirals can be likened to musical spirals. One form of geospiral occurs in multiples of seven from 3.5 to 49 coils, which resonate to the 3/2 harmonic. For example, in Cornwall, Boscawen-un stone circle has a 14-coiled spiral at its near centre, and the Hurlers' central circle has a 21-coiled spiral. The Cuckoo Stone, near Stonehenge, marks a 49-coiled geospiral and the Bush Barrow, south of Stonehenge on Normanton Down, marks a 3.5 coiled geospiral (as surveyed by Guy Underwood, shown in *Fig. 135*), which resonates to the 3/2 perfect fifth. Birds and animals use the 3/2 harmonic and the octave 2/1—they make overtones of the original base note—this is also used for overtone singing. While not all geospirals are associated with musical intervals, those that are add a quality that can be felt by the soul.

Fig. 136 Newgrange mound, Ireland.

197

Spiral Harmonics at Newgrange, Ireland

Newgrange is a 5,200-year-old passage tomb located in County Meath, Ireland. It is part of a complex of monuments built along a bend of the River Boyne, known collectively as *Brú na Bóinne.* The other two principal monuments are at Knowth, which is the largest, and Dowth. However, throughout the area there are as many as 35 smaller mounds. Dating to 3200 BC, Newgrange is a Neolithic kidney-shaped long mound 279 ft (85 m) in diameter and 43 ft (13 m) high, covering an area of about one acre. A passage measuring 62 ft (19 m) leads into a chamber with three alcoves. Both the passage and the chamber are aligned with the rising Sun at around the time of the Winter Solstice. The mound is surrounded by 97 large stones called kerbstones, some of which are engraved. The most famous and striking is the entrance stone that displays a triple spiral, shown (faintly) in *Fig. 136.* Newgrange is more than a passage grave, it is an acoustic temple, a place of astronomical, spiritual, religious and geomantic importance. The far chamber is located above a 7-coiled geospiral which equates to the perfect fifth, giving New-grange energising and healing properties. Also, a 5-coiled spiral is sited to one side of the mound. These energy-spirals, shown in *Fig. 137,* are carved onto one of the kerbstones, showing the Neolithic geo-mancers were aware of earth energy harmonics.

Fig. 137 The perfect fifth and perfect fourth spiral carvings at Newgrange.

Acoustic Discoveries

Paul Devereux, in his fascinating book *Stone Age Soundtracks* (2001), notes that Newgrange's chamber complex resonates to 110 Hz. During his research he made an astonishing acoustic discovery that would have made the Winter Solstice an unforgettable event. When sound from the chamber is driven into the long passage it creates a standing wave pattern along its entire length. Due to the partial reflection from the stones surrounding the entrance to the passage, the standing wave displayed twelve antinode/node pairs and acted rather like a musical wind instrument, where sound travels through the passage entrance and dissipates in open space beyond. Devereux noted that a rarely mentioned feature of Newgrange—a separate rock slab that fits the aperture of the passage entrance perfectly—could have been put into place and then removed. If this closing stone was fixed in place during important rituals, then any sound made would create a stronger standing wave within the passage. If this is what happened, then deep otherworldly sounds from inside the mound would have emerged with particular power out through the roof-box, which sits above the passageway and main entrance. Devereux suggests this was enacted at the time of the Winter Solstice when sunlight enters through the roof-box. It would have created, he says:

"...an alchemic exchange of light and sound: regenerating solar light for the ritualists and the ancestral spirits within, awesome sounds announcing the cosmic moment for the congregation outside."

Devereux concluded, from most of the chambered tombs he tested, that they fell into the 110-112 Hz band. He surmised that:

"...the chambers were probably used for chanting, singing, or oracular pronouncements at the resonance frequency of the chamber would enhance the volume and reverberation of the voice. Such a maximised vocal effect would be appropriate for creating the commanding sense of the presence of supernatural agencies, whether gods or ancestral spirits, moreover, the male voice in the frequency range concerned can generate a high intensity."

In a previous chapter, I went further by arguing that a programmed standing stone, possibly triggered by sound involving the voice, could aid in manifesting not just a *sense* of the presence of a god, but mysterious sounds, or a ghostly corner of the eye fleeting image. Belief in magic, the gods and the power of place, would generate a mirage or a paranormal experience at the centre of Stonehenge. This would happen at other monuments such as Newgrange too. As Devereux and I have both demonstrated, sound played an important part in the ritual use of monuments. And so did creed.

Fig. 138 Fourknocks passage tomb.

Fourknocks Passage Tomb

Located 10 miles (16 km) southeast of Newgrange is Fourknocks, built around 5,000 years ago and today close to the village of Naul in County Meath, on the Dublin border. Private access can be gained by obtaining a key from local resident, Mr Fintan White, who lives nearby, and leaving a cash deposit. He allows you all the time you wish to awe and wonder at this incredible passage tomb. 'Knock' comes from the Gaelic word *cnoc*, meaning hill. Excavated in 1952, the monument is now covered by a concrete dome to protect the rich artwork inside. As the chamber is too wide for corbelling, it is speculated that the original roof was wooden with a central pole, which was evidenced by a post hole found during excavation. To enter the monument, a short stone passage widens into a large pear-shaped chamber with three smaller chambers that contain breath-taking megalithic artwork. Excavation also uncovered cremated and unburnt fragments pertaining to 65 individuals, both adults and children, along with beads, pendants and decorated pottery, now housed in Ireland's National Museum. Originally, the mound was about 62 ft (19 m) in diameter, surrounded by a dry-stone kerb wall. Contained within are twelve decorated stones, comparable to Gavrinis Passage Grave in France. Author James Swagger points out that one of the most striking features of Fourknocks is that it features a sculpted human-like face, the earliest known example from the Neolithic period in Europe. Situated on the left side of the chamber and standing 3 ft (0.91 m) high, the carving is eerie to look at, as if it has diamond eyes and a pointed chin, not unlike the 21st-century mask of Spiderman. Surprisingly, although Fourknocks appears small, its central space is the largest in Ireland.

Harmonic Artwork and Alignments

Bar one, the stunningly decorated stones at Fourknocks, some of which have zig-zag carvings that encode harmonic sequencing, are comprised mostly of green sandstone. The patterned stone found originally over the passageway interior has now been placed to the

left of the entrance. Another stone with similar patterning, shown here in *Fig. 139*, forms the harmonic sequences of 3/2 and 4/3 which represent male and female balance and union. Geodetic energies that resonate with the 4/3 harmonic flow with ease and are strongly influenced by the Moon.

Swagger discovered that Fourknocks has an alignment 17 degrees east of north, and he noted that other passage graves have this unusual alignment, which

Fig. 139 A decorated lintel stone with zig-zag patterning.

provokes enquiry. Ireland is not the only country with a heritage of astronomically aligned buildings, as many pre-Columbian structures are aligned to this exact azimuth. He ruled out the usual solar and lunar activities and calculated that at the time of construction, around 3000 BC, Fourknocks passageway was pointing at two constellations: Cygnus 'The Swan' and Cassiopeia. Normally, these constellations are circumpolar, but Swagger noted that during this epoch they fell below the horizon. Interestingly, this is the *only* time period when this occurs over an entire 26,000 precessional cycle. In 3000 BC, Deneb, the brightest star of Cygnus, does something spectacular at Fourknocks—it skims the horizon as it revolves around the pole star. The internal layout of this and most other passage graves are cruciform, which happens to be the same shape as the Cygnus constellation. In astronomical terms, the main star Deneb is also a good point of reference for the Sun on the very night before Winter Solstice, and this date happens to be when Cygnus perfectly aligns to Fourknocks.

Harmonic Earth Energy

Geodetic spirals and circles were incorporated into numerous sacred sites worldwide, releasing a tonal earth energy that speaks to the soul and can put us on the path towards our spiritual destiny. The geodetic system of earth energy is truly spectacular because all of its surface patterns relate to a particular harmonic. Earth energy currents such as aquastats and track lines that interlace the planet were integrated into ancient sites. Aquastats emerge and converge on geospirals and, as I discovered many years ago, they are associated with deep underground yin streams or underground yin rivers. These consist of four sets of triads, each of which are separated by a gap, and due to their numerical sequencing some resonate to 4/3, the perfect fourth. Invariably, harmonic aquastats were also incorporated into megalithic and earthen avenues; examples can be found at Stonehenge, Avebury, Stanton Drew, Dartmoor's stone rows, and the Sphinx Avenue at Luxor, Egypt. In one guise, they charge the avenue stones with harmonic energy. *Fig. 140* illustrates that the standing stones of West Kennet Stone Avenue were set on aquastats, which resonate to the 4/3 Moon harmonic. Of particular interest is the powerful geodetic spiral energy associated with avenue Stone 20 (Underwood's unofficial numbering system). Likewise, the avenues at Stonehenge and Stanton Drew were set on, or close to, aquastat flows. This also applies to the portal entrances of some Cumbrian stone circles and to the Rollright Ring in Oxfordshire.

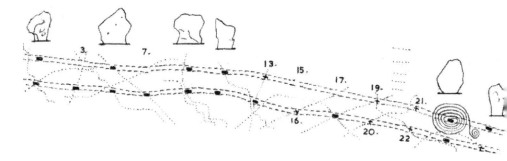

Fig. 140 Underwood's survey of aquastat flows along
West Kennet Stone Avenue.

Track Lines
Track lines are earth energy flows and are not associated with underground water. They consist of two triad lines of energy that interlace the planet and often exist in sympathy with the ratio 3/2, which is the most powerful shaping force in music after the octave. Track lines were incorporated into the ceremonial landscape and these solar geodetic energy flows relate to old tracks and country lanes, hence their name. During the Iron Age (c750 BC-AD 43), the Druids utilised tracks to link hillforts in a vast energy network. Animals naturally follow track lines with little resistance, and so Iron Age 'drove roads' (small lanes for moving livestock) were aligned upon them, making moving cattle across the landscape trouble-free. Track lines can bring an energising boost to the physical body, and this is why migrating animals can follow them for days on end as their energy levels are gently replenished. In the ceremonial landscape, they were often dug out to create hollow ways that sheltered people from the elements. In the Stonehenge environs, one hollow way track line is 7 miles (11 km) long and runs from a hillfort to an earthen enclosure.

The Celtic Triquetra
Harmonics can be also found in Celtic artwork, creating a pleasing form and energy. The name 'triquetra' is from the Latin adjective *triquetras* meaning three-cornered. The triquetra is over 5,000 years old and in Europe has been used since the Bronze Age. In Celtic art this triangular figure, composed of three interlaced arcs or three

overlapping *vesica piscis* lens shapes, is usually found as a design element, or part of a more complex composition in manuscripts and knotwork, but rarely on its own. This has led some historians to believe that it wasn't a primary symbol of belief. However, in the

Fig. 141 Interlaced triquetra.

Christian tradition, primarily since the Celtic revival of the 19th century, the symbol became used as a sign of the Trinity: Father, Son and Holy Spirit. In Paganism, it is hard to identify a precise meaning: Celtic Pagans and Neopagans use the interlaced triquetra (see *Fig. 141*) to symbolise a variety of concepts and mythological figures, usually related to the importance of the number three. In Celtic cosmology this generally refers to the three realms of Earth, Sea and Sky. It is not unusual for symbols to be multivocal in this way. The triquetra also represents the triple goddess: Maiden, Mother and Crone, and in modern Wicca it symbolises life, death and rebirth. The symbol displays the 8/5 ratio, a complement of the 5/4 harmonic, the major third, which is the ratios of 9/8 and 10/9 combined. The 5/4 would make a triangle within a circle, whereas when 8/5 is repeated thrice it makes the more interesting triquetra.

Fig. 142 Silbury Hill exhibits harmonics.

Silbury Hill: Sun and Moon Harmonics

Originally, Silbury Hill was built as a seven-tiered chalk pyramid, which was then smoothed over to form a white chalk mound. It is the largest manmade mound in Europe, and people from all over the world sense its energy and wonder. Silbury is sited on an aquifer that emits a large 7-coiled geospiral, which relates to the musical spiral of 3/2 i.e., C-G. From this emerges numerous underground yin streams that bestow the mound with geodetic energy. In the 1940s, Underwood claimed to have seen and recorded the faint remains of an earthen avenue connecting Silbury Hill to Avebury. He noted that aquastats flowed each side of this lost avenue, beginning in the northeast sector, as shown in *Fig. 143*. Associated with the aquastat lunar 4/3 geodetic harmonic, this was a distinctly feminine avenue. Possibly, during the Bronze Age, it was used solely by women as a guided processional route to and from Avebury. The lost avenue seems plausible—rather than simply wandering into Avebury, formal megalithic avenues were created to guide people across the ceremonial landscape. This would seem an imperfect premise were Silbury excluded.

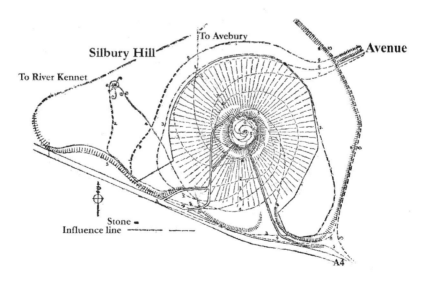

Fig. 143 Underwood's survey of underground streams at Silbury and a lost avenue.

Adding strength to this claim, I noted that LiDAR may have detected the lost avenue. Light detection and ranging, or LiDAR, is a remote sensing technology that uses a laser pulse to collect and/or record variable distances to the Earth. These are used to create 3-D models and maps of various objects and environments. LiDAR is one of archaeology's most exciting modern tools which has changed the face of the landscape by making it possible to measure and map objects and structures that would otherwise remain hidden from view. Note that from the northeast sector skirting around Silbury Hill, a meandering line, shown in *Fig. 144*, matches the location of the lost avenue which appears to be coursing towards Avebury, although the LiDAR map only extends to New Bridge. The avenue may have taken a right-hand

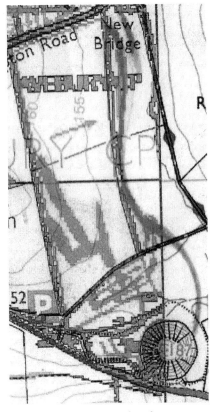

Fig. 144 LiDAR results show an anomalous meandering line: the lost avenue?

turn on its approach to Avebury's southeast entrance. Additionally, Hamish Miller's and Paul Broadhurst's Mary earth current flows through the mound, as does the 'Planetary Ley System' that designates the Earth as Silbury Hill (see my book *Divining Ancient Sites*, 2014, available from my website).

From the very beginning of its construction, Silbury Hill incorporated mathematical ratios: Silbury 1 was the primary mound having a ratio of 4/3, the perfect fourth, associated with the Moon and the ancestors of time past. The final phase was the completion of the summit, with a potential ratio of 3/2, the perfect fifth, that corresponds to the Sun, time present and time future. This is illustrated in *Fig. 145* below. Using harmonic allegory, time past is *within* Silbury and future time is on the summit *outside* of Silbury. Placed centrally within the mound, music can be seen as symbolically filling the mound with the feminine lunar energy of the perfect fourth i.e., C-F. We are sure that other large mounds, such as the nearby Merlin's Mount in Marlborough, and Grave Creek Mound, West Virginia, USA, were also constructed to incorporate similar ratios.

The following figures relate how the construction of Silbury Hill corresponds to harmonic ratios:

Diameter of mound (Silbury 3 and 4)	192 MY 192/48 = 4/1
Height of mound (Silbury 3 and 4)	48 MY 144/48 = 3/1
Maximum diameter of ditch deepest section	144 MY 144/88.5 = 8/5
Diameter of mound (Silbury 2)	88.8 MY 88.8/44.4 = 2/1
Diameter of mound (Silbury 1)	44.4 MY 192/144 = 4/3
Diameter of the external summit (flat)	36.75 MY 36.5/24 = 3/2
Diameter of the wattle fence (Silbury 1)	24 MY = 24/6 = 4/1

The measurements used in the calculations are taken from Michael Dames' *The Silbury Treasure* (1978), and Alexander Thom's *Megalithic Yard* (1969).

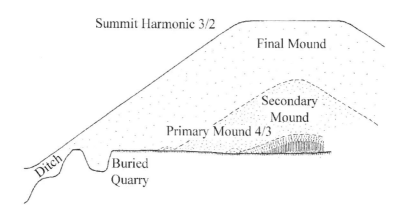

Fig. 145 Internal and external harmonics of Silbury Hill.

Lighting Up the Darkness

Accompanied by a retired engineer, we conducted several experiments at Silbury Hill using an electrostatic field meter [Chubb i.c.i.] to record the electrostatic field. A measurement was taken at the top of Silbury and another at the bottom of the mound. As soon as the digital instrument was switched on (range setting-20000 volts), a surge caused the meter to malfunction which has never happened before. A normal reading from atmospheric charges, which can vary with the degree of cloud formation, is 200 volts when 6 ft (1.82 m) from the ground. This was indeed the case when a 'control' measurement was taken at the foot of the hill. Constructed mainly of alternate organic and inorganic compounds, Silbury was effectively a high voltage capacitor and potentially could store a high electrostatic charge built up from the atmosphere. If the mound originally had a metal cap, as is sometimes claimed at the tops of pyramids, particularly if pointed, a corona discharge caused by ionisation would create a blue light, but only in darkness; although there may have been an exception when moonlight struck one side of the mound, leaving a dark shadow on the far side. Archaeological records exist of tunnels being dug into Silbury Hill that might have severely damaged its structure and ability to maintain this high charge. Corona from very high electrical discharge causes ionisation of fluids, which would be present in the form of water from rain and dew covering the surface of the hill with moisture. Similar blue flashes can sometimes be seen from national grid power lines, as well as high voltage electrical equipment, also from equipment such as old TV cathode ray tubes and radio transmitters. When the mound was in pristine condition, the effect of this blue light would have appeared even more spectacular, as would our view of the night sky during earlier periods in our history in the absence of artificial light. If we are correct, then during the Bronze Age, Silbury Hill could have emitted light—lighting up a dark night like a beacon mound. I also propose that other large mounds, such as Merlin's Mount in Marlborough and the Enford Barrow, near Stonehenge, were likewise designed to produce blue light. In the distant past, the landscape was beautiful by day and by night.

Harmonics of the Serpent Mound

The Serpent Mound in Ohio, in the American Midwest, has seven half bends, shown in *Fig. 146*. These, we suggest, each represent one musical scale, say C, D, E, F, G, A, B, and because they are half bends, they equate to 3.5 coils, which is a fraction of the perfect fifth, 3/2 harmonic. The tail makes 2.5 bends, which is a harmonic of 4/3, the perfect fourth. As previously explained, the perfect fifth corresponds to the path of the Sun, whereas the harmonic of 4/3 relates to the Moon, time past and yin energy. This suggests that the Serpent Mound is an effigy of a figure whose coils represent time,

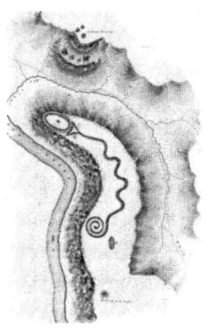

Fig. 146 Serpent Mound, Ohio.

as well as male/female energies, day/night, union and balance. Challenging emotions, attitudes, and memories of our past, can be lovingly released when working with the 4/3 harmonic, so the spiral tail can assist in clearing any lingering emotional energy that may be causing blockages. This enables the body of the snake to be walked with clarity, free of psychic and emotional 'pollution', keeping the serpent mound energetically pure. The seven bends may encourage the seven chakras to open, and the solar aspect of the mound, like an oracle, can encourage insight into one's future. The 3/2 harmonic also balances the male energy within. Walking from the past towards one's future, beginning at the tail and then along the serpent's body, could assist in the manifestation of one's dreams and visions.

In conclusion, harmonics, whether born of mathematics or of Gaia, can quietly influence sacred sites, creating a musical gateway or portal through which humanity can commune with higher energies, the earth and the ancestors, or receive healing as an echo of a long-lost aspect of the Old Religion. Geodetic harmonics can restore balance and be likened to a universal key to humanity's modern salvation. Gaia's hidden harmonics offer a new and alternative interpretation of stone circles and the use of sound at ritual or ceremonial events.

Richard noted that harmonic ratios are found at Stone Age sites worldwide, but our research may place these findings in the same field as the speculations of Erich Von Daniken. For this reason, despite the mathematical evidence and content, Gaia's harmonics will probably continue to remain outside the scope and interest of the current generation of academics and archaeologists. The truth is that earth energies express themselves in musical proportions, and the 'Song of the Earth' is a sacred aspect of Gaia's deep, fluidic body. Sadly, the science of harmonics vanished from our monotheistic religions. Plato respected the work of Pythagoras, but to a degree he rejected the old mystery tradition of harmonics which had been taught to the initiates of Egypt and spread into Europe. Harmonics were used on many levels to align the mind, voice and soul with a specific site, ultimately to resonate with its 'Spirit of Place'—where place and humanity unite. Gradually, the use of harmonics faded, and, unlike stone circles, temples and pyramids, modern constructs became silent and sacred practices ceased.

Chapter 11

Stonehenge Transformed

Science News: *Ancient DNA shows that the culture which brought Bronze Age technology to Britain was connected to a migration that almost completely replaced the island's earlier inhabitants.* (July/August 2021)

L et us now return to Stonehenge in an attempt to understand what happened to the long headed people. Across the ancient world, Stonehenge's reputation must have spread far and wide. Stories of people seeing a blood-red moon rise above the Heel Stone, the southernmost Full Moon framed by the Greater Trilithon's upper window, and sound emanating from the stones; people receiving divination from oracles and being healed—all would have generated awe and wonder. Stonehenge stood intact in this form for around one hundred and forty years, and five generations of long headed people worshipped there. However, a dark cloud was about to engulf the landscape that would transform the course of British prehistory, and no doubt the long headed people sensed a chill wind of change in the air.

DNA Evidence

From around 2700 BC, the European Bell Beaker migration began to enter Britain and the country was about to see significant population changes. Generally speaking, the integration was a peaceful process with the exchange of ideas and new technologies—but this was not so at Stonehenge. The Beaker culture refers to people that lived in Europe whose ancestors had previously migrated from the Eurasian Steppe. This group continued to migrate west and finally arrived in Britain around 4,400 years ago. The DNA available data suggests that over a span of several hundred years, the migration of peoples from continental Europe led to an almost complete replacement of Britain's earlier inhabitants—the Neolithic communities who were responsible for building the huge megalithic monuments, such as Stonehenge. The DNA also shows that the Beaker people had different pigmentation than that of the population they replaced, who had olive-brown skin, dark hair and brown or blue eyes. In comparison, they brought genes that had a significant reduction in skin and eye pigmentation, with lighter skin, blue eyes and blonde hair becoming more commonplace.

Professor Ian Barnes, a research leader on ancient DNA, says:

"Large megalithic structures such Stonehenge were built in Britain by Neolithic (or New Stone Age) people, who were replaced by the Bronze Age Beaker population."

He goes on to say:

"This parallel situation in which both peoples (ancient Britons and the Beakers) were living and interacting, but not mixing much biologically, lasted for perhaps up to 500 years. Then, there was a tipping point when the populations started having children together more extensively. What caused this tipping point is hard to discern. By 2000 BC people living in Britain derived more than 90% of their genes from ancestors who, before 2450 BC had lived on the European mainland."

Furthermore, new diseases spread by the Beaker settlers may have caused depopulation; this and intermarriage over several generations appear to have caused the long headed culture to vanish. Britain was transformed. To the Late Neolithic long headed people, the new incomers would have looked radically different in terms of head shape and stature. An average round headed man was around 6 ft 2 in (1.88 m) to 6 ft 6 in (1.82 m) tall and heavily built compared to one male from Wor Barrow, Dorset who was just 4 ft 10 in (1.47 m), almost dwarf-

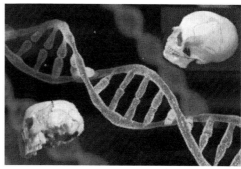

Fig. 147 Long skulls and DNA. Professor Ian Barnes.

like in comparison. *Figs. 148* and *148a* demonstrate the difference between a typical Beaker male's head shape and size contrasted with a long headed male from West Kennet Long Barrow. Beaker men were much taller, which has led some researchers to suggest they were giant-like. Certainly, their femur bones gave an average height of 6 ft 6 in (1.82 m), whilst others may have been taller. Recorded in the 16th century, a skeleton from a Bronze Age round barrow near Stonehenge was said to have measured 13 ft (3.96 m). Once again, I think it was the ancestors who inspired legends of elves, the fey and giants. By the time of the Druids c750 BC, I am sure stories of people that were likened to mythical beings began to circulate, yet their genesis is rooted in historical fact!

The forgotten story of these two cultures can finally be told. During these changing times, Stonehenge was not at peace and some of the long headed elite were murdered. The beheaded men of Boles Barrow and Rodmarton Long Barrow were killed with a metal sword. These killings, and the murder of the Neolithic High Queen, may have been the last of the long headed royalty to rule at the time of the Beaker immigration. Perhaps, the long headed people were fighting for Stonehenge—their spiritual capital—and their lands. Elsewhere in the country, long headed people were buried alongside the round headed in newly constructed round barrows, suggesting a peaceful alliance. For example, placed within Three Lows Round Barrow in Wetton, Staffordshire, a round headed female and a very long skulled man were buried together. Yet, in the Stonehenge environs not a single long headed person was buried in a round barrow.

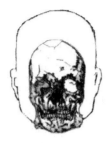 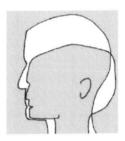

Figs. 148 & 148a Head size comparison of a long headed and Bronze Age male. *Illustrations:* Caroline Morgan.

Posthumous Grave Attacks

In the Early Neolithic, burial did not consist of immediate interment; it was a protracted ritual sometimes extending over months before the bones were taken to their final resting place. Safe from predatory animals, the deceased were often left exposed on a scaffold close to a long barrow's entrance, then when the bones were fleshless they were regularly buried in a sitting or flexed (foetal-like) position within a long barrow. Archaeologists have noted that some long barrow deposits around Stonehenge were callously disturbed. Analysis shows that long after burial the long headed deceased were violated; certain skeletons were *killed* by destroying parts of the skull. Aubrey Burl informs us:

> "Some skeletons had been buried, dug up and then apparently 'killed' by destroying part of the skull, maybe as an additional safeguard to ensure the total extinction of the spirit."

If this violent act was an "additional safeguard" as Burl proposed, then why wasn't it a common funereal rite practiced throughout southern England? It is unlikely that the long headed would violate their own dead, so I offer an alternative explanation. Did the tall and round headed culture want to destroy Stonehenge's long headed ruling elite; both the living *and* the revered dead, and is this why some burials were posthumously attacked?

The area around Stonehenge houses the largest concentration of burial mounds in Europe and within one mile of Stonehenge lies Amesbury 14 Long Barrow, which is 100 ft (30.4 m) long. Excavations uncovered the remains of three skeletons to the southeast of the mound, and two of the skulls had been smashed. Burl states, "the blows were thrust long after death." On the edge of Salisbury Plain lies Oxendean Down Long Barrow, north of Battlesbury Iron Age enclosure. This is where Cunnington found a deep grave and the curious remains of a man: "his skull lay chiefly upon the breast, literally beaten." Near the centre of Knook Long Barrow, 99 ft long (30 m) and 50 ft (15 m) wide, four headless skeletons were found—although these may have been a later Saxon burial. Six miles (9.5 km) from Stonehenge, on East Down, a large long barrow contained eight skeletons, of which it was noted the bones had been previously dug up and unceremoniously reburied. South of Stonehenge, further desecration occurred at Corton Long Barrow, where another eight skeletons lay in a state of disarray, "as though they had been thrown on a heap without ceremony," commented Burl. That a child of seven to eight years old was laid to rest alongside several adults reminds us that this is not a cold archaeological report but a warm, human story. We read earlier that Norton Bavant 13 Long Barrow housed eighteen people, many of whom were murdered; some had missing long bones that excavators found unusual, although they may have been selected bone relics. In *The History of Ancient Wiltshire, Vol. I* (1812), Colt Hoare's 'Stations' indicate there were around 2,000 long barrows in Wiltshire. He and Cunnington opened nineteen and Thurnam opened twenty-five between the years 1855 and 1868; four barrows had been previously opened by other early excavators. Shockingly, by 1914 only 86 long barrows remained. In the early 20th century, Maud Cunnington quoted as few as 32 long barrows remained unopened. Some, at least, of the long headed still rest in peace.

Monuments Sealed

Writing in *British Archaeology* magazine, July-August 2021, Barnes states:

> "From an early stage these recently arrived communities, the Bell Beaker, took an interest in, and in some cases directly adopted, monuments and places with which they had no ancestral connection."

My research shows that the Beaker culture not only adopted existing monuments, they closed thousands down and reformed others. In some parts of the British Isles, this may have been collaborative. However, evidence suggests that from 2500 BC the Stonehenge landscape was being systematically transformed. Long barrows that contained open chambers were infilled with earth and debris and permanently sealed off. Across Britain, a new burial practice of constructing round barrows, predominately for the round headed elite, replaced the old Neolithic long barrow tradition. Crowning the hilltops, the long headed culture had constructed ceremonial centres called *causewayed enclosures*, consisting of one to four concentric rings of interrupted internal banks and external ditches, covering an area of between 3-24 acres. Across the Thames Valley, causewayed enclosures were regularly spaced every 5 miles (8 km), showing a sophisticated planning system. Three miles (4.8 km) northwest of

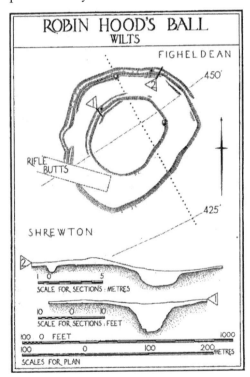

Fig. 149 Archaeological survey of Robin Hood's Ball, 1955.

Stonehenge, Robin Hood's Ball causewayed enclosure consisted of two circuits of high chalk banks with several deep ditches that enclosed eight acres. The inner ring was an ellipse shape; on the north and west sides the ditch is still partly visible with a width of 30-40 ft (9-14 m). In contrast, along the northern side, the bank is only 18 in (45 cm) high, and there were at least fifteen ditch causeways.

Not unlike the decommissioning of the long barrows, the ditches at Robin's Hood's Ball were infilled, and the process was rapid. Archaeologist Nicholas Thomas concluded that the levelling of Robin Hood's Ball, and in Dorset Mount Pleasant and Maiden Castle, was deliberate. Archaeologists suggest that these centres were abandoned between 3000-2500 BC. I disagree, and suggest they were not deserted but deliberately demolished by the Beaker elite to end the long headed culture's reign. After targeting their earthen monuments, they turned their attention towards Stonehenge, which would never be the same again. For decades, archaeologists and scholars have puzzled over why Stonehenge underwent so many alterations—such as the resetting of the bluestones—some of which were intrusive and damaging, whilst other stone circles were left intact. By acknowledging there were *two* different cultures living in the Stonehenge environs, a bigger picture emerges. Barnes notes:

"There are loads of Neolithic structures around Stonehenge and it's this landscape, that the Beaker people use as a prestigious place to bury their dead. What is interesting is that even though it wasn't these people's biological ancestors who built Stonehenge, they referenced and incorporated these monuments into their belief systems very quickly and they were adapting parts of the local culture."

Dr Selina Brace, another leading researcher in ancient DNA, explains:

"Just before the point where we can infer interbreeding, there was a hybrid culture between what came before and what came after."

STAGE 3 THE COPPER AGE 2460-2280 BC

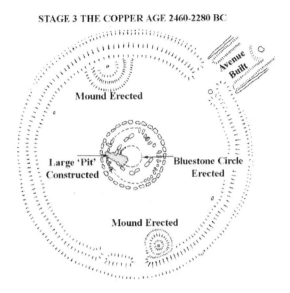

Fig. 150 A large unsymmetrical pit was dug by the Greater Trilithon.

New People, New Designs

My own evidence shows that the round headed Beaker culture were aggressive and disrespectful of the long headed; they attacked the dead, slaughtered the living, including the petite Neolithic High Queen, and sealed off their monuments. To lay claim to Stonehenge, the round headed destroyed certain features and they built earthen mounds over the timber temples that housed a Station Stone, which was uprooted and re-erected on its summit. At the centre of Stonehenge, on the northern side of the Greater Trilithon at the holy of holies, a large pit was dug that cut into the bluestone stone setting, shown above in *Fig. 150*. This pothole was an ugly unsymmetrical shape that was over 10 ft (3 m) long and around 2 ft (60 cm) deep. It sullied the heart of Stonehenge as rainwater would have filled this hole, making a large muddy, soggy mess. This was not design, this was vandalism.

Sometime between 2500-2200 BC, Parker Pearson notes that one of the concentric circles of bluestones was probably rearranged in a circular design *inside* of the trilithons; originally, they were both on the *outside*. Additional changes transformed the night-time lunar goddess temple into a solar 'masculine' temple. Originally, the narrow entrance was 35 ft (10 m) wide and incorporated the moon's Metonic cycle. The round headed culture were solar worshippers and in order to make the Sun *appear* to rise above the Heel Stone at Midsummer, the northeast entrance was widened by levelling a 25 ft (7 m) stretch of the bank to the east of the entrance and infilling this section of the ditch. Now, from Stonehenge's centre, the Midsummer Sun rises *close* to the Heel Stone, but was never exact, as shown in *Fig. 151*.

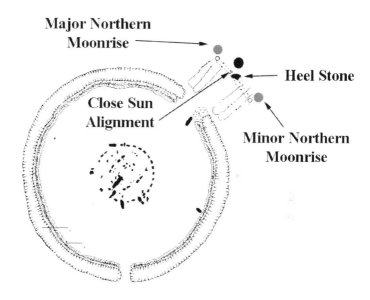

Fig. 151 The inaccurate Midsummer Sunrise.

Over the course of the next two and a half centuries, from 2280-2020 BC, Parker Pearson et al describe Stonehenge Stage Four, when the bluestones were once more rearranged into an inner oval—later on six were removed to make a horseshoe. Other alterations may have included removing one of the Slaughter Stone's partners (Stone holes D or E). The only features that remained in situ, because they were too heavy to move, were the sarsen lintelled ring, the giant trilithons and the Altar Stones. Stonehenge had been transformed.

Parker Pearson notes that during this time frame, a 1.5 miles (2.4 km) long earthen avenue was constructed that coursed from the River Avon at West Amesbury to Stonehenge's northeast entrance. Close to the entrance there was probably a megalithic avenue. William

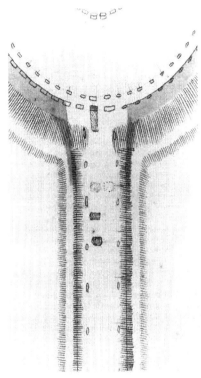

Stukeley, visiting Stonehenge in 1719 with his friend and colleague Roger Gale, noted that an earthen ditch and bank formed the avenue; they also saw several large stone holes that Stukeley drew in 1721, as shown in *Fig. 152*. However, when Stukeley's book was published in 1740, he omitted any reference to them. A bemused Roger Gale wrote to him:

"I think you have omitted a remarkable particular, which is that the avenue up to the chief entrance was formerly planted with great stones, opposite to each other, on the side of the banks of it, for I well remember we observed the holes where they had been fixt, when you and I surveyed them."

Fig. 152 Stonehenge's megalithic avenue, recorded by Stukeley.

Five years earlier, Stukeley suggested that the avenue stones had been removed by local people for development of the nearby village of Amesbury. Why he should have omitted any reference to the stone-lined avenue, shown in his drawing, is totally perplexing, especially when both he and Gale observed the stone holes. A more recent geophysical survey agrees with his findings and shows that the avenue was given emphasis by paired standing stones, just as Gale had reminded Stukeley in 1740. Later, I will demonstrate that Stonehenge once had three avenues.

Bronze Age Bell Barrows

As well as bringing metallurgy to the British Isles, new forms of burial rites were introduced by the tall Beaker people who constructed large *bell barrows*: these were large earthen mounds with encircling ditches. There are around 36,000 surviving round barrows in the British Isles. During the Chalcolithic period, Francis Pryor notes that bell barrows often contained a single male burial. Later, around 2100 BC, mounds were raised for men, women and children, commonly known as *bowl barrows*. About 3 miles (4.8 km) northwest of Stonehenge, on Net Down, near the village of Shrewton, a Bronze Age cemetery was sited along a chalk ridge that extended to Stonehenge's Greater Cursus. Excavations of twelve plough-damaged round barrows unearthed one of the earliest and best-preserved Chalcolithic burials in the area, known as the 'Shrewton Beaker burial'. Placed in a 7 ft (2 m) deep pit beneath a large barrow, a male skeleton was found in the flexed position alongside a decorative Beaker pot and a copper dagger, surrounded by a neat kerb of chalk blocks (see *Fig. 153*), and covered by a low mound. Around 300 years later, the burial of a crouched young man with a Beaker pot was inserted, followed by two other burials: that of a young woman and a young girl. After a further 600 years, three Middle Bronze Age cremations were inserted, and finally, the skeleton of an Anglo-Saxon male was added. This tells us that early round barrows were reused time and time again, often centuries after the primary burial.

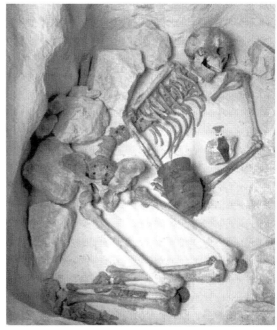

Fig. 153 Shrewton Beaker burial, Salisbury Museum.

Stonehenge Royalty and Healer-Priests

Around 1950-1750 BC a new Beaker elite ruled Stonehenge known as the Normanton dynasty. They made dramatic changes to Stonehenge and were buried in large bell and bowl barrows that overlooked Stonehenge. These were the ruling priesthood of the area who dressed in a particular manner—the healers and seers who appear to have invented a proto-type set of runes millennia before the Germanic Goths or Vikings. During this period, the healer-priests were men and women who used certain gemstones and exotic substances that became a standardised medical kit for both healing and ritual purposes. In 1962 numerous Bronze Age Beaker burials were analysed and it was noted that the different styles of burial determined social status. A regular Beaker burial consisted of a flexed skeleton accompanied by a Beaker pot or cremation remains placed inside or beneath grave goods such as bronze artefacts. In contrast, a shaman was placed in an extended position alongside certain artefacts that displayed magical-spiritual properties; this practice was repeated throughout Britain, especially in the Stonehenge environs.

Shamanic burial traditions belong to a well-defined series of interments, stretching across Eurasia from the Baltic Sea to Lake Baikal in Siberia. Archaeologists have noted that extended burials are rare, and there are no more than six or so in Wessex which include the well-known burials of the Bush Barrow man and the Upton Lovell Stonehenge shaman. However, this interpretation may be incorrect, as whilst Colt Hoare often described flexed burials, sometimes he termed an inhumation as "lying north and south", which may imply an extended burial. If so, in one Bronze Age round barrow cemetery there are eight extended burials alongside specified artefacts that indicate shamanic status or—as I prefer to call these ancient people —healer-priests. Furthermore, I have located and analysed numerous examples of shamanic/healer burials around Stonehenge (and at other ceremonial landscapes), also mapped them, which has not been done before. One possible reason why extended burials were adopted in Britain is that the Bronze Age German Unétice culture in central Europe, contemporary with Wessex, buried their elite in an extended position under huge barrows, whereas normal burials were flexed. Published in *British Archaeology* magazine, July-August 2021, tin alloy isotope analysis of the Unétice Nebra Sky Disc found the gold and tin originated from Cornwall. In 2019, cultural contact between the Unétice and Wessex was firmly established, providing clear evidence of a connection between both cultures. Bronze Age associations between Europe and southern England can also be found in human burial remains. For example, oxygen isotope analysis established that the 'Amesbury Archer'—a burial not far from Stonehenge—originated from the Alps region in probably what is now Switzerland. Elsewhere across Northern Europe and Southern Scandinavia, the same burial rites were adopted.

Neolithic Shamanic and Warrior Grave Goods

Earlier, I explained that a Neolithic royal burial consisted of an ex-tremely elongated skulled person who was buried alongside lesser-elongated skulled people, most of whom had been immolated along with their ruler. I propose there were two other distinctive Neolithic burial practices: the shaman-healer and the warrior-hunter. Animal bones have been associated with shamanic style burials. Neolithic medicine men and women were found buried in long barrows alongside stag antlers or cow skulls and bones, clay pots, sharp bone or flint instruments, and sometimes iron pyrite for starting fires. Outstanding examples are Norton Bavant 13 Long Barrow, near Warminster, Wiltshire, where the primary burial was an extended skeleton deposited with a shallow black pottery 'vase' with two handles, probably an incense burner (the clay sourced from clay beds in Hampshire), one large red deer tine and flint nodules. Near-by, at the centre of Warminster 6 Long Barrow, a small pottery 'cup' was found next to a skeleton. Similarly, at Brixton Deverill 1 Long Barrow, a cup and a bone pin were found next to a skeleton, and at Cherhill 1a Long Barrow, situated just outside of the ramparts of Oldbury Camp, near Avebury, three skeletons were unearthed in the extended position. Fragments of two black pottery pieces were found alongside human remains at Edington 7 Long Barrow, and at West Kennet Long Barrow an exotic circular black flint knife with a short projecting handle was found. I believe these artefacts could indicate the burial of a Neolithic healer-priest. The third type of Neo-lithic burial is the warrior-hunter; interments are predominantly males buried alongside neatly executed arrowheads. Examples can be found at Adam's Grave Long Barrow, the Giant's Grave near Pewsey, and at Wayland Smithy Long Barrow in Oxfordshire.

The Healers' Medicine Kit

In the Bronze Age, a healer's equipment became the standardised medical kit categorised today as shamanic, although these people were not what we might consider shamanic looking. They were glamorous and wore fine clothes, carried rare gemstones and were adorned in gold and fine jewellery. Today, we might call them herb-alists, crystal healers or holistic therapists. Their 'kit' was kept in a linen bag, often fastened by a beautiful jet or gold button, or clasp. Among Beaker communities, these pouch bags are thought to have been an important ritual component of a special form of dress. Items included flints and iron pyrite, beautiful incense cups, amber beads and large amber pieces, pieces of jet often fashioned into rings, beads made of rare minerals and piercing blue glass, fossils and shells of fascinating shapes from dis-tant lands, even the teeth of wild animals. Small bronze knives or daggers, such as the one found in the Manton mound at Marlborough, shown in *Fig. 154*, were used for cutting and chopping herbs for cooking and burning in-

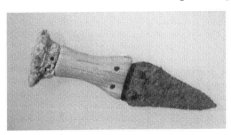

Fig. 154 A miniature bronze knife. Manton Barrow, Marlborough.

cense. Whetstones, many of which were perforated for suspension and made from special stone, were utilised as a cutting block. There were bone tweezers for the sorting and handling of substances, stone palettes for mixing ointments, body paint and cosmetics, as well as finely pointed awls, traditionally associated with leather working but now thought to have been used to inscribe symbols and patterns on wood and leather, and for tattooing human flesh. Such 'tools' would have been effective in all kinds of healing, medical, religious or divinatory encounters.

Healing Crystals

Specific coloured crystals and stones were selected for the medicine bag. The authors of *Ritual In Early Bronze Age Grave Goods* (2015), Ann Woodward and John Hunter, with David Bukach, Stuart Needham and Alison Sheridan, catalogue excavated Bronze Age artefacts of ritual significance. Their extensive research shows the preferred colours to be red, black, gold, blue and white. The favoured colour was red with red stone beads and the use of amber. Stunning bronzework that with age now looks brown or green was originally a highly polished red-gold colour. The next most occurring colours were black and white. The black category consists of items made from shale, jet and black polished stone, whilst creamy white objects are a myriad of items made from bone, shell, chalk, and other white stones such as flints and whetstones. Brown items include battle axes, polished stones and fossils, which may have been selected for their shape and texture rather than colour. Blue and green faience beads were also popular among healer-priest assemblages. Worldwide, in many different societies, some basic colour contrasts are associated with a similar symbolic meaning. The most common examples are the correlation of the colour red with blood and danger, flesh and fertility, and black with darkness and death. White denotes bones, hardness and light, but can also relate to human milk. In Bronze Age Wessex, red and black or red and white items often occur together, whilst black and white combinations are rarer. The objects tend to be smooth and cool to the touch and the workmanship is outstanding. I found a Bronze Age pre-coinage money ring which I often wear around my neck, as did my ancestors. Although no longer red-gold in colour, it is exceptionally smooth to the touch and is my physical link to the past.

Magical Amber

Amber beads deposited in round barrows were once thought to be characteristic of a female burial. However, Woodward notes that the majority of beads were not always perforated or strung:

> "[They] were a special collection of carefully gathered heirloom items which might have uses other than [for] the

adornment of the body. Perhaps most of the beads from the barrows were not necklaces at all."

Extremely large collections of amber beads are rare, though they can be found in quantities ranging from 50-100, but most deposits are fewer than twenty. Amber was imported from Estonia, also from the eastern shores of Britain, and crafted to make figurines, beads and amulets. Exotic amber breastplates, like the one shown in *Fig. 155* below, could be removed and rubbed to display magical effects. Amber can produce a triboelectric effect—electrification—by rubbing two similar materials together to increase the contact between their surfaces, this creates a triboelectric effect. Combing through hair with a plastic comb can build up triboelectric charge and amber can likewise acquire an electric charge by contact, separation or friction with textiles and wool. The word 'electricity' is derived from William Gilbert's initial coinage 'electra', which originates from *ēlektron*, the Greek word for amber. Historically, amber and crystal breastplates were worn by high priests, and ancient scribes thought amber was the solidified rays of the Sun. Amber has the appearance of gold, yet it is a fraction of the weight, is easily carved, burns well and the effused vapours give a sense of well-being. Amber beads with no evidence of perforation may have been used as incense for relaxation and to restore health; they could also have been placed on the body to sooth aliments.

Fig. 155 Amber breastplate with six plates 7 in (17 cm) long, 2 in (5 cm) at the widest point.

The Greek physician Hippocrates was one of the first to record the use of amber in medicine, but it had been used therapeutically for a long time before that. In the 18th century, many other fossils were also used as medical cures. The Scottish author, Martin Martin of Marrishadder, recorded that on Scotland's Isle of Skye, Jurassic ammonites and belemnites were infused in water to relieve dysentery, diarrhoea, tuberculosis, worms and cramps. A piece of amber (called lammar in Scotland), now in the National Museum of Scotland, was used to relieve failing eyesight by rubbing it on the eyelids. Several amber beads and amulets were used to cure a variety of ailments: one from Argyllshire was also said to cure poor eyesight and another to relieve cattle from a host of diseases. One of amber's medicinal properties that resulted in its everyday use in mainstream Western medicine, right up until the 1950s, was as part of the embrocation for treating whooping cough. Other descriptions of amber's therapeutic properties say that worn as a necklace it will give the wearer great protection, and it is said to bring good luck to warriors. To the Native Americans, amber is a sacred stone used in certain fire ceremonies. In medieval England, amber was burned as a fumigant to clear the environment of negativity and would cleanse the area where it was placed. Today, crystal healers believe that its properties can help calm the nerves, enliven the disposition, and transmute negative energy into positive energy. Amber is versatile as it can be worn, carried on one's person, burned or used as an elixir.

Magical Jet

Sourced from Whitby Bay in East Yorkshire, jet was worn and revered by the Wessex priesthood. Often called black amber or lignite, this fossilised charcoal (wood) has a velvety black colour and a resinous lustre that can be enhanced by polishing. Like amber, jet can produce a triboelectric effect. Easily carved, in the Bronze Age it was fashioned into belt rings, buttons, rings and made into elaborate spacer-plate necklaces. The rings have been described as 'pulleys' and some are ornate, but others may have been placed on the body for healing purposes or worn by the patient or healer. Jet is believed to have magical properties and can be used to dispel fearful thoughts or worn to protect against illness and violence, especially to regain one's strength when feeling vulnerable or when external forces are attacking you. According to Pliny the Elder (AD 24-79) in his *Natural History*:

> "...when jet is burnt it smells of sulphur and what is remarkable is that it is ignited by water and quenched by oil. The kindling of jet drives off snakes. Moreover, when thoroughly boiled with wine cures toothache."

Today, crystal healers use jet to treat headaches, migraine, epilepsy, colds and swellings.

Faience Beads

Strikingly blue faience beads were also a part of the healer's kit. Faience is a glass-like material with a glazed surface, coloured by traces of copper compounds that provide a bright turquoise blue colouration. Some of the earliest precious stones found to have been used for certain purposes in the world were those displaying similar shades of blue, such as lapis lazuli in the Middle East around 3000 BC. About 250 faience beads have been found in Britain, some of which were imported from the Mediterranean and as far away as Turkey, whilst others were made locally.

Fig. 156 An unusual stone found alongside a tattoo awl, beads and a beaker.

Unusual stones were also revered. Two examples were found in round barrows close to Stonehenge, one of which was long and flat, 4 in (10 cm) by 2 in (5 cm), as shown at the bottom of *Fig. 156*. It looks like fossilised wood with dark green and white stripes, was very neatly polished and felt silky to the touch. Placed next to the skeletons of an adult and a child was a sardonyx kidney-shaped pebble that had transverse alternating stripes and was spotted all over with very small white specks. After dipping this into water, it changed to a sea green colour.

The High Priests of Stonehenge

Men exhibited their high priest status by carrying tall staves and they wore elaborate gold-studded armbands. Their regalia was not only visibly stunning, it personified regal power that was as much spiritual as temporal. As Stuart Piggott points out:

> "For priests [and priestesses], kings, and queens, magicians and healers were not in the ancient world so sharply separated as they are in our latter-day scientific minds. In Celtic Gaul, Diviciacus was not only the ruler of the Aedui but a Druid priest; and we scarcely need the Coronation service to remind us that kingship and the gods have never been far removed from one another."

The healer-priests also carried exquisite gold objects in their medicine bags. For thousands of years gold has been regarded as miraculous as it never tarnishes. Gold was used by the Wessex healers and gold objects have been found in Bronze Age barrows. Today, gold is considered a master healer and is used for the puri-

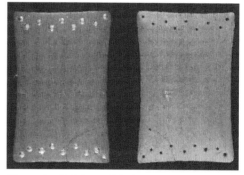

Fig. 157 Gold-studded arm bracer from a male Beaker grave, Barnack, Cambridgeshire.

fication of the physical body. Accompanying high-status male burials were large gemstone and gold-studded bracers. Originally, these were wrongly interpreted as archers' bracers or wristbands, applied to the inside of the forearm or wrist to ensure protection while practising archery. But for the bracer to be functional and allow an arrow to fly smoothly, the surface needs to be a smooth and flat; most bracers found in Bronze Age round barrows are like the one shown in *Fig. 157*. However, not all bracers fit this category as many are curved and were made to be worn on the *outside* of the forearm, unlike archers' bracers that are worn on the *inside*. Curved bracers were invariably made from an attractive jade-coloured

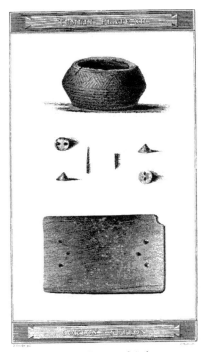

Fig. 158 The Corton high priest's gold artefacts with an emblematic bracer.

Langdale tuff stone, sourced in the Lake District. This is the same type of rock used for Neolithic ceremonial axe heads. Archers' bracers were often crafted from an actinolite-bearing amphibole rock that commonly has one or two holes, whilst larger curved bracers have numerous holes that held gold studs. Made by expert craftspeople, these emblematic bracers were highly polished. Some were permanently placed on a staff, such as the gold-studded bracer from Kelleythorpe, Yorkshire, and were a symbol of male power and authority. From a round barrow near Corton, Wiltshire, an emblematic bracer located under the right hand and close to the breast of a male skeleton, found alongside other items indicating healer-priest status such as a copper awl and an incense cup, is now housed in the Wiltshire Heritage Museum (see *Fig. 158*).

Incense Cups and Trance Consciousness

An essential item of the healer-priest's medicine kit was a miniature incense cup used for burning aromatic and intoxicating substances.

Research by the late Andrew Sherratt suggests that it was highly likely Europe's early inhabitants used the opium poppy, which is native to the Mediterranean and was grown by Neolithic farmers. Opiate seed capsules have been found in Neolithic deposits in Spain and Switzerland, and opium was known to have been burnt in

Fig. 159 Exquisite incense pot from Yorkshire.

incense cups in Wessex. An exquisite incense pot from Yorkshire is shown in *Fig. 159*. There is convincing evidence that from the beginning of the Neolithic the usage of hemp seed and cannabis to produce vapours for inhalation was widespread across the Black Sea. The habit undoubtedly spread across Europe where cannabis may have been infused as well as smoked and drunk in combination with fruity alcoholic concoctions.

Fig. 160 Left: Elaborate incense pot (top) and a Grape Cup (bottom). Right: Incense burning colander, holed for suspension.

The style of miniature incense cups used to release psychoactive smoke and to burn aromatic materials, were called by Piggott 'Aldbourne Cups'. Many in the British Museum collection show clear signs of burning, the most famous example being the Grape Cup, shown in *Fig. 160*. Distinguishable from open bowls and dishes, incense cups have incurving rims with pairs or rows of holes—perforations allowing the vessel to be suspended and swung from side to side like a church censer (see *Fig 161*). The base of the

Fig. 161 Ornate incense burners were used like church censers.

vessel was highly decorative and designed to be seen; some had colander-like bases with numerous holes, as shown on the right of *Fig. 160*. Archaeologists suggest these incense cups were used with psychoactive burning substances in small, confined spaces such as a tent. However, I suggest they were more likely used in specialised constructs at places such as Durrington Walls and within timber temples, perhaps to induce altered states of consciousness. Some of the finest incense cups were found close to Stonehenge and they were probably also used prior to divination and oracle readings.

Tattooing

Another important priestly item was an awl that was used for tattooing. Some of these have been found alongside small 'ink' pots. Around the second century BC, tattooing was practiced by the pastoral Scythian culture, nomadic people who also buried their dead in mounds. The Pazyryk mounds belonged to an elite group of men and women and probably formed a family dynasty cemetery. The excavators noted that all the bodies were tattooed, and it was suggested the patterns may have represented a symbolic or magico-religious language that was regarded as sacred; a known example is shown in *Fig. 162*. Findings published in *The International Journal of Paleopathology* in 2018, reveal that tattoos have a long and complex history. Evidence suggests they may not have been solely used for decorative purposes but also applied to record medical treatments.

Ötzi, also known as 'The Iceman', was discovered in September 1991 in the Ötztal Alps (hence his nick-name), on the border between Austria and Italy. He is the natural mummification of a man who lived between 3400-3100 BC. Due to the discovery of an arrowhead embedded in his left shoulder, Ötzi is believed to have been murdered at about 45 years old, and he also suffered from various other wounds and ailments. The

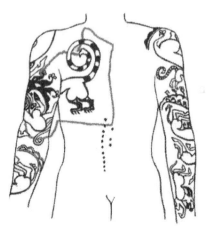

Fig. 162 Scythian tattooing.

nature of his life and circumstances of his death are the subject of much investigation and speculation. His body and belongings are on display in the Museum of Archaeology in Bolzano, South Tyrol, in Italy. At the time of his death, Ötzi was just 5.3 ft (160 cm) tall, of average size for a Neolithic/Chalcolithic man, and weighed about 110 lb (50 kg). Remarkably, he had a total of 61 tattoos, consisting of nineteen groups of black lines ranging from 1-3 mm in thickness and 7 mm long. These included parallel lines running along the longitudinal axis of his body and to both sides of the lumbar spine, also around his left wrist as well as a cruciform mark behind the right knee and on his right ankle. The greatest concentration of markings is to be found on his legs, which together exhibit twelve groups of lines. A microscopic examination of samples collected from these tattoos show they were created from pigment manufactured out of fire ash or soot, which was rubbed into small linear incisions or punctures applied using an awl. New research reveals that Ötzi consumed medicinal herbs prior to his death. Albert Zink, head of the Eurac Research Institute for Mummy Studies in Bolzano, told *LiveScience.com*:

> "The ancient society of the iceman most likely already had a considerable knowledge about medical treatments. It seems that they used different forms of therapy, including physical treatment and using medical plants. This definitely requires a certain knowledge of the human anatomy as well as how diseases arise and develop."

Ötzi had been repeatedly tattooed in the same bodily locations; the majority are quite dark, and, given their placement, the researchers think the markings were a form of repetitive medical treatment. The tattoos are located on bodily regions where the Iceman had some health issues, including degenerative diseases of the hip, knee, ankle joints and lower back—most of the tattoos are located on these areas. The chest tattoos may have been to soothe belly discomfort as he also had intestinal parasites and an infection. Several of the inked spots correspond to traditional acupuncture pressure points, which led some researchers to suggest that he underwent a form of Neolithic acupuncture. Although the first written description of acupuncture comes from China around 2,200 years ago, it was possibly practiced much earlier in Europe. Nonetheless, at the time of his death, Ötzi had a medicinal mushroom known as Birch Polypore in his digestive system, which is thought to have anti-inflammatory and fever-reducing properties. He'd also consumed certain ferns as a remedy to kill off the parasitic worms that plagued him. He was certainly consuming the correct medicinal herbs to treat his various health complaints.

It is not beyond the realms of possibility that the copper awl instrument of the Wessex healers was also used for acupuncture pressure points, and that the tattoos are an identifiable record of each treatment. Interestingly, the copper alloy awl was prominently found alongside female burials, which suggests the tattooists or acupuncturists were mainly women. Out of fourteen known cases, ten burials were women, two more were probably female and only two were men. The awl could also have been used for ritual scarification or other medical procedures.

The Wessex Seers of Sixpenny Handley

Let us now meet the healer-priests and seers of the past and explore their royal burial grounds. One of the finest ceremonial landscapes in Wessex is at Sixpenny Handley, situated on Oakley Down, Cranbourne Chase, in Dorset. This burial ground contained twenty-four round barrows and two Neolithic long barrows that housed approximately 40 individuals. I noted that 42% (17) of the individuals were buried with items denoting healer status, eight of which may have been extended burials. There were three or four warrior status burials and only eight were regular, making this a burial ground of the priestly caste. *Fig. 163* is a 19th century map of the barrow grouping drawn by Philip Crocker, who accompanied Colt Hoare and Cunnington. I recommend visiting this diverse barrow grouping which has easy access from the A354 road. You will not be disappointed, and it feels as if one is walking through time on the soft downland grass to be greeted by six magnificent disc barrows, sixteen bowl barrows, a rare saucer barrow and three oval barrows.

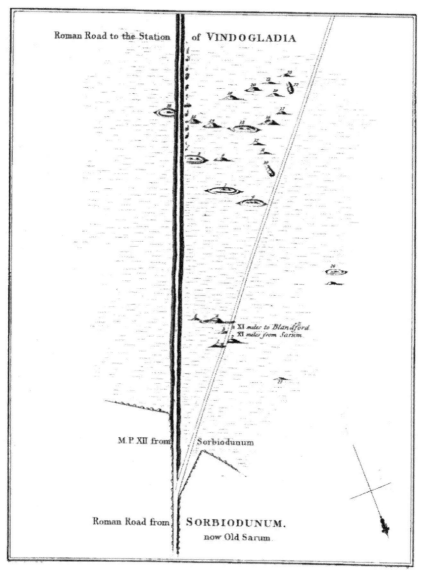

Fig. 163 Sixpenny Handley Bronze Age burial ground.

The mounds that contained remains of the priesthood were exceptionally well-constructed disc barrows, consisting of a circular or oval area of level ground defined by a bank and an internal ditch. Each contained one or more central or eccentrically located small, low mounds covering what were usually cremations in chalk cists, accompanied by pottery vessels, tools and personal ornaments.

Nationally, disc barrows are rare with only 250 known examples, of which 29 are located within the Stonehenge landscape. In Mound 1 (*Fig. 163*) were two interments of a man and a woman. The primary burial was described by Colt Hoare as "a tall and stout man" found in a flexed position, indicating regular social status. A secondary extended burial of a woman just 2 ft (60 cm) from the surface was laid to rest facing the direction of the rising Midsummer Sun. This woman was an Early Iron Age high queen or priestess; she wore an unusual necklace with traces of iron that depicted a human head wearing a triangular wizard-style of headdress—this is the only piece of jewellery found in Wessex that depicts a human face. Other artefacts included faience beads, twelve amber beads, two rings, a brass hair clasp and an iron ring, all of which are indicative of healer-priestess status. Mound 4 is a magnificent bell barrow that housed three important healers, one of which contained a "large skeleton and was lying north-south" (possibly extended like Mound 1 as Colt Hoare did not describe it as being in the flexed position). Two other skeletons, also possibly extended, were deposited with an exquisite incense burner, a highly polished black bead, and a large urn. Rich artefacts belonging to the priesthood were found in all of these disc barrows, dated to 1600-1200 BC. Mound 6 is remarkable as within its circular depression are three mounds: two had been ransacked prior to the 19th century, whilst the other one contained a cremation alongside a very large urn, inside of which were numerous faience and amber beads. Another impressive disc barrow containing two inner mounds is Mound 7; one had been plundered but the other had an interment of burned bones with large amber beads alongside.

The richest amber finds were, however, unearthed from Mound 8, which is my favourite disc barrow in Wessex, and has two small inner mounds surrounded by a large ditch 190 ft (58 m) in diameter. The inner mound closest to the Roman road contained a cremation with several faience, jet and amber beads, an incense cup, and a fragment of a flat section of an amber breastplate. The other mound also contained a cremation, accompanied by one hundred amber beads and a large amber breastplate (see *Fig. 155*). Applying Lethbridge's dowsing method to these mounds revealed that they both contained female cremations of high priestesses. I laid on the barrow and felt their presence within and around me; their forgotten beauty and knowledge of natural magic reached out to me, and I replied softly, "I've found you. You are not forgotten."

Fig. 164 My favourite disc barrows at Sixpenny Handley. The barrow of the high priestess is in the foreground.

Two other disc barrows, Mound 13 and Mound 28, both contained amber beads, and Mound 26 is likely to have housed a woman priestess and tattooist; alongside a large urn were pieces of jet, amber, bone, a brass awl-pin and a beautiful incense cup. Animal bones have been associated with shamanic style burials and in Mound 14, which is a very finely made bowl barrow, a cremation was found alongside a cow jaw. In Mound 18, the primary burial of a flexed male skeleton was accompanied by a large deer's tine that was perforated and clearly designed to be suspended, possibly indicating a long forgotten Early Bronze Age shaman. Nearby, an unusual find was unearthed from a bowl barrow. It was a large urn that contained a cremation. On its base was "some ornamental work in high relief, resembling a wheel or a star with six rays," the only one of its kind in Wessex.

Warriors

Warrior-style artefacts were un-earthed from three large mounds: Mound 9 is a magnificent bell barrow that covered two second-ary burials. Beneath a layer of flints the primary burial of a large skeleton lying in the flexed posi-tion was found with shamanic and warrior grave goods, com-prising large pieces of stag tine, half a stone celt, a beautiful bronze gilded dagger that had been protected by a wooden scab-bard, a large jet button, a jet pully-ring, four perfect flint arrow-heads, and a small brass pin (*Fig. 165*). Described by Colt Hoare

Fig. 165 A warrior's grave goods.

as a 'British Hero', when Cunnington opened the barrow there was a sudden thunderstorm that forced the excavators, including Rev Bowles, the illustrator Philip Crocker, and Colt Hoare himself to take refuge in the barrow they'd dug into. Colt Hoare reported:

> "...the lightning flashed upon our spades and iron instru-ments and the large flints that poured down upon us from the summit of the barrow so abundantly and so forcibly, that we were obliged to quit our hiding place, and abide the pelting of the pitiless storm upon the bleak and unsheltered down."

The unforgettable experience inspired the Rev William Lisle Bowles to write a long poem, which begins:

> Let me, let me sleep again;
> Thus, me thought, in feeble strain,
> Plain'd from its disturbed bed
> The spirit of the mighty dead.

I'd like to think the storm was divine intervention of an old Thor-like protector god for disturbing an ancient warrior's grave. Although out of the 400 or so barrows opened, only about three storms occurred. Mound 19 may have belonged to a warrior as arrowheads were found next to a cremation containing large pieces of bone, probably male; and in Mound 20 a similar cremation was found with a bone arrowhead. Later, we will explore the warrior women of Stonehenge—the 'shieldmaidens'—who also bore weaponry.

At Sixpenny Handley, Colt Hoare found a high proportion of "tall and stout men" (and possibly women, as Woodward points out the sex of the so-called 'Bush man' has never been ascertained, only *presumed* to be male). The femur bone of an individual can be used to ascertain the height by applying a simple mathematical formula, used by both anthropologists and the police. The femur bone of one of the "tall and stout men" that Colt Hoare described, measured 20 in (51 cm), which would give him a height of around 6 ft 4-6 in (1.82-1.95 m). I would like to measure one of these bones; certainly, femur bones of large individuals that were measured in Derbyshire and in Staffordshire gave a similar height. Nonetheless, as previously stated, some may have been much taller, which has led to the suggestion they were giants. At Sixpenny Handley, I noted a significant number of large urns were found compared with more isolated finds, such as the Stonehenge urn which is 22 in (57 cm) high by 15 in (38 cm) diameter. One of the Sixpenny Handley urns measured 19 in (73 cm) by 11 in (28 cm). Could large urns containing, or associated with, cremations, have symbolic meaning—perhaps representing a tall, large (stout) person? At Stonehenge, I noted that next to a large skeleton a large decorative urn was found that may validate my speculation. Not far away, on the right-hand side of the old Roman road, there were once three other barrows. One was a large circular barrow, and at a depth of 2 ft (60 cm) a secondary burial of two skeletons was discovered; at 4.5 ft (1.37 m) another large urn alongside a cremation was found. Unusually, on the bottom of this urn was a depiction resembling a wheel, or a star with six rays. All of the other barrows at Sixpenny Handley held simple, regular cremations.

The Stonehenge High Priestesses

I have found only five amber breastplates in Wessex, all of which are associated with cremation burials, so the gender is unknown. However, what we do know is that more women were cremated than men, and accompanying grave goods suggest the breastplates were associated with high-ranking women. Four of these came from disc barrows and the other came from the 'Golden Barrow', which is a bowl barrow at Upton Lovell, in Wiltshire (recorded as Upton Lovell 2e by Goddard). It contained a secondary cremation or cremations, with lavish grave goods including gold beads, a rectangular gold plate, two small gold cones (see *Fig. 166*), over one thousand amber beads and an amber breastplate similar to the one shown in *Fig. 155*, as well as a bronze awl (indicative of a female), a grape incense cup for burning intoxicating substances, and a small flat bronze dagger for cutting and chopping herbs.

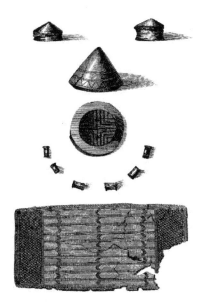

Fig. 166 Finds from Golden Barrow, Upton Lovell.

On Middle Hill, just outside of the village of Kingston Deverill, a remarkable disc barrow contained a cremation along with a beautiful six-section amber breastplate about 7 in (17 cm) long, around 40 amber beads of various forms and sizes, jet beads, jet pulley beads and two horn pulley beads. Hoare thought these belonged to "a distinguished female" and he is probably correct. The energy of this mound retains something of its past and calls deeply to the soul.

A High Priestess and the Stonehenge Runes

In search of amber breastplates and forgotten priestesses, I turned my attention back to Stonehenge and found the largest in Wessex, south of Stonehenge at the Bronze Age cemetery called the 'Lake

Group'. Take a walk around this ancestral landscape, as the view of Stonehenge is spectacular. Prior to the A303 road being constructed in the mid-1700s, this is the route taken by most people to reach Stonehenge. The largest amber breastplate was found in Wilsford G49 (or G50) bowl barrow. It is 10 in (25 cm) in height, about 3 in (7 cm) wide, and was made of eight instead of the usual six amber tablets. Colt Hoare, in *The History of Ancient Wiltshire, Vol. 1* (1812), lists this as Barrow 21, although various websites incorrectly state it as Barrow 20. It was opened in 1806 by the Rev Edward Duke, who described the barrow as:

> "...a wide and low tumulus, over which the plough has performed its agricultural rites for many years. The very rich and numerous trinkets discovered in this barrow, seem to announce the skeleton to have been that of some very distinguished British female."

This is one of the best examples in Britain (*Fig. 167*), with an amber necklace alongside four perforated gold ornaments, perhaps earrings, two small incense cups, a bronze awl, and a dome-shaped gold-plated artefact, probably a button.

Fig. 167 The Stonehenge runes and other artefacts.

The Runes

Nearby, Duke opened another barrow, listed by both Colt Hoare and Leslie Grinsell as Barrow 20 (although Goddard officially lists it as Hoare's Barrow 17). It survives as an earthwork mound nearly 5 ft (1.5 m) high, although as a result of ploughing appears square-like with a levelled ditch. Next to a cremation, some small bone artefacts were found. These, I would suggest, are prototype runes that predate the Nordic runes by nearly two thousand years.

It is believed that runes were developed around the time of Christ, probably in Scandinavia, and by AD 500 they were being used by the Germanic peoples, the Norse and the English. The Stonehenge set consists of four neatly polished rectangular-shaped pieces of bone that were smoothed, carved with symbols and then painted. Each piece had a particular symbol on the flat side and on its concave, reverse side, was a cross-like symbol. When selected from a bag

there would have been a total of eight symbols for interpretation. When cast, this gave several permutations, depending upon which way the runes fell. The symbol of the cardinal cross may have represented the four directions and the seasons: the Equinoxes and the Solstices.

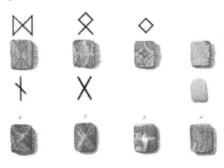

Fig. 168 The Stonehenge runes and corresponding Viking rune symbols.

The Stonehenge symbols closely resemble some of the Viking rune stones, such as Dagaz, which means breakthrough, transformation and prosperity; Inguz, the rune of fertility; and Othilia, the rune of separation, retreat and inheritance. Two of the concave cross-symbols bring to mind Gebo, the rune of partnership; and Nauthiz, the rune of constraint, necessity and pain. In the Viking runic system, one rune is left blank,

Fig. 169 A Bronze Age jet rune and a Viking rune.

which is called 'Odin's Rune', representing the unknown. It cannot be coincidental that, likewise, there is a blank Stonehenge rune (see *Fig. 168*). Another runic symbol from Yorkshire was carved onto a piece of jet with dotted perforations that closely resembles the rune of fertility, shown in *Fig. 169*. At Flixton Wold, North Yorkshire, a young girl was

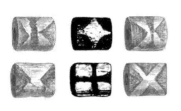

Fig. 170 Rune-like set from North Yorkshire.

buried with four beads of bone, three of which were ornamented on each side with symbols very similar to the Stonehenge runes. These symbols all meant something to the Bronze Age seers.

The Stonehenge Shaman and a Forgotten Shawoman!

Bronze Age men, such as the Bush Barrow man, the Boscombe Bowman, the Amesbury Archer and the Stonehenge Shaman, have all been widely documented and gained worldwide media attention. Yet the women of prehistory, with equally magnificent grave goods, meeting all the criteria for shamanic, priestly or royal status, have been largely overlooked. In the name of my sister ancestors, I want to address this inequality. For example, buried next to the famous Stonehenge Shaman was a woman who had her own shamanic artefacts, including beads of jet and ivory. However, she is only mentioned as 'probably his wife'. Likewise, next to the Bush Barrow man are high-status women, members of the Stonehenge priest-hood—women of wealth and power—who were undoubtedly equal in rank to their male counterparts.

Approximately 12.5 miles (19 km) west of Stonehenge and overlook-ing the River Wylye, two burials were found within Upton Lovell G2a round barrow. One became famous—the Stonehenge Shaman —but the other, who I suspect was a female shaman, has been over-looked. This barrow was excavated by Cunnington in 1801, and in the chalk bedrock at a depth of 3 ft (91 cm), he found an extended skeleton lying on its back with the head towards the north; and just 10-12 in (25-30 cm) from the surface, he found another skeleton in a sitting posture:

> "The first, from the largeness of the bones, appeared to have been a stout man; the latter, being much smaller, was prob-ably a female, and perhaps his wife."

More than 36 pointed and perforated bones were found and have been interpreted as a 'cloak fringe' that would have clattered as he walked or danced, some of which are shown in *Fig. 171*. Adjoining these were three celts of flint or stone, one of which was made for sharpening or bringing the bone arrowheads to a point. Another stone of a larger size probably served as a whetstone in forming and polishing the celts, shown in *Fig. 172*. Analysis of one of the smoothers showed traces of gold, and it has been speculated that the shaman was, in fact, a gold-smith.

Fig. 171 Bones of fringed cloak.

Unfortunately, during the excavation a considerable quantity of the woman's smaller bones and artefacts fell upon the man's skeleton, causing difficulty in ascertaining to which of the bodies certain artefacts belonged. A large, ornamented jet ring that had rough sections on the inside was probably worn as an amulet, or it may have been a healing ring used in a similar manner to modern-day crystal therapists who treat ailments by placing certain gemstones on the body. There were also several imported stones and pebbles, a small brass pin or awl, jet beads, eagle stones and one bone bead. I suggest these belonged to the woman who was a healer and probably a midwife. This is suggested because the stones associated with midwifery and childbirth are eagle stones and jet. In the magical-medical tradition of Europe and the Near East, eagle stones were used to promote childbirth, prevent miscarriage and premature delivery, and could help to shorten labour. According to the Greek physician Dioscorides, an eagle stone could protect the baby at the time of birth. Pliny describes

Fig. 172 The celts of the Stonehenge shaman.

four types of eagle stones in his *Natural History* and outlines their medical uses for pregnant women to prevent a miscarriage. The fourth-century AD magico-medical text *Cyranide* also claims that an eagle stone worn as an amulet can prevent miscarriage. Ruberto Bernardi, in his 1364 book of popular medical lore, says that eagle stones should be carried by pregnant women on their right side. In the 1660 book *Occult Physick*, William Williams states:

> "...the aetite [eagle stone] is white and round like a tennis-ball and hath a stone that shaketh within it. Being worn it delivereth women in their extremity, but at any other time it is not to be used by them that are with child. It doth also dissolve the knobs of the Kings Evil (i.e., scrofula)."

Likewise, jet artefacts were sometimes used in midwifery. Pliny states that the kindling of jet stops the movement of the uterus and can ease tuberculosis. Thus, the jet amulet, eagle stones and awl could have been essential medicinal items belonging to the woman, who may or not have been the shaman's wife—a revered midwife and healer in her own right—and hence her burial next to a male shaman.

Chapter 12

Stonehenge's Ruling Dynasty

The archaeological record shows that during the Bronze Age the ruling elite was a hierarchy of high priestesses and priests. They practiced cranial deformation (as did the long headed) to make their skulls appear rounder than the populus, and they were buried in prestigious round barrows. Within a 10-15 mile (16-24 km) radius of Stonehenge, archaeologists estimate that there were once over a thousand round barrows, most of which have been dated to 2200-1700 BC with others constructed in the succeeding Middle Bronze Age (1500 BC). Throughout these times, the mounds continued to receive secondary burials, and these were usually cremations. In 1828, philosopher and astronomer, Mr Waltire, gave a series of lectures on Stonehenge. He had traced as many as 1,500 round barrows and suggested they represented the magnitude of the fixed stars, forming a complete planisphere encircling Stonehenge. Eight hundred stars can be seen with the naked eye, and the smaller barrows he proposed represented stars too minute to be observed without an instrument or telescope; therefore, he surmised, the ancients must have used such a device. This is an attractive idea, and, if correct, it must have been an ongoing project for more than one thousand years. It is tempting to think that the departed became associated with a star, immortalised in the star-spangled sky.

Stonehenge's ceremonial landscape is diverse and contains several Bronze Age cemeteries including Winterbourne Stoke Roundabout, Winterbourne Stoke East, Winterbourne Stoke West, Durrington Barrows, the Cursus Barrows, Normanton Down, Wilsford and the Lake Down groups. Numerous barrows were excavated by early antiquarians, but those least investigated are the Old and New King Barrows. I created a detailed map of the artefacts found in these mound cemeteries to establish the burial status of those interred, and I placed them into three main categories. Firstly, the royal ruling priesthood, who were denoted if the burial was found with classic priestly grave goods; secondly, warrior status if weaponry was present; and thirdly, Beaker cremations or inhumations with non-exotic or no grave goods present, which I classified as a regular burial. Interestingly, I noted a pattern emerged with the landscape divided into two distinctive sections: the south was reserved for burials of the elite, the royal healer-priests and warriors, while the north and northeast contained a high proportion of regular burials and only a handful of priestly or warrior status burials. For instance, the Cursus barrow grouping is situated just to the north of Stonehenge; this linear line of mounds contained seven primary burials that housed only two royal priests and one female warrior. Similarly, at Winterbourne Stoke Roundabout, of twenty-six barrows only two royal elites and two warrior burials were found. At Winterbourne East, which is an enclosed cemetery, eleven barrows contained only one royal priest, all the others being regular burials. However, this circular earthen barrow cemetery is unique as it consists of three non-burial mounds that form a triangle. Winterbourne West's cemetery has twelve round barrows and only four or five are potential elite burials. Mounds situated further north from Stonehenge contained less prestigious grave goods. On Durrington Down, beneath the Durrington Walls henge complex, only regular burials were found in all of the barrows. In contrast, directly south of Stonehenge on Normanton Down was an area exclusively reserved for the elite—this is one of the most important Bronze Age burial cemeteries in Britain. Significantly, the ridge overlooks Stonehenge and during a restrictive time span, 1950-1500 BC, which is known as Wessex Period 3, this area became a burial zone reserved predominantly for Stonehenge's 'Masters of Ceremonies', establishing a special place for these notable people. Although many burials in the vicinity are later than Period 3, there is currently no firm evidence of burial along the Normanton Down ridge after this period. The ridge is associated with the Winter Solstice axis, linking the barrows and those entombed to rebirth, renewal and solar regeneration.

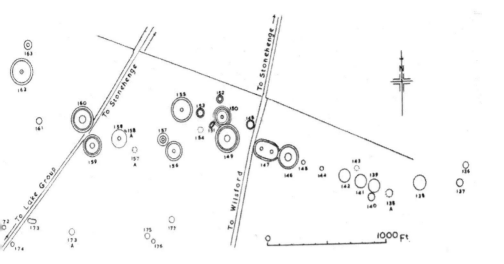

Fig. 173 Normanton Down round barrow grouping.

Revaluating the Normanton Down excavation reports, I noted that out of the thirty-five round barrows, shown in *Fig. 173*, Barrow Nos. 149-160 are unique; they are the largest mounds in the area that housed the super-rich—the royal healer-priesthood—with a direct view of Stonehenge. Further to the south, Barrow Nos. 139-148 contained individuals of warrior status, while the smaller barrows, Nos. 161, 163 and 172, held only regular Beaker burials that were mostly cremations with no exotic grave goods.

The Bush Barrow

Containing the richest burials are Colt Hoare's barrow 156 (modern numbering system Goddard (G7)), 155 (G8) and a bowl barrow 158 (G5), known as the Bush Barrow, which is 123 ft (37 m) in diameter and 11 ft (3 m) high. These were the people who oversaw the Stonehenge ceremonies, and, interestingly, there were more high-status women than men. Archaeologists such as Ann Woodward suggest these individuals "represented a dynastic succession that controlled access to Stonehenge and presided over the ceremonies therein." The Bush Barrow (G5) unearthed a skeleton of "a tall and stout man lying south to north" which implies a supine shamanic burial, although Needham argues for a flexed position. The femur bone of this man measured 20.5 in (52 cm), giving a height of 6.4 ft (1.95 m). The skeleton was found with elaborate grave goods, including a mace that was made out of a rare, flecked fossil originating in Devon, with a wooden handle with bone zig-zag decoration that survives. Mace heads are extremely unusual grave goods in southern Britain and were more common among the regalia of high-status rulers in northern regions. Alongside the skeleton were two bronze daggers with the largest blades found of that period; a third dagger had a 12 in (30 cm) long wooden hilt, originally decorated with up to 140,000 tiny gold studs forming a herringbone pattern, each of which are around 0.0079 in (0.2 mm) wide and 0.039 in (1 mm) long—over a thousand studs would have been embedded in each square centimetre. The gold is thought to have come from Ireland and the dagger was made in Brittany.

This hilt lay forgotten, having been sent to Atkinson at Cardiff University in the 1960s, and was later found in 2005. Research has shown that the design of the famous artefact known as the Bush Barrow lozenge, and that of a smaller lozenge, is based on a hexagonal construction; a similar gold lozenge was excavated from Clandon Barrow in Dorset. Remains of a knife that would have been

at least two hundred years older than the other items found has been dated to around the time of the construction of Stonehenge's trilithons. This suggests that it was a treasured antique or heirloom and was buried alongside the precious, newer items. Archibald Thom, J M D Ker and T R Burrows suggested the lozenge, shown in *Fig. 174*, was an astronomical calendar. They demonstrate that the Bush Barrow lozenge was not meant to be decorative but was intended as an aide memoire, belonging to an astronomer-priest. By fixing the flat lozenge on a table at eye level and orienting it with the shorter

Fig. 174 The gold Bush Barrow lozenge.

side on the meridian of longitude facing north, an observer could use the gold device whilst watching the Sun's centre at sunrise and/or sunset throughout the year. The authors suggested the pattern of intersection points at the ends of the zig-zag arrangement of scribed lines were intended for practical use. They calculated that the sight lines radiating outwards could have been used to fix the dates of Alexander Thom's 16 epochs in his 16-month calendar, and that the eight additional lines identified lunar standstill risings and settings. The lozenge conforms in size to instruments later used as astrolobes. However, astronomer Clive Ruggles outlines the evidence against the alignments calculated by Thom et al, given that the round barrows are of a much later construction than Stonehenge, therefore the device would not have been used in its construction as was suggested. Further evidence given by the authors against its use as a calendrical device is that initially they thought its wooden backing was flat, enabling practical use of the lozenge to the alignments, but it turns out that originally the lozenge was domed. Thus, the curved-shaped lozenge makes it unlikely to have ever been used as a calendar. Burl explains what had happened:

"In 1878, the entire collection [of Bush barrow finds kept at Stourhead House, Wiltshire] was loaned to the Wiltshire Archaeological Society... Then came the irony. In 1922 it was loaned to the British Museum for safe keeping. Despite the confidence [it would be protected as it originally was found] the lozenge suffered reconstruction even though no approval to smooth out [flatten] the object was made and no permission given. In 1984-1985 the lozenge was irreversibly restored and flattened by the British Museum."

Stonehenge's High Priestesses

Close to the Bush Barrow are two large barrows known as G7 and G8, both of which contained a high priestess. Personifying their power, both had a battle-axe bead like those from Ireland or the north of Britain. G7 is a large bell-shaped barrow measuring 102 ft (31 m) in diameter and is 10 ft (3 m) high. Within a very shallow cist the remains of a female skeleton were found, her head placed facing towards the west, which is anomalous in the region. She was buried with healer-priest items, including a grape cup incense burner of the local Wessex variety. Undoubtedly, she led mind-altering ceremonies as well as giving oracles at Stonehenge. Her medical kit consisted of two round amber beads, rare spherical-shaped jet beads, two gold beads, several pieces of jet and amber, as well as two pieces

of flat amber, one plain and the other marked with transverse lines; both were perforated and are shown at the bottom of *Fig. 175*. Nearby is barrow 156 (G8) that Colt Hoare recorded as a bell barrow, which stands 11 ft (3.3 m) high and is 92 ft (28 m) in diameter. However, today it is referred to as a bowl barrow. Alongside a cremation were found several articles of gold and deep-coloured amber, beautifully crafted gold pendants and an elaborate incense cup, also illustrated in *Fig 175*. These are characteristic of the southern coastline bordering the English Channel, linking to a maritime network that brought influences and materials from continental Europe.

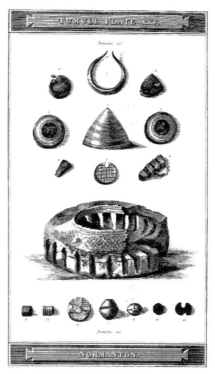

Fig. 175 Beautiful jewellery from Barrow 156 (G8).

The elegant gold cone shown above (No. 1), is similar to one found in the Golden Barrow at Upton Lovell. It is ornamented with four circular indentations, all of which were dotted with a pointed instrument, the base covered with gold plate that was indented with concentric circles. Perhaps, for special Stonehenge ceremonies, this priestess wore a horn-like pendant made of brass and covered with a thin plate of gold, which was designed to be worn with the points downwards. In her honour, I often wear an exact replica.

In a high state of preservation are two beautiful disc pendants: No. 3 is composed of deep-red amber set with gold, and No. 4 shows an unusual pendant also made of red amber, decorated with fluted stripes of gold, one of only three found in Wessex and which imitates the form of Aunjetitz halberds from Saxo-Thuringia. No. 5 is a chequered pendant of plate gold laid over a piece of polished bone, with holes for stringing on the back part. Most of these pendants are unique and have not been found anywhere else in Wessex. Many of the gold items appear to have been made by a single hand, or by a very closely knit school of craftsmen, and the pieces are not especially worn. This suggests that all the gold objects may have been made and deposited in a very short period of time, or they were carefully stored and only worn for special occasions. Nearby, in another disc barrow (G3), a further high-status cremation, probably a woman, was found alongside six shale, eleven amber and two faience beads. With fine views towards Stonehenge, these wealthy rulers were placed on the Winter Solstice axis that passes along this ridge, marking the rebirth of the year and which may have formed a spiritual solar pathway connecting them to the Sun, the gods, and to Stonehenge.

Closer inspection of these artefacts, which are now housed in the Wiltshire Heritage Museum, Devizes, suggests that these wealthy individuals may not have originated from Wessex. The orientation of the female's head position, the battle axe pendants, and the Bush Barrow man's mace, all indicate connections to the north of England—possibly to the ceremonial centre of East Riding, Yorkshire, and to the Rudstone monolith, the tallest prehistoric standing stone in Britain. This monolith is sited by a dramatic bend in what is known as the Gypsey Race, a *winterbourne* or intermittent stream that flows (mostly in winter) through the chalk landscape of East and North Yorkshire. Its unpredictable flow may have been revered in prehistory as the stream can suddenly change direction both above and below ground, as well as disappearing then reappearing; its bend became the focal point for four Neolithic cursus monuments. Not far away is Whitby Bay, the source of the jet worn by the Wessex elite, which may indicate a trade route or forged alliances.

Certainly, there is a connection with East Riding to Avebury. Pottery sherds from the West Kennet Palisade complex, close to the stone circles, have been matched to those found at Rudstone. Also, 77 pieces of grus stone, originating from either Yorkshire or Northumberland, were brought to the Palisade and placed in former postholes. Weighing around 49 lbs (22 kg) each, about the weight of a bag of cement, they were transported from the north of England, perhaps to establish a firm identity. I believe there was a deep, ongoing relationship between these two megalithic capitals and to Stonehenge.

In East Riding, the shaman or elite also adopted the extended burial position with the head placed to the west, often alongside iron pyrites for making fire, awls and elaborate incense pots (illustrated in the previous chapter, see *Figs. 160 & 161*). The jet articles discovered in the area, such as the pretty jet buttons engraved with a cross pattern and the jet rings discovered at Thwing and Rudstone, were exquisite and surpassed those found in Wiltshire in both design and workmanship. As well as short distance contacts, long distance alliances were forged. For example, the Halberd pendant found in barrow G8 indicates continental connections, and/or inter-regional marriage. An alternative explanation is that the people themselves were not outsiders but the objects symbolised their contrasting allegiances.

Fig. 176 Yorkshire Beaker pots.

The Normanton Barrows and Earth Energies

Until recently one could visit Normanton Down barrow cemetery, but it is now a nature reserve that denies public access. At a location of intense and powerful earth energies, these prestigious barrows were first surveyed by Underwood in 1954, although he did not interpret or publish his findings. At first, Underwood thought that each of the barrows was placed on a blind spring or geospiral. However, he soon realised that this was impossible and must be incorrect. I noted the barrows are connected to one another by yin and yang underground streams, and are placed above large geodetic energetic circles that are themselves said to be 'protective'. Barrow G8 that housed the gold hoard of pendants is associated with six energy circles, G7 has five and G4 disc barrow has numerous circles as well as yin/yang underground streams, whereas the Bush Barrow is sited above a 3.5 coiled geospiral (see Chapter 10, *Fig. 135*).

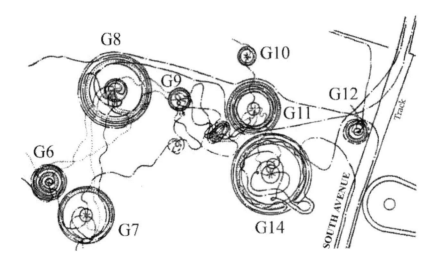

Fig. 177 The royal priesthood barrows and energy flows.

It is interesting to note that mounds containing females are located above circles of earth energy, and bell barrows (or large bowl barrows) that are placed above geospirals often house males. I have dowsed this same phenomenon at the Toltec Mounds, Arkansas, USA, also in Sardinia, France, Ireland, Scotland and Wales. In England, the royal family continued this tradition: in Westminster

Abbey, London, echoing the Pagan death rites of the ruling elite of Stonehenge, the tomb of Elizabeth of York, the wife of King Henry VII who died in 1503, was placed within protective circles of earth energy, and the tomb of King Henry V is sited above a geospiral.

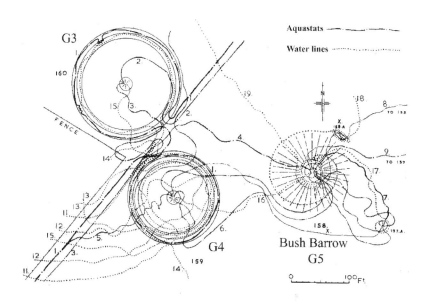

Fig. 178 Normanton Down round barrows 'protected' by energy circles.

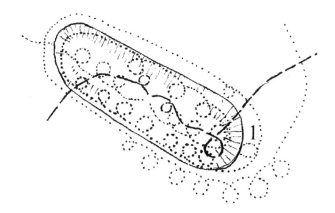

Fig 179 Normanton Long Barrow with chakra loops. Survey by Underwood, 1951.

Long Barrows and the Chakras

Two thousand years before the Stonehenge royal dynasty, the long headed people selected Normanton Down for the location of an extraordinary long barrow, known as Amesbury 14 (Colt Hoare's Barrow 165). Although containing only three burials, this barrow was placed on a rare and distinctive geospiral which Underwood called a *Culie spiral*. Along its summit are loops of energy that could suggest the barrow was used for chakra healing and/or balancing. Along the mound are two flows containing seven loops that pulse with energy, which I associate with the seven chakras (see *Fig. 179*). From starting point 1, you can walk down the left-hand side of the mound with a dowsing rod in the 'search' position—pointing straight ahead and parallel to the ground—and upon detecting the loop the rod will spin. Standing on the first loop will balance one's base chakra and this process can be repeated for the other chakras. After doing this, turn and walk down the middle of the summit and locate the seven pulse points that will gently stimulate each of the chakras, ending back at point 1 where you began. This clearing and stimulating processional walk can be a profound spiritual experience. Other long barrows, such as Wayland Smithy in Oxfordshire, have similar pulse points that gently activate or balance the chakra system. Only 328 ft (100 m) to the south of Amesbury 14 is Sun Barrow G15. Beneath this enormous bell barrow was an extended burial of a man laid to rest on an elm plank with antlers at his head and feet, denoting shamanic status.

The Normanton Shieldmaidens and Warriors

Normanton Down's ruling elite were placed in large round barrows and exotic disc barrows that roughly formed pairs. In contrast, 'warrior' barrows were arranged in a singular linear fashion and orientated roughly east-west, as shown below in *Fig. 180*. Indicative of warrior status are weaponry and regalia such as daggers, spears, javelins, knives, axes, maces, arrowheads, belt buckles and belt-hooks. Of seventeen out of twenty belt-hooks found with cremations, the age and sex of only six individuals have been determined: two known inhumations were identified as male and four cremated remains were probably males. There was also an unsexed adult with

Fig. 180 Linear line of barrows containing the Normanton warriors.

a child and an unsexed teenager. It was presumed that cremations with weaponry were men. However, although recent analysis of cremated remains shows that women were generally cremated, while men were more likely to be inhumed, women too were often buried with weaponry. I noted that at Hay Top round barrow in Monsal Dale, Derbyshire, a woman was buried alongside several flint arrowheads, jet beads and a bone pendant. At Barrow 16 on Barrow Hill, Oxfordshire, an adult female was buried alongside an awl, knife dagger and an amber, jet, faience and shale necklace. Artefacts alone cannot ascertain the gender of an individual. For instance, at Little Cressington, Norfolk, a male inhumation was found with a decorative gold plate, similar to the one found in Golden Barrow, and a beautiful amber necklace, which we have seen was part of the healer-priest's regalia for both men and women.

When 19th-century antiquarians were excavating mounds, women of this era tended to adopt conventional roles, such as housekeeping, cooking, sewing or working in the family business; these domestic occupations consequently influenced the limited view of the early antiquarian, thus their interpretation of barrow finds regarding gender. Historically, Iron Age women fought alongside men, such as Queen Boudicca and her warrior daughters, and this may have been an inherited tradition from the preceding Bronze Age. Much later, the daughter of King Alfred, Æthelflæd, Lady of the Mercians, led an army against the Danes, and after a savage battle she took Derby in AD 917. Her reputation grew and the following year she advanced on Leicester, but it surrendered without a fight. After the death of her husband, Æthelflæd ruled as queen but she was never officially given a royal title. Old Viking legends describe a shield-maiden as a warrior woman who chose to take up arms in battle and whose temper was equal to the bravest of men. Armed only with a handful of clues and a passionate heart, I went in search of Stone-henge's shieldmaidens and warriors to uncover their lost legacy.

Looking to the past, three mounds on Normanton Down held cre-mations alongside which were warrior belt-hooks: Normanton 139 contained two brass daggers, a perforated whetstone, a swan bone pipe, a belt-hook and belt buckle. A belt-hook was also found in Normanton 145 alongside a kidney-shaped black pebble; and from Normanton 147 a beautifully crafted ivory belt-hook and a small ivory lance that may well have been worn by a woman as a pendant, were interpreted as male artefacts. Yet, as we read earlier, crema-tions are invariably associated with women—were they shield-maidens? I suggest that a shieldmaiden's weaponry may have consisted of javelins, daggers and possibly what Colt Hoare de-scribed as smaller-sized axes, celts or lances heads. Situated close to Stonehenge, a documented example of a shieldmaiden's barrow is the Cursus twin barrow No. 29, where a teenage girl was buried with faience beads, amber of all shapes and sizes, a brass javelin spear and a jet belt-hook. The latter two items are associated with male warrior status, yet here we see them with a young woman.

South of Normanton Down, with Stonehenge just visible to the north, lies Wilsford Down barrow cemetery. Today, the barrows are mainly hidden in woodland; the planting of box within the wood as cover for game birds has largely obscured the barrows, especially Nos. 15 and 16. Shamefully, barrow No. 13 is so densely covered that it could not be surveyed in modern times. Colt Hoare's illustration (see *Fig. 181*) shows eighteen barrows of which fourteen survive as earthworks; some of the grave goods are associated with the Early Bronze Age, and some of the smaller barrows may be of a later date.

Six mounds had been previously opened but the contents were unrecorded, five or six housed regular burials, two or three were healer-priests, and there were five impressive warrior status burials.

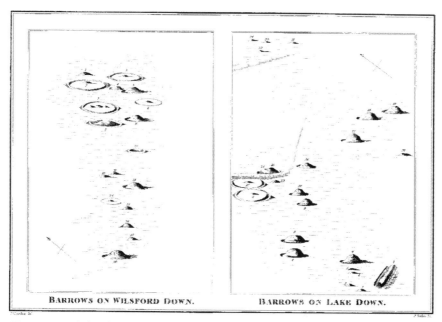

Fig. 181 Wilsford and Lake Down Bronze Age cemeteries.

Wilsford G71 (Colt Hoare's Wilsford 2) is a large disc barrow that held a primary cremation alongside a brass dagger and a bronze awl. As previously stated, Woodward points out that women are mainly associated with awls—is this another forgotten warrior woman? In Wilsford G60 (Colt Hoare's Wilsford 16), a secondary cremation was inserted into the mound alongside antler pieces, two whetstones, two arrowheads, a small bronze dagger and a flint knife, illustrated in *Fig. 182*. This may be a contender for a shamanic shieldmaiden. It could be argued that Wilsford G64 (Colt Hoare's Wilsford 9), also contained a shieldmaiden. This bowl barrow contained a primary cremation with a bone awl or pin, a small bronze flanged axe, and a bone belt ring. The cist was covered by a flint cairn, on top of which was laid a dog inhumation that may have been a pet or a hunting dog. All of these artefacts with the exception of the ring are in the Wiltshire Heritage Museum, Devizes.

In the Early- to Mid-Bronze Age, axes may have been a woman's choice of weaponry; we saw earlier that battle-axe beads from Normanton barrows G7 and G8 were found alongside high-status females. Burl associates axes with a goddess cult. In Irish mythology, the Morrígan, also known as Morrígu, is a goddess of war and fate who foretells doom, death, or victory in battle. In her role as a warrior queen, she often shape-shifts and appears as a raven or crow, inciting warriors to battle. The Morrígan encourages warriors to do brave deeds, strikes fear into their enemies, and can also help bring about victory. Perhaps this goddess of war originates from the heroic Bronze Age shieldmaidens?

Fig. 182 Artefacts found in Wilsford barrows.

Fig. 183 Large bronze blade and artefacts found in the barrow of "a very tall and stout man".

Male Warriors

Burial assemblages suggest that Wilsford Down was a mixed sex warrior cemetery. Wilsford G65 (Colt Hoare's Wilsford 5), is a flat bowl barrow; on the floor by the side of a circular cist, a simple cremation was placed within a beautiful urn. Nearby was another oval cist containing a cremation alongside a large brass spear head, which appeared to have been almost melted in the heat of the pyre. This may have been a male burial, and the food vessel and dagger are both in Devizes Museum. Wilsford G58 (Colt Hoare's Wilsford 18), is a large bell barrow that contained a primary inhumation of "a very tall and stout man" buried with a flanged axe, a massive hammer of dark stone, a perforated battle-axe, bone haft, grooved whetstone, bone tube, a large boar's tusk, and what was once suggested to be a bronze cauldron handle, but is more likely to have been used as an ox goad with hanging chain (see *Fig 183*).

Further south is the Lake Group of barrows that began with a Neolithic long barrow and developed into a vast Bronze Age cemetery, consisting of twenty-four round barrows. The large bowl or bell barrows, Nos. 7, 8, 16, 17 and 18, are associated with warrior burials and several may have been shieldmaidens. No. 7 is a well constructed large barrow that held a primary cremation alongside which was a bronze awl, bronze dagger, a bone bead, and a large, red-stained stone bead; once again, an awl may indicate a woman who was buried with weaponry. If we are looking for other shieldmaidens, Nos. 16, 17 and 18 each held a cremation with a "small lance-head of brass" (or dagger). No. 8 is known as the 'Prophet Barrow' that apparently acquired its name in the early-18th century after French prophets set up their standard on it and preached to the local people. It may have been constructed for a male burial as next to a cremation was a wooden box in a long cist measuring 8.5 x 2 ft (2.59 x 0.60 m), with a large, grooved dagger and a perforated whetstone—a shamanic item used as a cutting block or palette. In total there are six elite priest/ess healers, two of which have been previously discussed: Barrow No. 20 held the Stonehenge runes, alongside which there was also a small lance; and Barrow No. 21 housed an exceptionally large amber breast plate, belonging to a high priestess.

Other priest/ess-healer barrows are No. 2 where a beautifully perforated incense burner was found next to a cremation; No. 5 held a cremation alongside 20-30 polished jet beads; and No. 24 may have been an extended shaman's burial beside some large stag tines. There were also four regular burials, whilst barrows 1, 3, 4, 11, 12,

14, 21 and 22 had been previously opened. One unusual barrow that stands out is Barrow No. 10, which was constructed for a dog and the head of a deer. Similar deposits were repeated at Winterbourne Stoke Down at Barrow 25, where a human skeleton and a secondary cremation were buried with shamanic items, deer bones and several dogs. In ancient cultures, dogs, wolves and jackals were often associated with the Underworld, such as the Egyptian Anubis and the Greek Cerberus. In Mesoamerica, a common belief is that a dog carries the newly deceased across a body of water in the afterlife. Large black dogs are said to be the guardians of ley lines, and Australian aboriginals call the guardian of song lines 'Boss Dog'. Perhaps the ancients placed a dog in the barrow to guard all those who were laid to rest at Lake, Wilsford and Winterbourne Stoke.

Masters of Ceremony: Regalia and Style

Colt Hoare and Cunnington took away rich and lavish grave goods, but they did replace the skeletal remains and cremations. When visiting the ancestors' mounds, I sensed their loss and so I photocopied the artefacts that Colt Hoare's companion drew, and I lovingly returned these items to their rightful barrows by placing the recycled paper inside mole hills or natural holes. I feel that they still guard Stonehenge far more than the security guards who are paid to do so. To reawaken their beauty and style in their memory, I want to show you just how majestic-looking these people were. Archaeologists invariably portray prehistoric men and woman, such as the famous Amesbury archer, with bare legs wearing a knee length cream and brown tunic and carrying a basket or a bow and quiver. This image, shown in Fig. 184, is quite inaccurate.

Fig. 184 The Amesbury Archer.

The fabrics and styles of Bronze Age clothing were, perhaps, surprisingly sophisticated and some garments appear modern-looking. Remnants of Bronze Age fabric show that linen was made with threads as thin as a coarse human hair, some were 100 microns (1/10 mm) in diameter. Other fabrics were so finely woven, with a thread count of 28 threads per centimetre, fine even by modern standards. Textile remains were found at Must Farm, Whittlesey, in Cambridgeshire—a place often described as Britain's equivalent to Pompeii—where a Bronze Age village was suddenly abandoned after a fire. People fled, leaving behind their belongings, meals half-eaten, salted and dried meats still hanging from the rafters, and garments neatly folded, some of which were perfectly preserved in peat. This was once a prosperous community and the houses that survived at Must Farm have allowed archaeologists to examine its structure, artefacts, ceramics and textiles. The archaeological team at the University of Cambridge have unearthed unspun fibre and yarn, and hundreds if not thousands of flax seeds—commonly used to make linen—some of which had been stored in containers. The presence of unspun processed fibre, yarn and finished textiles, as well as these seeds, strongly suggest that the village was involved not only in using and wearing textiles but in manufacturing them, perhaps for other communities also. They are among the finest Bronze Age samples found in Europe.

So far, no evidence of any extensive patterns or coloured dyes have been found on any of the linens, although the edge of one piece of fabric, perhaps a cowl or cape, seems to have been decorated with fringes, rows of knots and stripes featuring different styles of weave. One method of altering the colour of the natural light brown linen would have been to bleach it in a mixture of urine and milk to achieve a creamy colour or even a dazzling white, or by simply laying out the fabrics on wet grass on a succession of sunny days. Linen would have been the most common fabric used to make numerous garments and domestic items, including drapes for beds and wall hangings. A glamorous fabric discovered at Must Farm was made from nettle fibre, which I suggest was reserved for the priesthood. In traditional folklore, various types of nettles were regarded as having magical powers, able to protect both humans and animals from sorcery and witchcraft. What's more, garments made of nettles were believed to protect the wearer from negativity and evil. Indeed, one of Europe's most famous fairy tales, *Wild Swans*, written by Hans Christian Andersen, whose tales are thought to be based on traditional folk stories, reveals how shirts made of nettle yarn enabled their wearers to break a witch's spell. Nettle yarn may well have had additional benefits in the eyes of those who used such fabric, such as aiding their magical arts.

Archaeologists at Must Farm noted that the Bronze Age fabric weavers and designers processed nettle stems from a locally available non-stinging subspecies, known today as fen nettles. The extracted fibres are white in colour and are fine, long and very strong, measuring up to 1.9 in (50 mm) in length. The fibres are silken-like and hollow, which means they have insulating properties due to the air being trapped inside, so fabric created with nettle fibre will keep its warmth but will also be breathable. Additionally, its dye does not stick to the fibres and when blended with dyed wool, the yarn takes on a slightly mottled appearance which creates an interesting fabric. Nettle fibres have been labelled the material of the future, being ecologically friendly, sustainable and a good alternative to synthetic materials. Here is one instance where we can learn from the past.

Fig. 185 A high priestess with regalia. *Illustration:* Fiona Hughes.

For the Ancestors

Let us step back in time to 1950-1750 BC and see the splendour of the priesthood in their finery. They probably wore clothing made from white nettle textiles that was silky and stylish, with contrasting jet or gold buttons, a large amber spacer plate necklace and gold jewellery, and had golden hair tresses. We know these people were probably tattooed, perhaps with motifs revealing knowledge of healing earth energy patterns, or with chevrons, Sun and Moon and other symbols that we can only begin to imagine. Individual members of the priesthood carried a medicine bag and walked with swaying incense burners that released exotic smells and intoxicating substances; no doubt they delivered oracles and healing above the geospiral energy centre at the heart of Stonehenge.

Male high priests and warriors were frequently described as "tall and stout men" by Colt Hoare, which has led some authors to call them giants. They too probably wore white nettle fabric robes, perhaps as a toga-style garment. Some of the fabrics found at Must Farm were of a very substantial size; we know this because they had been folded, in some cases numerous times, up to ten layers. If intended to be worn, such garments may well have been designed as large capes or cloaks, not unlike those in the ancient world known as the Greek chiton, Roman toga and Indian sari. Alternatively, in some parts of Europe, men wore trousers, tunic tops and cloaks. At Stonehenge, a high priest would also wear an amber or jet necklace, or gold plate such as that found at Upton Lovell, a belt with ornate jet or ivory belt hooks and gold trusses in the hair. Green coloured bracers studded

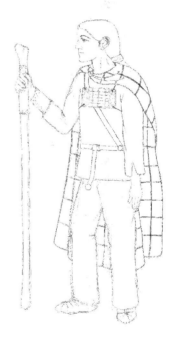

Fig 186 Bronze Age high priest with regalia. *Illustration:* Fiona Hughes.

with gold adorned one or both outer forearms, and a tall wooden staff was often also decorated with a gold-studded green bracer. We can imagine that at Midwinter ceremonies they would have worn thick woollen capes, fastened with jewelled pins or gold buckles, similar to those that have been unearthed. The Stonehenge high priest and priestess had both style and presence. Shieldmaidens and warriors, like the priesthood, were probably tattooed. They wore leather or linen trousers and tops with leather or woollen jackets fastened with ivory, gold or jet buttons, or brass pins. Numerous

examples have been unearthed in warrior status barrows. Leather belts were fastened with carved ivory or jet belt-hooks, fasteners to which were attached a leather dagger sheath. Skilfully crafted, their daggers were embossed with gold or brass studs, and some warriors carried spears or javelins. Certainly, they had swagger.

Evidence shows that Bronze Age adolescent girls wore outfits not unlike modern-day teenagers, such as short skirts, crop tops and jewellery, as shown in *Fig. 188* which is historically accurate. The design of the mini skirt is often credited to Mary Quant in the 'Swinging Sixties', while some point to Frenchman

Fig. 187 A Stonehenge shieldmaiden. *Illustration:* Fiona Hughes.

André Courrèges, but archaeologists say the origin of the mini goes back more than 7,500 years. A series of stone figurines that capture prehistoric fashion were unearthed at one of Europe's oldest known villages, a community that nestled between rivers, mountains and forests in what is now southern Siberia.

"According to the figurines we found, young women were beautifully dressed, like today's girls in short tops and miniskirts and wore bracelets around their arms,"

said archaeologist Julka Kuzmanovic-Cvetkovic. The Vinca civilisation that made the figurines flourished between 5500-4000 BC in Bosnia, Serbia, Romania and Macedonia. In all probability, a similar fashion may have been worn at Stonehenge.

At Must Farm the ancients also made fabric from lime bast. Could the symbolism and meaning of lime hold a clue to how the fabric was used? I think so. The heart-shaped lime leaf is associated with the heart, love and fidelity. The lime is a feminine tree of love, that often plays a key role in myths, fairy tales and appears in old customs. In the legend of Philemon and Baucis, the couple are turned into an oak and a lime tree respectively, symbolising their great love for one another. The lime tree is also associated with Freya, the Scandinavian goddess of love; and with Frigga, the goddess of medicine who protects marriage and binds faithful lovers together. In Greek mythology, the mother of the centaur Chiron, who taught medicine to mortals, was called Philyra,

Fig. 188 Bronze Age teenager in mini skirt and crop top.

which means lime tree in Greek. This tree, the bark of which was used to weave textiles and to make rope, is one that ties and binds, linking together individuals and communities. Perhaps lime fabric was woven as a marriage or partnership textile or worn by couples to symbolise their commitment and love for one another. It may have been worn by a proto-Druid judge, as the lime tree is also associated with justice. The components of its bark, sapwood, leaves and flowers are used in many medicines, making the lime especially valuable. Its hidden meanings lie in stones, trees and flowers.

Although I am speculating here, in trying to reach back in time to understand the lives of our ancestors, there is some indication of prehistoric fabric dying having taken place on a grand scale. If the combination of what were known as the 'ancient three': madder (red), weld (bright yellow), and woad (blue) were used, then it is possible to produce an almost complete range of colours. Ringing in a new era, the stylish Stonehenge priesthood transformed past traditions and created a new way of entering the stone circle—they did it their way.

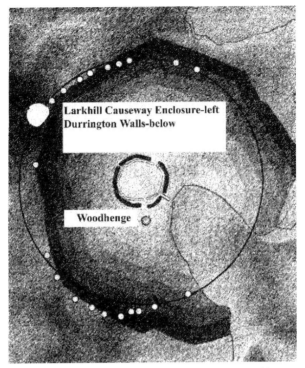

Fig. 189 Large pits encircled Durrington Walls,
constructed by the round headed Beaker people.

Entering Stonehenge

Prior to the Normanton dynasty, according to both Pitts and Parker
Pearson, during the second half of the third millennium BC, at ceremonial times of the year, people began their journey to Stonehenge
from Durrington Walls. This was a superhenge, 1,600 ft (487 m) in
diameter, that once accommodated over one thousand houses. It
was probably constructed by the round headed culture to make a
visual impact on the landscape, and to display their power and
authority. On the inside of the henge ditch there were over 300
wooden posts with two inner timber circles, timber temples and
enclosed areas. The same distance that the Heel Stone is from
Stonehenge, a large timber outlier was placed outside of Durrington
and orientated, as was the short-paved avenue, to the Summer
Solstice Sunset. Forming an intimate relationship, the two monuments mirror each other. At a later date, a massive circle of deep pits
was dug by the round headed Beaker people, encircling Durrington

(see *Fig 189*). At Durrington Walls people walked down its short avenue and boarded boats to sail along the River Avon to West Amesbury's henge, where they disembarked to walk the 1.5 miles (2.4 km) along the Stonehenge Avenue(s) to the northeast entrance, from where they would enter the monument. This processional route was used for nearly a thousand years.

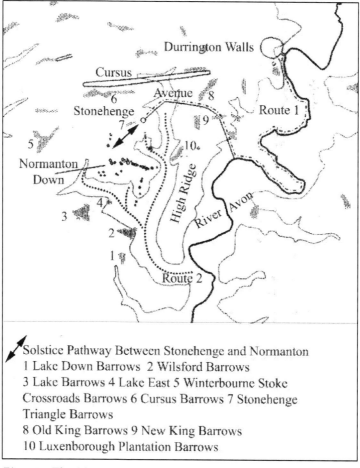

Fig. 190 The Normanton dynasty's new route to Stonehenge.

Significant changes occurred at the beginning of the second millennium BC. The Normanton dynasty transformed the way Stonehenge was entered and fashioned a new way, creating a tactical switch from the relationship between Stonehenge and Durrington Walls to one between Stonehenge and Normanton Down—their land. To establish a new authority over Stonehenge, I suggest an avenue was either constructed or extended that led to the southern entrance. This was not an arbitrary placement as it courses towards barrows G11, G14 and G8, dividing the Normanton barrows into two groups: the ruling elite and the warriors. Strategically, the Normanton ridge has visual surveillance of Stonehenge with an overview of the passages along the valley routes. A route that archaeologists say led from the River Avon along the dry valley, and I suggest onto my proposed southern avenue, is shown as Route 2 in *Fig 190*. Route 1 is the earlier Durrington Walls to Stonehenge processional route.

Fig. 191 The new entrance to Stonehenge c1950-1790 BC.

Originally, the southern entrance led to stone Nos. 10 and 11 of the lintelled stone circle and into its inner realms. The Normanton elite rejected this established approach. I suggest they were responsible for breaking Stone 11, which is why it is much shorter compared to the other outer stones, and deliberately damaged the stone circle to create a new and novel entrance (*Fig. 191*). Beside entrance stones 10 and 11 are the fallen stones 8 and 9. Parker Pearson points out that these stones are recumbent because of an intentional act of toppling from the inside of the circle so they would fall outwards. Walking through the fallen stones creates an avenue-like approach, leading to the gap between Trilithons 51-52 and 53-54 and on to the Altar Stones. However, by doing this a magical element of Stonehenge was lost. There are only thirty concentric stone circles in the British Isles, meaning they commonly have two rings of stones; Stonehenge, ever the maverick had three, two of which still existed in 1950 BC. Circles generate an energy called *form energy*, whether this is an occultist's circle of salt or a stone circle that can aid manifestation is an ancient occult lore. A circle can emit seven etheric circles that radiate towards its centre. Stonehenge's form energy was the most powerful ever created, as it emitted twenty-one of these form circles; it is tempting to think that ghostly images of the healing Sun god and oracle Moon goddess once manifested. Showing a lack of re-spect for the outer circle and the long headed geomancers that constructed it, the Normanton rulers were conveying a new dynastic

authority over Stonehenge. It was officially theirs, and, as previously stated, they altered the inner features of Stonehenge by uprooting one of the concentric bluestone circles and its small avenue, to create an oval, and later a bluestone horseshoe by removing some of the stones. Finally, the Y and Z holes were constructed during the Middle Bronze Age 1680-1520 BC and certain stones were carved with daggers and axe heads,

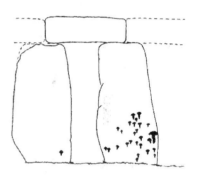

Fig. 192 Stone No. 4 carved with axe blade symbols.

as shown in *Fig. 192*. Stonehenge had been changed forever. Adding wonderment to their new approach, as the 'Masters of Ceremonies' walked from Normanton Down, they would have witnessed a spec-tacular Midsummer mirage that undeniably added to Stonehenge's sacrosanctity—perhaps predicted to their attendees. On very hot days when walking from the dry valley near Normanton Down, just as Stonehenge comes into view an optical illusion can be seen: the stones of the monument appear to dance off the ground in the shim-mering hot air. This could be the origin of 'The Giant's Dance' at Stonehenge. Certainly, it would be an amazing sight to see!

Chapter 13

Round Headed Cranial Deformation

In prehistoric times, cranial deformation was common. Just as the preceding long headed culture, the round headed elite also practiced cranial deformation to accentuate the roundness of their skulls. This has been referred to as parieto-occipital flatness—making the back of the head appear flatter and, in some instances, the head rounder and more elevated. This should not be confused with plagiocephaly without synostosis (PWS), which is infant cranial deformation due to a constant supine sleep position. That said, from the North of England, several skull examples show a distinctive asymmetry of the parieto-occipital region, an area shown in *Fig. 193*, produced by one-sided carriage during infancy, as shown in *Fig. 194*.

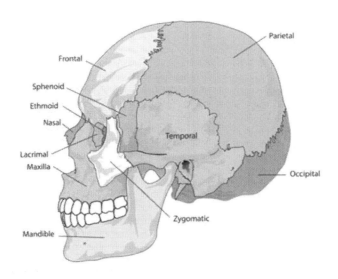

Fig. 193 Skull showing the parieto-occipital region.

An examination of 146 prehistoric skulls revealed that cranial deformation performed in infancy was commonly more marked on one side, with increased flattening towards the back of the head (the occiput) and a flattening of the forehead (frontal region), whilst the side of the head (peripheral parts of the spheroid) bulged out. Additionally, several skulls show prominent superciliary ridges: for instance, one male from a mound on Hitter Hill in Derbyshire. For clarity, these areas of the skull are shown in *Fig. 193*.

The authors of *Ages of the Giants: A Cultural History of the Tall Ones in Prehistoric America* (2017), Jason Jarrell and Sarah Farmer, noted the Adena of North America likewise practiced a form of cranial deformation. Some skulls exhibited a similar flattening of the occipital and frontal regions, known as fronto-occipital modification, which

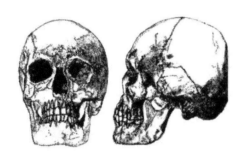

can result in a heavy superciliary ridge and protruding, wide jaws. Elsewhere, other Native American skulls exhibiting fronto-occipital deformation were excavated from the Humber Site in Mississippi, and belonged to the Late-Mississippian period, roughly AD 1400.

Fig 194 Male skull with signs of one-sided carriage distortion.

This is comparable to the British Bronze Age elite that underwent cranial manipulation. Interestingly, both cultures were tall, strong and muscular, in England averaging 6-7 ft (1.8-2.1 m) in height, and 7-8 ft (2.1-2.4 m) in America. Whilst excavating Bronze Age round barrows, Colt Hoare constantly remarked that he had unearthed, "a very tall and stout man".

I have researched numerous instances involving babies, small children, teenagers, adult men and women, all of whom bear the distinctive signs of Bronze Age artificial cranial deformation. These individuals were often found to be buried in close proximity to the stone circles they probably ruled over, such as Avebury, Arbour

Low in Derbyshire, the East Riding complex in Yorkshire, and in Staffordshire, as well as in Ireland, Scotland and Orkney.

Thanks largely to the research of authors such as Brien Foerster, the Peruvian cone-shaped skull is well known. Cranial deformation practiced throughout the British Isles did not produce the large, pointed head shape of Paracas fame. However, as we shall soon see, there are exceptions such as the 'cone headed king of Avebury' whose reign was long. Interestingly, coinciding with the decline of the long headed and the rise of the round headed cultures, I found an unusual burial site from this transitional period containing numerous examples of cranial deformation that produced a hybrid type of skull.

The Avebury Hybrid Skulls

Not far from Avebury was an exceptionally large long barrow known as Mill Barrow. An excavation by Alasdair Whittle in 1989 unearthed a unique feature of double ditches on either side of the mound. Postholes and pits containing human remains appeared to pre-date the mound, and several pieces of human bone and antler produced radiocarbon dates from the late-4th millennium BC. Close by were ten or so large sarsen stone blocks

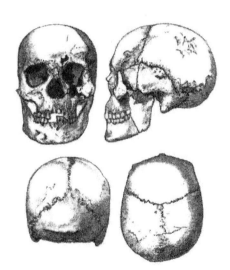

Fig. 195 Exceptionally round shaped skull that is flatter at the back. Cranial deformation of a tall man.

sited to the north and south of the old road, between Monkton and Yatesbury. When these were removed during the 19th century, four circular burial cists were discovered; one was neatly paved with small sarsen stones and a skeleton found placed in a sitting position, not unlike a burial from Parcelly Hay barrow in Derbyshire, shown in *Fig. 196*. This cairn is similar to the Avebury cist.

Fig. 196 Parcelly Hay stone cairn.

From numbers one and two of the Avebury cists, twenty-seven skeletons were found, and one-third had mesocephalic shaped skulls—a head of medium proportions, neither round nor long. In Cist 1 there were six skeletons: two males of about thirty years old, two or three teenagers aged twelve to seventeen, and a five-year-old child. Cist 2 contained around twenty-two skeletons.

The majority of the skulls, including those of all the small children, had a narrow depression that crossed the skull immediately behind the coronal suture. According to anthropologists, these markings were the result of cranial deformation:

> "The existence of a coronal depression in so large a series of skulls as that from Monkton, is perhaps most easily reconciled with the idea of its artificial production."

The markings resulted from covering the head with a long bandage that was carried under the jaw, by which the coronal region and sides of the skull were constricted and compressed. Possibly, these were the lesser-long headed that were ensuring their skulls appeared rounder. This burial is unusual, as in this era a single burial (normally a round headed person), was placed into a chalk cist before a round mound was constructed above it. Later, secondary burials, invariably cremations, were inserted into the mound. Yet here we have a hybrid type of skull in an unusual stone cist marked by a large sarsen stone, which is unprecedented. Perhaps there are more of these hybrid cist burials waiting to be found?

Fig. 197 Avebury's southeast entrance, constructed by the round headed Beaker culture c2400 BC.

Avebury's Cone Headed High King

During the Beaker period, head binding was common amongst the round headed elite, producing foreheads that appeared more elevated, the top of the head more pointed and the back of the head flatter. Just like the preceding civilisation that lengthened their heads, this culture made them distinguishable from the general population—their heads were rounder and more regal looking. Although the round barrows surrounding Avebury did not contain the rich gold artefacts found at Stonehenge, they did house the tall Beaker elite. One of the finest examples of cranial deformation can be found 5 miles (8 km) from Avebury's stone circles. Unfortunately, the barrow no longer exists but an excavation report does. It tells us that in the chalk bedrock there was an exceptionally smooth oblong cist 5 ft (1.52 m) long by 2.5 ft (0.76 m) wide; inside was a male skeleton in the flexed position, lying on his left side with the head towards the north. Grave goods found included a small flint arrowhead next to his skull, and a highly ornamented beaker containing loose chalk was placed by his feet. Near his left hand was a large 10 in (25 cm) long bronze dagger with a neatly bevelled edge, and between the bones of the left forearm an oblong green coloured bracer 4 in (10 cm) long and nearly 2 in (5 cm) wide, pierced with two holes at each end. This single bracer suggests it adorned a staff, and undoubtedly this man was once a High King or 'Master of Ceremonies' at Avebury. His grave and skeleton, with some of his burial goods are illustrated below, in *Fig. 198*.

Fig. 198 The grave of Avebury's High King:
"a very stout and tall man".

This man lived to be 70-80 years old and his reign at Avebury was undoubtedly long. His thigh bone, measuring 20.5 in (52.07 cm) and described as being "strong and massive", indicates a stature of over 6 ft (1.82 m) tall. He was clearly a robust man, his head appearing exceptionally round and pointed, but narrow from behind. Cranial deformation gave him an extremely elevated forehead, particularly in the centre, giving his skull a conical appearance. I can imagine him standing within Avebury's stone circles dressed in his finery, wearing silky clothing, regally holding his adorned staff of office. He has laid forgotten for 4,500 years, lost to time, but now his story can be told.

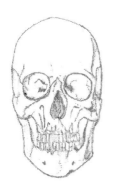

Fig. 199 Morgan's Hill: "a tall and stout man" underwent cranial deformation.

Nearby on Morgan's Hill, another 70-year-old, "a tall and stout man", underwent cranial deformation. His skull was exceptionally oval with a considerable depression in front of the coronal and lambdoidal sutures, showing that bandaging or boarding of the skull had occurred during childhood. His forehead would have looked very narrow although full and high, and the side and back of the skull appeared expanded. Shown in *Fig 199*, he would have been noble-looking to his peers.

Fig. 200 The Sanctuary on Overton Hill.

Not far from Avebury, near Marlborough, is the Manton Round Barrow, where a high-status priestess-healer was laid to rest with a bronze knife or dagger with an amber pommel, a small dagger blade for cutting herbs, 150 shale beads, some amber beads, a gold-bound amber disc, a gold-bound shale bead, a rare gold Halberd pendant, some bronze awls and two incense cups. I suspect her skull may have been manipulated to display her regal status as a high queen or priestess of Avebury, and she too had a long life.

The Avebury Priestly Caste
Near Avebury, opposite the Sanctuary on Overton Hill, is a round barrow cemetery that contained members of the Avebury priesthood. Colt Hoare noted ten barrows, but today only a handful survive. Six barrows contained cremations, two with incense burners and a small knife for chopping herbs—the tell-tale signs of a healer-priest. One barrow grouping was exceptional: three bell barrows were enclosed in an hourglass shape that held a healer-priest. Unusually, one of these barrows contained a lesser-long headed male who was laid to rest with white and green glass beads

alongside long pieces of amber, possibly from a breastplate or necklace. Another mound contained a male in the flexed position with the marks of cranial deformation, alongside a lance, a long pin and a celt. Described as being "tall and stout" with an estimated height of 6 ft 4 in (1.95 m), his skull is illustrated below, in *Fig. 201*.

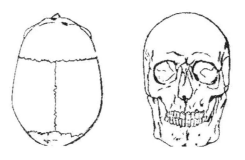

Fig. 201 Overton Down male displaying cranial deformation: "a tall and stout man".

Close to the end of the Beckhampton Stone Avenue were once nine barrows, one of which contained two jet rings, undoubtedly a priestly burial. Overlooking Avebury, other healer-priests were buried on Avebury Down as some barrows contained pieces of copper and jet. Others were buried inside of Windmill Hill's causewayed enclosure, where there is a group of four barrows—one of these mounds may have borne the windmill which gave the hill its name. Either or both Winterbourne Monkton 1 and 2 (a large bell barrow and nearby bowl barrow) were excavated before 1849, yielding seven skeletons, perhaps Saxon secondary interments. A grape cup incense burner and a stone battle axe were unearthed, hinting at priestly status. I also found a cranial deformation at Codford, some 10 miles (16 km) from Stonehenge, where yet another skull was exceptionally round. Throughout Britain, my research has shown that during the Bronze Age cranial deformation was commonplace.

Royalty and Arbor Low Stone Circle
Arbor Low is a recumbent stone circle in Derbyshire, known as the 'Stonehenge of the North' that still appears grandiose and has spectacular views and energy. Containing around 46 white limestone

blocks, it encircles an earlier cove feature. Nearby, south of Long Rake (SK1541 6383), a round barrow, now ploughed out, contained

a 40-year-old woman with a small, four-year-old child. Around her neck was one of the most elaborate necklaces ever discovered in Britain. It consisted of 420 beautifully crafted jet pieces, some of which were ornamented with puncture patterns. Cranial deformation had given her skull several distinctive features: a more elevated and rounder skull and a large, expanded forehead that passed upwards into an arch shape on top of the skull. Described as being beautiful and feminine looking, the sides of her skull bulged outwards and descended rather suddenly towards the

Fig. 202 Jet necklace of the high priestess of Arbor Low.

occiput (back of the head). Buried in such close proximity to the stone circle suggests she may have been a high queen or priestess of ceremonies, who sadly died in the prime of her life.

Five miles (8 km) from Arbor Low, is Hitter Hill Barrow, its elevated position offering outstanding views across the upper Dove valley.

Fig. 203 Arbor Low stone circle, Derbyshire.
Photograph: John Harris, dowser.

Excavations in 1862 revealed a primary burial of a 70-year-old man whose skull also showed signs of cranial deformation. Another Derbyshire woman's skull from a round barrow on Hay Top, in Monsal Dale, likewise displayed the distinctive bandage and boarding cranial markings. The barrow covered several cists, one of which held a flexed male skeleton and, unusually, two female skulls with no lower jaw or skeleton. Called 181Ta and b, they are believed to have been the servants of the male who were sacrificed when he died. I disagree, as skull 181Tb shows extensive cranial deformation, slightly inclined on the

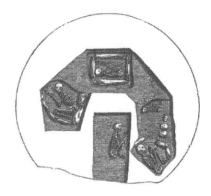

Fig. 204 Monsal Dale, Derbyshire: cranial deformation burials.

right side making the skull exceedingly round and indicating elite status. None of the other skulls showed signs of cranial manipulation. However, in the north-eastern cist, a 60-year-old male skeleton with a large skull was "of considerable stature". His femur bone measured 18¾ in (48 cm), giving an approximate height of nearly 6 ft (1.83 m). These burials are shown above, in *Fig. 204.*

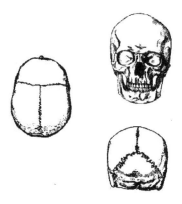

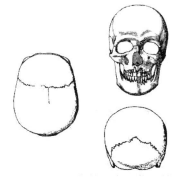

Fig. 205 Middleton Wold, near Arbor Low: male skull showing lightly one-sided cranial deformation.

Fig. 206 Hay Top Barrow, Derbyshire: male skull showing perfect cranial deformation.

Fig. 207 Nine Stone Close stone circle. *Photograph:* John Harris, dowser.

The Wetton Shaman

Nine Stone Close stone circle, near Middleton-by-Youlgrave, contains the tallest megaliths in Derbyshire. Only 2 miles (3.2 km) away, an 18-year-old woman was found in a barrow on Smerrill Moor. Her small, contoured skull was very elevated, and the back of her head flat due to artificial compression. From a round barrow in Bostorn, near Dovedale, yet another skull displayed the tell-tale signs of cranial deformation, showing the practice was widespread. Just across the border in Wetton Hill Barrow, Wetton, Staffordshire, a male had an unusually high and elevated cone-like skull due to intense cranial manipulation. Close by, a similar skull with coronal depressions was found, alongside a stag tine and an incense burner, indicating priestly status. The largest barrow at Three Lows, near Wetton, was reserved for an important shaman. When it was opened in June 1845, what were described as numerous red deer horns, stag tines, large pieces of stag horn and spear heads, along with a crema-tion were found. The unusual amount of stags' tines, the largest number found in Staffordshire, makes this burial remarkable.

The practice of making the skull appear rounder and flatter at the back was commonplace across Bronze Age Britain, and there are several examples from Scotland. A male burial in Newbigging, Orkney, an unsexed skull from Juniper Green, near Edinburgh, and a male skull from Lesmurdie in Moray, all had the distinctive markings of cranial deformation. They did, however, appear to lack symmetry as there was a bulging to one side. Other examples showed more sophistication, creating a similar look to those skulls previously mentioned.

Childhood Cranial Deformation

There are also several examples of childhood cranial deformation. From a barrow on the edge of Salisbury Plain, near Collingbourne Ducis, a three-year-old child showed exceptional flattening of the occiput. In Derbyshire, the skull of a four to five-year-old from End Low Barrow, as well as young children from Green Low Barrow and Galley Low Barrow, all displayed signs of cranial manipulation. On Ballard Down, the Isle of Purbeck, in Dorset, the skull of a fourteen-year-old boy revealed the tell-tale signs of cranial flattening. It was noted that he bore the marks of artificial flattening of the occiput. This calls to mind the artificial lateral flattening of the skull, characteristic of the ancient people called Macrocephali or Long Heads, of whom Hippocrates tells us:

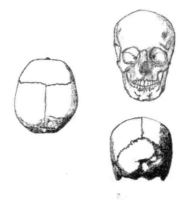

Fig. 208 Skull of a teenage boy from Ballard Down, Dorset, showing cranial deformation.

> "…while the head of the child is still tender, they fashion it with their hands, and constrain it to assume a lengthened shape by applying bandages and other suitable contrivances, whereby the spherical form of the head is destroyed, and it is made to increase in length."

Evidence shows that the practice of cranial deformation extended well into the Iron Age. Interestingly, two male skulls from barrows in Acklam Wold, East Riding, and an Iron Age skull from the area of East Yorkshire that became known as Arras—a culture that adopted the unusual practice of burying its dead in square, rather than round mounds—as well as a male skull from End Low, near Harlington, in Derbyshire, were very similar to the skulls of Africans, which may imply the interconnectedness of people from distant lands coming to the British Isles.

From Roundway Hill, near Avebury, the skull of a 50-year-old man that showed the marks of cranial deformation was buried with thirty pieces of ivory, rather like children's marbles cut into two. These may have been used as counters in a game resembling draughts or backgammon. *The Dictionary of Greek and Roman Antiquities* states that the ancients, "played with two sets of latrunculi or draughts-men, having fifteen pieces on each side." The decayed wood found with them could have been the remains of the board on which the game was played. Another set of twenty-eight convex bone objects that were ornamented with dots or dots within circles, was un-earthed from a barrow in Derbyshire.

Never Leave Me: Powerful Women Revered

Female bones were associated with fertility and rebirth, and from 1950 BC the practice of cremation became more widespread. Exam-ination of remains reveal, as mentioned, that cremations were pre-dominately women, while men were more likely to be inhumed. Placed within or beside a pottery vessel, cremation remains were not always those of the entire body, but small deposits known as *token burials*. There is evidence of the reopening, in the Early Bronze Age, of a mound's internal grave and the removal of certain bones that were to be used, it is presumed, as ancestral relics. On Crichel Down, in Dorset, a mound was reopened and the skull removed soon after deposition. The cremation bones of women were commonly subject to this same process. All of the skull bones were missing from a cremation contained within Barrow VI at West Heath, Harting, in Sussex, and the pelvis bone was absent in another female cremation. Pollen analysis found that an adult woman's bones were moved around the landscape for many years; it seems that the bones of certain females were being circulated or retained by their families or communities—cremation makes it easier to possess and transport fragments of a person, for whatever reason.

Research has shown that some indigenous societies have different ways of thinking about oneself than we do today, and that a sense of self is not always located within the boundaries of the human body but in relation to, and part of, other significant people, places and things over the course of a lifetime—*a dividual* within and beyond the body, as opposed to 'an individual'. It has been suggested that the circulation of fragments of human bone indicate the development of the concept of self. Parts of women's bodies were curated and may have circulated as dividual elements of exchange; the fragmentation process may have symbolised death, fertility, and a new life. Archaeologist and lecturer, Lisa Brown, noticed the theme of death and rebirth occurring in Bronze Age ceramics. Pieces of old broken pots were mixed into fresh clay for new pottery production in a continuation of life, and food vessels are associated with nourishing life-giving properties.

Despite the era's masculine solar cult dominance, I suggest that relics in the form of women's bones may have been a part of a continuing and widespread goddess cult. The bones of females, perhaps of those who had given birth, may have been seen to retain their life force, fertility and feminine power, bringing rebirth to the land and its people. We noted earlier that many round barrows contained female remains and were associated with circles of earth energy flowing around the barrow. Archaeologist Sir Cyril Fox suggested that flat floored ditches, which surround most round barrows, may have been intended for the ceremonial movement of people, perhaps mourning the deceased. He noted that at Collingbourne Kingston the barrow's ditch was kept impeccably clean for months after an interment; other excavated ditches also yielded similar observation. It could be that the ceremonial movement around the ditch was to *charge* the mound and the bones with its encircling earth energy.

Women clearly played a major role in society—from daughter, mother, wife/partner, to seer and shieldmaiden—even after death they were not forgotten. By the Mid Bronze Age (1500 BC) cremations were commonplace; there was a move away from inhumation (burial) accompanied with lavish grave goods that exhibited wealth, ego and self-importance, to simple cremations associated with an urn and no grave goods. It is widely accepted that this indicates a move away from expressing social status, suggesting that women's cremation relics facilitated this social change.

The Mysterious Mounds of Ashton Valley

Whilst studying the barrows of Wessex, I came across two unusual barrows at Ashton Valley, in Wiltshire, that may have been constructed as initiation or acoustic centres. Interpreted as a family mausoleum, there is a large bowl barrow 80 ft (24 m) in diameter and 6 ft (1.8 m) high, that contained eleven cremations. Directly beneath the mound's summit were two skeletons and five crushed urns, and 3.5 ft (1 m) from the surface four more urns and another skeleton was found in the flexed position. To the right of the deposits was a tunnel leading to the south, large enough to admit a slender man. It ran for 6 ft (1.8 m) before separating into two lesser corridors to the right and the left, but these were not investigated. Unfortunately, the excavation partly destroyed the tunnels that probably led to a room which may have once been used for ritual purposes prior to burial. Mound No. 3 is an anomaly as it was only 18 in (45.7 cm) high, and beneath it, at the unusual depth of 11 ft (3.3 m), an area the size of a small room had been cut out of the chalk bedrock. Its walls were smooth but as hard as stone, with sharp angles. At the centre, a skeleton had been placed in the extended position, indicating a shaman burial. This mound stands alone and was undoubtedly used for ritual purposes—like a proto-type fogou—an underground dry-stone structure, many of which are found in Cornwall. I suggest that at a later date it was reused as a burial chamber, and a small earthen mound constructed to conceal its entrance.

Chapter 14

Lost Features and Ancient Rites

The long headed culture placed all of their monuments on earth energies, grid lines and ley lines. This practice was continued by later cultures such as the round headed Beaker people, the Templars and other secret societies. Prehistoric geomancers selected locations that exhibited a combination of earth energies; this would determine the monument's primary function, its overall size, and dictate the positioning of the stones. Locations where numerous forms of earth energy meet, converge and emerge, constitute a geodetic power place. Thus, there is far more to a sacred site's placement than what may be termed today as a ley line or a crossing of leys.

Primary Design Canons: Spirals, Circles and Horseshoes

Earth energies were fully integrated into a stone temple's architecture, uniting it with Gaia's life-force to ensure a profound connection with the 'Spirit of Place', breathing life into a manmade monument. The primary requirement for construction was the location of underground aquifers, rivers and streams, as well as deep springheads or *blind springs*, and there is scientific reasoning for this. According to Professor Y Rocard, underground water produces changes in the Earth's magnetic field, and this is what a dowser's muscles respond to. Water can do this because it has a magnetic field of its own that interacts with the magnetic field of the Earth. A deep aquifer or springhead is easy to identify because it generates an electromagnetic energy pattern, called a *geospiral*.

To briefly recap, geologists correctly inform us that rainwater replenishes the underground water table, aquifers, rivers and streams, and this is called *groundwater*. However, there is another type of water called *primary water* (sometimes referred to as a *blind spring*, though a *pressurised springhead* is a better description), which can be found deep beneath the Earth. I have always stated that this water's energy field is alive, feminine, healing and sacred. As described in my previous books, I call this water *yin* water as it is produced chemically deep within Gaia, and it is completely independent of rainfall, which is *yang* water. Internally, the Earth continually produces yin water, so a springhead will never run dry. Pressure forces this upwards through vertical fault lines, and when yin water eventually gets close to the surface, it often blends with groundwater and is revered as a healing spring. To the geodetic dowser, each kind of water can be recognised by its energy pattern: yin water's geospiral produces geometrically perfect *spiral coils* in multiples of 7 (although recently I found a lost manuscript of Underwood's that shows another numerical form of especially powerful geospiral); and yang water produces 3, 6 or 9 energy lines known as a *stream band*. In the geodetic layout of megalithic sites, the geospiral pattern marks the esoteric centre. At Stonehenge, the Altar Stones were placed above a large 7-coiled geospiral—a highly charged electromagnetic zone.

Fig. 209 Deep pressurised water produces a three-fold energy pattern.

Underground springheads or aquifers that are under sustained pressure from the surrounding rock, can generate additional patterns. This pressure causes a circular and sometimes semi-circular pattern to surround the geospiral, known as a *primary* and *secondary halo* respectively, shown in *Fig. 209*. Primary haloes have three concentric circles or ovals of energy, although exceptionally strong sources can generate six. It is these primary haloes that originally dictated the size of a stone circle, the perimeter of temple walls, and the placement of large earthen mounds, such as Silbury Hill, in Wiltshire. In early Christian times, features such as church spires or the perimeter of a churchyard, were often dictated by the primary halo; this is why medieval church grounds are often circular.

In America, circular Anasazi sites, such as the great kivas at Wupatki and Bonito, are likewise associated with the geospiral or primary halo pattern. A secondary halo was incorporated into the outer walls of Pueblo Bonito at Chaco Canyon, which accounts for its seemingly odd 'D-shape', shown below in *Fig 210*, and this became the template for the surrounding great houses that mirror the site, which was constructed in stages between AD 850-1150.

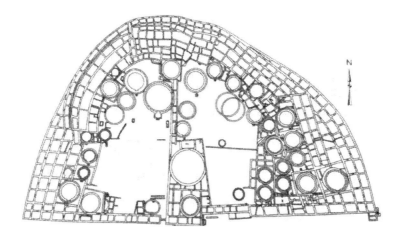

Fig. 210 The secondary halo forms the shape of Pueblo Bonito, Chaco Canyon.

Deep below Stonehenge, a highly pressurised aquifer generates six primary haloes; it was these that set Stonehenge's main features: its size, shape and placement of the ditch, bank, Aubrey Holes, sarsen circle and part of the Z and Y features. The halo's gaps dictated the northeast and south entrances, as well as a lost entrance which is shown below in *Fig. 211*. We read earlier that these energy circles form musical intervals—the music of Gaia. The idea that the surface patterns of underground water have musical power adds another dimension to our understanding of earth energies.

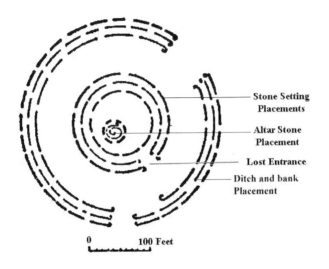

Fig. 211 This circular energy pattern dictated the stone settings at Stonehenge.

Vatican Hill

Another holy place associated with deep yin water is Vatican Hill, in Rome. According to the British Druid Order, its name has Celtic origins. Druidry has three grades: Bard is the first, Vate the second, and Druid the third. Vates are the order of healers, seers, diviners and prophets that gave its name to Vatican Hill. This was originally the site where the Druid Vates (today spelt and pronounced *Ovates*) delivered their inspired prophecies.

St Peter's Basilica is the largest church in the world. It is associated with a geospiral and a section of St Peter's Square is associated with a primary halo. Many springs are found at its base, some of which are considered to have medicinal properties. To gain hallowed protection, sections of the ancient city of Rome incorporated the semi-circular secondary halo pattern that was believed to ward off evil.

Symbolically, when a secondary halo is integrated into a sacred site, it serves to 'protect' the area from unwanted influences. Separating the sacred from the profane outer regions, the halo was an essential component of monumental planning. Stonehenge has all three energy patterns, which is rare, and shares geodetic similarities with the Great pyramid at Giza. Circular walled cities and sites were also set, or partially set, upon a secondary halo, for the purpose of its energetic safety. Research has shown that outdoor hens and geese that nest on this energy pattern rarely get molested by foxes as it 'grants protection'.

Deep Underground Yin Streams

Groundwater emits a recognisable dowsing pattern of three lines, known as a *triad water line* or *stream band*. In monumental planning, ditches and dykes were often located above groundwater streams, as are some of the Nazca lines in Peru. Much deeper underground streams are called *aquastats*, a word that was coined by Underwood, although he never defined its meaning. However, after years of dowsing this energy, I discovered that aquastats flow with yin water that emits a surface pattern of twelve parallel lines of electromagnetic force, and an energy field 15-30 ft (4.5-9.1 m) to either side. Underground yin and yang streams emerge and converge at geospirals (aquifers), similar to surface rivers that flow onwards to the sea. Stonehenge is a textbook example of this. *Fig. 212* below shows aquastats emerging at the Altar Stone(s) and converging at the Heel Stone, making these locations especially healing—as aquastats emit healing energy, standing stones sited above them can be classified as healing stones. And, as we shall see, I discovered they can also enhance seed germination and plant growth.

Underwood surveyed Stonehenge over three hundred times and noted that stones sited above aquastats transmit energy via grooves or cup marks. Dowsers all agree that underground yang water can emit toxic energy, termed *geopathic stress* and long-term exposure is injurious to health. However, when yang water flows in close proximity to yin water, the geopathic stress is negated and a third energy pattern is emitted, discussed in Chapter 17.

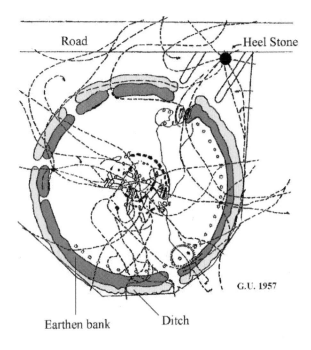

Road — Heel Stone

G.U. 1957

Earthen bank   Ditch

Fig. 212 Aquastat convergence and emergence survey of Stonehenge.

Mass Healing and Aquastats

Chislehurst Caves in Kent contain over 20 miles (32 km) of underground galleries, some of which are thought to be prehistoric. During World War II the caves were used as air raid shelters and over 15,000 people took refuge there, many of whom lived underground for long periods of time when their homes were bombed. In 1959-60, it was widely reported by the media that many mature people who had stayed in the caves were cured of rheumatism, toothache and general aches and pains. We discovered that the caves and many other manmade galleries that are in close proximity, or aligned upon aquastats, create healing zones.

An example of mass healing occurred on the eve of Ascension Day in 1770, when a miraculous healing of sixteen children occurred after being placed onto the sepulchral slab of John and Isabella Colmer (died c1376). Although no longer in situ, the original location of the sepulchral slab, which became famous for its healing properties, was found to mark the crossing point of two aquastats. When I met with the church warden, he had not heard of this story, which made famous the church of Holy Trinity, Newport, in Wales.

Aquastat crossing points are ideal locations that are a healing gift from Gaia to humanity. They can be observed at the Rollright Ring in Oxfordshire, England; Mnajdra Temple in Malta; at the temples of Abydos, Hathor, Karnak and Edfu in Egypt; and at locations in the USA, such as at Chaco Canyon in New Mexico, Woodhenge in Illinois, Wupatki in Arizona, and America's Stonehenge, near Salem.

Dowsing Reveals Stonehenge's Long-Lost Features
The underground springs and streams dictated to the geodetic architectural planners of Stonehenge not only the placement of its avenues but the surrounding barrow cemeteries. Underwood was a dowsing pioneer, but he also made mistakes. His final survey of Stonehenge's underground water lines (see *Fig. 213*) was criticised by Dragon Project author, Don Robins, and by Master Dowser, Tom Graves, both of whom pointed out that his survey of Stonehenge showed dense so-called 'water lines' in the car park area that were actually *remanence trails*—the dowseable traces of where people have walked in the past. Being unaware of this dowsing phenomenon, some of Underwood's energy lines are in fact pathways. Using traditional water divining methods, I dowsed Stonehenge for its primary water lines and plotted their courses. When we compare my survey (which includes and excludes some of Underwood's underground streams) to Stonehenge's ceremonial landscape, the match, shown in *Fig. 214*, is almost identical. Could geodetic energies be a vital key to unlocking Stonehenge's long-lost ceremonial landscape?

An Avenue for the Gods
According to archaeologists, Stonehenge originally had only one earthen avenue that coursed for 1½ miles (2.4 km) from the River Avon, at West Amesbury, to the northeast causewayed entrance, shown in *Fig. 214* to be located above a wide underground stream (Main Avenue 1). Did Stonehenge once have other avenues set above underground streams?

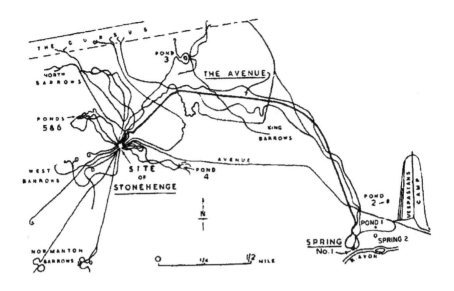

Fig. 213 Underwood's underground streams and remanence trails at Stonehenge.

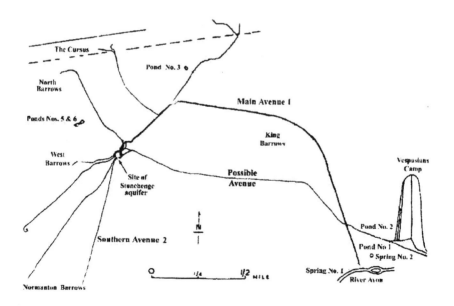

Fig. 214 Waterscape: underground streams at Stonehenge (after Underwood).

If I am correct, one lost avenue may have also led to the northeast entrance, now associated with part of the A303 road and the former A344. Interestingly, this speculative avenue almost mirrors the course of the main avenue as if it were its twin. Although, as I have previously suggested, the southern causeway has never been associated with an avenue, I think it started at an energetic underground springhead on Normanton Down, and an earthen avenue followed an underground river that marked its course and width.

Many Wessex henges have two or more avenues. Avebury has two known stone avenues, and archaeologists suggest that it originally had four due to the fact there are four entrances. Stanton Drew stone circle has two avenues, both of which follow the course of wide underground yin streams. Therefore, Stonehenge's lost avenues are not out of context, and they may have been designed for specific people, even the gods. Stonehenge's southern causewayed entrance aligns to the Equinox Full Moon, and as the moon represents feminine energy, perhaps it was used by females. During the Normanton dynasty, however, which I described earlier associated with the royal healer-priest elite (c1950-1750 BC), this entrance was used by both sexes. After it was widened, the northeast entrance was closely aligned to the Midsummer Sunrise—the Sun being associated with masculine energy, when it may have been used by men. The other avenue may have been exclusively reserved for Stonehenge's main deities—the oracle goddess and the god of healing. Interestingly, and in support of this concept, Alexander Keiller's early excavations of Avebury's West Kennet Stone Avenue found compression marks *outside* and *alongside* the avenue, but not inside. Additionally, the inside of the avenue was naturally littered with many half-buried sarsen stones that would have made procession difficult. This 1½ mile (2.4 km) stone avenue connected a stone circle called the Sanctuary on Overton Hill to Avebury's main stone circles. Water diviners, including Guy Underwood and Reginald Smith, claimed numerous underground streams set the avenue's course, whereas Hamish Miller suggested it was the Michael earth current. Archaeological theories of its use range from a processional way for fertility rituals to a reserved route to commemorate an ancestral trackway.

In New Mexico, the Chacoan roads associated with Pueblo Bonito were not always typical roads; some have been interpreted as sacred shrine roads, possibly for the gods. Typically, they often have a stone shrine, or deliberately broken pottery heaps placed in the centre, which makes procession difficult. During the Babylonian spring festival of Akitu, deities were believed to inhabit a stone statue that travelled to Babylon along specially designated roads. The infrastructure was designed for the gods, who even had their own living quarters in the temple area. I suggest Britain's major stone circles were designed in a similar fashion. If Stonehenge's avenue was not for the gods, perhaps it was intended to be used by the priestly caste?

Stonehenge's Avenues Sacred Springs

Two of Stonehenge's avenues are associated with surface springs, and those attributed with healing powers often contain minerals such as calcium or iron. Clean water springs have been revered since the dawn of time, and one such example is Blick Mead, near Stonehenge. I suggest that the spring, which is located close to the main avenue, as well as its twin, were venerated and used as an integral part of a long-lost preparation ritual. Prior to walking to Stonehenge, a member of the priesthood may have sprinkled or anointed the participants with sacred spring water. In 2006, Spring No. 1 was a garden feature in the grounds of a large house at West Amesbury, but sadly it has since been destroyed. Spring No. 2, shown here in *Fig. 215*, survives and is situated in a field close to both avenues. This spring has incredible energy.

Fig. 215 Sacred Spring No. 2.

Occasionally, a surface spring is located above or in close proximity to an underground aquastat springhead. When this pairing occurs, a beautiful and exceptionally powerful geospiral is emitted, called a *multiple geospiral*. It consists of six three-and-a-half coiled geospirals, and the largest stream to emerge from it, I call a 'Mother Line'. The six outer spirals are associated with deep yin streams, although yang streams also flow from the springs. Perhaps, after experiencing a water preparation rite, people stood in the field to absorb its effects, as the spiral appears to enhance perception and intuition; it feels like its water cleanses one's own body. After I had interacted with this vibrant energy, I felt radiant, clear and strong.

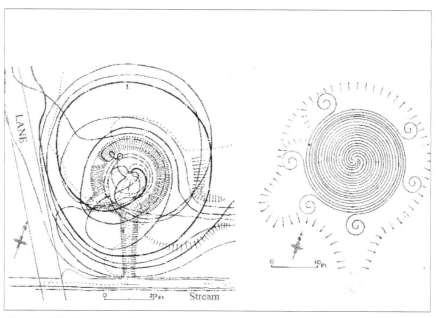

Fig. 216 Underground streams and multiple geospiral of Spring No. 1.

Author Laird Scranton pointed out to me the work of Mae Wan-Ho. She describes water as integral to the biology of life and explains that water exists naturally in two states: one high density and coherently aligned, and the other low density and more chaotic. Within our bodies, interstitial water—water at an interface—takes the coherent form that exhibits the same qualities of superconductivity. Likewise, I think Gaia's body water is similar. The constant replenishment of groundwater and its seasonal fluctuations is a candidate for low density water energy, whereas Gaia's deep water corresponds to the coherent form. Certainly, the meeting point, or interface, of these two waters produces the high energy field of the multiple geospiral, which is divine.

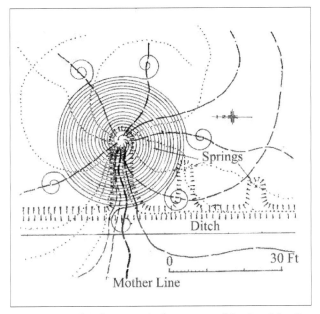

Fig. 217 Multiple geospiral pattern of Spring No. 2.

Europe's Ancient Water Goddess

Underground water emits several other patterns. I noted geodetic lines that cross one another imply fast-flowing energy called *reticulation*. Stonehenge's avenues are associated with reticulated lines that are highly energetic, shown in *Fig. 218*. Walking along the avenue will increase energy levels, so the walk can be regenerating and healing.

In occult terms, the element of water is feminine, and rivers and springs are often associated with a goddess. The Thames which famously flows through London derives its ancient name Tamesis from the Thame that rises from its source in the Cotswolds and joins the Isis. Hafren is the Welsh goddess of the River Severn, her Latin name is Sabrina. The Irish goddess Dana and her British equivalent Don share the same ancient Indo-European root word as the Hindu River goddess Danu, whose name means *primeval water*—she is mother to a group of gods called the Danavas. The existence of a primeval water goddess is believed to account for the numerous rivers with names like Don, Danube and Dneiper. Irish bards were known as *Aos Dana*—people gifted in the Art of Craft—and bear the name of the water goddess Brigit (Bride). Many of the qualities of the goddess Brigit were transferred to an early Irish saint of the same name who was popular in Irish Catholic homes, and Brigid's role as the mother goddess was subsumed as the Christian Mother Mary. Dressed in blue, green and white Brigit/Brighid is associated with holy wells, mead and ale, childbirth, healing, fertility, the harvest, protection, the sacred fire, smithcraft and 'fey folk'. Her festival is Imbolc (1st February) when, according to Scottish folklore, the white serpent of Bride rises from its hole in the ground, heralding the first stirrings of spring and life renewed. Water and Earth goddesses were seen as powerful aspects of Mother Nature and moreover, I believe that underground water, Gaia's patterns, were also revered as an aspect of the divine feminine.

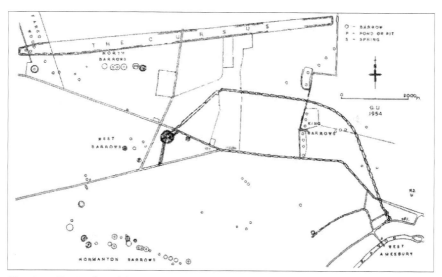

Fig. 218 Reticulated lines indicate fast-flowing energy.

Some ancient temples are surrounded by water and create a *water temple*, an island with mirror-like properties. The Osireion at Abydos in Egypt, constructed of huge blocks of Aswan granite, sandstone and limestone, has been interpreted as a cenotaph to Osiris, or possibly Seti I (as Osiris). Rather like an underground vaulted hall, it is reached by a subterranean passage that contains a central platform with ten monolithic pillars, surrounded by a channel of water. Its hydrogeologic setting is unique as the water channel intersects the water table beneath the desert; its outer walls surround

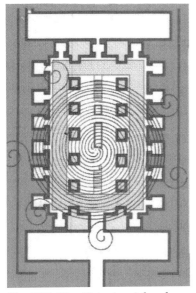

a water-filled channel that creates a large rectangular central stone island. It was discovered that it also incorporates a highly pressurised artesian springhead. My dowsing located a nearby underground springhead that generates a multiple geospiral (see *Fig. 219*). Another island temple is the Temple of Évora in Portugal, incorrectly called Diana's Temple, which was constructed at the historic centre of the city in the first century AD during the reign of Caesar Augustus. Still impressive today are the giant columns, and this Roman temple was also surrounded by water.

Fig. 219 The Osireion island and multiple geospiral pattern.

Silbury Hill: A Water Mirror

We have seen that Silbury Hill lies at the heart of Avebury's ceremonial landscape that was roughly contemporary (orthodox dating) with the pyramid building of Egypt. The smooth, chalk white mound resonates, musically, to the perfect fourth and the perfect fifth. Past excavations have revealed nothing of its purpose and many authors suggest the gigantic mound represents Mother Earth. Archaeological analysis has revealed that the mound was once surrounded by water all year round, and to cross the moat a long earthen causeway was constructed, shown to the right-hand side of *Fig. 220*. Using Wessex Water's well boring data, I calculated that in prehistoric times Avebury's deep ditch would have filled with water, possibly creating an island mirror-like effect.

Universal Energy: Orgone Energy at Silbury Hill

Decades ago, my late father proposed that Silbury Hill was an orgone generator. In the 1940s and 1950s, the Australian born

American, Dr Wilhelm Reich, experimented with a universal source of energy which he called *orgone* and claimed that it could be freely generated. His orgone accumulator consisted of a container filled with alternate layers of organic and inorganic materials, which he used to publicly demonstrate the power of orgone. On one occasion, in a cloud-busting exercise, he disintegrated clouds. He also showed that orgone could heal the physical body. Unfortunately, Reich and his 'invention' was seen as a direct threat to the power corporations, and he was eventually jailed on trumped-up charges of peddling quack cures for cancer. Police raided his home, and his manuscripts and research notes were destroyed. His orgone device was simply replicating a 5,000-year-old Neolithic technology!

Fig. 220 Silbury Hill: a water mirror with causeway.

The Silbury pyramid structure was infilled with many alternate layers of organic and inorganic materials, similar to the way that Reich created his orgone generator. Other energies also played a part in orgone production at Silbury, as its mound is located above a vast source of underground water. This generates a 7-coiled geospiral where numerous underground yin and yang streams converge and emerge. A diagram of Underwood's survey of underground streams is shown in *Fig. 143* (Chapter 10), and in detail in *Fig. 221* below.

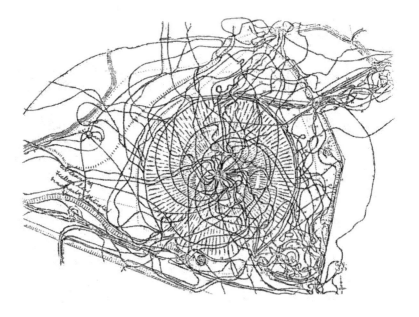

Fig. 221 Underwood's survey of yin and yang underground streams at Silbury Hill.

Additionally, coursing through the mound are narrow earth energy currents, the much wider Mary current, and other ley lines. Although invisible to the naked eye, within and beneath the mound perpetual activity is going on. Under the planet's unrelenting bombardment by cosmic rays, the small nuclei of water molecules disintegrate, and in the process release fast-moving beta particles, slower moving alpha particles, and ultra-high frequency gamma rays at the top end of the electromagnetic spectrum. Most of these particles would never reach the Earth's surface but the negative ions and gamma rays would, creating a highly energised cocktail at the regional power centre. If this energy was harnessed by the mound's geometric shape, as I suggest it was, then Silbury Hill was generating a continual source of geodetic energy. This would charge the surrounding area with its invisible power.

Reich stated that orgone energy is mass free, that it permeates all of space in different concentrations and is in constant motion, either pulsating or flowing along a curved path; it is taken into the body through breathing and is especially drawn to water. Silbury Hill's moat may have been constructed for a similar purpose. To ensure ultra-high levels of moat water all year round, a channel was constructed connecting the moat to the nearby Beckhampton stream. Many witnesses state they have seen large balls of plasma energy emerge from the mound, and on one occasion, several years ago, a ball of light, the size of a football, was seen at the Winter Solstice. Earthen mounds are a worldwide phenomenon. America's Grave Creek mound located in West Virginia is strikingly similar to Silbury Hill, and also had a surrounding moat.

Water has memory and the deep yin water at a sacred site can hold memories of past and present events, rather like an Akashic record of space and time. Tapping into the past is one way of spiritually working with a site's sacred inner waters. As humans, we are made up of over 75% water, and over the years I have developed effective ways of cleansing and rejuvenating one's own body water above a geospiral. I suggest that our bodies hold on to good and challenging memories as well as emotional trauma, which is something I have previously written about in my book *Divining Ancient Sites* (2014). Geodetic energy patterns relating to water are, in effect, transmitting a universal language. It is well known that Australian aboriginals used symbols in ancient rock art to map the songlines. Four concentric circles represent an encampment, a camp fire, or a water hole, which manifests as a geospiral and a primary halo pattern; a group of four straight lines represents a trackway, and in the geodetic system a track line is similar; wavy lines linking concentric circles represent a watercourse, and mirrors old water divining lore. Across the ancient world, waves or chevrons are a symbol of water; an underground stream can flow in meandering wavy streams in a zig-zag pattern or as small and large loops, depending on the geology.

Fig. 222 Aboriginal symbols are similar to geodetic energy flows.

Vortex Energy and the Goddess

Transformative *vortex energy* was also integrated into sacred sites. Sedona is often regarded as a vortex capital. However, some of the most exotic examples can be found on the island of Bali in Indonesia. This is because Bali marks the crossing point of two global earth energies: the Rainbow Serpent (Mary and Michael) and the Plumed Serpent, that imbue the island with extraordinary energy. Vortex energy is classified as a geophysical anomaly and in dowsing terms there are several distinctive types. Mild vortex energy occurs above the crossing points of leys, grid lines, geodetic spirals, geochimneys and geodetic magic squares, and often cause a dowsing rod to spin. Strong vortexes can assist spiritual expansion and produce incredible earth energy patterns, one of which is associated here with a Balinese goddess. Some dowsers interpret vortex energy as an *electric* vortex that is highly energising and can boost energy levels; these patterns draw energy into the earth and can therefore assist in letting go of old emotional or mental patterns and karmic trauma. *Magnetic* vortexes can be soothing, and both types encourage an altered state of consciousness. Sometimes these vortexes are called *earthbound* and *cosmic vortexes* respectively.

Fig. 223 The Durga's eight-armed vortex.

Many decades ago, at Oxford University, a European Master Dowser introduced me to vortex earth energy patterns and their frequencies (earth colour). On the island of Bali, vortex energy was incorporated into many Hindu Pura Dalem temples. A Pura Dalem is a temple of death—when someone dies in Bali they are temporarily buried and their spirit resides in the Pura Dalem; not until a cremation ceremony has taken place is the person free to be reincarnated. Dated to the 14th century, the Pura Dalem Puri temple is inhabited by the Durga, who deals with the Underworld and her colour is red. Her popular form is as Rangda, a monstrous witch-goddess who has eight arms and appears at night in the temple. Located inside the temple and symbolically mirroring the characteristics of Rangda is a red vortex. It too has eight arms, a strong anti-clockwise motion and covers the entire temple. In one guise it is associated with the ancestors, the Underworld and time past, and can be seen as an entrance to such realms. Guru figure, Ketut Arsana, told the Master Dowser, "the vortex is Durga's!".

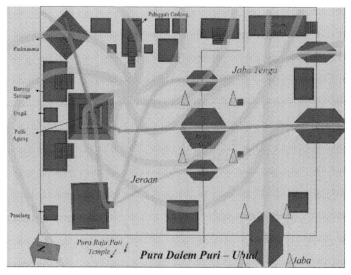

Fig. 224 The Durga vortex within Pura Dalem Puri temple.

Spiritual Involution and Evolution Vortexes

Especially transformative are evolution and involution vortexes and these are often associated with temples and stone circles. A clockwise flowing vortex is called an *evolution vortex* that encourages development of the self and a deep awareness of the planet and its life forms. The anti-clockwise *involution vortex* can bring deep spiritual understanding, higher consciousness and a connection to the planets, stars and galaxies—the cosmos. The Mnajdra temple complex in Malta and the Temple of Hathor in Egypt both have powerful involution female vortex energy—this commonly has four arms, and its energy rises upwards from the ground and radiates outwards. Sometimes a swastika symbol placed within a temple can reveal the presence of a four-armed vortex, and this can be seen in the stonework at Peliatan Pura Desca temple's courtyard in Ubud on Bali, where inside there is an evolution vortex. At Pura Tirta Empul, a famous holy spring temple, there is an involution vortex.

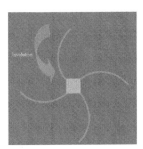

Fig. 225 The Bali swastika (above) represents a vortex,
an evolution and an involution vortex.

When combined, the clockwise and anti-clockwise vortex can sometimes generate a portal that may or may not be active. Within the
Pura Puseh temple is Wisnu's shrine set above a four-armed clockwise vortex and a four-armed anti-clockwise vortex, creating a
gateway or bridge into another dimension or realm. Wisnu, the
Manifestation of the Trimurthi, focuses on preservation and displays
geomantic understanding. The Wisnu discus reflects the fused
vortexes, as shown below in *Fig. 226*, and Wisnu's double vortex or
portal shrine in *Fig. 227*.

Fig. 226 Wisnu's discus,
the fused vortexes.

Fig. 227 Wisnu's double
vortex or portal shrine.

At Stonehenge we can encounter an involution vortex. Stone 28 of the linteled stone circle has a curious facial feature and the natural cracks appear extenuated to form a swastika—the symbol of a vortex. Strangely, the standing stone appears buckled and distorted, yet the area around this stone is highly active with involution spiritual energy. Another exceptionally powerful vortex can be found close to the Greater Trilithon. Close to this stone downloads can occur that can literally take you to great heights!

Earth Chimneys: Archway Energy

Balinese temples are known for their *candi bentar*, which is a split gateway entrance that is often elevated and reached by a flight of steps. Throughout the island, the gateways are placed above a pair of *geochimeys* or *earth chimneys*—a powerful earth energy consisting of seven concentric circles of energy with radiating petals or arms that form a flower-like pattern. Some have energy going upwards from the Earth to the cosmos and others going downwards from the cosmos to Earth. Their unique feature is that they articulate in three dimensions rather like a tree, and some make energy arches. When one walks through the entrance upon an earth energy current, energy rises up through the feet and simultaneously comes down through the crown chakra, so one is showered in earth and spiritual energy (see *Fig. 228* below).

Fig. 228 Energy arch with an earth current coursing through the entrance.

Earth Currents: New Discoveries

Meandering earth currents are always present at sacred sites world-wide. Research has shown that there are two main types of earth currents: one that runs close to the surface and another that rises from deep underground. John Burke and Kaj Halberg, authors of the ground-breaking book, *Seed of Knowledge, Stone of Plenty* (2005), describe an earth current, which they call a *telluric current*, as flowing within 3 ft (0.90 m) uppermost in the ground. In contrast, another type of earth current is generated deep within the earth that has a male or female polarity. Their experiments demonstrated that at dawn, which brings a change in magnetic field strength, a weak DC electrical field is generated that could be utilised in seed germination (to be discussed later). Hamish Miller says of these currents:

> "...they issue from deep within the planet, perhaps con-densing as streams of biomagnetic energy from the molten magma in the heart of the Earth."

Their association with rocky outcrops led Burke and Halberg to believe that on a purely physical level they were, at times, connect-ing with geological fault lines in the Earth's crust, whilst other re-searchers hint that plasma could interact with this electromagnetic energy. It is widely documented that in the 1980s, Miller and Broadhurst discovered the St Michael ley line had entwined yin and yang earth currents, which they called Mary and Michael. Other major leys are also associated with twin currents, and at places where these currents cross the land is imbued with harmony and balance. At such *node* points, the widths narrow and taper to form a cross. Manor houses, Templar sites, medieval Christian churches, cathedrals and Masonic lodges are often associated with a yin/yang earth current. Those that course down the axis of smaller chapels in Christian churches are invariably defined by the gender of the saint to whom they are dedicated. Likewise, the gender of the deity in Egyptian temples will often affect the nature of the earth current.

Earth currents can also be found at medieval castles, such as the impressive Renaissance structure in Büren, Germany, Wewelsburg

Castle, which after 1934 was used by Heinrich Himmler and served as the central SS mystical castle. It is said that this was to be the Grail Castle of the Nazi regime, having established itself as world rulers. Wewelsburg was, for Himmler, not so much about the location where the Grail was hidden, but where his Grail Order— the SS, the Schutzstaffel and its sacred treasures, rumoured to include the 'Spear of Destiny'—would be brought, and from where the magical power of the Nazi regime would radiate outwards. Underlying this belief, the estate was to be in the shape of a spear, reflecting the power of the 'Spear of Destiny'. One story goes that Hitler saw his future when he visited the museum in Vienna where the spear was on display, and he became convinced that whoever possessed it would control the fate of the world. Wewelsburg was to be the 'New Jerusalem' at the centre of Germany and, as is evident from 1941 onwards, the architects called the complex the 'Centre of the World'. In line with sacred mythology, the triangular-shaped design would sit on a mountain, surrounded by a lake, from where there were plans to flood the valley below. In terms of earth energy, it is located on an intense red vortex and has emerging red and white male/female earth currents, mirroring the colours of the Nazi flag. Representing the colours of the warrior, this was a place where these currents could be used to create an active geomantic occult arena for rituals, bestowing strength and power to those that knew how to work with such frequencies. Himmler certainly did, with sickening consequences for humanity.

Earth Energies: Ancient Egypt

Not all ley lines have twinned earth energies. Whilst dowsing energies in Egypt I made a remarkable discovery. Abydos Temple has a strong solar ley that is associated with *three* earth currents. I called this the *Ra Line* as it targeted Ra's chapel, and the triad currents that course through the chapels are dedicated to Horus, Osiris and Isis —thus, I named the currents after them. Other Nile temples are also associated with these currents, as shown in *Fig 229* below. Likewise, a European Master Dowser noted that triad currents were associated with some temples in Bali, supporting my discovery of the triad of earth currents in Egypt.

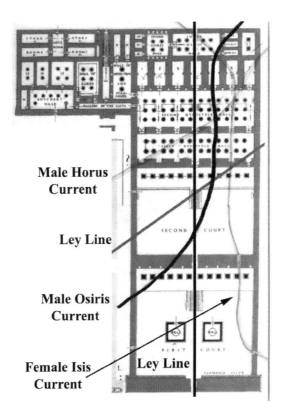

Fig. 229 Abydos Temple: the Ra ley and the
Isis, Osiris and Horus earth currents.

One does not need to visit a sacred site to experience earth current
energies, as there are narrow currents about 2-4 ft (0.60-1.5 m) wide
that interlace the planet and can be found within our homes and
gardens. Wide earth currents can be likened to mighty rivers; they
have arteries with smaller tributary veins joining them. Lunar
female currents are calming and soothing and can balance the emotions, whereas solar male currents can be energising—both are
healing. Often these tributary currents emerge or terminate at sacred
sites, which I call *Alpha* and *Omega* currents or lines. These were first
noted by Miller and Broadhurst at Boscawen-Un stone circle in
Cornwall, and although they never fully investigated them, these
lines fascinated me. The Mary female current passes through the
central leaning stone alongside a male and female Omega current
that terminates near this stone. Cobra-like, a female Alpha current

emerges from the area and flows eastward. Interacting with these energy points can be rewarding and alchemical. Endings, releasing, letting go, and turning points in life, can all be worked through at Omega termination points, after which new beginnings and emergence meditations can be the focus at an Alpha energy area. All male and female earth currents are influenced by the cycles of the Sun and Moon, respectively. I also noted that some currents have a sympathetic connection to Mars and Venus.

Earth Currents, Sound and Radiation

Could an Omega termination point play a vital role in the acoustic properties of a Neolithic monument? Doctors Aaron Watson and David Keating of Reading University conducted acoustic investigations in Aberdeenshire, Scotland, an area that contains around 99 recumbent stone circles (RSC). RSC is a term that refers to the presence of a large altar-like stone that is set horizontally between two flanking standing stones, surrounded by a circle of stones. Why these altar-like structures were erected is a mystery, but the Reading duo think they have an answer, and I can elaborate on their findings.

Fig. 230 The Easter Aquorthies. *Photograph:* Martin Morrison.

The Easter Aquorthies stone circle, a name that may be derived from the Gaelic term for *field of prayer*, is over four thousand years old. Contrasting grey and red granite stones were symmetrically placed within the 62 ft (19.5 m) diameter ring; on the east side pinkish-white stones are opposite other dark grey stones. The impressive light grey flankers are 7.6 ft (2.5 m) tall and the recumbent altar-like stone 12.6 ft long by 4.6 ft high (3.8-1.4 m), shown in *Fig. 230*, is an attractive reddish granite with flecks and lines of white quartz. Similar to other RSC, these stones are often aligned to the Southern Moonset.

In 1994, Watson realised as he walked around the circle that he could hear clearly what other people were saying—a strange type of echo was being reflected across the stone circle by the recumbent and flanking stones, yet in other parts of the circle the sound was faint. Alongside Keating, using acoustic recording equipment that utilises *pink noise* (a sound not unlike a distant waterfall), the pair discovered that the effect generated by the megalithic setting was similar to a theatre. Sound created inside the stone circle was projected towards the interior and contained within the circle so that no-one outside could hear what was going on. Furthermore, the recumbent megalith acted like a rostrum that would have made sound ceremonies spectacular. The Easter Aquorthies has a strange characteristic that science cannot explain. In 1987, the year of the most Southerly Moonset that occurs every 18.61 years, Dragon Project researchers, Cosimo and Ann Favaloro, measured the radioactivity both within the stone circle and at control points outside of the circle. Having taken readings continuously throughout a twelve-hour period, inexplicably, at one point in the afternoon, the readings within the circle soared for a few minutes, whilst those outside the circle remained constant. Defying explanation, at 9 pm, the precise moment of moonset, the radiation level of the external environment soared higher than that within the stone circle. Some form of geophysics was occurring that influenced the radiation readings, accounting for the variations.

Camster Round and Long Barrows

One of the most impressive sound experiments conducted by Watson and Keating involved two cairns in Caithness, Scotland. One of these, Camster Round Barrow, is a spectacular circular cairn with a diameter of 55 ft (17.5 m). Its central 10 ft (3 m) chamber is accessed via a narrow passageway, some 19 ft (6 m) long. The pair discovered that sound reflected off the chamber walls was amplified and created echoes. Sound was also transmitted along the narrow passageway and could be heard outside of the cairn, emerging from the entrance, and this faded away by the time it reached the edge of the forecourt. Using a tone generator at various frequencies and pitches, the tone was often unclear, appearing to come from different parts of the chamber and at other times from *inside* the listener's head. By changing the frequency, if the listener moved, even slightly, the volume and pitch could change, and speech inside of the chamber would become distorted. Sound from drumming inside the chamber passed down the passageway and could be heard in the forecourt; higher frequencies were filtered out, leaving just the hypnotic-sounding base notes.

It was noted that sound created inside the chamber travelled a maximum distance of 328 ft (100 m). Intriguingly, drumming within Camster Round Barrow could be heard twice this distance away, *inside* Camster Long Barrow as a distant booming sound that rose from the floor—yet outside all was quiet. Keating and Watson suggest this explains why megalithic complexes such as Knowth and Loughcrew in Ireland have satellite cairns centred around a main cairn, to create an acoustic soundscape. My dowsing reveals that an Omega current courses through Camster Round Barrow and terminates inside Camster Long Barrow, as does an underground stream. Could the electromagnetic energy field of the flowing Omega line attract sound waves that can carry from one barrow to the other? Or is the sound carried on the underground water which conducts sound five times more readily than air? Either way, I think earth energies can explain these mysterious acoustic properties.

The Long Headed, Leys and Kingship
Neolithic monuments such as long barrows, causewayed enclosures and cursus enclosures are the oldest monuments in the ritual landscape, all of which are placed above earth energies and leys. The long headed civilisation began this tradition that was utilised by later cultures, such as the round headed priesthood of the Bronze Age. Then came the Iron Age Druids, Knights Templar and the medieval Masonic brotherhood, all of whom added to the existing leys by way of building churches, cathedrals, stately homes, medieval castles, large barns, town halls and Masonic lodges.

Numerous earth mystery authors and various websites state that Alfred Watkins was the first person to research and write about ley lines. Certainly, in 1925 he published his seminal findings in a book titled *The Old Straight Track*, having rediscovered the ancient British ley network. Watkins noticed that old tracks and pathways sometimes formed straight lines, linear alignments across the countryside, upon which ancient manmade structures were often sited. He called these simple linear alignments *leys*. However, my own research reveals that one of the earliest references to leys and earth currents was by Dr John Dee (1527-1606), the Royal astrologer to Queen Elizabeth I. He wrote:

> "The true mathematical science is that which measureth the invisible lines and immortal beams which can pass through cold and turf, hill and dale… It was accounted by all ancient priests the chiefest science; for it gave them power both in their words and works."

Dee's documented occult observations predates Alfred Watkins' by centuries. At various castles he appears to have located feminine and rejuvenating earth energies for his queen. Although ruinous, the dark red sandstone walls of Kenilworth Castle still have presence. It was here that Queen Elizabeth I often visited Robert Dudley, 1st Earl of Leicester. Dudley was a Knight of the Order of Saint Michael from whom John Dee enjoyed patronage, and both may have known about the leys and earth currents associated with the castle and its grounds. Knowing how to work with the "invisible lines" (leys) and "immortal beams" (earth energies), Dee could perhaps have acti-

vated the female earth current associated with Queen Elizabeth's chambers, giving her power both in her words and in her works. It seems that activation did occur, as close by there is a magic square that can increase the 'energy of place', which will be discussed in the next chapter.

Fig. 231 Kenilworth Castle, Warwickshire.

The priestly caste, including shamans, were thought to have once used the lines for magical purposes; in more hierarchical times, this was the king or emperor. Earth mysteries enthusiast Jim Kimmis noted that the proto-Indo-European linguistic root word *reg*, once meant 'movement along a straight line', and this eventually found its way, in one form or another, into the structure of words associated with kingship such as rex, raj, reign, reich, roi and regent. Also, it was associated with order and behaviour, through words such as recht, regime, erect, regiment and regular. Today, in the English language, we have the word *ruler*, which means both a straight edge or measure, and queen, king or leader. Hierarchical societies reserved the straight lines for the king or emperor, who literally *ruled the land*. During the 17th and 18th centuries, the ruling elite continued to create straight pathways within their stately grounds. This is evident at Badminton House in Gloucestershire, which has been the principal seat of the Dukes of Beaufort since the lines were originally positioned within the design, more about which will be said shortly.

Thousands of miles away, Chinese Feng Shui Masters were likewise utilising leys on behalf of their rulers. A north-south alignment was anchored into the Imperial Palace in the (purple) Forbidden City. The rectangular plan of the city had four cardinal gates that represented the directions of the emperor's kingdom—and the entire world. At its centre was the old Imperial Road that was oriented to the northern Pole Star. Every wall, court and hall in the palace was bisected by the meridian, so that when the emperor sat on his throne he was merging with the axis of the world. It is documented that the Han Dynasty (205 BC) reserved the exclusive right to place imperial tombs upon the straight ley network to ensure the prosperity of their descendants. Straight lines also feature in the ceque system of ritual pathways in Cuzco, Peru. Dated to around AD 1200, the Inca civilisation shares similarities to China's cosmological city. The Temple of the Sun was the hub or physical centre of the ceque system from where the network of paths or roads, which have been linked to straight alignment shrine roads, radiated out into the landscape. In Quechua, Cuzco means the *navel of the world*. The Coricancha (Inca ruler), like the Chinese emperor, sat at the centre of his empire.

Writing in the 17th century, Spanish missionary Bernabé Cobo recorded 333 shrines or *huacas* with three to thirteen shrines along any single line. Several lines followed underground watercourses as many were located by springs, some functioned as astronomical sightlines and others sited on leys. From the long headed elite of Stonehenge to the Inca Empire, the ruling elite have long been associated with ley lines. As John Dee informs us, these lines were known to ancient priests as "the chiefest science; for it gave them power both in their words and works."

Feminine Power

Although seemingly connected to kingship, historically a considerable proportion of Old English place names that relate to the land are feminine, and many early medieval English women wrote their names onto the map of England. For example, the word for clearing or meadow was *leah* (modern English *lea* and *ley*), and Kimberley in Norfolk was Cyneburgh's clearing. One of the most common forms of early English place names is the definition of a natural feature, or its establishment, such as a grove, clearing, dairy farm and so on, with a personal name in the possessive form. The name given may indicate the owner or founder of a place, or perhaps they were connected by some kind of exploit, like the later Nan's Clark Lane, in Mill Hill, London, so-called because Nan Clark was supposedly murdered there and continues to haunt the lane.

Signifying women's independence are names that relate to property, especially landed property. For example, *ham* refers to a dwelling: Babraham in Cambridgeshire was Beaduburh's *ham*. A *tun* is enclosed land around a dwelling and could later mean an estate within a village or community, such as the manor in Wollaton, Shropshire, formerly Wulfwynn's *tun*. A larger property, a *worth* or *worthing*, is an enclosed homestead with surrounding lands that may encompass estates of great extent and importance; it is the suffix often used to denote royal estates such as Kenilworth Castle, which was formerly Cynehlid's *worth*. Denoting power and wealth are a *burh* or *burg*, later *bury* or *borough*, that was originally a fortress. Bamburgh, we know from Bede, was the royal stronghold of the Bernicians, named after an early queen called Bebbanburh, thus Bebbe's fortress. Great monasteries were also often named after women, such as Tetbury in Gloucestershire, which was Tettanbyrig: Tette was a royal abbess.

A predominance of feminine earth energies at these medieval sites cannot be coincidental, rather a geomantic acknowledgement of a powerful female ruler. But there is more to sacred sites than earth energies, as major sites were also encoded with a *Magic Square*. John Michell has pointed out that magic squares are found within many ancient sites as a form of sacred mathematics. Decades ago, my late father and I were shown how to dowse for the magical planetary squares that served to connect a site to the heavens above. Dennis Wheatley was the first British dowser to begin working magically with these mysterious grids, which can raise the energetic level of a sacred site by a factor of 15 or even as much as 666.

Chapter 15

Geodetic Magic Squares

*For decades I have dowsed geodetic Saturn and Sun squares
at Stonehenge. They are truly Magical!*

Esoteric geomancers connected major sacred sites to the heavens, and this was achieved by using two techniques. Firstly, to incorporate a solar, lunar or stellar alignment that would create a spectacular visual display, a physical connection was necessary. Secondly, a planetary *magic square* would allow a metaphysical connection to harness a particular force of nature. A planetary square is called a magic square if the sums of the numbers in each row, column and both main diagonals are the same. The order of the magic square is the number of integers along one side and this constant sum is called the *magic constant*. The magic constant or magic sum is the sum of numbers in any row, column, or diagonal.

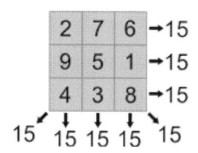

Fig. 232 Magic square of Saturn: magic constant of 15.

For example, the magic square of Saturn, shown in *Fig. 232*, has an order of 3 x 3 and a magic constant of 15. These squares were used by the medieval masons to design the above ground architecture of cathedrals. John Michell pointed out the three spires of Lichfield cathedral were based on the mathematics of the Mars square.

A magic square attracts a particular planetary energy. This is key to energetically working with the consciousness of the planet to which a monument is aligned. To quote my late father, Dennis Wheatley, who was *the* expert Master Dowser of magic squares:

"These squares of antiquity [which I call geodetic magic squares] appear as patterns on the Earth's surface and one wonders if this is how the ancient Chinese initially discovered them. As a surface entity the Saturn square is by far the most numerous. Master geomancers can create them, as I have done, within my own home."

In my late twenties, I was fascinated by geodetic magic squares, and I was shown how they are utilised as 'entrance squares'. Often, they were placed upon earth voltages or earth energies and this geodetic rite is still employed by some secret societies. My father went on to say:

"The magic constant is the timing key to interaction and so when one finds a Saturn square one can only stand on it for the maximum of 15 seconds. No more. This gives the aura a gentle boost and in one guise they are the gateways to the realm of the devas [and the 'fey']. One can open and close the squares and this is the origin of the saying *Open Sesame* and *Close Sesame*—not from the mouths of story tellers but from the works of Arabian magicians."

Yet, according to academics, the phrase "Sésame, ouvre-toi" first appears in Antoine Galland's French edition of *One Thousand and One Nights*, in twelve volumes between 1704-1717, which translates into English as, "Sesame, open yourself". In the story, Ali Baba overhears one of the 40 thieves saying, "open, says me". In 1673, Galland had travelled in Syria and the Levant and copied a great number of inscriptions and, in some instances, removed historical artefacts. Mystery surrounds the origins of some of the most famous tales as there are no Arabic manuscripts of *Aladdin* and *Ali Baba* which pre-date Galland's translation. He had, in turn, heard these tales from Syrian storyteller Hanna Diyab, who was a part of an Eastern Catholic tradition known as the Maronites.

American folklorist Stith Thompson says that *Open Sesame* has been classified as a motif element, "mountain opens to magic formula". In nature, sesame seeds grow in a seed pod that splits open when it reaches maturity, so the phrase may allude to the unlocking of hidden treasures. 'Sesame' is an imitation of the Hebrew *šem*, 'name' i.e., of God, or a Kabbalistic word representing the Talmudic *šem-šāmayīm*, "shem-shamayim", 'name of heaven'. Clearly, in the Middle East, the word 'Sesame', which is associated with Babylonian magical practices, had magical and heavenly connotations. The phrase is also used in esoteric geodetic dowsing.

Geodetic magic squares can be found either inside or outside of certain sacred sites and their purpose is to link the *planetary genii* to the monument. This is because the primary concern when building a temple was to attract the gods, or forces in nature, to which it was dedicated. This was achieved by the occult lore of 'like attracts like'. Michell says:

> "Each temple or construct included symbolic reference to the appropriate deity and was orientated according to the season and the heavenly body corresponding to the deity, whose characteristic numbers were expressed in the dimensions of the building."

In esoteric dowsing, geodetic magic squares—those that appear as surface patterns—are the opening gateway to connect with a deity's spiritual power, a supreme location where one can summon its energy and bring it down to Earth. The square allows the Earth and the structure to resonate with the deity's inpouring energy. One needs to prepare oneself for working with magic squares and know how to open and close the gates. In the British Isles, Avebury has the largest magic square, and Stonehenge's lintelled circle is squared by a magic square.

The Seven Wonders of the Ancient World

In 1531, the occultist Heinrich Cornelius Agrippa, drawing on the Hermetic and magical works of Marsilio Ficino and Pico della Mirandola, expounded on the magical virtues of planetary squares in much the same way as the older texts. Agrippa inspired the work of Alphonse Louis Constant (1810-1875), known as Eliphas Lévi, a French magician and a brilliant occultist who influenced the mystery school movements, including the Hermetic Order of the Golden Dawn. Adept at the magical arts and with medieval grimoires at his disposal, Lévi states that the 'Seven Wonders of the Ancient World' formed an astrological system that was laid out to a cosmological order, each planet associated with a magic square and radiating from central points on the Earth's surface—natural centres of terrestrial currents.

Fig. 233 The tomb of Mausolus at the British Museum, London.

Each magic square harnessed a particular planetary force, and the 'Seven Wonders of the Ancient World' were designed as instruments for the *control* of that particular aspect of cosmic energy. Lévi wrote that:

> The Colossus at Rhodes equates to the Square of the Sun.
> The Temple of Artemis at Ephesus to the Square of the Moon.
> The Tomb of Mausolus to the Square of Venus.
> The Pyramids of Egypt to the Square of Mercury.
> The Towers and Gardens of Babylon to the Square of Mars.
> The Statue of Jupiter of Olympus to the Square of Jupiter.
> The Temple of Solomon to the Square of Saturn.

Most dowsers and ley line researchers know of the existence of large global grids which appear as lines that cover the planet from pole to pole, like giant fishnets. The crossing points of these grid lines often connect site after site, worldwide. However, despite being far smaller, planetary squares are actually stronger grids, likened to a magical key that can unlock and activate a temple's power.

Back in the 1990s, my late father and I were the first British dowsers to be shown how to detect and interact with magic squares. Magic squares draw in planetary energy and each planet has a *sigil* or *seal* that is designed to block that planet's energy. A seal is a geometric sign designed to touch all of the numbers in a mystical embrace, and which seals or negates the energy of that planet. These sigils are used in talismanic magic to represent the entire square and to act as a witness that governs it. A planetary seal is a useful tool that can be likened to an 'on/off' button. Blocking a planet's energy at times of retrograde motion may be useful if one feels that its negative effects are likely to be experienced. Mercury's retrograde motion, for example, invariably affects communication, so if one has an important job interview or lecture during a retrograde period, by placing a planetary seal over the planetary square this will diminish the effects. One must, however, remain mindful that when blocking a planet's square, you are blocking *all* of the effects of that planet, the more positive energies as well as those considered potentially harmful.

Additionally, using gematria, each planet has an *Intelligence* and a *Spirit* derived from the key numbers of its square. The Intelligence refers to a planet's consciousness, viewed as an inspiring, evolutionary or informing entity, while the Spirit is considered a more blind, baleful and chaotic force. Each has a divine name that was listed by Agrippa: Saturn's Spirit, for example, is Zazel. Some magicians use the grid-like square to entrap, but the Spirit is crafty and can easily outwit its antagonist. The planetary Intelligence cares little for its jail, becoming silent, and 'open and close sesame' are the gateways that *invite* its energy. Agrippa called the magic square a *compass* as it brings forth direction for each of the symbols. The divine names of the Intelligence and Spirit of a planet are calculated by adding up the value of each letter of its name in Hebrew—each letter can represent both a sound and a numerical value.

Chinese Magic: The Saturn Square as Lo Shu

Geodetic Saturn squares are often located in the ceremonial landscape, and they are the most common of all the planetary squares. At the Rollright Ring, in Oxfordshire, several are found within the stone circle. Likewise, they can be found just outside of Woodhenge (near Stonehenge), also in front of a megalith at Avebury, at Karnak in Egypt, and Hagar Qim in Malta. Unlike a mathematical Saturn square, the energy level of a geodetic Saturn square can be raised to the power of 5, 10 or 15. The number 15 happens to be the number of days it takes for a New Moon to become a Full Moon, representing the growth of power and luminosity.

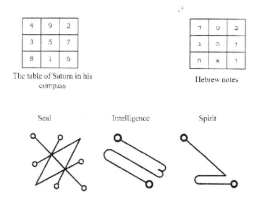

The table of Saturn in his compass

Hebrew notes

Seal   Intelligence   Spirit

Fig. 234 The Saturn square.

After studying the power of the squares with a European Master Dowser, my late father wrote:

> "By manipulating the squares of the opening sesame square
> I can raise the energies of a site by a factor of 5, 10, or 15,
> then close the energies back to normal by manipulating the
> closing sesame gate."

Utilised in one Masonic rite, a Saturn square has a yin/yang polarity and a vortex motion. Prior to entering a religious construct, or Lodge, the initiate would stand on a Saturn square for 10 or 15 seconds to experience aura expansion. The Master Mason's Saturn square is shown in *Fig. 235*. By constructing a straight horizontal line from the tip of one of the compass points to a point one-half a unit away, one can add the value of one-half to the line from G-A. This results in a line segment which is equal in length to the divine proportion, Phi, shown as a dashed line in the diagram.

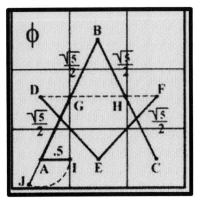

Fig. 235 The Mason's magic mathematical Saturn square.

The Saturn square's total number of 45 resonates to man, and 15 is the Hebrew *jah*—a name of God. The Saturn square has the colours of contrast, the black of midnight and the white of the midday Sun; the dark earth and life brought forth through the fertile earth that promises a fruitful harvest. To the ancient Chinese geomancers, the Saturn square had a mythical birth, and is intimately associated with Feng Shui or the 'art of placement'. In the history books of ancient China, it is written that sometime around 2000 BC, a noble turtle emerged from the legendary river Lo, carrying on its back a Saturn square. This became known as the *Lo Shu square*. The 'Magic of Three' exerted a powerful and mythical influence on Chinese cultural symbolism. The grid corresponds to the Pa Kua of the eight directions, which is centred on a ninth pivotal point and used in the 'art of placement'. Number 1 is north and 9 is south, as shown in *Fig. 236*. The numbers also create connections with the four celestial animals: the dragon, phoenix, tiger and the turtle.

The Lo Shu Saturn square became the foundation of Taoist magical practices, with which many of Taoism's magical rituals continue to be synchronised. Scholars studying the origins of the Lo Shu grid have speculated on the striking similarities between the grid's numbers and certain potent symbols from other cultures, especially the ancient Hebrew seal for the planet Saturn, which is similar to the symbol created by the

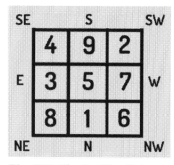

Fig. 236 The Lo Shu Saturn square and the directions.

sequence of numbers in the Lo Shu. As with all the seals, the Saturn seal, shown in *Fig. 234*, is constructed by drawing lines that intersect every number within the magic square. When used in the art of placement, the seal creates terrestrial harmony. A geodetic Saturn square found in a domestic setting is called *hara*, which is an aspect of its Intelligence. Chinese geomant Mike Chan dowsed one of these in my home; he designed highly sensitive dowsing rods to detect geodetic squares and vortex energy. I still use and sell these rods, as they are perfect for this type of esoteric dowsing.

The Jupiter Square: the Magick of 4

Jupiter is called the great benefactor by ancient astrologers; it rules money, growth and success. Its colours are blue and purple. Containing 4 squares and 4 columns that have a sum row of 34 and a total of 136 makes this square fortuitous. In temple design, Jupiter squares were favoured for large statues to personify the planet's genii (soul), imbuing the statue with planetary power. At Karnak in Egypt, on the Sagrada Familia church façade there is a manipulated Jupiter square.

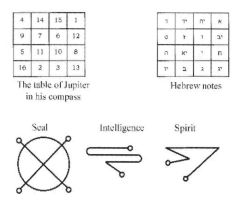

Fig. 237 The Jupiter square.

Fig. 238 Albrecht Dürer's magic square.

In 1514, Albrecht Dürer depicted the Jupiter 4 x 4 square in his engraving *Melancholia*, which represents the indecision of the intellect. According to scholars, the Jesus-Jupiter square, shown above in *Fig. 238*, contains a subliminal message hidden within the numbers. Adding up the numbers that repeat and converting them to their corresponding Roman letters, gives the initials INRI which means *Iesus Nazarenus Rex Iudaeorum*, 'Jesus of Nazareth King of the Jews'. This is the title the Roman Emperor, Pontius Pilate, wrote on Jesus' cross.

The Mars and Templar Squares: the Magick of 5

The Mars square can relate to male sexuality, fertility, destruction, conflict and anger. Its colour is red, and it also rules over one's energy levels, ego and the divine masculine. The Mars 5 x 5 square contains the 25 numbers from 1 to 25. Each row, column and diagonal adds up to 65, and all of the numbers total 325. This planetary square is often called the *Sator-Rotas square* or the *Templar magic square* because the Knights of Malta cross fits into the square that connects all of the letters from 'A' to 'O' and unites with 'E'. The letters 'A' and 'O' are said to represent the Alpha and Omega, which

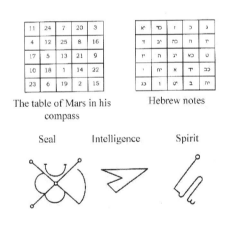

Fig. 239 The Mars square.

are also embedded within the anagram of *Pater Noster*, an old power charm. One of the earliest examples was discovered scratched onto the wall of a buried house in Pompeii. The early Christians used this square as a powerful amulet, which has surfaced all over the world.

In Rome, during the Middle Ages, this magical square was inscribed onto everyday objects such as cups and over doorways, to ward off evil spirits. In France, at the 11th-12th century collegiate church of Saint Ours, overlooking the medieval town of Loches, in front of the altar is a mosaic beneath thick glass that reads: *Sator Arepo Tenet Opera Rotaso*, linking it to a Templar square.

Fig. 240 Templar square.

Some years ago, when I was asked to help 'heal' a house, I was told that the former occupant was a Madame and a witch, who had placed a strange symbol close to the entrance. It turned out to be a Mars square, used to attract men, sex and money, and to ward off negative energy. I said to the present owner, "She is no witch, but rather a knowing and clever Magician!". Having cleared the house and dissolved certain aspects of the square's energy, today their legitimate business thrives.

The Sun Square: the Magick of 6 and the 'home' of 666

The Sun square relates to health, vitality, the heart, creativity, power, success and leadership. Its colours are gold and yellow. Stonehenge, like the Colossus of Rhodes, the bronze statue of the Sun god Helios, houses the square of the Sun with the High Magic of 6, having 6 rows and 6 columns containing the numbers 1-36. Each row adds up to 111 and the total to 666. The Biblical King Solomon knew the magic of the squares and noted the number 37 is one third of 111, said to be 'the highest life', 'to burn', 'splendid', 'a flame', 'a blade' and 'greatness'. 111 is the Intelligence of the Sun, Nakiel. The Spirit of the Sun is Sorath.

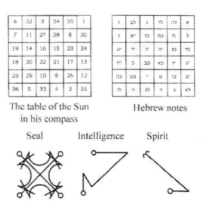

Fig. 241 The Sun square.

Historically, royalty and the priesthood had magic squares woven into their residences to ensure solar protection. The Sun square was carved onto an iron plate and used in AD 1273 for the protection of the palace of Prince Anxi, and today can be seen in Shaanxi Museum, dating from China's Yuan dynasty. The Masons continue to incorporate planetary squares into their buildings. The main Masonic building in Washington DC which serves as the headquarters of the Scottish Rite of Freemasonry, officially home of the Supreme Council 33°, has a Sun square window that allows sunlight to flood into the temple room. Hidden within the ground plan is a geodetic Sun square, which can be activated and used at times when the Sun is at its most powerful, or a numeric code such as 111 or 666 applied. Adepts can raise the power of the square by 11, 111 or 666, but I would suggest leaving that to them as the Sun square contains not only the 'Number of the Beast' (Spirit) but the 'Smiting Power of God' (Intelligence)—the darkness within the light.

The Venus Square: the Magick of 7

Corresponding to love, female sexuality, art and music, the energy of Venus is highly creative. Its colours resonate with pink and green. Hagiel is the Intelligence of Venus, meaning the 'murmuring of God, murmuring of doves, lamenting or sighing, the purring of a lion over its prey and the muttering of enchanters'. This 7 x 7 square has the numbers from 1 to 49, which add up to 175 and total 1225. The Intelligence of Venus can be contacted in one of Stanton Drew's stone circles; its placement is encoded by a square-shaped stone found in the great circle that also contains a Venus square. Interestingly, in the northeast is a Venus stone circle: its eight stones mark the 8 years and 99 Full Moons of the Venus pentagonal cycle. When summoned, the Spirit of Venus can provoke violent, tumultuous storms.

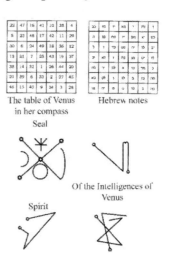

The table of Venus in her compass

Hebrew notes

Seal

Spirit

Of the Intelligences of Venus

Fig. 242 The Venus square.

The Mercury Square: the Magick of 8

The high magick of Mercury is communication with worldly and otherworldly beings, information, science and writing. Mercury is the psychopomp who escorts newly deceased souls to the afterlife, not to judge but to guide them. Mercury's correspondences also relate to buying and selling, wisdom, cleverness, creativity and memory. Associated herbs and oils are rosemary, amber, lilac, lemon, sage and cherry. The magic square of Mercury contains 64 numbers ranging from 1 to 64, and each row, column and diagonal adds up to 260, with 2080 in total.

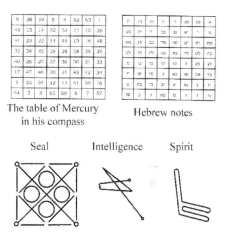

The table of Mercury in his compass

Hebrew notes

Seal   Intelligence   Spirit

Fig. 243 The Mercury square.

Lévi stated that the Great Pyramid was associated with a Mercury square embedded into its square foundation, resonating to the Intelligence of Thoth/Mercury for all time. The Spirit of Mercury is chaotic and has a darkness that should not be invoked as it is the supreme Master of trickery and illusion.

The Moon Square: the Magick of 9

The Moon square correspondences are dreams, psychic energies, secrets revealed, birth and fertility. Its colours are white and silver, and the Moon rules the feminine. Containing 9 rows of 9 squares of numbers that equal 369, the sum of all the numbers used is 3,321. Large and energetically powerful, early secret societies encoded this square into churches dedicated to Mother Mary and Mary Magdalene, to commune with the Intelligence of the goddess.

37	78	29	70	21	62	13	54	5
6	38	79	30	71	22	63	14	46
47	7	39	80	31	72	23	55	15
16	48	8	40	81	32	64	24	56
57	17	49	9	41	73	33	65	25
26	58	18	50	1	42	74	34	66
67	27	59	10	51	2	43	75	35
36	68	19	60	11	52	3	44	76
77	28	69	20	61	12	53	4	45

Fig. 244 The Moon square.

In occult tradition we have seen that the planets possess ethereal souls responsible for baleful and beneficial influences. Likewise, a geodetic magic square always contains both qualities. The qualities of the Sun square can lighten the darkest of nights, yet it also houses the number 666, the darkness within the light. It is said by some Magicians that the summoned Spirit of Venus, as an earthquake, destroyed the mausoleum at Halicarnassus. The Knights of St John of Rhodes invaded the region and built Bodrum Castle (of Saint Peter) that was fortified in AD 1494 using the stones of the mauso-leum. Some researchers list the lighthouse of Alexandria as one of the 'Seven Wonders'. However, occultists insist that the true wonder of the ancient world was Solomon's Temple which stood on Temple Mount and once housed great treasures. After visiting Egypt several times and exploring its magic squares, I noted that like 'The Seven Wonders of the Ancient World', the temples of Egypt are a divine reflection of the solar system and several temples correspond to a planetary geodetic square.

Planetary Squares and Egyptian Temples

Below I give a list of some examples of magic squares and their cor-responding temples. However, this list can be extended to include many other temples and old city complexes throughout the world.

The Sphinx and obelisks—the Sun.
Hathor's Temple—the Moon.
The Great Temple of Thoth/the Great Pyramid—Mercury.
The Temple of Isis—Venus.
Edfu Temple—Mars.
Temple of Amun-Re, Karnak—Jupiter.
The Serapeum of Saqqara—Saturn.

One might ask if these enigmatic small grids are a reality? Saturn squares were my late father's favourite dowseable energy, and so we wanted to prove or disprove their existence. At Avebury, in the southern inner circle, a Saturn square of great power can be found. Rodney Hale conducted an ionising radiation test over the square in the company of my father and myself. We noted that over the square the count was lower at 67.1 counts per minute (cpm), and the control higher at 70.4 cpm. Rodney suggested the test was worth repeating, "to see if there really is a lower count at the centre that somehow changes the environment." Using a spectrum analyser, a retired engineer and I conducted an additional frequency test. We noted a 2495 Hz emission over the square, and the control was 1748 Hz. In another experiment, the millivolt reading was lower than the control. Rest assured, this square is extraordinary as it can change energy and frequency levels, expand one's aura and consciousness, and it also contains a portal gateway. It should be pointed out, however, that although planetary squares are seemingly hidden and obscure, they are often in plain sight.

Chapter 16

New Discoveries ~
Ancient Agriculture and Earth Energy

Millennia ago, the ancients lived in harmony with Mother Earth, and they understood that the earth force was a vital key to ensure a successful harvest. Earth energies can stimulate growth, and this is how crops were successfully cultivated on cold northern hill slopes, as prehistoric lynchets and field systems attest. Geo-pathic stress zones (toxic earth energies) were marked out as areas to be avoided as they can be injurious to some plants and living organisms. It was not until the 1950s, with the advent of manmade fertilisers, that food production of the Late Bronze Age (c700 BC) was surpassed. Working in harmony with Gaia's energies, the ancients knew the geomantic secret of how to enhance seed germination, and they constructed a particular kind of monument solely for this purpose. Additionally, they knew where to plant to gain maximum yields, understood the most favourable locations to store seeds, ripen fruits and vegetables, and where to stable livestock for the benefit of their health. Geodetic integration of farm and field became as complex as the ritual landscapes that preceded it. I suggest this agrarian knowledge was handed down to the medieval aristocracy who became wealthy landowners, as they too often adopted a similar farming template.

During the 1990s, the late John Burke and Kaj Halberg conducted a series of experiments to investigate the relationship between ancient sites and seed germination. Using an electrostatic voltmeter, ground electrodes and a fluxgate magnetometer to measure electrical currents, ionisation and magnetism (the same equipment used by a retired engineer and myself), they investigated various sacred sites worldwide. Having recorded high levels of electromagnetic energy within a New England stone chamber sited in magnetite country, one of their experiments demonstrated that seeds placed within this chamber germinated earlier, grew straighter, faster and were more uniform in growth compared to the laboratory control samples. The chamber's energy somehow influenced germination and plant growth beneficially. Further analysis showed that the air inside the stone chamber close to the ceiling included negative ions and the more positively charged ions were closer to the floor; this separation of charge set up a measurable pulse within the chamber.

After investigating numerous monuments worldwide, from pyramids to henges, the authors realised that invariably ancient sites were located at places that geologically had high electrical and magnetic fields. Also, at locations where there is *conductivity discontinuity*—when a geological zone conducts electricity well and meets an area that conducts an electrical current less well—these locations, it was noted, produced strong surges of geomagnetism and ground electrical currents. At dawn, magnetic field levels are at their peak, producing high levels of electrostatic field strength as well as ground electrical currents—telluric currents. This makes it an ideal time to charge seeds within a sacred site, such as a stone chamber or upon a mound. Later, I shall challenge this model and demonstrate that earth energies assist in the charging mechanism and that magnetic field levels and ground electrical currents at dawn are not necessary for plant growth. I have extended Burke's work which focused on seed germination, but I have not examined *where* to plant seedlings, or *how* to successfully store surplus grain. Advancing Burke and Halberg's initial research, I reveal how earth energies were successfully integrated into a prehistoric farming template.

Neolithic Cenotaph Long Barrows
There is a particular kind of a monument that has defied explanation and baffled archaeologists for decades, and so it has been largely ignored. The monument in question is called an *unchambered earthen long barrow* or *cenotaph long mound*. I am going to propose that this was used to enhance seed germination. Its characteristics are that it contained no burial deposits and was inaccessible; it is just a long

mound. Yet, great lengths were taken to identify it from other long barrows that were used for ceremonies and burial deposits.

Burke noted that the Olmec civilisation of Mexico constructed earthen mounds and pyramids with well-engineered electrical properties. He says, "Villages with a mound enjoyed a better standard of living than otherwise identical villages nearby." Alongside an engineer, I used an electrostatic voltmeter, as did Burke, and our measurements show that some of the Wessex cenotaph barrows have similar, and often far greater, ground electrical properties than those recorded by Burke.

Long Barrows and Soil Boundaries

Archaeologists generally interpret cenotaph long barrows as either a boundary marker to distinguish different regional tribal areas, or as a memorial to those who died in war, conflict or accident when their bodies could not be retrieved for burial; thus, a mound was raised. However, excavations in the Avebury area tell a different story. As mentioned earlier, over 8,000 years ago, if not longer, the Mesolithic geomancers conducted a detailed land survey to identify soil boundary zones. Then, during the Neolithic, the long headed people constructed a cenotaph long barrow at these locations. For example, one of Avebury's cenotaph long barrows was placed on a former Mesolithic site, on the *exact* boundary between rendzina and brown soil, and another long mound was raised on the boundary of chalk and gault clay. I noted that cenotaph mounds were colour coded to distinguish them from chambered long barrows that had been finished with gleaming white chalk and used as temple spaces and for burial deposits. In contrast, a cenotaph long mound incorporated two colours, and geodetic energies were boosted by planetary magnetism. Combining astronomical knowledge with geomantic awareness, the long headed people developed an advanced agricultural mound-based technology of a kind the world has never seen.

An excellent example of a cenotaph barrow is the Beckhampton Road Long Barrow, which was solid and inaccessible. Centuries before its construction, the Mesolithic geomancers created a notable axis-line of pits on a soil boundary between rendzina and red-brown earth. I discovered that soil boundaries produce a strong geodetic energy flow of 15 lines. Marking its precise geological edge, the earthen long barrow was raised above it. Internally, the long mound was sub-divided along its axis with several internal bayed structures, each of which was filled with 'contrasting material' (the actual material was not described and may have been layers of organic and inorganic material akin to an orgone generator), and a large sarsen stone was positioned within the mound. Its north and south sides were located on a former Mesolithic cultivation site; clearly not all Mesolithic people were hunter gathers. Material extracted from the flanking ditches created asymmetrical colouring: the north side consisted of compacted brickearth soil making it a reddish-brown in colour, and the south side was chalk white. When first constructed, the mound would have been noticeably different to the chambered temple burial mounds in both composition and colour.

Around 7 miles (11 km) away and similar in construction, was the South Street cenotaph long mound. A remarkable crescent-shaped zone of massive chalk pieces defined its frontage. Creating a noticeable textural and colour contrast, its north side consisted of coombe rock (chalk and flint fragments contained within a mass of chalky earth, making a kind of gravel), and again its south side was smooth white chalk. Once again, beneath the mound were deep grooves forming a criss-cross pattern; these were identifiable plough scars from early Mesolithic cross-ploughing, overlaid by earth ridges for tillage using a spade or hoe. Still think the Mesolithic were hunter gathers? Beckhampton Firs Long Barrow was identical in construction to Beckhampton Road, and it too had several base pits and was finished in reddish brown brickearth and contrasting white chalk. Close to Windmill Hill causewayed enclosure, near Avebury, yet another cenotaph mound was placed on pre-mound activity of seven large pits, some of which were 16.5 ft (5 m) wide. Although their original function is uncertain, these pits were clearly an integral part of cenotaph mound construction. Unfortunately, most of the earthen long mounds have been ploughed away, and only notes from early excavations record their former existence.

Stonehenge's Cenotaph Mound

Located half a mile (800 m) to the north of Stonehenge, the Greater Cursus, dated to around 3800 BC, formed a large enclosure consisting of two roughly parallel chalk banks and ditches around 310 ft (100 m) apart that coursed for nearly 2 miles (3 km). These take their name from William Stukeley, who believed them to be Roman racetracks. Today, little exists of the once gigantic monument which was aligned roughly east-west towards Equinox Sunrise. Located 65.5 ft (20 m) from its eastern end was a cenotaph long mound, 265 ft (81 m) long by 70 ft (15 m) wide and 4 ft (0.9 m) high. Further afield in East Riding, Yorkshire, as mentioned earlier, is one of Britain's most unusual long barrows. Excavated in 1860 by William Greenwell (1820-1918), it consisted of two long mounds joined together to form a dramatic V-shaped earthen structure. The north mound contained a cremation area with disarticulated human bones, but the southern mound was a solid inaccessible cenotaph mound. Notably, all cenotaph long barrows are sited on a geospiral energy pattern as well as earth currents and, as previously noted, if located upon a soil boundary, a 15-fold geodetic energy line will be present.

Cenotaph Barrows and Celestial Magnetic Storms

Burke realised that ancient cultures placed seeds upon mounds and within stone chambers to enhance seed germination. I propose that in the British Isles the cenotaph mound was constructed *solely* for this purpose. I will demonstrate its unique connection to the wider agricultural landscape and show that stone chambers are not necessary for seed enhancement. Burke was unsure of the exact timing required for this process, suggesting "summertime or during thunderstorm activity," which he observed produced exceptionally good results, especially at dawn due to telluric currents. However, I noted that a reliable timing system using certain planetary alignments may have been employed—this is because when two or more planets form a major astrological *aspect*, then celestial magnetism occurs. Astrological aspects are the conjunction 0°, sextile 60°, square 90°, trine 120°, and opposition 180°. In the 1950s, when John Nelson checked radio signal records going back to the 1920s, he noted that the conjunction, square and opposition coincided with, or could produce, magnetic storms that can cause radio disturbances. Interestingly, some of these aspects were at times deemed problematic by ancient astrologers, yet during periods of more favourable aspects such as the sextile and the trine, he noticed that no magnetic storms occurred, and shortwave radio reception was good. Nelson's findings gained support in both astronomical and meteorological circles. Yet, despite the fact that his predictive forecasts on magnetic storms and radio disturbances were 93% accurate, his findings were largely dismissed by the wider scientific community.

Some twenty years later, supporting evidence from Drs A A Boe and D K Salunkhe of Utah State University, confirmed that the movement of celestial bodies can cause magnetic fluctuations; they noted an increase in the fertility of plants as the chemistry of the mineral content of the soil was changed. When the Sun is 90 degrees from the Moon, at its first and last quarter, it coincides with a magnetic storm. However, on the previous day—six days after a New or Full Moon—a geospiral changes its rotation from clockwise to anti-clockwise motion (or vice versa), a movement that rests at the Quarter Moon. To determine the influence of a particular aspect, astrologers refer to an *orb of influence*. This defines the range of degrees before and after the exact aspect, where its effect is thought to extend. For example, some astrologers recommend an orb of 6 degrees for major aspects between planets (the distance apart), but 10 degrees when involving the Sun and the Moon. Using this system renders the sixth day after a New or Full Moon especially potent as the magnetic storm is waxing, coinciding with a geospiral beginning, before ending its rotational cycle within the orb of influence at the Quarter Moon. That said, charged seeds at the Quarter Moon also grow more robust and taller than a control batch. Unlike Burke's suggestion of dawn, any time of the day is effective, in any season or weather pattern, as this planetary timing sequence utilises both earth *and* celestial energies.

Dolmens and Conductivity Discontinuities

Another type of Neolithic monument is called a *dolmen*; they too were constructed by the long headed civilisation. I believe these were also used for seed enhancement as well as other agricultural practices. Burke focused on seed charging for cultivation, but looking at the wider picture, dolmens may have been used to charge seeds prior to underground storage which was standard practice in the Bronze and Iron Ages. Most dolmens are associated with three or more aquifers that generate an intense interfluve. Burke explains:

> "…interfluves are usually powerful conductivity discontinuities with abnormally large daily surges of electric current and geomagnetic field strength."

More than that, as mentioned, they produce an incredible rotational energy surge twice a month, six days after a New and Full Moon.

The Devil's Den
The following survey shows that the Devil's Den dolmen, near Marlborough, in Wiltshire, was placed above the meeting point of three large aquifers and three lesser ones (see *Fig. 245*). all of which are at various depths with emerging underground streams that flow towards a nearby trackway. In terms of earth energy, when aquifers merge, they generate intense concentric circles of energy—this is the most powerful interfluve in the Avebury area as it generates 224 concentric circles. That's powerful! Burke described interfluves in

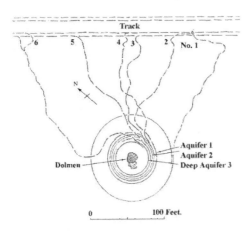

Fig. 245 The Devils Den: the meeting zone of three deep aquifers.

scientific detail, but to date no one has shown what an interfluve actually looks like in water divining terms. Additionally, due to its strong and vast circular electromagnetic energy field, I think a dolmen's primary function may have been to ripen fruit or other foodstuffs. Boe and Salunkhe noted that when green tomatoes were placed within a magnetic field, they ripened four to six times

Fig. 246 The Devil's Den.

faster than under normal conditions. Prior to storage, perhaps seeds were also charged to encourage longevity. With such metaphysical agricultural knowledge, it is little wonder that Diodorus of Sicily remarked in the first century BC that the ancient Briton's had two harvests a year and supplied Greece with an enormous amount of produce.

Spinster's Rock

Spinster's Rock, standing in a field near Drewsteignton, Dartmoor in Devon, is another dolmen associated with intense aquifer energy. Supported by three uprights at a height of 9 ft (2.7 m), the capstone weights 16 tons. Legend says that it was constructed one morning before breakfast by three spinsters. Perhaps they relate to the Fates, the Moirai of the Greeks. The three spinsters are the daughters of Mother Night, conceived without a father: Clotho was the spinner, Lachesis the measurer, and Acropos, whose name means 'she who cannot be avoided', was the cutter. Together, they wove the destiny and length of a mortal's life, and their decisions could not be changed even by the great god Zeus. Creating a powerful interfluve that undergoes electrical surges twice a month, Spinster's Rock is the meeting point of one large groundwater aquifer and two exceptionally deep aquifers, each of which generate a geospiral of 35, 21 and 7 coils respectively, shown in Underwood's survey in *Fig. 247*. There are also four lesser 'pools' of water, and in total 140 concentric rings are generated, making this monument an ideal location for agricultural purposes.

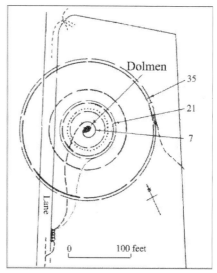

Fig. 247 Spinster's Rock. Survey by Guy Underwood.

Pentre Ifan

Pentre Ifan is a stunning dolmen set in the heart of bluestone country in Pembrokeshire, Wales. There are six upright stones, three of which support the giant 16½ ft (5 m) long capstone that weighs around 16 tons. Incredibly, it is located above the meeting place of four aquifers emitting 112 concentric rings. Perhaps these monuments were multifunctional and served those that constructed them in more ways than one.

Fig. 248 Pentre Ifan dolmen.

Plant Germination and Surface Water

In 1930, V Kiviera experimented with plant germination and demonstrated a relationship between water and accelerated plant growth. He germinated plants in closed glass vessels that were sunk in water to depths of 4.9, 49 and 492 ft (1.5, 15 and 150 m) respectively. After ten days it became apparent that the growth of seedling germination increased the greater the depth of water. One of his conclusions was that seedlings at a greater depth were screened from ionising cosmic radiation and, despite the lower temperatures, their growth was accelerated. He suggested that:

> "…this obeys a general rule, that whereas heat, infra-red and Hertzian rays tend to hasten metabolism and cell division (and suppress disease therewith), the actinic, ultraviolet and yet higher frequency electromagnetic radiation tend to suppress and retard vital processes, owing to their ionising character."

Could this explain why some monuments are associated with rivers? Archaeologist David Fields noted:

> "…the siting of long barrows on Salisbury Plain appears to be remarkably riverine, with examples set on the slopes and above the River Avon, by the Winterbournes and springs of the River Till and elsewhere."

Numerous long barrows on Salisbury Plain, some of which are cenotaph barrows, were situated close to rivers and water sources. For example, Stonehenge's main avenue joins the River Avon at West Amesbury; Marden Henge consisted of an earthen henge with the Avon forming a significant part of the enclosure, and Avebury's Beckhampton Avenue crosses the River Winterbourne. The Late Neolithic Palisade Enclosures at West Kennet, contemporary to Avebury's stone circles, incorporated the River Kennet. In Somerset, Stanton Drew, the world's second largest stone circle, has an avenue that once led to the River Chew. Whilst seed germination enhancement was taking place at cenotaph mounds, the possibility that growth acceleration may have occurred by placing certain species of seedlings into river water cannot be ruled out. Perhaps these technologies may have assisted in food production requirements for the large and extensive megalith building programme—there were many mouths to feed!

Long Barrow Experiments

The geospiral *and* the mound are the principal elements required for seed enhancement. It is apparent that a mound's construction, and invariably its soil boundary location, appears to boost the geospiral's energy. Within a megalithic chamber, Burke noted that heavily charged positive ions sink to the lower levels and negatively charged ions rise, which, he said, assisted in germination and thus plant growth. Additionally, his laboratory experiments using metal plates with an opposite charge supported these findings. However, I suggest the primary factor is the electromagnetic energy released by the geospiral the mound is sited upon. Compared to a long barrow that was used for ceremonial and burial purposes, extra care was always taken in the construction of a cenotaph mound—while inaccessible they were clearly built for a reason. Although Burke pointed out that the best time to charge seeds is at dawn, due to the heightened magnetic and electrical telluric currents in the ground, especially when wet after rain or during a thunderstorm, I would like to again stress that the time of day is *not* critical. I personally believe that the ancients utilised the sixth day after a New or Full Moon to charge seeds, or the seventh day when the Sun is square to the Moon.

Fig. 249 Tidcombe Long Barrow.

To verify this, 27th June 2020 was selected as a suitable date, when the geospiral's rotational switch occurred on the sixth day after the New Moon. For 15 minutes, at 11.30 am BST, close to the hottest part of the day, I placed some parsley seeds above the Tidcombe Long Barrow's geospiral. The following day, at First Quarter Moon, the control seeds and the charged seeds were planted in identical pots containing exactly the same amount of soil. The experiment was conducted outdoors in natural sunlight and the same amount of tap water was used to maintain growth. Interestingly, the geospiral charged seeds were slightly slower to germinate than the control sample, which surprised me. However, they soon overtook the control sample with vigour. Growing perfectly straight, their stalks appeared thicker, taller and stronger than the control batch. Additionally, the charged seedlings were the first to flower. Burke noted that his charged seed samples germinated faster, and likewise grew straighter. From each batch, the tallest and healthiest looking seedling was selected for measurement. The charged parsley seedling grew to 2.9 in (7.5 cm) and the control to 1.9 in (4.9 cm). This is shown in *Fig. 250*. Other experiments carried out at these lunar phases will be described shortly, which also yielded excellent results. I also experimented with *soil charging* at the Devil's Den dolmen, near Marlborough. Organic soil was used and charged for 15 minutes inside the dolmen. Uncharged seeds were placed within separate plant pots that contained charged and uncharged soil. Interestingly, once again the seeds in the charged soil germinated slower but then grew faster, stronger and straighter than the control batch.

Could it be that our ancestors were charging seeds and potting soil at sacred sites, and this is why Britain, according to its chroniclers, was renowned for two harvests a year? I noted that the ancients had developed a sophisticated farming pattern, and that seed germination was only a small part of this. Whilst studying with archaeologist Lisa Brown at Oxford University (CAT points degree course), I realised there is far more to these ancient agricultural practices, and that a Bronze Age farming template once existed that identified earth energies and decoded the land prior to farming crops and husbandry activities. Through an intimate understanding of Gaia's earth and cosmic energies, prehistoric farmers could harvest 1.7 tons per hectare. This is a little-known fact!

Fig. 250 Charged seedling (right), uncharged (left).

Chapter 17

Geodetic Agricultural Templates

During the Middle Bronze Age (c1500 BC) there was an agricultural revolution. The landscape was divided into open and enclosed field systems. Archaeologist Lisa Brown explains:

> "Britain was being transformed like never before and the reorganisation of the British landscape became the island's greatest communal effort to date that outstripped the monumental efforts of the Neolithic and Early Bronze Ages. Thousands of square miles of land, especially the lowlands were transformed from informally worked tracts and short-lived settlements that were overtaken by linear land divisions, larger farms and a network of field systems."

The status and value embodied in this agricultural paradigm replaced the old economies of the Neolithic and Early Bronze Age exchange networks, which were based on trade in cattle and exotic objects such as jadeite axes, jet, shale, gold, amber, pottery vessels and bronze. The new 'money' was in farming. Communities benefited from living in harmony with the land as geodetic energies dictated the placement of tracks, roads, field boundaries, entrances and enclosures, as well as ponds. Intensive year-round agriculture gave a vast amount of surplus produce, and an extensive European trade network in commodities was established. Writing in the sixth century BC, Hecataeus, an early Greek historian and geographer, stated that Britain reaped two harvests in one year, which, as mentioned, was later retold by Diodorus. Reaping spelt grain in winter and emmer (prehistoric wheat) in summer, Britain was sending regular supplies to mainland Europe and to Greece. Thus, Wessex farmers became rich in a land of plenty. Remarkably, despite the passage of time, we still live amidst prehistoric land divisions. Archaeologist Bob Clarke pointed out to me that the positions of some of our modern-day parish and county boundaries, trackways and hedges can be traced back to their Bronze Age origins. After studying numerous ancient farmscapes, I realised that a persistent pattern recurred, which I believe is based on this prehistoric template that produced plentiful harvests and surplus trade.

Cenotaph Seed Experiments

The Bronze Age Beaker people continued to use seed enhancement technology. However, instead of reusing the existing long barrows, some of which may have become ruinous as they were now two thousand years old, new cenotaph round barrows were raised. Yet again, archaeologists explain these as memorials for the dead and for those whose bodies could not be returned for burial. As it was standard practice to bury personal artefacts with Bronze Age inhumations and cremations, then why weren't items belonging to, or representing, the deceased deposited in these barrows? Furthermore, it was common to insert secondary burials into a round barrow long after the primary burial. Rarely were such burials put into cenotaph mounds, which makes this a strikingly different kind of monument in its own right. Cenotaph round barrows may have life-increasing and life-enhancing properties.

Fig. 251 Cley Hill and its Bronze Age cenotaph round barrow.

Crowning Cley Hill earthen enclosure near Warminster, in Wilt-shire, is a large cenotaph round barrow, shown above in *Fig. 251*. During an earlier excavation, beneath its summit and towards the lower section, undecayed emmer ears were found that were perfectly intact after 4,000 years of being entombed. One presumes they would have rotted and died; the fact they did not is astounding, hinting at the mound's life-enhancing energies.

Close to Stonehenge, Colt Hoare called Amesbury 55 round barrow "The Monarch of the Plain". It is the largest cenotaph mound in the area, standing 10 ft (3 m) high and 162 ft (58 m) in diameter. I chose this mound to repeat my seed enhancement tests to ascertain if the results would be similar to my previous long barrow experiment. On a *very* hot summer's day, on the sixth day of the New Moon on 24th August 2020, at 3 pm BST (avoiding dawn and any telluric current surge), cress seeds were placed on its summit for 15 minutes and a control sample from the same batch was left uncharged. Once again, the seed samples were planted in the same size pot and given equal amounts of water. Just as in the previous experiment, the charged seeds were slower to germinate. However, like the parsley seeds, they soon grew faster, straighter and stronger. Compared to the uncharged seeds, they were on average 0.78 in (2 cm) taller. For two hot days the seedlings were deliberately not watered, and it was noticeable that the charged seedlings suffered far less wilting than the control batch. Clearly, they were more resilient and robust.

Scratchbury Camp's Cenotaph Mound

About 7 miles (11 km) from Cley Hill is Scratchbury Camp, a magnificent Iron Age ceremonial enclosure that was fortified during the Roman invasion. With extraordinary views, this earthen enclosure consists of a single rampart which is over a mile (1.6 km) in circumference. Originally, it had brilliant white chalk banks and, according to Colt Hoare, a deep ditch that at its greatest height was 66 ft (20 m). The main entrance faces northwest towards the Midsummer Sunset and a narrow entrance in the east faced the Equinox Sunrise. An older Neolithic earthwork lies at its centre, and seven round barrows grace its summit.

Fig. 252 Scratchbury cenotaph barrow.

Conspicuous for miles is Scratchbury barrow, a large cenotaph round barrow, 12 ft high (3.5 m) and 100 ft (30 m) in diameter, shown above in *Fig. 252*. To put its size into perspective, Stonehenge's lintelled circle is 108 ft (33 m) in diameter. Notably, when cenotaph mounds are found in round barrow groupings, they are always the largest and most well-constructed, and always sited on a geospiral pattern, whilst the others are not.

On the sixth day following September's New Moon in 2021, a batch of parsley seeds was charged on the mound. Once again, the charged seeds were slower to germinate but they soon caught up and out-grew the uncharged batch. Measuring the tallest in each batch showed the charged seedling was nearly 2.95 in (7.5 cm) tall, whilst the uncharged seedling was shorter at 1.85 in (4.7 cm) (see *Fig. 253*), and the charged plants were always the first to flower. Offering support for cenotaph barrow agricultural usage, Burke pointed out that the larger mounds produce the best seed enhancement. Several exceptionally large cenotaph mounds can be found in Wiltshire, such as Silbury Hill, near Avebury; Merlin's Mount, in Marlbor-ough; Enford Barrow on Salisbury Plain; and Hatfield Barrow at Marden Henge, the largest henge in Britain with a huge diameter of 1,738 ft (530 m). Prior to its destruction, the Hatfield cenotaph barrow stood 30 ft (9 m) high and was 200 ft (70 m) in diameter.

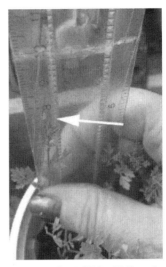

Fig. 253 Left: control seedling, nearly 1.85 in (4.7 cm).
Right: charged seedling, nearly 2.95 in (7.5 cm).

Cultivation Template

From the Middle Bronze Age, a spectacular agricultural template was adopted that consisted of several crucial monuments: a *cenotaph mound* that was invariably placed close to, or within, an earthen enclosure or hillfort; lengthy serpentine earthworks called *ranch boundaries*; earthworks called *cross-dykes*; large ditches known as *boundary markers*; cultivation areas termed *Celtic field systems*; and vast strips of *cultivation lynchets* that are linear earthwork sections, usually found on a hillside, some of which were reused in the Roman, Saxon and medieval eras.

I noted this monumental patterning is repeated, time and again, and persists across the country, creating numerous farmscapes. A good example can be found at Cley Hill. As previously mentioned, this hilltop earthen enclosure contains a huge cenotaph mound that is surrounded by Bronze Age ditches and ranch boundaries, numerous Celtic field systems and cultivation lynchets. Certainly, there are many Late Bronze Age lynchets associated with hilltop farms that are round or sub-rectangular. An excellent example, according to archaeologist Eric Wood, can be found at Ogbourne on the Marl-borough Downs, in Wiltshire. Others of a pastoral kind are to be found at Thickthorn, Dorset; Martin Down, Hants; and Albury in Surrey. Battlesbury Camp, on the edge of the Salisbury Plain, also has an earthen enclosure, inside of which is a cenotaph mound, with nearby Celtic field systems and extensive hill lynchets sited on the northeast and southeast slopes. Other examples in Wiltshire include the vast Celtic fields, lynchets and boundary ditches associated with Barbury Castle earthen enclosure, near Wroughton. This is repeated on Salisbury Plain at Bratton Castle and Sidbury Camp. Likewise, another can be found at Scratchbury Camp and at Whitesheet Hill, some 10 miles (16 km) to the southwest, a large cenotaph mound is sited within an earthen enclosure and surrounded by fields.

Fig. 254 Cultivation terraces, near Battlesbury hillfort.

Interestingly, early Celtic field systems that were not associated with an earthen enclosure, some of which span hundreds of acres, always incorporate cenotaph mounds, ranch boundaries and ditches. These are not random farming activities but a prehistoric agricultural design canon—a template. This is because the layout of Celtic field systems, mounds, lynchets, ditches and ranch boundaries were not arbitrary; the ancients knew exactly *where* to plant. Today, we dictate to the land where we choose to plant, imposing our own desires, whereas in prehistoric times awareness of the land's harmonious and disharmonious earth energies was made visible and planted accordingly. Archaeologists are often puzzled as to why lynchets and low banks that mark the outline of some Bronze Age fields are seemingly randomly placed and "straggle down the hillside in no regular pattern" either in the upper or lower section, not the entire hill; some even curve in a serpentine manner when it would have been labour-saving and easier to make them straight. Prehistoric cultivation lynchets are remarkable, given that some face the cold, harsh north with areas of shade for much of the day, yet would have still yielded a harvest. This is because they were sited upon aquastat earth energy flows. *Fig. 255* below gives a linear mound as surveyed by Underwood, who incorrectly interpreted them as processional ways. They were cultivation terraces, which I suggest were used to enhance agricultural production, as most plants thrive on these harmonic earth energies.

Most linear mounds and some cross-dykes, which are often believed by archaeologists to be 'just' boundary markers, are always aligned upon aquastats and are sometimes accompanied by a water line (underground

Fig. 255 Linear mound and aquastat placement (Underwood, 1950).

stream of yang water) that generates an energy field conducive for farming. Despite flowing at different depths, when in close proximity or they cross at right angles, these set the width of the lynchet, imbuing it with unseen energy, as shown in *Fig. 256*.

Fig. 256 Earth energies set the width of the lynchet (Underwood, 1951).

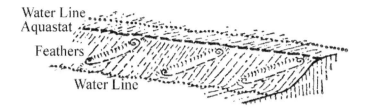

Fig. 257 Fast flowing underground streams generate feathering energy.

When the underground water is fast flowing, or if an aquastat is located between two water lines, a secondary earth energy pattern called *feathers* is produced (see *Fig 257*), creating a highly charged and beneficial energy field for crop cultivation, especially root vegetables. I have found growing radishes and onions on this energy especially productive.

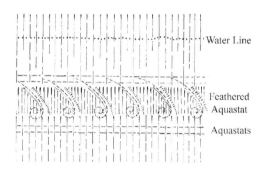

Fig. 258 Feathered aquastats generate spiral energy fields.

When two or more aquastats flow closely together, one will produce feathers and this is called a *feathered aquastat*, shown in *Fig. 258*. Found on old lynchets and cultivation terraces they are especially beneficial to plant life. Underwood thought these were hillside sacred walkways, but most archaeologists agree they were created for agricultural usage. In the medieval period, some lynchets were reshaped and reused. Likewise, in Peru, the Incas were aware of aquastat energy flows, and living in the mountains they incorporated these energies for farming by creating elaborate terraces in flat land, in a similar way to that shown here in *Fig. 259*.

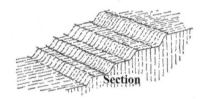

Fig. 259 Cultivation terraces and aquastats.

Celtic Field Systems

Unlike prehistoric field systems, modern fields are not laid out in a sacred manner. Looking like a patchwork quilt, Celtic field systems blanketed the sloping ground of hillsides. They incorporated earth energies and solar alignments connecting the Earth to the Sun and integrated astronomy and geomancy, as did the stone circles that preceded them. The ancient field systems of Salisbury Plain have been carefully surveyed and excavated, to

Fig. 260 An example of a Celtic field system.

find that many mirrored Stonehenge's astronomical axis. Six co-axial field systems were aligned to the southwest and northeast, facing respectively the Midwinter Sunset and Summer Solstice Sunrise. Co-axial field systems are a complex design in which the boundaries of adjacent fields form a series of roughly parallel lines that serve as trackways or droveways, and they are often associated with cenotaph barrows. These too are associated with ley lines, underground streams, aquastats, feathers and earth currents.

Serpentine Fertility Earthworks: Ranch Boundaries

Revered by our ancestors, earth energies were seen as a divine manifestation of Gaia's life force. Although invisible to the naked eye, earth energy flows were made recognisable to the initiated, whilst remaining visible yet incomprehensible to outsiders. Monumental in scale and size, ranch boundaries—also known as *linear earthworks*, although they are not usually straight—can be up to 50 miles (80 km) long and some were 10 ft (3 m) high, the height of Avebury's henge bank, and were likewise chalk white. Many of the shorter and straighter examples are called *cross-dykes* or *cross-ridge dykes*, an integral part of the agricultural template that span narrow necks of land, running between steep slopes or sheer escarpments. For example, Hampshire hilltop enclosures, such as at Woolbury,

Danebury, Quarley Hill and Sidbury Hill, were all established at junctions or terminals of linear earthworks. Constructed from the Early Neolithic onwards, one of the earliest examples can be found on Hambleton Hill in Dorset, dated to around 3600 BC.

Interpreted as land division markers by archaeologists, *serpentine ranch boundaries* are often associated with either a wide aquastat or a powerful earth current that courses through field system after field system; they can be seen as fertility serpents and *serpentine mounds* were often sited above them. Another form of earthwork called a *hollow way* has large banks to either side that are said to be *drove-ways* for the movement of cattle from one enclosure to another, and sometimes created sheltered trackways. This distinctive type of hollow way followed an earth energy flow called a *trackline* which consisted of two triad lines that animals such as sheep, cattle and horses naturally follow. However, other hollow way earthworks sited upon aquastats led to rich and fertile farmland that was associated with cenotaph mounds, lynchets, cultivation fields and terraces. Antiquarian reports state that these were single, double, or even had spectacular triple banks with an accompanying ditch, and

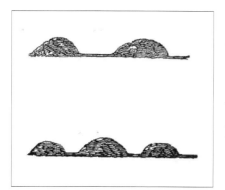

Fig. 261 Antiquarian drawing of mounds that led to fertile pastures.

the largest bank was centrally placed. An excellent example can be found close to Tidcombe Long Barrow on Chute Causeway, in Wiltshire, where parallel triple-banked mounds targeted fecund pastureland. Several antiquarians and early archaeologists noticed that the mounds invariably led to fertile fields. One farmer told an antiquarian: "The soil in the neighbourhood of these works was remarkably fertile." Colt Hoare documented such mounds before they were ploughed, and noted:

"The whole surrounding country clearly demonstrates, by numerous banks and enclosures, a very remote and extensive cultivation. The banks and ditches are so confounded with the lynchets, that it becomes a difficult matter to separate them, one ditch section forms an angle round a large and fine bell barrow [cenotaph], then ascends the hills towards Twin Barrows, near which we find another bank and ditch steering westward towards the River Avon and which is visible for some distance across the down and fields."

What he describes is geomantic farming—marking the flow of aquastats and earth currents that imbued the land with fertile energy. Consistently, the template of cenotaph barrows, hollow ways, ditches, serpentine ranch boundaries, Celtic field systems, cultivation terraces and lynchets is repeated. Farmers in the 19th century reported that "near these earthworks the land was *always* rich and fertile." This is no coincidence; it is geodetic engineering.

Agricultural Experiments and Underground Streams

Snaking across the land, earthwork mounds were set above underground yin streams that could generate a 30 ft (9 m) wide harmonic energy field either side of its main flow, irrigating the landscape with life-enhancing energy. Previously, it was noted that when two aquastats flow near to one another, a vast feather energy pattern is produced. Six days after the New and Full Moon the feathers reverse their position, i.e., those which face right turn left, and vice versa. They are actually double triads which assist fertility and growth, but for simplicity only one was drawn in *Fig. 257*. However, when flowing alone, groundwater (yang water) generates *geopathic stress* (toxic earth radiation). Ingeniously, ancient geomancers made these flows visible by digging deep ditches upon them, thus identifying potential areas to be avoided. Archaeological surveys of agricultural landscapes confirm that if a wide ditch is present, there was little farming activity or the land was left fallow.

Modern-day dowsers are aware that groundwater has a detrimental effect on some living organisms as it emits a Hertzian energy field that can stunt growth and cause plant disease. This was investigated

Fig. 262 Aquastat mound courses for miles and marks fertile energy zone.

in the 1940-60s when numerous experiments were conducted above various underground streams, some of which involved seed germination and electrical field analysis. It was concluded that plant growth was influenced by ionising rays, whether naturally or artificially produced. Sixty years before Burke, it was observed that electrical earth currents benefited plant growth, whereas groundwater created localised positive ionisation that was injurious to plant growth, animals and humans. Other experiments noted that during maximum sunspot activity and at the Full Moon, the growth rate of trees increased. It was demonstrated that crops such as parsley, different cabbage varieties, turnips and sweet peas, grown above an underground stream, and for several feet on either side, showed reduced growth compared to their control groups.

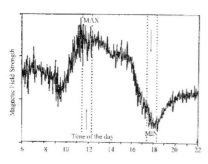

Fig. 263 Graph showing magnetic peaks detrimental to plant growth.

An underground stream flowing with 300 gallons per hour at a depth of 45 ft (13.7 m) can produce a toxic field up to 60 ft (18 m) wide. Experiments have shown that potted parsley grown directly above an underground stream that flowed with 1,000 gallons per hour in 20 ft (6 m) of limestone, grew 50 percent better when placed several metres away from the underground stream. My own experiments confirmed that potted parsley grown above a fast-flowing underground yang stream likewise resulted in reduced growth. Magnetic intensity recordings above the stream also showed variations in strength. In this instance, minimum peaks occurred in the early morning and around 5 pm, with maximum peaks around midday and midnight, and at 11 am and 11 pm. It is these peaks that are detrimental to plant growth.

The variations of electric earth potential between an open stream and the adjoining moist grass-turfed ground were also studied. Results showed how the electrical field peaked at 4 ft (1.2 m) away from the stream. Another experiment was conducted above an underground stream for electrical and magnetic variations. New analysis revealed that the magnetic changes may be more fundamental than the electrical current in this regard. The same relationship was observed in underground streams where it was noted that

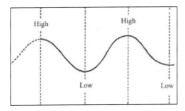

the field strength 30-40 ft (9-12 m) above ground level was almost as strong as at ground level. When ionisation levels over underground yang streams were recorded, it was noted that at certain times they peak and trough, as shown in *Fig. 264*. Ancient farmers were aware of these detrimental effects and marked the course of large underground streams with deep, wide ditches, knowing the land on either side produced geopathic stress, and so, invariably, as mentioned, it was left fallow.

Fig. 264 Ionisation levels showing peaks and troughs.

Geodetic Farming
One example of geodetic farming can be seen at Sidbury (Chidbury) Camp on Snail Down, close to the town of Tidworth. This heart-shaped double banked earthen enclosure lies on the eastern edge of Salisbury Plain; sections of the Iron Age hillfort are located within the MoD impact zone, making parts of it inaccessible to civilians. Enclosing 17 acres, its once tall ramparts have been mutilated by military tank manoeuvres which have disfigured the monument.

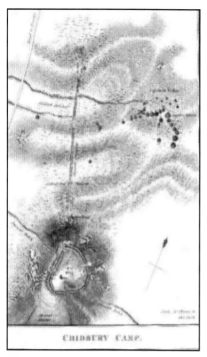

Fig. 265 Antiquarian drawing of Sidbury Hill and earthworks.

Beneath this enclosure stands the largest cenotaph mound complex in Wiltshire that may have been used for charging seeds on a vast industrial scale. Of the twenty-six round barrows, nine are cenotaph: 5, 10, 11, 12, 13, 21, 22, 23 and 25, and the largest, No. 25, known as King Barrow, stands 13 ft (4 m) high and is 98 ft (30 m) in diameter. Cross-dykes and serpentine ranch boundaries course through its adjoining field system and a Late Bronze Age/Iron Age town was located north of the mound cluster. My geodetic survey of the area reveals that the ancients divided productive earth energy cultivation areas from intense geopathic stress zones. Fig. 266 shows this area enclosed by two deep ditches, also a lengthy ditch to the south, all of which mark wide underground yang streams or rivers and were set aside as fallow land; notably only two small fields were placed within these zones. Coursing through the extensive Celtic field system are double aquastats that produce a rich feathering pattern, nourishing the land with harmonic energy. Ancient man clearly would not have repeated this practice if it were of no value. There is no doubt that in antiquity the entire country was covered with numerous earthworks that served an important purpose in marking major geodetic track lines, aquastats, earth energy currents and groundwater areas, creating a nationwide geodetic farming network.

Fig. 266 An agricultural template.

Field Systems and Solar Alignments

Overton Down, near Avebury, contains a variant template consisting of a vast Celtic field system spanning miles of chalk downland. Many of these survive as co-axial square-shaped fields adorning the hillsides, edged with sarsen stones to form low stone rows. The stones were positioned to mark the aquastat energy peaks or nodes, as shown in *Fig. 267*. In 1948, Underwood surveyed the area for aquastats, which alongside their 15-30 ft (4.5-9 m) parallels and large feathers make the entire area fertile. The sides of the fields all line up to form a giant pattern that once stretched symmetrically across the countryside. Each field faced the path of the Sun at its zenith, giving life to the plants that grew in its radiant warmth. Crops also benefited from the electrically charged earth currents that brought a daily surge of energy and guaranteed a plentiful harvest. Once again, deep ditches that followed geopathic stress flows were avoided. Holistic understanding of the land avoided manmade interference so that Gaia and the Sun breathed life into the land and its crops—geodetic fertility at its finest.

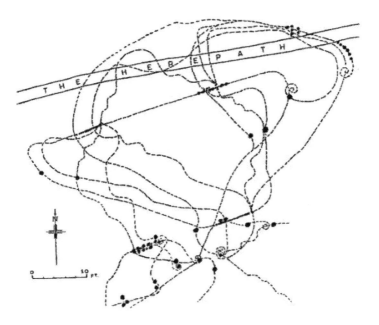

Fig. 267 The Harepath on Overton Down.
Aquastats create a fertile field system.

Our research shows that electrical currents (AC and DC fields) are emitted by groundwater and aquastats. According to old water divining lore, a current of electricity is said to flow from the mouth of the river, which is negative, of any stream or river towards the source, which is positive. This may be one of the ways in which the negative charge of the Earth is dissipated. My dowsing discovered that underground streams, springheads and aquifers share this characteristic, emitting an additional electrical current that flows from an aquifer to an underground springhead/blind spring. Studies have shown that a DC electrical field can influence plant growth, seed germination and weight change. Tests have also shown that applying a DC field to daikon radish and thale cress improved their seed germination rate and resulted in an increase in length and weight. In the past, the DC fields emitted by earth energies may have been utilised in this manner.

Across the British Isles there were similar agricultural templates. At Gib Hill, in Derbyshire, sited 98 ft (300 m) from Arbor Low stone circle, is the largest cenotaph mound in the county. The two sites were once connected by a serpentine earthen mound that marked the course of a strong earth current. Not far away, and discovered by aerial photography, are extensive field systems known as Cow Low that show probable integration of geodetic energies, as does the largest settlement in Derbyshire, on Gibbet Moor. Further north in the Yorkshire Wolds, serpentine earthworks and cultivation terraces can be found, where there is extensive evidence for prehistoric settlement and land use, including substantial boundaries dating from the Neolithic period. Crop marks in Durham and Northumberland suggest field systems were interspersed with enclosed and unenclosed farmsteads. Without a doubt, the evidence in the landscape is unambiguous and shows a deep metaphysical awareness of Gaia's invisible earth energies.

Prehistoric Fertiliser and Grain Storage

Burke stated there was no evidence for prehistoric fertiliser usage. This, however, is incorrect as Late Bronze Age fertilisers were found to have been created in Wiltshire at large midden sites, such as East

Chisenbury, All Cannings Cross, and Pottern, near Devizes. Some middens were used for hothouse food production, whilst others were monumental in size covering some 6,5616 ft (20,000 m). That some modern-day farms are still benefiting from the fertile midden sites created in the Bronze Age is a little-known fact.

Another key component to successful farming is grain storage. Today, whole grains are usually stored in airtight containers with tight-fitting lids or closures. The type of container used is a matter of preference: glass, plastic and aluminium canisters or zip-top plastic bags can all be effective, as long as they remain airtight. These are all above ground storage facilities, whereas in the distant past storage was always below the ground—in the womb of Gaia. Archaeological experiments conducted at Buster Farm in Hampshire, by Dr Andrew Fitzpatrick of the University of Leicester, demonstrate how grain was successfully stored in prehistoric times. Applying Late Bronze Age techniques, he used underground sealed circular and beehive shaped storage pits to determine that grain could be stored for many years without spoiling. Furthermore, he noted that grain stored underground has twice the germination rate of that stored above ground. Recent research at Buster Farm has shown that yields of emmer wheat and spelt, with the correct competitive weed flora, likely averaged over 1.7 tons per hectare. Not only is this comparable to early 20th century yields, but it also suggests that the harvest from one hectare will fill, in threshed form, more than one storage pit. Furthermore, if the grain is stored in the ear, it will fill at least three pits. These yield figures indicate the need of our ancestors for intensive bulk storage facilities.

During another excavation in Hampshire, at Danebury Ring, an Iron Age hillfort which was an occupied site for nearly four centuries and a major grain storage facility, Sir Barry Cunliffe found 2,400 storage pits and he estimated another 2,000 in the unexcavated area. These pits were of a variety of shapes, the most popular being circular and conical. One pit was nearly 10 ft (3 m) deep, 18 in (80 cm) wide at the mouth, and 8 ft (2.4 m) across at the base, with chalk walls and floors cut completely smooth.

Segsbury Camp, an Iron Age earthen enclosure in Berkshire, will be my last example of geodetic farming. Its farmland has a series of so-called boundary ditches, some of which course for thousands of feet, whilst others are short and do not always appear to function as a boundary marker; with reduced field and fallow areas they relate to geopathic stress zones. Aquastats are a main feature and course through the Celtic field systems with some water lines showing they generate feathering. There are also several cenotaph as well as burial mounds. Interestingly, the outline of the whole system at Segsbury (see *Fig. 268*) appears as the side profile of a young woman's head.

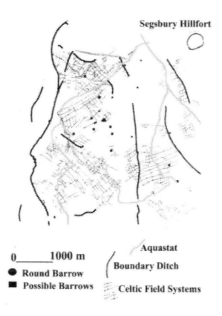

Fig. 268 Segsbury farming template.

I have noted the criteria for intensive Bronze Age farming, from cenotaph mounds and ranch boundaries to solar aligned Celtic field systems and ditches that marked the flow of chronic geopathic stress zones, injurious to plant life. My own careful examination by dowsing in areas on chalk downland shows that when groundwater flows are over 2,000 gallons per hour, no arable fields were present. When a crop was grown close to a ditch, it was likely to be one that thrives on geopathic stress, such as peas. Prehistoric farmers clearly understood the nature of earth energy emissions.

Ley Lines and Reduced Plant Growth

In the 1970s, agricultural scientist, Dr J Havelock Fidler, studied how ley and megalithic energy affected seed germination. His professional expertise offers valuable insight through the eyes of a scientist into dowsing ley energy. Havelock Fidler discovered a geodetic energy pattern called a *petrostat*. This is similar to Underwood's aquastat (12 hairlines) and my own geodetic soil boundary line (15 hairlines). A petrostat has nine hairlines of an aerial type of energy similar to a ley line and is released from a *charged* stone. Following the same procedure used in his agricultural trials, Havelock Fidler developed several experiments to determine if petrostat energy influenced seed germination. He used Lethbridge's *long cord* pendulum, which differs from the modern *short cord* pendulum that relies on 'Yes/No/Maybe' answers in response a question.

With a short cord pendulum, if one wants to know, for example, the depth at which water occurs at a site, one has to ask the question: Is the depth of the underground water deeper than (say) 250 ft (76 m)? If the answer is 'no', the figure is reduced to (say), 200 ft (61 m) and so on, until a number is obtained using progressively smaller units of, for instance, 5's or 10's. Using this procedure, the conscious mind is directing a specific question to the subconscious mind, which replies through the medium of the pendulum by either going back and forth or round in circles. The long cord pendulum is different in that the conscious mind is not concerned in any way; instead, it is the *field* around the object being dowsed that is reacting. One can use a long cord pendulum even when thinking about something else, or when the mind is blank, which is preferable, as the mind can easily influence the pendulum's movement if one has a preconceived idea or notion of the likely answer—a well-known pitfall of short cord pendulum dowsing and the reason why it can be inaccurate.

Using the long cord pendulum, Havelock Fidler began a series of tests to determine if petrostat energy influenced plant life. Three stones, with a male charge, a female charge, and no charge (control), each weighing 3 lb (1.5 kg), were placed into a 7 lb (3 kg) tin so they would be shielded from outside influences (the charging process is explained in Chapter 7). On each stone was placed a 2 in (5 cm) plastic plant pot containing identical weights of compost, each pot having been planted with seven mustard seeds that received an equal amount of light and water. After twelve days, the seedlings were large enough to be removed, washed and dried, and weighed to the nearest milligram following agricultural trial protocol. The seedling growth above the male charged stone was 56 percent of those on the uncharged stone, and on the female charged stone it was 69 percent. When Havelock Fidler applied an 'Analysis of Variance', the mean reduction in the weight of the seedlings on the male charged stone was 27.5 percent less than on the uncharged (control) stone, whilst those on the female stone were 31.5 percent less. There appeared to be no difference in germination rates, although there was a significant difference in weight—the growth of the plant. To rule out chance, the trial was repeated three times and the results were the same. Havelock Fidler decided to increase the 'charge' of the stone to see if this would further damage the mustard seedlings' growth rate, and he discovered that the weight of the seedlings was inversely proportional to the charge of the stone. However, this did not prove the 'charge' was responsible as it could have been the power of the stone in the first place. So, to find out, another trial was set up using uncharged stones weighing 0.44 lbs (200 g) to 3.5 lb (1.6 kg), upon which new seedlings were placed. The seedlings showed little difference in growth and weight, proving the factor concerned was the charge and not the actual stone itself.

As charged energy is similar to ley energy, an experiment was designed to test if it too had a detrimental affect by placing potted seedlings on a ley—to the best of my knowledge, this test has not been duplicated. The experiment was repeated several times to ensure that chance could be ruled out and the results unambiguous. The ley line had the same influence as the charged stones, and the mean weight of the seedlings was reduced by 20.3%. However, there was one new factor, which was that germination was noticeably reduced in the plants located on the energy line when compared to the control plants; the mean reduction was as large as 52.9%, a highly significant result. This puzzled Havelock Fidler as he knew that germination generally takes place when seeds come into contact with water in the presence of oxygen, and if oxygen is removed from the air the seeds will not germinate in nitrogen. Warmth is required and the seedlings were given all the necessary requirements for successful germination. Certainly, atomic radiation can harm seeds, but the radiation from charged stones or ley lines surely could have no such power, yet his scientific trial proved otherwise. I repeated this experiment by charging seeds on a local ley line and again the control batch was healthy whilst the ley seeds exhibited stunted growth. Other types of seedlings were used such as peas, beans, cress and turnips; the latter, a member of the mustard family, was affected in a similar manner, but the others were less affected.

Many ley hunters have noted that Caledonian Pine trees grow well on leys and European dowsers are aware that certain trees thrive in geopathic stress zones. Havelock Fidler mused that fractured ley lines, due to modern roads and buildings, may behave in a similar manner, producing geopathic stress. He suggested that in laying down the ley system, megalithic man may have been trying to rid an area of undesirable forms of energy. Ancient Chinese geomancers were well aware of this potential danger and avoided living upon straight dragon lines. As previously mentioned, Burke was unsure of an accurate timing system for seed enhancement and suggested that the summer months may be the most beneficial or during thunderstorm activity. However, to see if this was correct, using the same equipment as Burke, on a cold February morning, we repeated one of his experiments and obtained dramatic electrostatic readings on

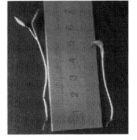

the summit of Silbury Hill, far greater than Burke's summertime reading, so questioned his initial findings.

On 29th November 2022, a bitterly cold and foggy winter's day, six days after the New Moon, I returned to Tidcombe Long Barrow to conduct another seed enhancement test. Could seeds be charged to hasten germination during the coldest and darkest time of the year?

Fig. 269 The charged seedling (left) grew faster and taller.

Parsley seeds were charged for 15 minutes longer than previously. Seven charged and uncharged seeds were planted in identical pots containing the same amount of compost and placed on a window sill. Remarkably, five of the charged batch of seeds germinated first and grew much faster, but only one of the seeds from the uncharged (control) batch germinated. By 1st January 2023, the tallest charged seedling was 2.89 in (7.4 cm), but the control seedling only reached a height of 1.96 in (5 cm), as shown in *Fig 269*.

Land Division and Geodetic Energies
Natural land boundaries are formed by the sea, rivers and chains of hills. In times past, due to the permanent nature of geodetic energies, these undeveloped features became boundary markers that were utilised for field and land division, the placement of droves and roads. Many old walls, hedges and tracks were also aligned to geodetic lines, which is why some are crooked, curved or winding, when it would have been easier and less costly to make them straight. Whenever possible, field entrances were aligned on geo-spirals or primary spirals, from where geodetic lines diverge and flow out into the landscape. Cattle and other farm animals regularly follow tracks when passing from one field to another, and these routes invariably follow geodetic flows that consist of two triad lines of energy. Cattle naturally sense these energies and leave through those entrances, so they rarely break out through fences as some-times happens with modern-day field division.

Historical documents show that land division was the concern of the priestly caste; their ability to tell with certainty whether or not a boundary had been altered would have enhanced their reputation as possessing supernatural powers. Caesar says that the Druids ad-judicated in all disputes relating to boundaries, and other writers attest that Druidic training included the art of measuring the Earth's surface. Similar training in geometry and geodesy may have been given during the preceding Neolithic and Bronze Age periods.

Professor A L Tchijevsky was the first to state that negatively charg-ed air which animals breathe in and plants absorb leads to increased cellular activity and metabolism, whereas positively charged air has the reverse effect or a depressive action. My experiments with a retired engineer show that converging aquastats change the air quality by producing negative ions. Air ionisation tests over a *power point*— where numerous geodetic aquastat lines and/or primary haloes converge—show a loss of positive ion(s) (electrons). We discovered that negative ions gain an electron from tests at Stone 4B along Avebury's West Kennet Stone Avenue.

Research has shown that certain animals are sensitive to different types of earth energy: horses, cattle and sheep are attracted to geodetic energies that emit negative ions. These animals, as well as pigs, dogs, cats, badgers, moles, hares, rabbits, tortoises, lizards, geese, owls, rooks, wild bees, ants and gnats are all aware of geodetic energy flow in the ground. Cats, ants and some gnat species are, however, attracted to geopathic stress emissions. That wild animals tend to follow tracks is an established fact, demonstrated by the buffalo and caribou trails of North America that extend for hundreds of miles, and those made by the elephant, deer, kangaroo and other game familiar to hunters and trappers. The reason why animals follow these tracks has never been satisfactorily explained. Our ancestors recognised life-enhancing geodetic emissions and aligned country lanes upon them, which is the reason why they meander. I also discovered that some of these trackways equate to musical ratios such as the perfect fifth, which allows ease of movement.

Many farmers are aware that animals kept in confined or enclosed spaces frequently break out to give birth; research has shown that they locate a geospiral or an aquastat primary spiral above which to give birth. There is some indication that a geospiral's energy can ease labour and produce healthier offspring. Mountain sheep excavate bays and scarps in hillsides as secure places to lamb, which are almost always associated with the spiral phenomena. Free range geese and hens seek out secondary haloes on which to nest and poultry keepers have admitted to Master Dowsers that their resulting broods are healthier than those hatched in coops. These outdoor geodetic nesting places are seldom molested by foxes; as mentioned earlier, the secondary halo is seen as a protective force. Birds such as owls and rooks nest above geodetic energies and horses favour such places to graze, especially 'pensioner' horses kept on farms. Animals would not behave in this manner unless it were of advantage to them, and it is difficult not to conclude that such places must have health-gaining or restorative properties, which is instinctively recognised by animals. Cows gather and sleep above geodetic spirals and, interestingly, cows have played an important role in the founding of cities. The Greek city of Thebes was founded by Cadmus who, having listened to the great Oracle of Delphi, as instructed founded the city where a sacred cow came to rest. The site of Troy was similarly selected by Ilius, and some legends say that Antioch was built over the place where Io died after she had been changed into a white cow by Zeus. Geospiral energy also appears to assist rheumatism, and in the 1940s a medical friend of Underwood said that during the Peninsular Wars the old campaigners sleeping rough always chose a place where a cow had lain because to sleep there meant they would not get rheumatics. Instinctively, animals know what is good for them and ancient civilisations also sensed and dowsed geodetic energies.

Geodetic farming continued into the Dark Ages. The Saxons were village dwellers and managed open field systems of furlongs that were not always straight; their vestiges can still be seen today, and they too followed earth energies. Later, during the medieval period, ploughing strips called *ridges* and *furrows* became common farming practice. Although some of these may originate from much earlier, they often show signs of a main crop growing area associated with aquastats and feathers. My family own ancient land that has ridge and furrow mounds, and I have noticed the buttercups appear far healthier and taller on several of the mounds associated with geodetic energy. In middle England, until the 18th and 19th centuries, the land reflected former open fields systems that were cultivated in strips; some were kept for orchard planting whilst others were left fallow. Most villages comprised houses with crofts attached, located along a narrow street or facing onto a green, behind which were back lanes with local roads determined by the field system. Some known examples of different types of village green may still be seen at Finchingfield, in Essex, the street at Long Melford, Suffolk, and the square village at Piercebridge, County Durham.

By ploughing separate furlong strips, this built them up in ridges; in many places these are separated by *balks*, narrow grassy boundary banks or footpaths. During the Inclosure Acts from the early 17th century, old farming methods of open field systems were replaced by enclosing the land with boundaries and hedgerows—the onset of the Industrial Revolution changed England's rural landscape and communities beyond recognition. From the 1950s onwards, chemical fertilisers were used to stimulate plant growth, cenotaph mounds were ploughed away, and memories of geodetic farming faded with only the unused lynchets to remind us of a time when humankind worked alongside Gaia. I would like this imbalance to be restored, and while some of this information compiled from Master Dowsers alongside my own dowsing and research may need adapting, I hope that much will be of interest and great worth.

Modern Geodetic Farming: Bali, Indonesia

Despite the passing of time, some ancient forms of geodetic farming are still being employed today. Traditional ways of growing rice in Bali were studied by a European Master Dowser, who dowsed numerous rice fields and noted a repetitive farming pattern, a template. Most rice fields house a shrine-like feature that is placed above a highly energetic earth energy pattern called an *earth chimney* or *geochimney*, which occurs every 33 ft (10 m). This can draw energy up from the earth or down from the cosmos. Interestingly, most geodetic energies emit a dominant colour frequency, and some colours can assist certain plant species—this adds a new dimension to geodetic farming.

In the 1980s, *earth colours* were discovered by two Belgian professors of physics and a Master Dowser German financier, who was an expert in macroeconomics. Their collaboration took dowsing to a new level. Independently, they undertook several experiments which determined a colour sequencing emitted by earth energies. I have been trained in this branch of 'High Frequency Colour Dowsing', as was my late father, who designed a dowsing aid that can quickly ascertain the colour, frequency and polarity of earth energies and leys. In total there are thirteen earth colours that can vary in strength and frequency. Each earth colour has a polarity: magnetic is positive and elevating, while electric is negative and enervating. Red, orange and yellow earth colours are said to be more earth-bound, and the geochimney associated with the rice shrine, shown below in *Fig. 270*, emits an orange magnetic frequency that stimulates rice growth. Dowsing investigations of house temples on Bali found that specific rituals, dedicated to the rice goddess Dewi Sri, appear to temporarily boost earth energy frequencies without permanently changing them.

Fig. 270 Rice fields contain a shrine feature set above a geochimney.

Likewise, Celtic field rituals were once performed to enhance crop growth. One such rite was recorded in the 11th century: an old Anglo-Saxon field charm, known as the Æcerbot, was to remedy poor yields. This healing spell that began at midnight and lasted for a day, honoured the Earth Mother and consisted of a partially Christianised prayer with its roots in Paganism. Four sods were taken from the field and a mixture of yeast, honey, oil and milk, mixed with parts of all the good herbs that grew in the field, save buckwheat and woody plants, was applied. The sods were taken to mass and returned to the field before nightfall, each with a small

Christian cross planted upon it. Back in the field, the healer faced the direction of the east and turned three times clockwise, calling upon "the holy guardian of the heavenly kingdom to fill the earth," so that the crops may grow. A plough was anointed with a sacred blend of oil, frankincense (imported frankincense was a Christian addition), salt and fennel. This was followed by chanting a song that began *erce, erce, erce, eorþan modor* (Earth's Mother), before the field was ploughed to a chant hailing *erce, eorthan modor*. The word *erce* may derive from the Old High German meaning "true, genuine", and refers to the true Earth Mother.

From Europe to the fertile rice fields of Bali, geodetic energies and their associated colour frequencies were integrated into sacred sites, domestic settings, farmsteads and fields. Miller and Broadhurst noted the earth currents they named *Apollo* and *Athena* correspond respectively to the earth colours of ultraviolet and red. Austrian hunters are aware that deer have their favoured sleeping spots, well hidden in the forest, and that their 'paths' cover vast distances. It has been observed that they tend to follow blue earth currents or lines, leading researchers to conclude that animals in the wild perceive these energies even during the darkest nights, when they tend to be at their most active. Likewise, four Alpine valleys were dowsed for sheep and goats, and traditional 'sheep paths' were also found to emit a blue frequency; this runs through the Rofental, the Niedertal, Schnals and part of the Timmelsjoch. Typically, these blue energy lines range between 3-32 ft (1-10 m) wide, with an often gentle and nurturing energy. Broadhurst and Miller also noted that the oldest pilgrimage paths to Mary sites follow blue earth energy currents; a similar blue energy line is associated with the old Kaltenbrunner pilgrimage site in the Tyrol. Without a doubt, an acute awareness of geodetic energies was utilised by our ancestors, creating a divine connection to Gaia's colourful energies. To return to this way of farming and restore balance to the land, is a way forward that could go hand in hand with other holistic farming methods.

Chapter 18

Endings ~ The Black Eclipse

O ur journey to understand Stonehenge has taken us near, far and wide. I travelled to various museums and universities to photograph skeletal remains and discovered that Stonehenge was constructed by a long-lost Neolithic civilisation that had vanished from the archaeological record. These small, possibly ethereal-looking people constructed this multi-functional stone circle that underwent several different phases. It is undeniable they moved the heaviest of stones; for example, the Cove Stones at Avebury have been dated to the Neolithic era and comprise some of the heaviest stones in Britain, weighing over 100 tons. And, as previously stated, often the femur bones of these people included an extra muscle attachment, developed as a result of carrying heavy loads. These are all clues that help to solve an age-old puzzle.

These enigmatic people knew the secret properties and language of stone. I have demonstrated that the lozenge-shaped stones were aurally programmed and probably thought of as being 'alive', just as the statues of ancient Egypt were thought to *contain* a god. At sunrise, at certain times of the year, the stones released ultrasound. Perhaps, due to their long skulls and unusual ear placement, this elusive sound may have been within auditory range, or possibly resulted in a corner of the eye apparition, as previously described by Dr Don Robins. Today, ultrasound is used in healing, as may have been the case thousands of years ago.

I discovered another type of inaudible sound was incorporated into Stonehenge: geodetic musical harmonics that are emitted by certain earth energies. These harmonics are what set the monument's circular features and brought Gaia's music to Stonehenge, which may have been complemented by ritual chants, songs or incantations in the same musical tone or interval. Musically, it is still possible to be at one with Gaia simply by knowing where at Stonehenge to stand. Alternatively, by walking any harmonic 3/2 line, as shown in *Fig. 271* below, you will resonate to the perfect fifth. Perhaps, our ancestors walked the entire 12-pointed star during important rituals, or they simply meditated upon a particular line or energy.

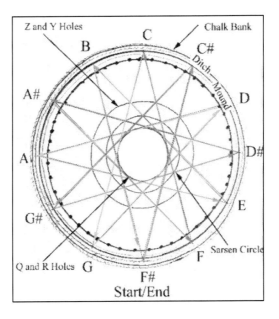

Fig. 271 Walking the harmonic lines at Stonehenge.

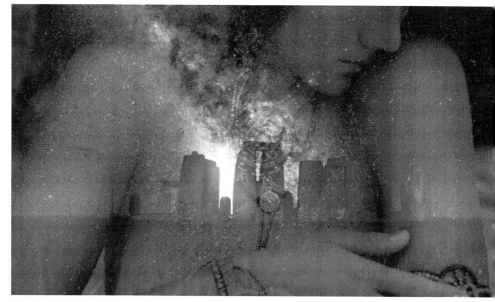

Fig. 272 The Celtic goddess Arianrhod was associated with Stonehenge (Phase 1). *Photograph:* Jonathan Womack.

Unearthing the secret history of Stonehenge has revealed many lost wonders, such as the bluestone circle of Phase 1 that was a secretive night-time temple. With its tall, chalk bank hiding the interior, those invited attendees witnessed a wondrous site. At certain times of the lunar cycle, the brilliant white chalk bank and temple floor reflected moonlight in the form of a caustic beam of light that gently shone upon a stone or a priestess, bathing them in soft moonlight. This phase of Stonehenge was associated with the Corona Borealis, the Celtic Pagan heaven, when, as we have seen, Alphecca was exactly overhead connecting the bluestone circle to Arianrhod, the goddess of reincarnation.

All these things allow us to gain a sense of what it must have been like at that time. There was, nevertheless, much more to come. During Phase 2, the long headed masons redesigned Stonehenge and constructed the lintelled stone circle that we are familiar with. Originally, it had colourful and mesmerising gem-like qualities that sparkled, diamond-like, in the light of the Sun and the Moon. The lintelled stone ring was highly polished—silvery-pink-hued sarsen stones formed a protective circle around the healing trilithon temple that had miraculous powers. Trilithons 51/52 and 59/60 were silvery-grey and known for their healing virtue, whilst 53/54, 55/56 and 58/59 were coloured pairs of pink and orange megaliths, as were lintelled Stones 4/5 and 6/7. The bluestones added an array of olive green and dark, midnight blue shades, which together with the pink and white flecked bluestones made Stonehenge one of the most colourful stone circles in the British Isles. At the holiest of holies, bejewelling the heart of Stonehenge, were two tall Altar Stones: one light green, the other dark green, both delicately spotted with mica and garnet. They represented the yin and yang energies and person-ified, respectively, an ancient British Moon goddess of divination and a healing, and a Sun god whose power culminated at the Winter Solstice. At this time of year, every 18.61 years, an exceptionally rare celestial event activated Stonehenge—the Moon's Minor Moonset—which was captured by the Greater Trilithon and the lintelled stone circle. We have seen that this was once part of a protracted Winter Solstice ritual that pivoted around the Midwinter setting Sun and the rising Dark Moon. It would have been a sight to behold.

Generation after generation of long headed people worshipped at Stonehenge. However, after their fall from power, the much taller round headed Bronze Age Beaker people took over, who to the long headed would have appeared like giants. Is it not possible that tales of elves, dwarfs and giants have their roots in Stonehenge's repress-ed history? We read earlier that the Beaker culture uprooted various bluestone settings and redesigned Stonehenge. For instance, the two D-shaped timber temples (illustrated by Fiona Hughes in *Fig. 101*) that housed a silver-coloured Station Stone, were destroyed by the round headed architects who then built grass mounds over them (see *Fig. 273*) and placed the Station Stone upon its summit—sacred healing temples lost to time.

Modern technology can help us to interpret the secrets of the past. The latest aDNA (ancient DNA) studies, backed by data from burials around Stonehenge, support my claim that during the Beaker settle-ment period the bluestones may have been deliberately smashed and destroyed at a time of social unrest and change, which the aDNA indicates spans four centuries. This was a time when the round headed migrants and their descendants were living side by side with an indigenous Neolithic long headed population—a time frame that coincides perfectly with the megalithic alterations and additions at Stonehenge and elsewhere. As archaeologist Mike Pitts points out, "Stonehenge could have been despoiled not that long after the last megalith was in place." This evidence outweighs the speculation that during the Mid Bronze Age, after the demise of the long headed, there grew a Beaker dominance and a flamboyant new royal dynasty ruled over Stonehenge. As we read earlier, their people had fine silky clothing, wore spectacular amber breastplates, gold, jet and amber jewellery, and their priesthood walked with gold-studded staffs. These were the healer-priests and priestesses of Stonehenge, and they carried a standardised crystal medical kit. They too damaged Stonehenge by toppling two of its stones, making a new 'avenue-like' entrance into the stone circle. Other sites were also vandalised.

Fig. 273 The D-shaped timber temples once housing a Station Stone were smothered by a grass mound.

Two or three days walk from Stonehenge is Mount Pleasant, near Dorchester, in Dorset, another great Neolithic henge complex. Mike Pitts and the late Geoffrey Wainwright found the remains of sarsen stones that had been raised within large concentric rings of oak posts. We see in *Fig. 274* an example of the skull of a small, long headed man from Wor Barrow, whose descendants may have

Fig. 274 Long headed adult male from Dorset.

constructed this vast complex. This Neolithic long headed male was 4 ft 10 in (1.21 m) tall. Notably, his skull is the same size as a modern-day child, aged 12 years. It was found that the stones had been uprooted, deliberately broken up and fragments dumped in a ditch that surrounded the structure. Only chips and a single jagged stump remained in the original socket hole; the temple had been destroyed.

Meanwhile, the decommissioning of the long barrows and causewayed enclosures ensured that the monuments of the long headed were unusable. I discovered that cranial deformation made the heads of the tall, round headed even more distinguished, and life was plentiful in their newly found kingdom. A devastating cataclysmic event would, however, soon put an end to this megalithic culture.

Archaeologists suggest that Stonehenge was abandoned in the Mid Bronze Age, around 1500 BC, as this date corresponds with the two rings of holes dug outside of the sarsen circle. Arranged in a double circle or spiral, these pits are known as the Y and Z Holes, and they diverted around the two toppled stones that were used as a new entrance. Possibly, they were intended for the bluestones during a redesign phase, but that never happened. After this period, it is

Fig. 275 Parch marks of Y & Z Holes.

apparent that no major stone monument was constructed, and numerous sites were abandoned in favour of farming. During one hot summer, I was able to photograph the parch marks of the Y and Z Holes, which are clearly visible here in *Fig. 275.*

But is this correct interpretation? I suggest that Stonehenge, as well as many other monuments, were still in use until the Late Bronze Age, 1100 BC, and their abrupt desertion coincided with a rare astronomical event that brought disaster and famine in its wake. No one to date has spoken of this episode or its aftermath. In former times, unusual celestial phenomenon such as eclipses, comets and nova were believed to cause pestilence, sterility of the earth, winds, earthquakes, floods, famine, wars and changes in kingdoms. Despite the dismantling of Stonehenge Phase 1, Hoyle demonstrated that the Aubrey Holes could have been used for predicating eclipses as late as the second millennium BC. During a total lunar eclipse, the umbral shadow of the Earth assumes a coppery-red tinge as it creeps across the full face of the moon, which is due to the refraction and absorption effects that occur when sunlight passes through the Earth's atmosphere. The colour can vary in intensity and in some instances, it is a dramatic blood red colour. This phenomenon was frequently documented, such as in *The Anglo-Saxon Chronicle* that for the year AD 734 records: "The Moon was if it had been sprinkled with blood". In AD 1044, French chronicler, Raoul Glaber, wrote of the partial lunar eclipse, on 8th November of that year:

> "In what manner it happened or whether a prodigy brought it to pass by the Deity or by intervention of some heavenly body remains known to the author of knowledge. For the Moon herself became like dark blood, only getting clear of it a little before dawn."

Although less well documented, there was a far earlier and more spectacular eclipse that was seen as an evil omen of disaster and death. It is this event we shall now focus on.

Hekla: Gateway to Hell and the Black Moon

Hekla is an active Icelandic volcano that has frequently erupted since time immemorial. In the medieval period, it was called 'Gateway to Hell'. I noted that a major eruption, known as Hekla 3, occurred around 1159-1141 BC, when 7.3 km^3 of rock and ash were spewed into the atmosphere. This is visible in the strata of tephra, and traces of this event are apparent in the peat bogs of Northern Britain and Ireland, where tree ring data shows minimal growth for well over a decade. Any violent volcanic eruption causes the Earth's atmosphere to become choked with suspended dust, and sunlight that is normally refracted through the upper atmospheric layers becomes absorbed. If such an event is followed by a lunar eclipse, when the moon is completely blotted out by the Earth's shadow, it will turn black—this is known as a *black eclipse* (not to be confused with a black moon). A black eclipse occurred on the night of 23rd January AD 753, when it was reported: "The Moon was covered with a horrid black shield." More recently, in the 1960s a black moon was seen after violent volcanic activity in the East Indies. For explanatory purposes, and because the exact date of Hekla 3 is unknown, I have selected the total lunar eclipse of 1155 BC, although *any* lunar eclipse coinciding with this eruption phase, and there were several in this time frame, would ensure a black eclipse. Let us envision the priest-hood in their finery, attendees gathering at Stonehenge to witness a total lunar eclipse which they anticipated would be like any other. It began in the darkening summer skies at 10.28 pm and ended just after midnight. However, instead of turning coppery-red, the moon unexpectedly turned ashen grey and then a deathly black.

Undoubtedly, people would have demanded to know why this wasn't predicted? The inhabitants of Britain would have known nothing of Iceland's volcanic event, though they experienced its ef-fects. After the eruption and following the foreboding black eclipse, the temperature plummeted by a degree, causing sudden climate cooling. In some parts of the northern hemisphere, the weather pattern became much colder and wetter, resulting in a period of dislocation, famine and disease. Was Stonehenge blamed for these devasting consequences? If so, this would explain why it was sud-denly abandoned—the priesthood had failed the people and the gods had forsaken them. Archaeologists suggest that towards the Late Bronze Age, Stonehenge's 'Masters of Ceremonies', the special-ist healer-priests, were at the cusp of social and political change; it is suspected they practiced important rites and ceremonies throughout the country. The only thing that is really different about Wessex is its concentration of round barrows that housed these ritual leaders, particularly at Stonehenge, Avebury, Cranbourne Chase and in the Wylye Valley. Possibly, because they failed to predict the black eclipse, climate change and famine, these magical practitioners lost favour and were supplanted. Ann Woodward argues:

> "...due to a particular historical process, whereby the practitioners of a particular cult was fast becoming obsolete, or their followers, chose to bury them in the areas of their ancient ancestral monuments. Thus, the concentration of burials of ritual equipment in Wiltshire may represent the final deposition of the most precious possessions of the last practising shamans of this particular cult."

This was the end of a spiritual and physical era, and the megalithic priesthood was no more. I agree with Woodward, but I would add that their downfall was the result of the black eclipse. During the social upheaval that followed, the healer-priests were replaced by warrior leaders; the heavens had decreed a change and life would never be the same. The megalithic building programme ceased.

Roundhouses in the area were also discarded and deterioration of the landscape caused vast areas to be deserted. The growing season was reduced and some regions that had been brought into cultivation or as pasture were left abandoned; the focus was now on lynchets on the drier hillsides. Other areas saw extensive development of the blanket bog—a peatland that forms in regions of high rainfall. In the Late Bronze Age/Early Iron Age, changing climatic conditions played a significant role in the evolving social order and consequently the cultural way of life. Stone circles became weed-choked and derelict, round barrows became smaller and then vanished completely. Collective labour turned away from mound and stone circle building to land ownership, farming and a greater focus on personal wealth. Around 1100-1000 BC, in response to the climate crisis and to appease the gods, perhaps also to safeguard the fertility of the land, strange and macabre death rites emerged. At Cliffs End Farm in Kent, an unusual Late Bronze Age burial was

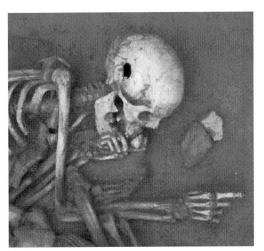

Fig 276 Unusual ritual burial of an old woman at Cliffs End Farm, Kent.

unearthed (see *Fig. 276*). Alongside animal bones were the bones of a disproportionate number of teenagers, although there was an absence of children under the age of six, and an abnormal female-male ratio 71%-29% with many more women than men. The burial focused on one elderly woman who had been killed by multiple sword blows to the back of the head. She was laid out in an unusual manner with brilliant white chalk up to her face, her index finger positioned in a pointing direction, and two lambs placed on her lap. Her violent end may have represented ritual sacrifice, but the nature of her death suggests deliberate cruelty and punishment, not consistent with mere sacrifice.

Other bizarre ritual burials found are the 'jigsaw' mummies of Cladh Hallan, South Uist, in the Outer Hebrides, where four mummies in the flexed position were placed in a row in the foundations of a roundhouse. They were manipulated body parts from several different people, possibly active members of the community from the same family, arranged to look like one person. The 'female' mummy was made up of a small baby, a young female adult, and a woman in her 40s with a male skull; likewise, the 'male' mummy was also a composite. The various body parts had been mummified by placing them in a peat bog for approximately one year. They were not buried immediately, and burial occurred some 300-500 years after the construction of the roundhouse, indicating their remains had been kept above ground for millennia. During this challenging time, ritual human burials—not ceremonies within stone circles—would ensure fertility, crop growth and a golden harvest. In the Stonehenge area, I noted that certain burials were likewise associated with fertility and farming. On King Barrow Ridge, two tightly flexed male burials were carefully placed in a deep boundary ditch associated with a nearby field system. A few miles away, at West Amesbury, the bodies of two other men that were probably curated were also ritually buried. At Porton Down, 5 miles (8 km) to the southeast of Stonehenge, two more tightly flexed burials were placed in a boundary ditch. Interestingly, a small number of tightly bound, or mummified bodies, are known from the Thames Valley and Cranbourne Chase, in Dorset. Perhaps these men were seen as *land guardians* offering their protection and fertility to Mother Earth. Near Normanton Down, at Druid's Lodge, a baby was placed into a palisade ditch, and may have symbolised the harvest child.

Until modern machinery redefined agriculture, corn was harvested by hand using sickles and scythes. Reaping gangs toured local farms, their leader known as the 'Lord of the Harvest'—the most skilled man present—who organised the harvest and the men's pay. Corn must be cut in dry weather as soon as it ripens, otherwise the grains shed from the ears and will spoil. A prolonged wet spell can destroy an entire harvest, so when the weather held every able-bodied man, woman and child would be out in the fields. The harvest is the reason for the six-week British school summer holiday and, until relatively recent times, the last sheaf of corn was always saved as it was believed to contain the 'corn spirit'. The following spring this sheaf was scattered on the fields, returning the corn spirit to the land. In some areas, it was hung up for hungry birds to peck on New Year's Day or made into a corn dolly. This tradition also existed across Europe. It is believed by many in Pagan communities to be a relic of the millennia-old belief in the dying and rising god

Fig. 277 The last sheaf was saved as it contained the 'corn spirit'.

—the Holly King and the Oak King—who dies in autumn to be reborn the following spring. The male burials placed in the boundary ditches may have symbolised such honorary 'tree' kings.

New Ceremonial Centres

The climate was now cruel and harsh. As Lisa Brown points out, "the wet and cold climate of the time would have resulted in multiple crop failures, possibly episodes of starvation or hardship." Around 1000 BC a new style of monument called a *midden*, often with an un-enclosed centre, was created for seasonal gatherings and ceremonies. According to Mike Parker Pearson, such centres were "stores of fertility" used for craft production, feasting and the deposition of some rare and exotic materials, such as gold, amber and glass. In prehistoric times, refuse and rubbish does not always seem to have had negative connotations, and could have been productive places with quite the opposite meaning. Excavations at the midden feasting site at All Cannings Down, near Pewsey, which replaced that at Avebury, shows that part of the midden was placed within an area reserved for seasonal livestock grazing and belonged to several communities. Life was slowly getting back to normal and cattle rearing and farming productivity gradually improved. Undoubtedly, due to the wetter climate, the element of water was woven into ceremonial life and watery places revered. It is also thought that the deceased were deposited in water, either as complete bodies, separate bones or as cremations. At Flag Fen in Cambridgeshire, preserved in wet-land is a 0.62 mile (1 km) long timber causeway, constructed across open water to a wooden platform that was built around 1365-967 BC as a place of ritual. Over 60,000 upright timbers and 250,000 horizontal planks were found buried under the ground, along with many offerings. Hundreds of weapons, including swords, leather objects, ornaments and personal items were cast into the water along the length of the causeway, at a site that maintained its ritual status for over a thousand years. It has been found that skilfully crafted swords were sometimes deliberately bent and placed into rivers and lakes, which Francis Pryor suggests is the origin of the *Lady of the Lake* of Arthurian legend.

In Gaul, bronze axes were sometimes left untrimmed after casting, denoting they were specifically made for ritual sacrifice. In England, one such axe was found buried near the doorway of a roundhouse in Dorset, and a collection of twenty plus were found in a similar position beside a roundhouse at Tower Hill, near the Uffington White Horse, in Oxfordshire. These new ceremonial places replaced the earlier stone circles—everything had changed.

In 2004, just north of Avebury, at Chiseldon, a hoard of seventeen Iron Age cauldrons were found—the largest deposit of cauldrons in prehistoric Europe. Analysis revealed that different types of meat and vegetable stews were cooked in them, giving an insight into the type of food served at communal gatherings, when alcohol was also consumed on a large scale. It was noted that the cauldrons were filled to the brim and calculations show that if all seventeen were used at once, they may have held enough sustenance for hundreds or even thousands of people. In Celtic mythology, cauldrons were not just used for cooking or as drinking vessels, they were intimately associated with the gods, magic, rebirth and knowledge. In one part of the *Mabinogion*, a cycle of myths relating to Welsh legend, Cerridwen brews up a potion in her magical cauldron for her ugly son Afagddu (Morfran), as it will give him wisdom. Having put Gwion in charge of guarding her cauldron, three drops of the brew fall upon his finger, blessing him with the gift of knowledge intended for her son. Cerridwen then pursues Gwion by shape-shifting into several different animals until, in the form of a hen, she swallows Gwion, who is disguised as an ear of corn. Nine months later, she gives birth to Taliesin, who becomes the greatest of all the Welsh bards. In another legend, Bran the Blessed has a magical cauldron, a vessel of wisdom and rebirth. This was one of the treasures the mythological Tuatha Dé Danann brought to Ireland as the Cauldron of the Dagda, known as the Cauldron of Plenty, or Undry, said to be bottomless and never ran dry, from which no one ever went away unsatisfied.

Shamanic Practices in Wessex
There was once a vast feasting site at Potterne, in Wiltshire, that was on par with the size of modern-day Glastonbury Festival. Remains of wild animals not intended as food were found, such as polecat, fox, wildcat, beaver and sea birds, along with deer teeth, perforated antler tine and the perforated claw of a white-tailed eagle. Whilst some of these relics were probably worn as personal ornaments, it

does suggest ceremonial usage for shamanic practices during the feast gathering. Wearing such items may have allowed celebrants to appropriate animal qualities, blurring the boundaries between the lives of human and animal. Rites of passage were also enacted, as over sixty shale armlets, of a size to fit an older child rather than an adult, had been deliberately broken in half or into quarter sections. This may have represented an initiation into adulthood, the breakage commemorating the end of childhood or a certain stage of life, when celebrations involved a shared feast. Cauldrons forged social cohesion through acts of communal cooking and eating, but also distinctions of social order between those who cooked and served, and those who ate together. During this period, burials in flat grave cemeteries containing cremation urns replaced the round mounds of the previous culture. Middens, springs, rivers, lakes and wells became locations for worship.

Fig. 278 Maiden Castle, Iron Age hillfort in Dorset.
Photograph: Busty Taylor.

Hillforts: Ceremonial Centres

The climate did not improve until about 700 BC, corresponding with the construction of hilltop enclosures and the rise of the Druids. In 1962, just over 1,360 hillforts were recorded. These were concentrated mainly in central Britain, from Wessex and Cornwall to the Cotswolds and Wales. In the Peak District and the Pennines, the spread of hillforts is fairly sparse, as it is in southeast England, whilst in Norfolk, Suffolk, the Fens and Lincolnshire, very few examples exist. Some hillforts were non-defensive whilst others were fortified, particularly during the Roman invasion. They were used for many purposes, including as spiritual centres, market towns and large production centres. For example, at Danebury in Hampshire, along-side neighbouring hillforts wool from extensive flocks of sheep was manufactured on an industrial scale. Many hillforts have one or more ramparts (banks) with ditches on the outside. Interestingly, according to John Michell, mountain ridges and elevated hilltops were conductors of the main energy lines, with smaller currents descending into the surrounding countryside. He says: "Each of these lines has its own particular colour and frequency that often dictated how the site was used."

(My next book on Dowsing will explain the use and importance of the colour combination of ley lines and earth energies.)

Having constructed ceremonial centres on high ground, the Iron Age Druids were undoubtedly 'rebooting' the former earth energy network, as described by Michell. Within a hillfort, the location of the holiest of holies, the Druid shrine, was sited on an earth energy pattern known as an *earth chimney* or *geochimney*, the shape of which resembled a Celtic Cross—this I suggest is its genesis. The Druids also revered trees that had two principal arms or branches that sprang laterally from the upright trunk and roughly formed a cross. It was the Druids who were responsible for land division; they divided England into forty sections reflecting the forty tribes, some of which are still recognisable as our modern-day counties. York-shire retained disproportionate magnitude to the other counties, being the territory of the large and powerful Brigantes. There were forty cors (colleges), each presided over by a chief Druid, and three Archdruids whose seats were in York, London and Caerleon-on-Usk. Caesar commented that the Gauls sent their youth to Britain to be educated; at times there were up to sixty thousand students at Druid colleges, comprising the youth and young nobility of Britain and Gaul. It required some twenty years to master Druidic knowl-edge, which included natural philosophy, astronomy, mathematics, geometry, medicine, jurisprudence and poetry. The Druids learnt by heart a great number of verses, since they did not feel it proper to commit these utterances to writing, although in almost all other matters and in their public and private accounts they made use of Greek characters. No Druid priest could be ordained until he had passed an examination in three successive years before the Druidic college of his tribe. We have inherited the concept of a three-year degree from the Druids, whose degrees were conferred after three, six and nine years of training. The highest award was that of Pencerdd or Athro—Master or Professor of Learning—awarded after nine years of study, similar to a PhD. The Druid physicians were skilled in the treatment of the sick, their practice far removed from the medicine-man cult so unfairly ascribed to them by their enemies. When Nuadha, an early Irish king of the Tuatha Dé Danann, lost his hand in battle to Creidne, a woman warrior of the Irish Fianna and an artificer, according to mythology she put a silver hand upon him, the fingers of which were capable of motion.

I suspect that some of the Druidic teachings were handed down by the preceding Neolithic and Bronze Age cultures, since they did not surface overnight. Despite constructing their own magnificent monuments, such as Yarnbury Castle, near Stonehenge, we know from Iron Age coinage having been unearthed that some Iron Age pilgrims still visited Stonehenge; likewise, the Romans offered votive coins to the stones. During the Dark Ages, the beheaded skeleton of a wealthy nobleman was buried at Stonehenge. Traces of lead were found in stable carbon isotopes, suggesting he came from a rich family that ate and drank from lead cups and plates. Stonehenge, named for its resemblance to a ring of wooden gallows, is not far from, if not precisely located, at the meeting of the *three hundreds* where the local government once held their courts. This man, known only as 4.10.4, would have had to walk from at least Amesbury, a distance of one mile (3 km) to the east, implying the location of his burial at Stonehenge was deliberate. A grave was dug for his body and post hole markers at each end delineated his location. This event echoes Geoffrey of Monmouth's tale of warring Saxon and British kings at Stonehenge, which was recorded some 500 years later and contains a garbled memory of actual events.

Stonehenge entered written history in AD 1129 when it was first mentioned in Henry of Huntingdon's *Historia Anglorum* (The History of England), as the Second Wonder of Britain:

> "The second [wonder] is at Stonehenge, where stones of extraordinary dimensions are raised as columns, and others are fixed above, like lintels of immense portals; and no one has been able to discover by what mechanism such vast masses of stone were elevated, nor for what purpose they were designed."

Some ten or so years later, Geoffrey of Monmouth wrote of how the stones were moved by Merlin from afar—as indeed some of them were—and that they had magical healing properties. Professor Tim Darvill, Geoffrey Wainwright and I agree that this was, and still is, a reality. In 1575, an unknown artist 'RF' made one of the earliest sketches of the monument and Stonehenge entered the minds of the curious, asking "How were the stones raised?" This is still a debatable question. We read earlier that the circle was documented in the 17th to 19th centuries by antiquarians Inigo Jones, John Wood, John Aubrey, Edward Duke, William Stukeley and the famous duo, Sir Richard Colt Hoare and William Cunnington, all of whom marvelled at the height of the stones and their power over the human imagination, and many theories arose. Their healing virtue was never forgotten, eventually leading to the misshapen appearance of the stones. This is because from the 16th century, reaching a climax in the 19th century, Stonehenge had changed irreversibly after more than two millennia of weathering. Tourists bought hammers from the nearby town of Amesbury and smashed off pieces of the healing stone. This dulled the monument and removal of the corners and angles that were the easiest to knock off resulted in rounder edges, the stones losing their precision and symmetry. A laser survey confirmed the shattered corners and revealed that large chunks of stone had been taken away. Pitts agrees that the monument once looked far more like Inigo Jones' straight edged temple. Having spotted a lump of stone known as the 'Boles Barrow bluestone' weighing more than half a ton, which is now in the Salisbury Museum, he said:

Fig. 279 Stonehenge, drawn by unknown artist in 1575.

"[It] was almost certainly taken from Stonehenge. We don't know when it happened, but we do know that around 1865 a 55 lb (25 kg) mass was broken off Stone 38, a dacite megalith in the bluestone circle by means of a sledgehammer."

Only in the early part of the 20th century, when Lieutenant Colonel William Hawley began to restore the circle at Stonehenge, did the hammering frenzy stop. Further restorations were carried out in the late 1950-60s by Professor Richard Atkinson, and I have shown that his restorations disfigured several stones that once had unusual features. On 26th October 1918, Sir Cecil Chubb gave Stonehenge to the nation—to us. Today, Stonehenge is a UNESCO World Heritage Site (an important landmark that has been recognised by the United Nations Educational, Scientific and Cultural Organisation) and it is now managed by Historic England (formerly English Heritage) and The National Trust. Yet, I feel that Stonehenge is owned by no one and is a place for everyone—it still attracts thousands of tourists and pilgrims each day. Stonehenge is an age-old wonder, and its secrets are ancient. I have uncovered a few of its mysteries and shown an alternative version of this mighty stone circle, and I have presented solid archaeological evidence for my claims.

My Closing Words

Stonehenge has stood for thousands of years, but the past is very close given the monument is approached in the right way. My journey to understand Stonehenge began when I discovered a Neolithic long headed High Queen. I sense her closeness and her need to have her people recognised—an ancient noble woman guiding a modern woman to uncover a lost history. Now I feel that finally, she and her people are more at peace. Stone circles were built using a technology lost to time. They are an expression of an ancient art and science so highly evolved that it can be barely recognised from our more primitive, modern level. A geomantic awareness of ley lines, earth currents, planetary and other invisible energies, brought Gaia's power to the stones. In a two-way exchange of energy and consciousness, ancient sites are about us too, what we can give and what is received can be a magical experience. From a heightened feeling of wellbeing to a life-changing download, anything is possible. I am thankful to have been given, whilst walking around sacred sites, divine inspiration—what the Celts called the *Awen*. This is an energy that flows with the essence of life, and I have felt Awen energy many times at Stonehenge. I could wander endlessly among these stones, were it possible to do so, and perhaps you could too. I thank the ancestors for raising this wonderful stone temple and I hope they approve of the words that I have penned on their behalf. Across time, Stonehenge is, and always will be, a truly magical place. It is a place where the veil between Mother Earth and humanity is at its thinnest and where, amidst the towering stones, you can dream your dreams awake.

Blessed Be,

Maria

For the Ancestors. Illustration by author Maureen Walton.
www.gooddarkness.com

For courses and tours with Maria Wheatley
TheAveburyExperience.co.uk
EsotericCollege.com

ESOTERIC COLLEGE